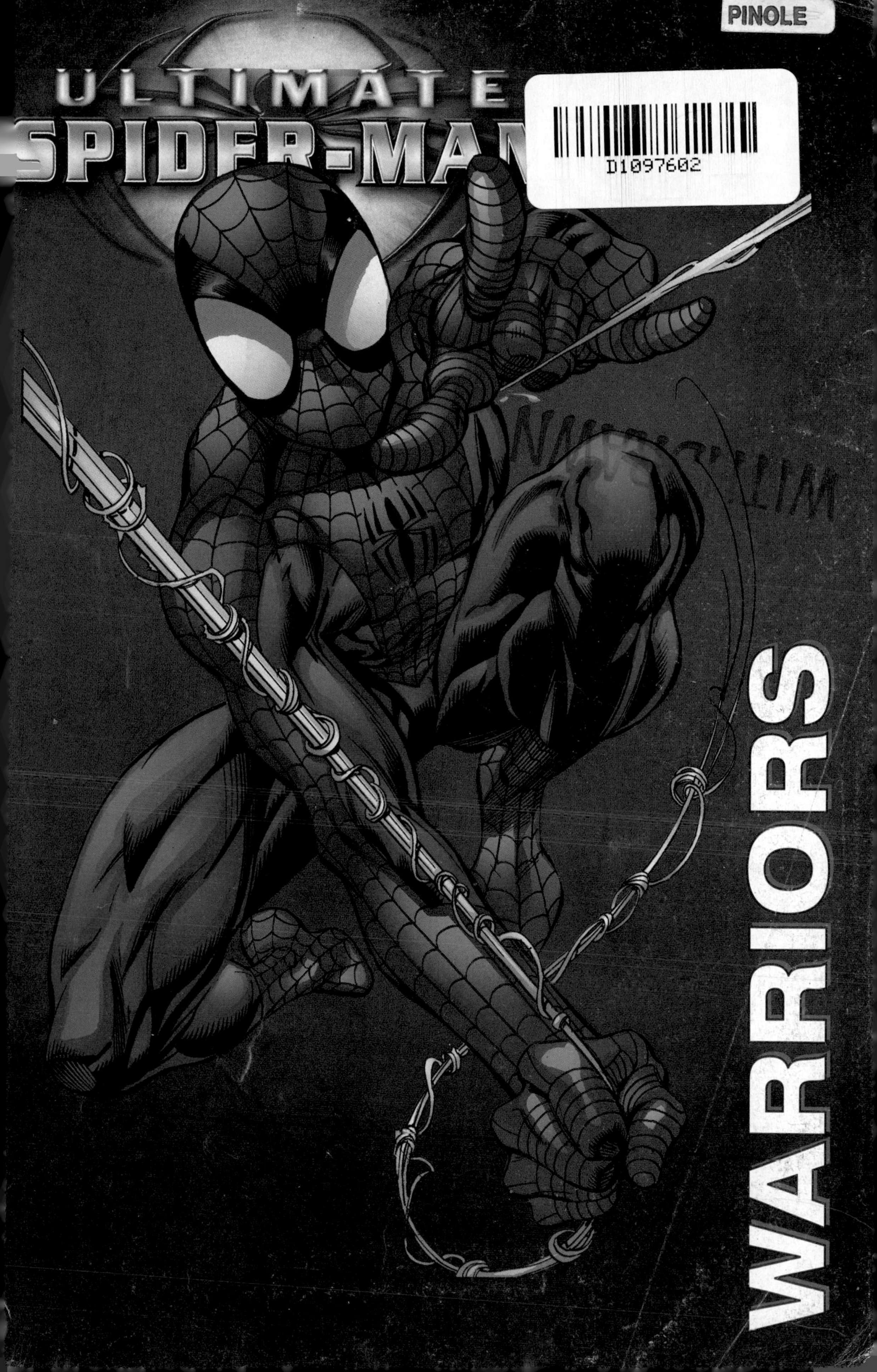
ULTIMATE
SPIDER-MAN
WARRIORS

ULTIMATE SPIDER-MAN

writer
BRIAN MICHAEL BENDIS

pencils
MARK BAGLEY

inks
SCOTT HANNA

colors
J.D. SMITH

letters
CHRIS ELIOPOULOS

covers by
MARK BAGLEY & RICHARD ISANOVE

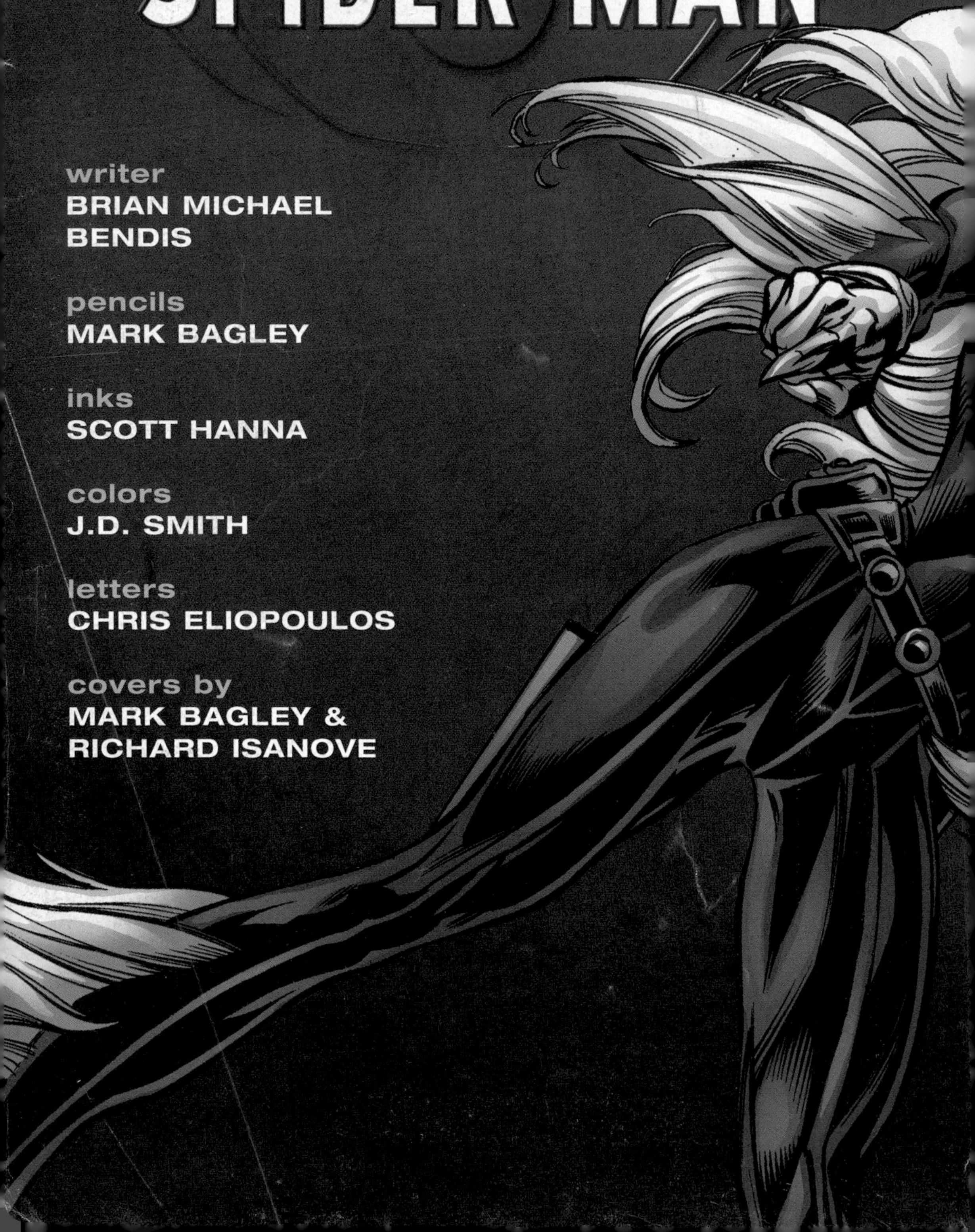

WARRIORS

assistant editors
JOHN BARBER & NICOLE WILEY

associate editor
NICK LOWE

editor
RALPH MACCHIO

collection editor
JENNIFER GRÜNWALD

assistant editor
MICHAEL SHORT

senior editor, special projects
JEFF YOUNGQUIST

director of sales
DAVID GABRIEL

production
CHRISTOPHER RAND

book designer
JEOF VITA

creative director
TOM MARVELLI

editor in chief
JOE QUESADA

publisher
DAN BUCKLEY

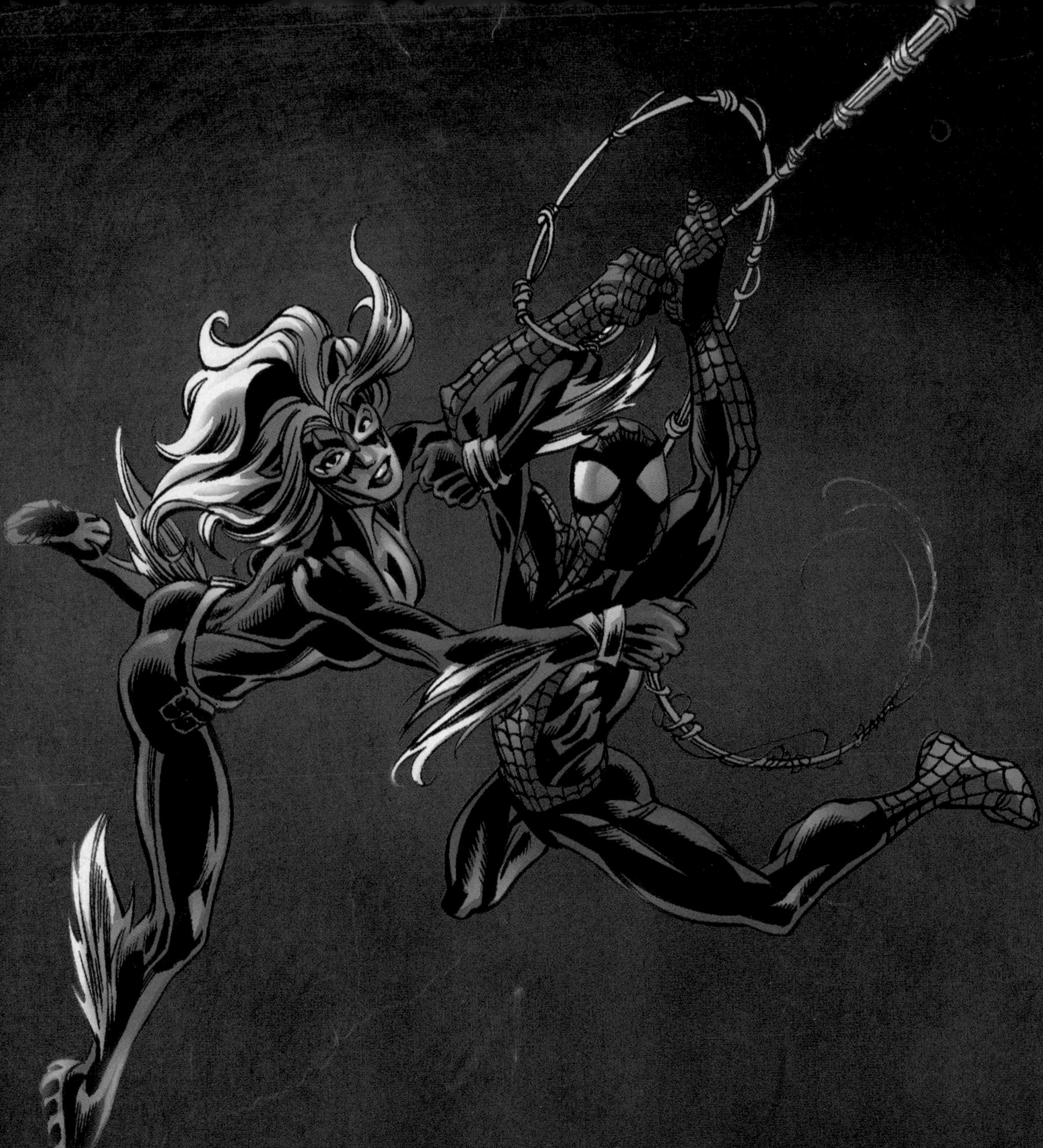

PREVIOUSLY IN ULTIMATE SPIDER-MAN ...

The past few weeks haven't been easy for Peter Parker. Tensions between Peter and his girlfriend Mary Jane come to a head when MJ is nearly killed during a battle between Spider-Man and the demonic villain, Hobgoblin. Realizing that his relationship with Mary Jane will always end up putting her in danger, Peter breaks up with her.

Meanwhile, New York City's underworld is in shambles. A government crackdown that forced Wilson Fisk—the Kingpin of Crime—to go into hiding has left his territory ripe for the taking. Rival mobsters, such as Allan Silvermane, are now faced with an unexpected opportunity: the chance to once and for all wrest control of New York's mob away from the Kingpin. However, the Kingpin might not be as helpless as he appears...

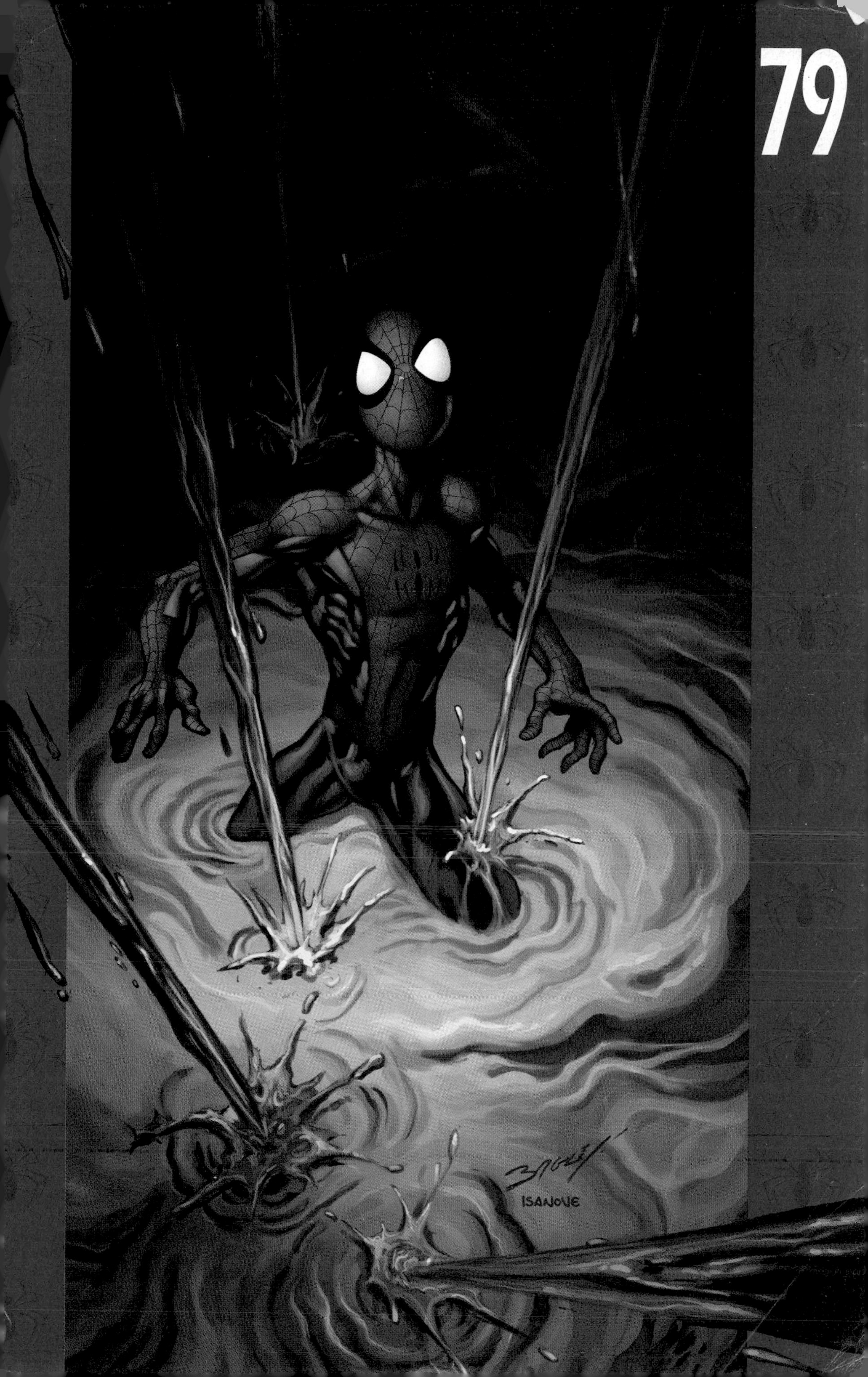
79
ISANOVE

I Tivo'ed this last night.

What the hell is a Tivo?

Watch.

--Federal officials indicted six men Tuesday on federal racketeering charges, alleging that they were members of the Fisk crime family.

Walter Dini, of New York, was among those named in the indictment, along with Samuel Silke.

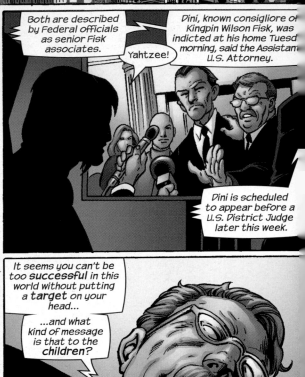

Both are described by Federal officials as senior Fisk associates.

Yahtzee!

Dini, known consigliore of Kingpin Wilson Fisk, was indicted at his home Tuesday morning, said the Assistant U.S. Attorney.

Dini is scheduled to appear before a U.S. District Judge later this week.

It seems you can't be too successful in this world without putting a target on your head...

...and what kind of message is that to the children?

So, huh?

What does that have to do with me, Silvermane?

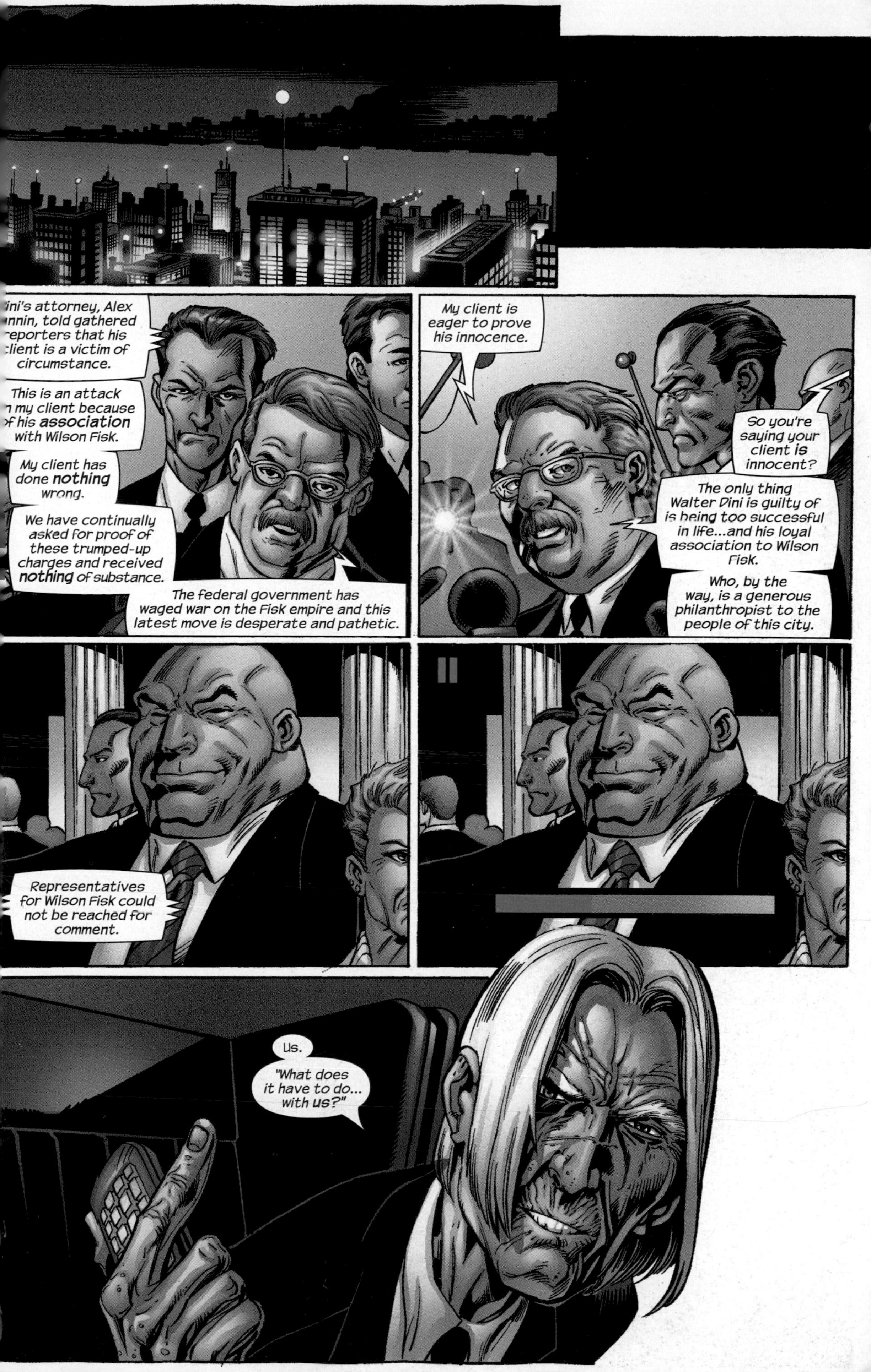
ini's attorney, Alex nnin, told gathered reporters that his client is a victim of circumstance.
This is an attack n my client because of his association with Wilson Fisk.
My client has done nothing wrong.
We have continually asked for proof of these trumped-up charges and received nothing of substance.
The federal government has waged war on the Fisk empire and this latest move is desperate and pathetic.
My client is eager to prove his innocence.
So you're saying your client is innocent?
The only thing Walter Dini is guilty of is being too successful in life...and his loyal association to Wilson Fisk.
Who, by the way, is a generous philanthropist to the people of this city.
Representatives for Wilson Fisk could not be reached for comment.
Us.
"What does it have to do... with us?"

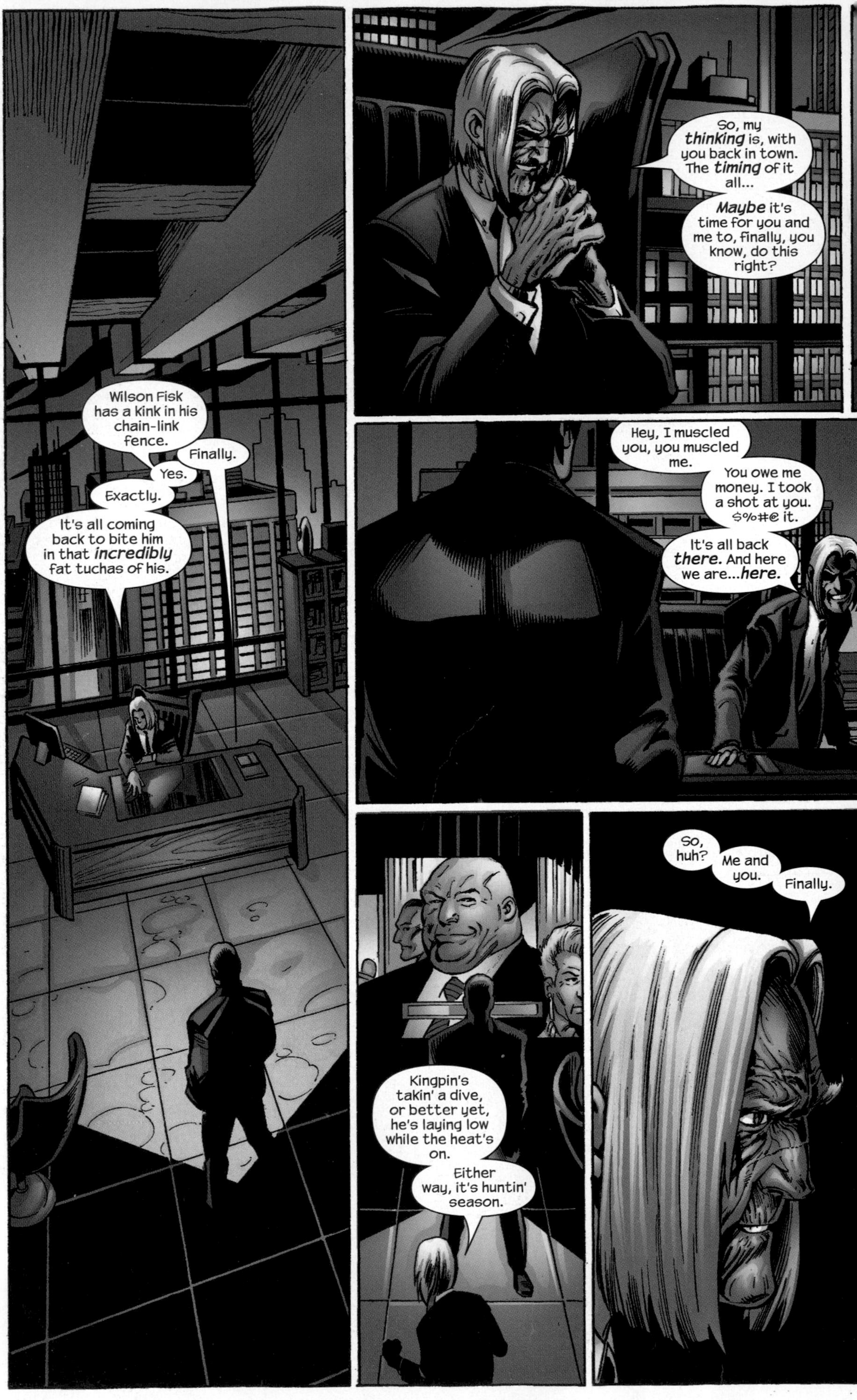

Wilson Fisk has a kink in his chain-link fence.
Finally.
Yes.
Exactly.
It's all coming back to bite him in that *incredibly* fat tuchas of his.
So, my *thinking* is, with you back in town. The *timing* of it all...
Maybe it's time for you and me to, finally, you know, do this right?
Hey, I muscled you, you muscled me.
You owe me money. I took a shot at you. $%#@ it.
It's all back *there.* And here we are...*here.*
Kingpin's takin' a dive, or better yet, he's laying low while the heat's on.
Either way, it's huntin' season.
So, huh?
Me and you.
Finally.

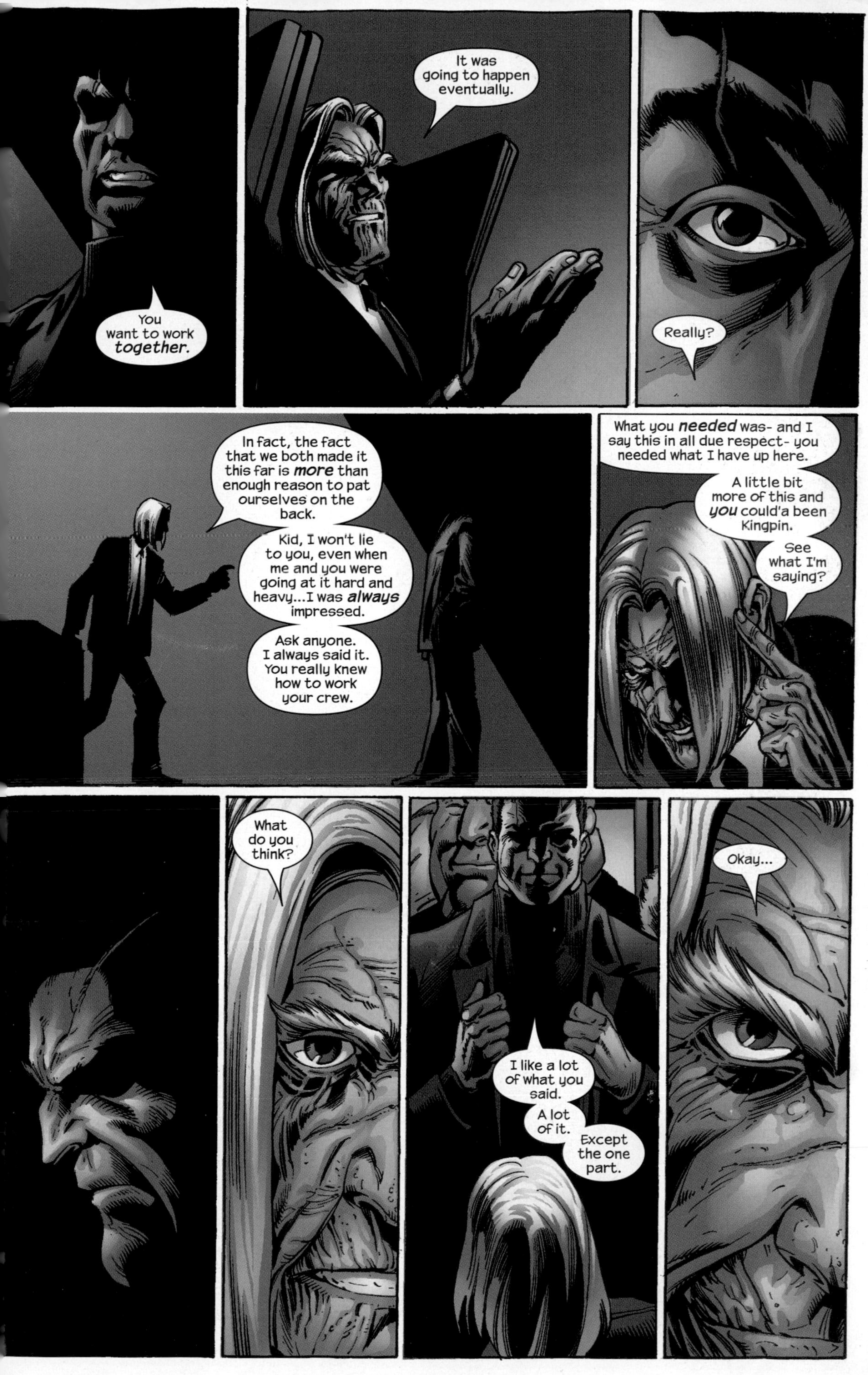
You want to work together.
It was going to happen eventually.
Really?
In fact, the fact that we both made it this far is more than enough reason to pat ourselves on the back.
Kid, I won't lie to you, even when me and you were going at it hard and heavy...I was always impressed.
Ask anyone. I always said it. You really knew how to work your crew.
What you needed was- and I say this in all due respect- you needed what I have up here.
A little bit more of this and you could'a been Kingpin.
See what I'm saying?
What do you think?
I like a lot of what you said.
A lot of it.
Except the one part.
Okay...

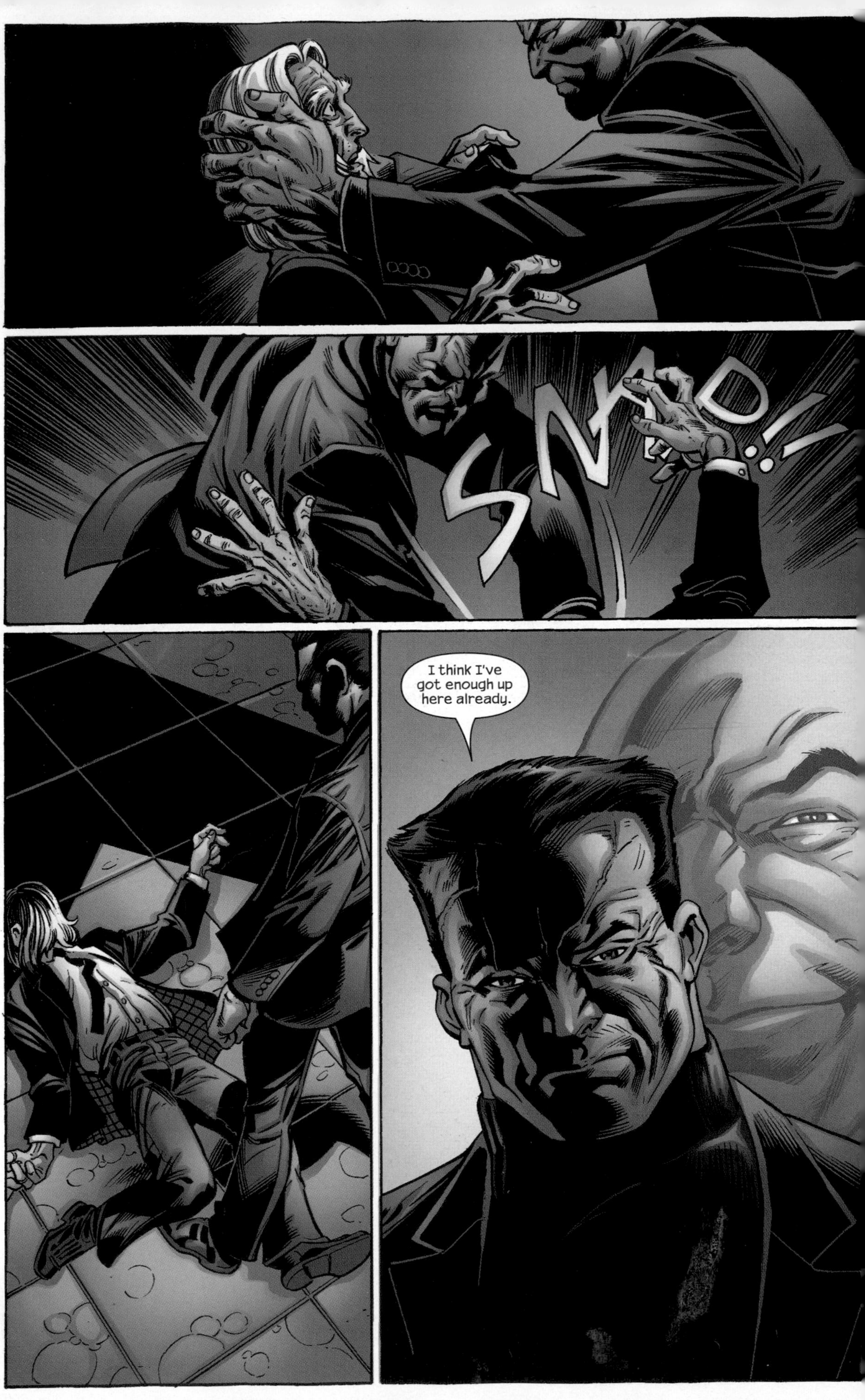
SNAP!!
I think I've got enough up here already.

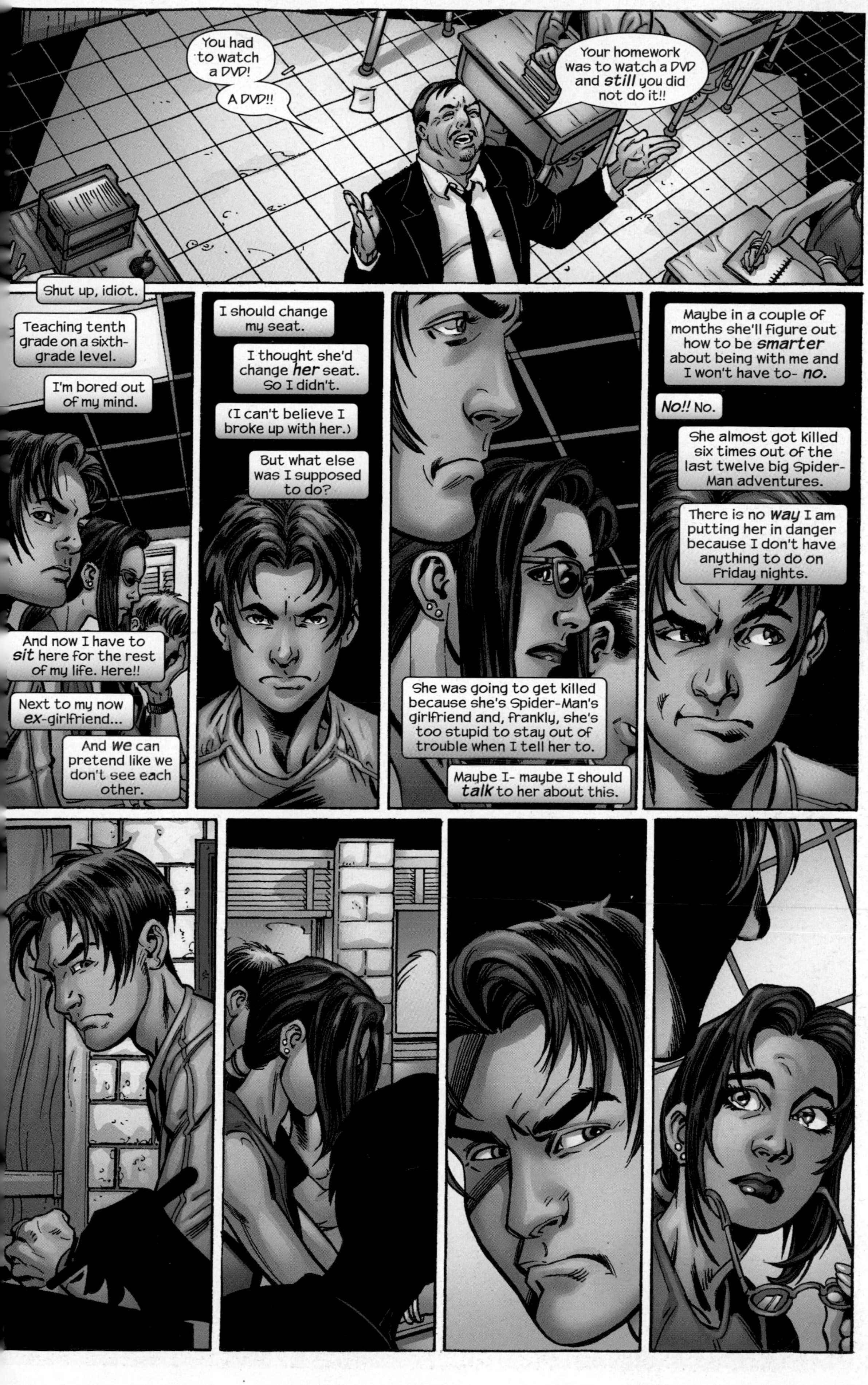
You had to watch a DVD!
A DVD!!
Your homework was to watch a DVD and still you did not do it!!
Shut up, idiot.
Teaching tenth grade on a sixth-grade level.
I'm bored out of my mind.
And now I have to sit here for the rest of my life. Here!!
Next to my now ex-girlfriend...
And we can pretend like we don't see each other.
I should change my seat.
I thought she'd change her seat. So I didn't.
(I can't believe I broke up with her.)
But what else was I supposed to do?
She was going to get killed because she's Spider-Man's girlfriend and, frankly, she's too stupid to stay out of trouble when I tell her to.
Maybe I- maybe I should talk to her about this.
Maybe in a couple of months she'll figure out how to be smarter about being with me and I won't have to- no.
No!! No.
She almost got killed six times out of the last twelve big Spider-Man adventures.
There is no way I am putting her in danger because I don't have anything to do on Friday nights.

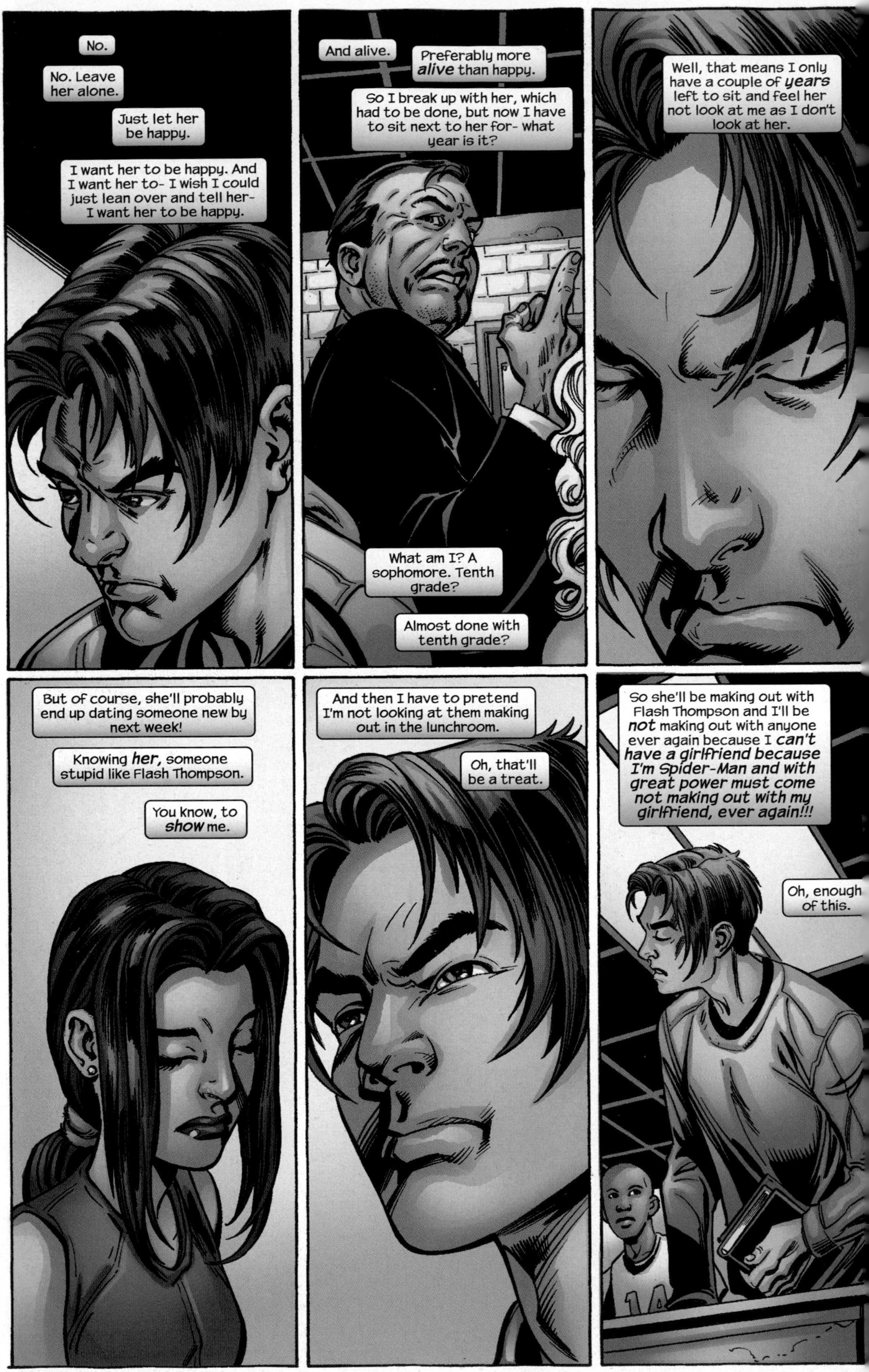
No.
No. Leave her alone.
Just let her be happy.
I want her to be happy. And I want her to- I wish I could just lean over and tell her- I want her to be happy.
And alive.
Preferably more *alive* than happy.
So I break up with her, which had to be done, but now I have to sit next to her for- what year is it?
What am I? A sophomore. Tenth grade?
Almost done with tenth grade?
Well, that means I only have a couple of *years* left to sit and feel her not look at me as I don't look at her.
But of course, she'll probably end up dating someone new by next week!
Knowing *her*, someone stupid like Flash Thompson.
You know, to *show* me.
And then I have to pretend I'm not looking at them making out in the lunchroom.
Oh, that'll be a treat.
So she'll be making out with Flash Thompson and I'll be *not* making out with anyone ever again because I *can't have a girlfriend because I'm Spider-Man and with great power must come not making out with my girlfriend, ever again!!!*
Oh, enough of this.

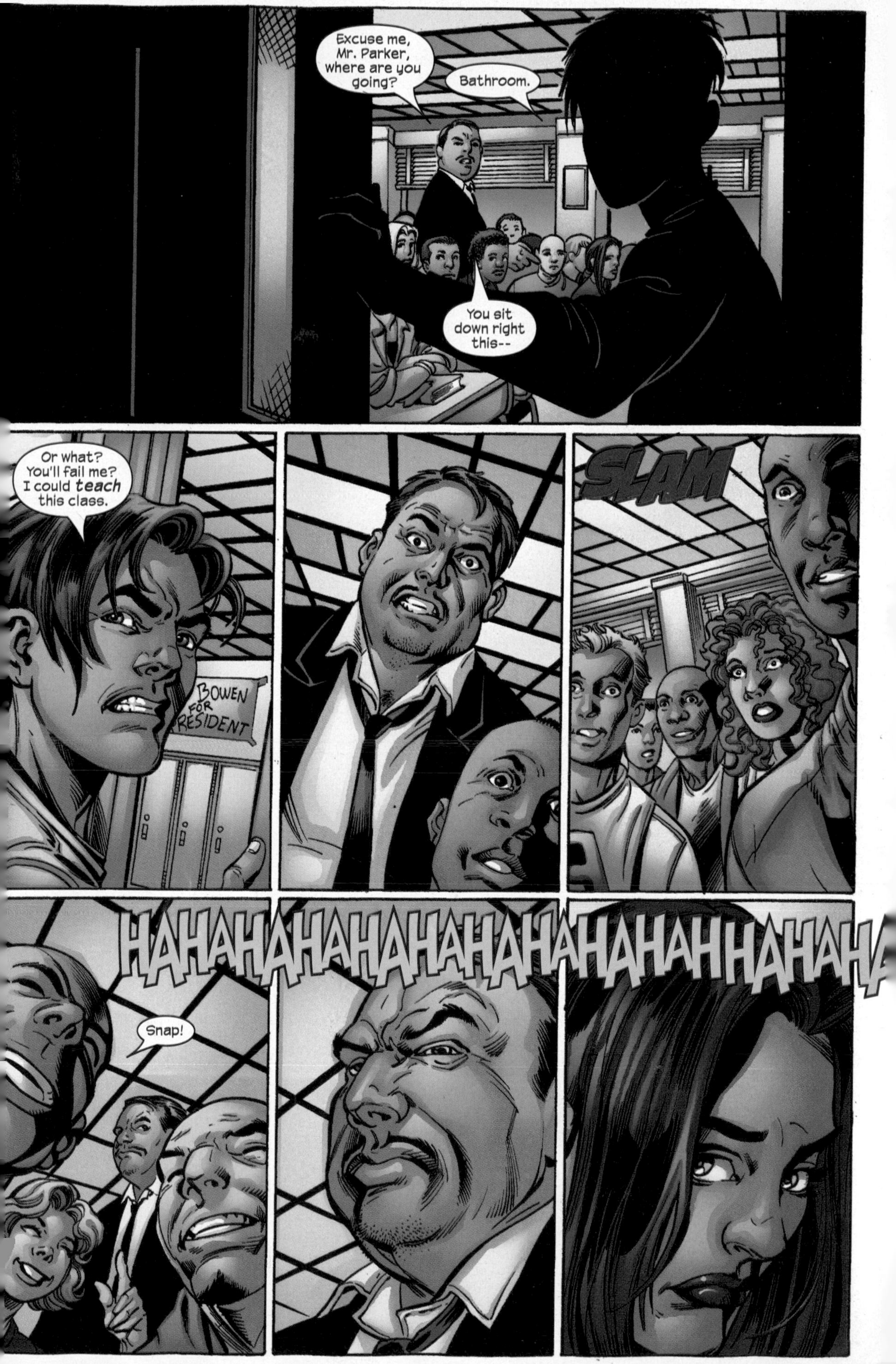

Excuse me, Mr. Parker, where are you going?
Bathroom.
You sit down right this--
Or what? You'll fail me? I could *teach* this class.
BOWEN FOR PRESIDENT
SLAM
HAHAHAHAHAHAHAHAHAHAHAHHAHAHA
Snap!

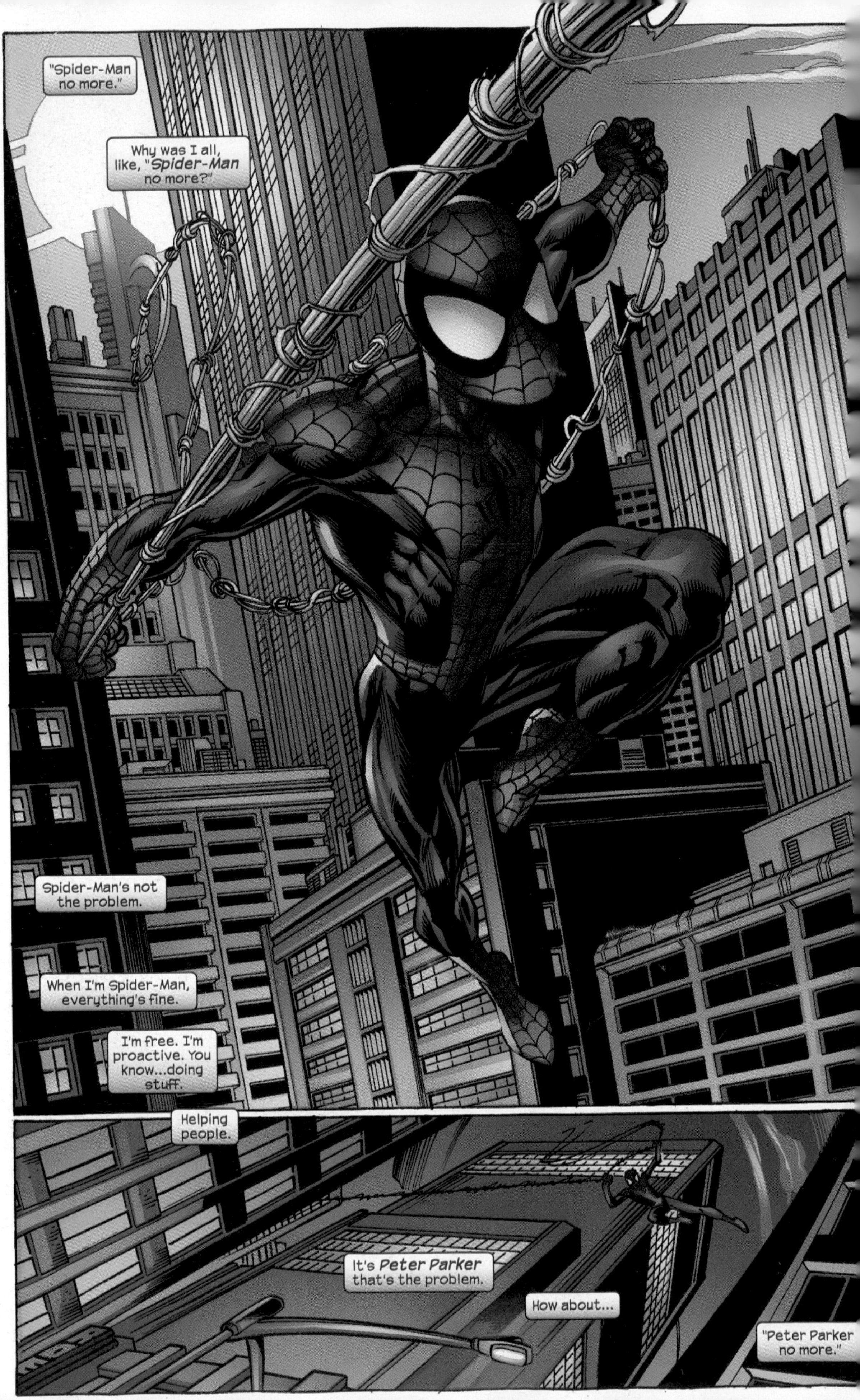
"Spider-Man no more."
Why was I all, like, "Spider-Man no more?"
Spider-Man's not the problem.
When I'm Spider-Man, everything's fine.
I'm free. I'm proactive. You know...doing stuff.
Helping people.
It's Peter Parker that's the problem.
How about...
"Peter Parker no more."

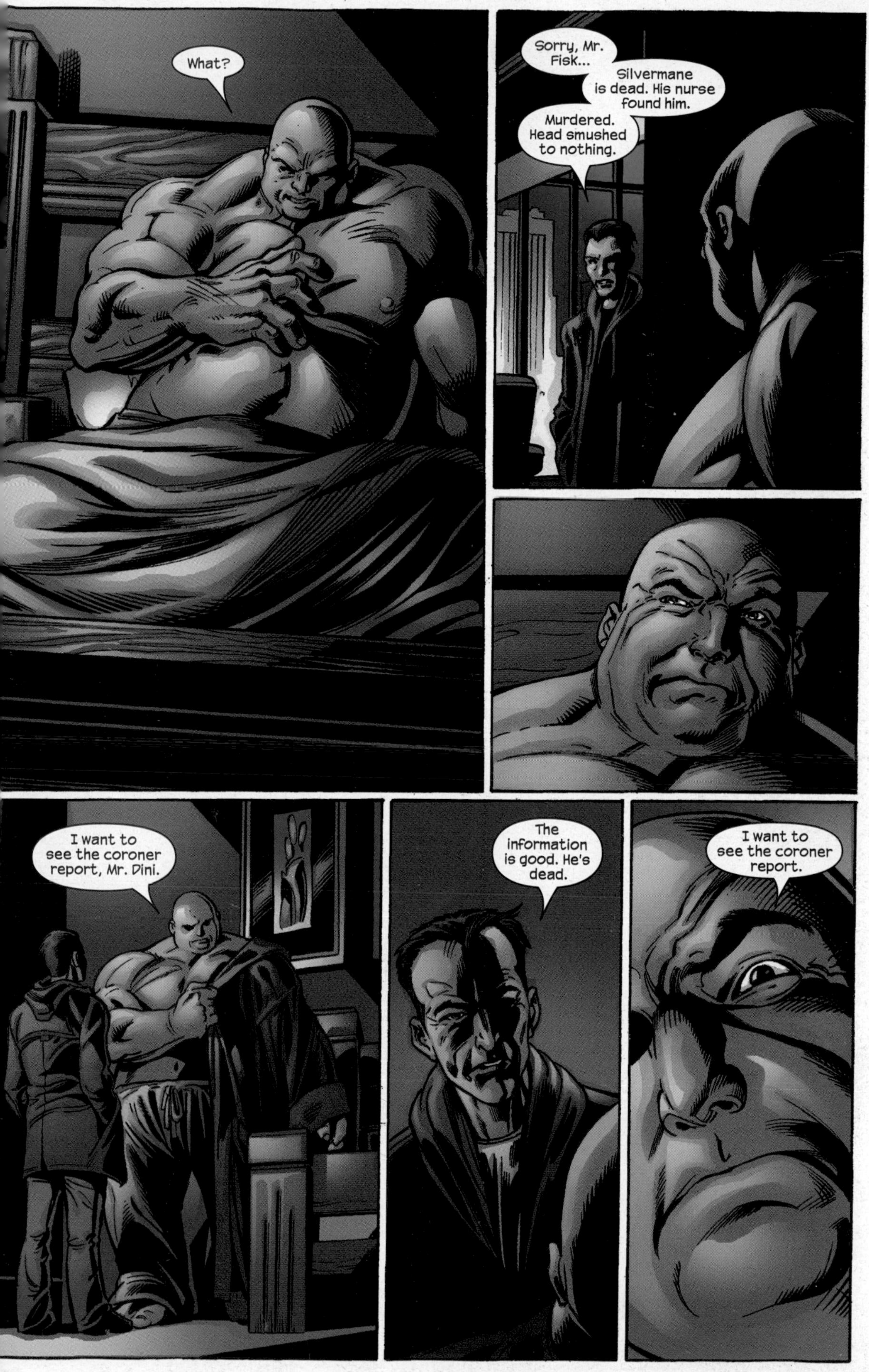
What?
Sorry, Mr. Fisk...
Silvermane is dead. His nurse found him.
Murdered. Head smushed to nothing.
I want to see the coroner report, Mr. Dini.
The information is good. He's dead.
I want to see the coroner report.

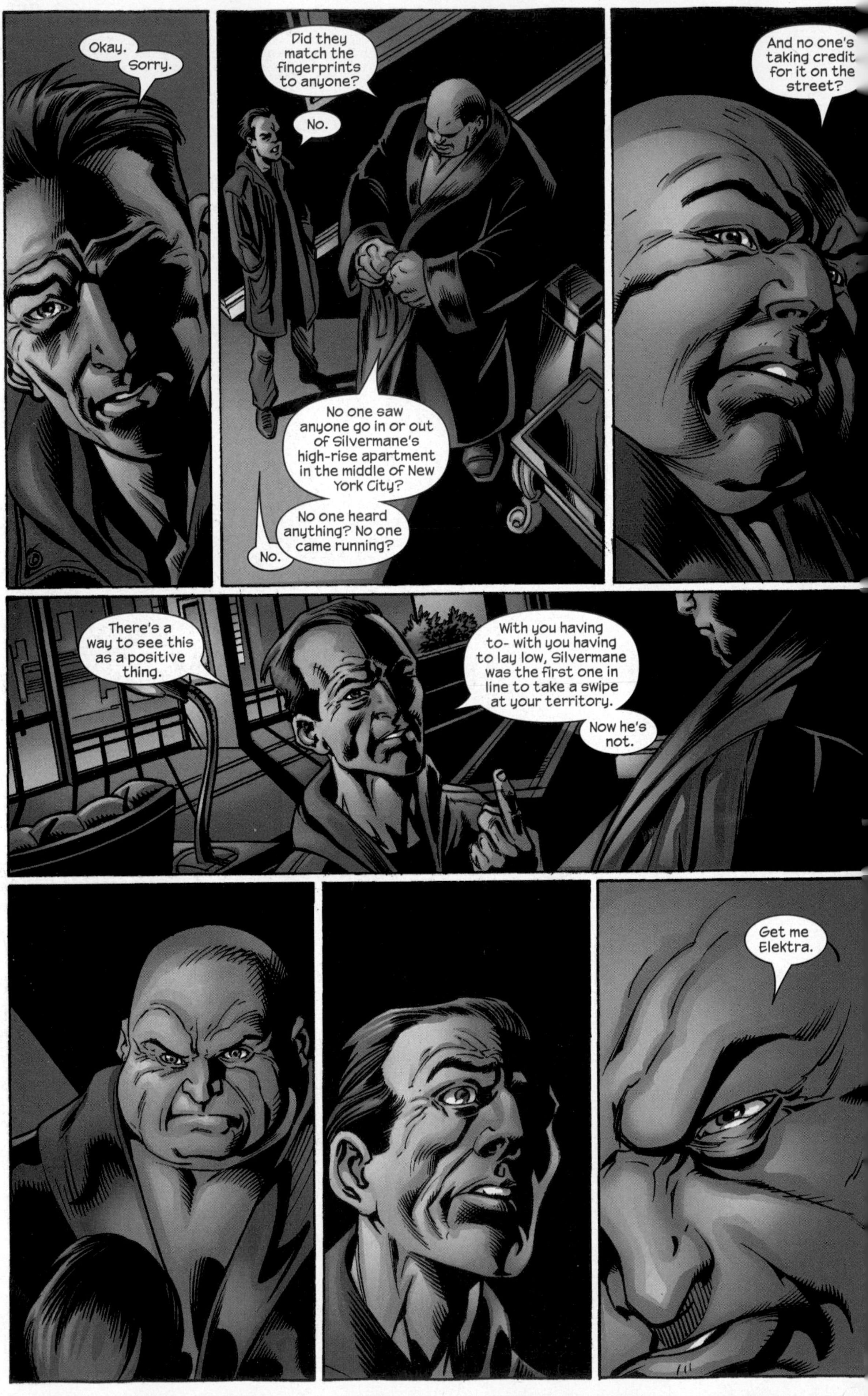
Okay.
Sorry.
Did they match the fingerprints to anyone?
No.
No one saw anyone go in or out of Silvermane's high-rise apartment in the middle of New York City?
No one heard anything? No one came running?
No.
And no one's taking credit for it on the street?
There's a way to see this as a positive thing.
With you having to- with you having to lay low, Silvermane was the first one in line to take a swipe at your territory.
Now he's not.
Get me Elektra.

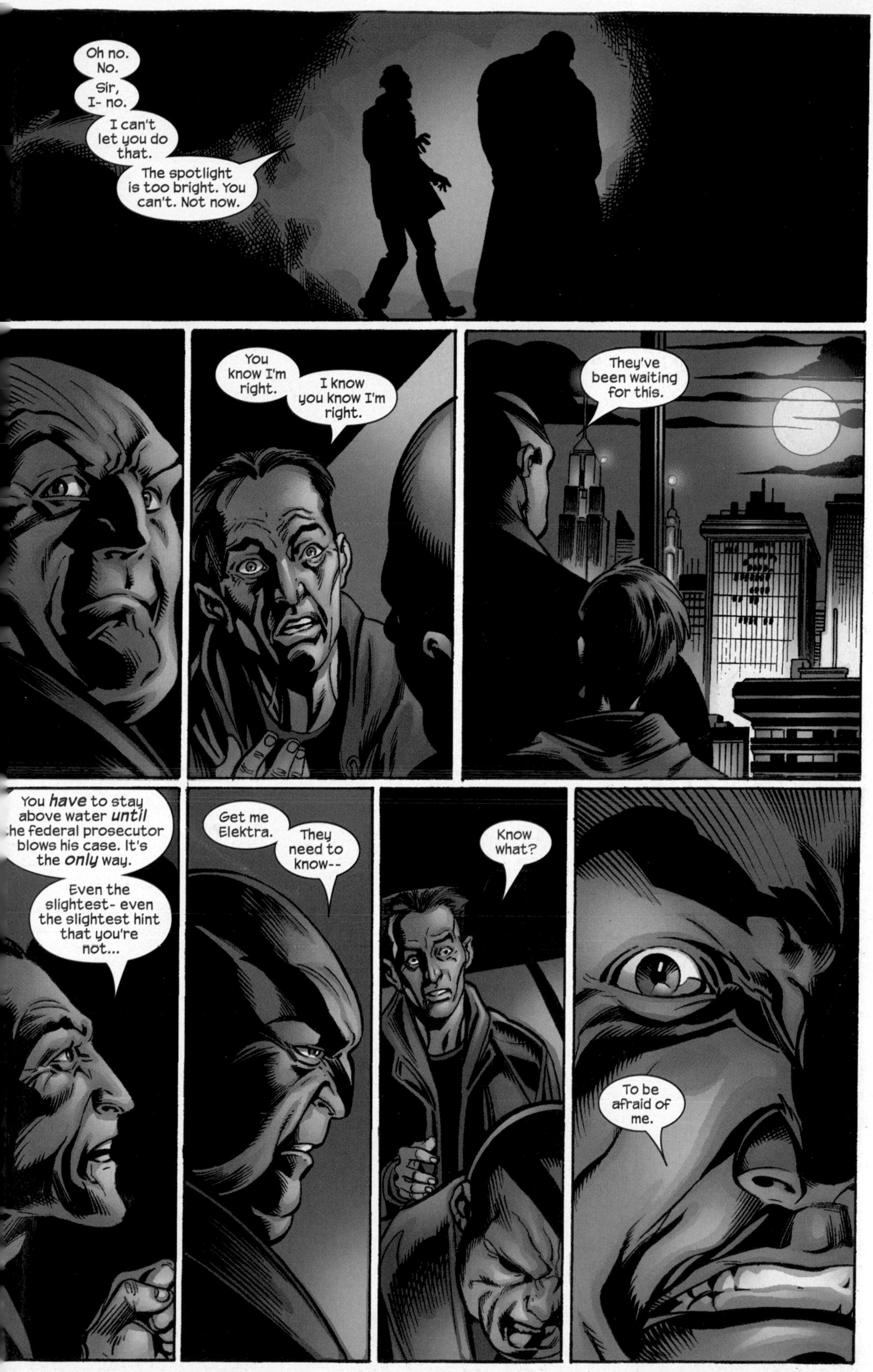
Oh no. No.
Sir, I- no.
I can't let you do that.
The spotlight is too bright. You can't. Not now.
You know I'm right.
I know you know I'm right.
They've been waiting for this.
You have to stay above water until the federal prosecutor blows his case. It's the only way.
Even the slightest- even the slightest hint that you're not...
Get me Elektra.
They need to know--
Know what?
To be afraid of me.

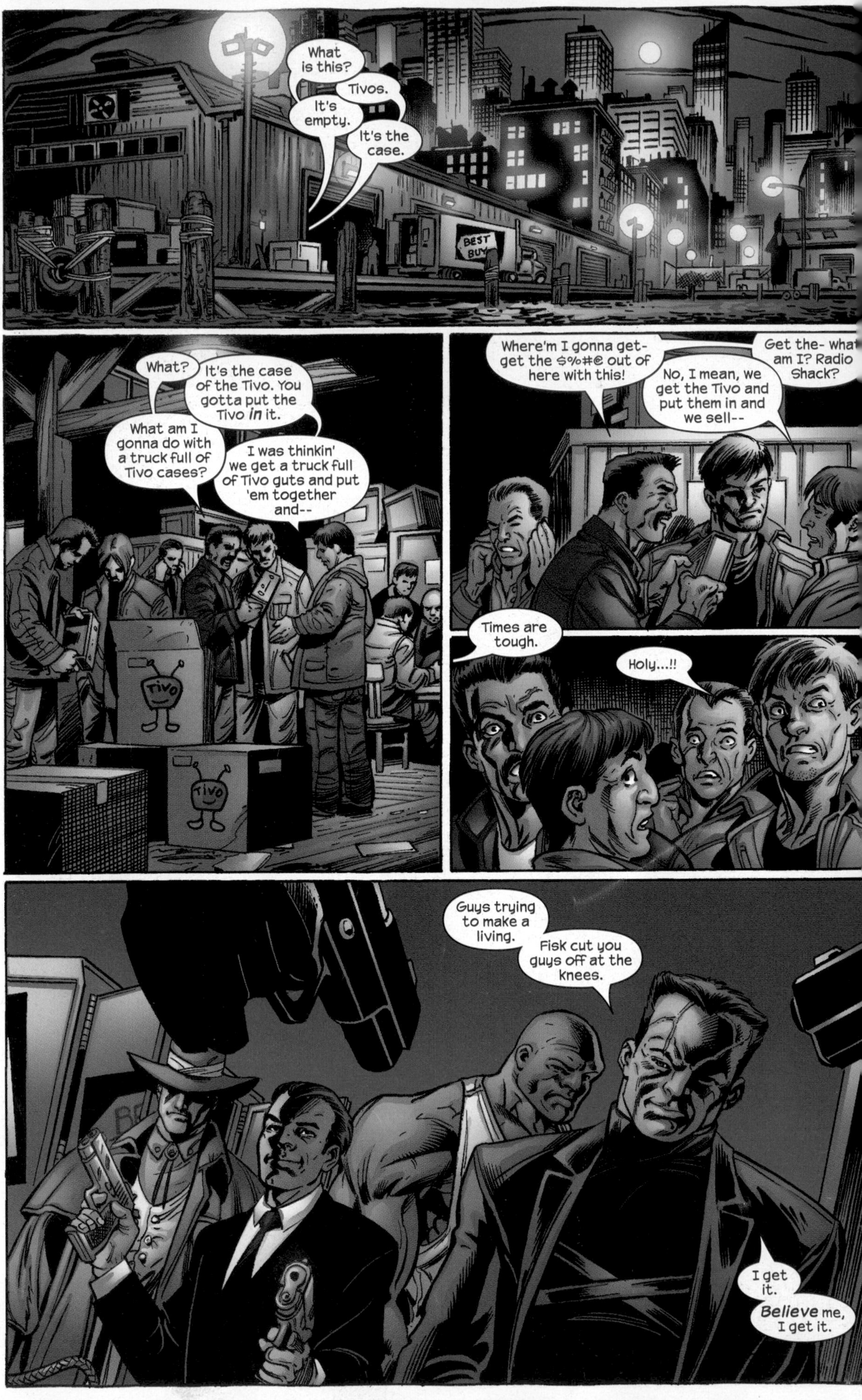
What is this?
Tivos.
It's empty.
It's the case.
BEST BUY
What?
It's the case of the Tivo. You gotta put the Tivo *in* it.
What am I gonna do with a truck full of Tivo cases?
I was thinkin' we get a truck full of Tivo guts and put 'em together and--
TIVO
TIVO
Where'm I gonna get- get the $%#€ out of here with this!
No, I mean, we get the Tivo and put them in and we sell--
Get the- what am I? Radio Shack?
Times are tough.
Holy...!!
Guys trying to make a living.
Fisk cut you guys off at the knees.
I get it.
Believe me, I get it.

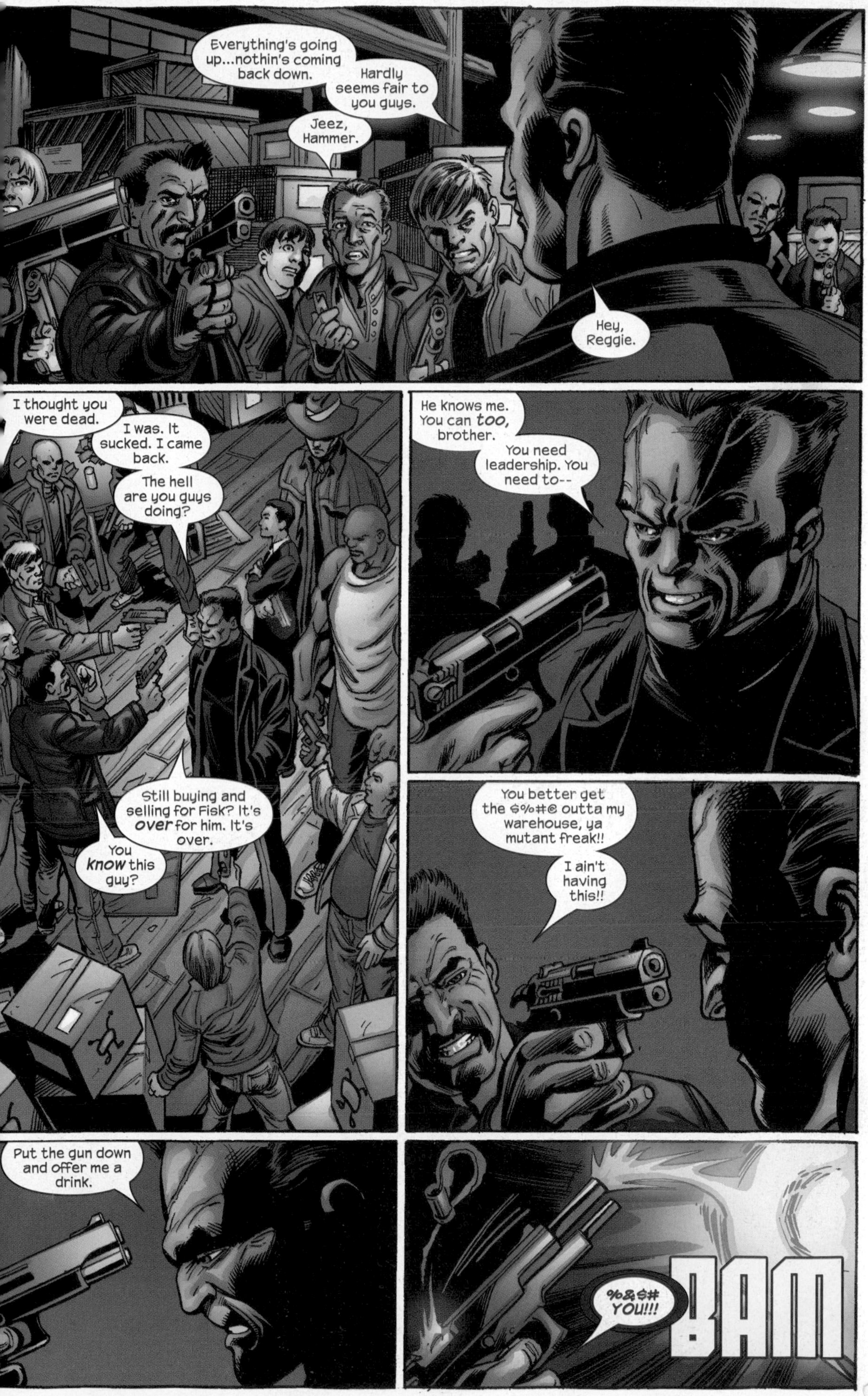
Everything's going up...nothin's coming back down.
Hardly seems fair to you guys.
Jeez, Hammer.
Hey, Reggie.
I thought you were dead.
I was. It sucked. I came back.
The hell are you guys doing?
Still buying and selling for Fisk? It's over for him. It's over.
You know this guy?
He knows me. You can too, brother.
You need leadership. You need to--
You better get the $%#@ outta my warehouse, ya mutant freak!!
I ain't having this!!
Put the gun down and offer me a drink.
%&$# YOU!!!
BAM

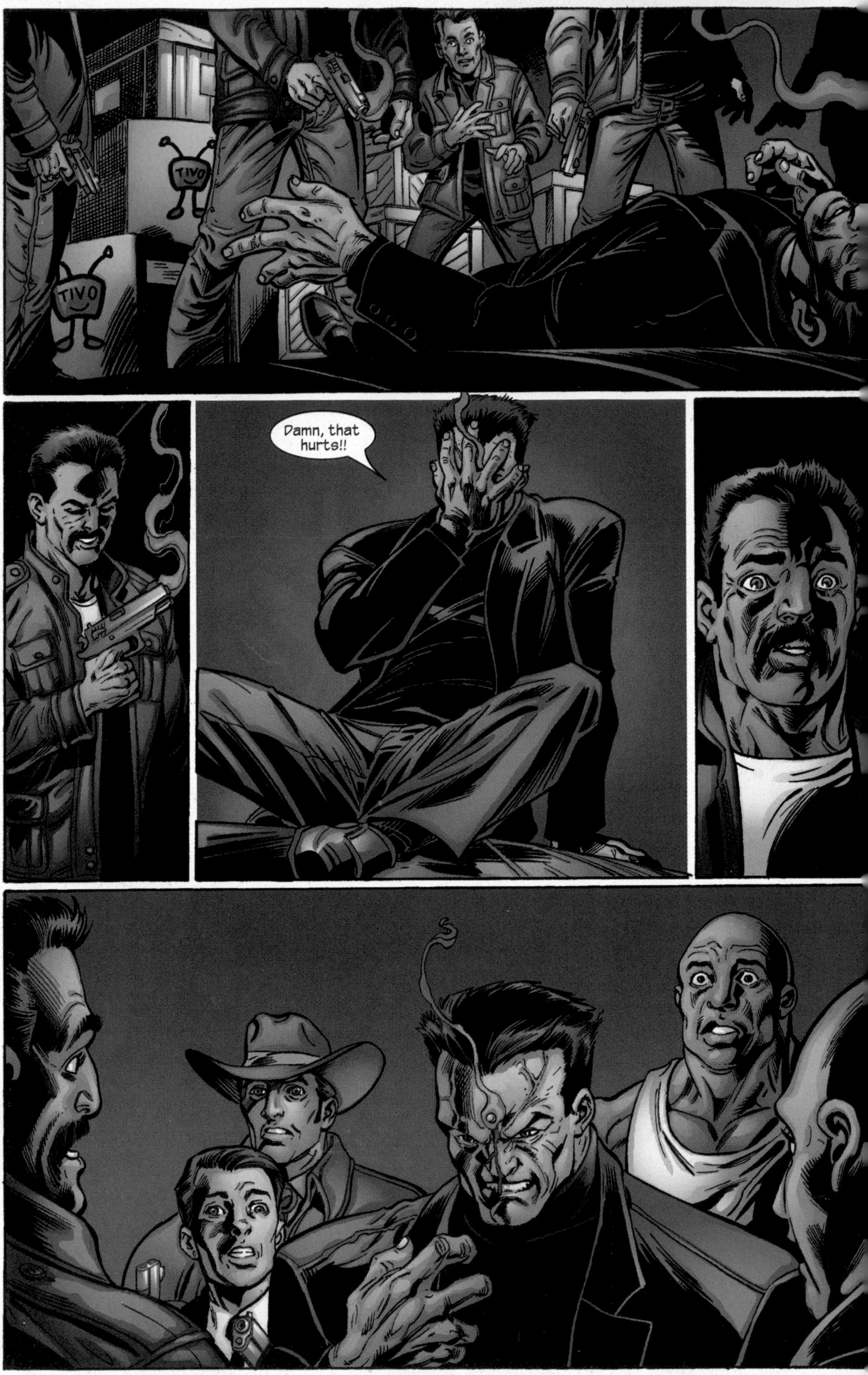
Damn, that hurts!!

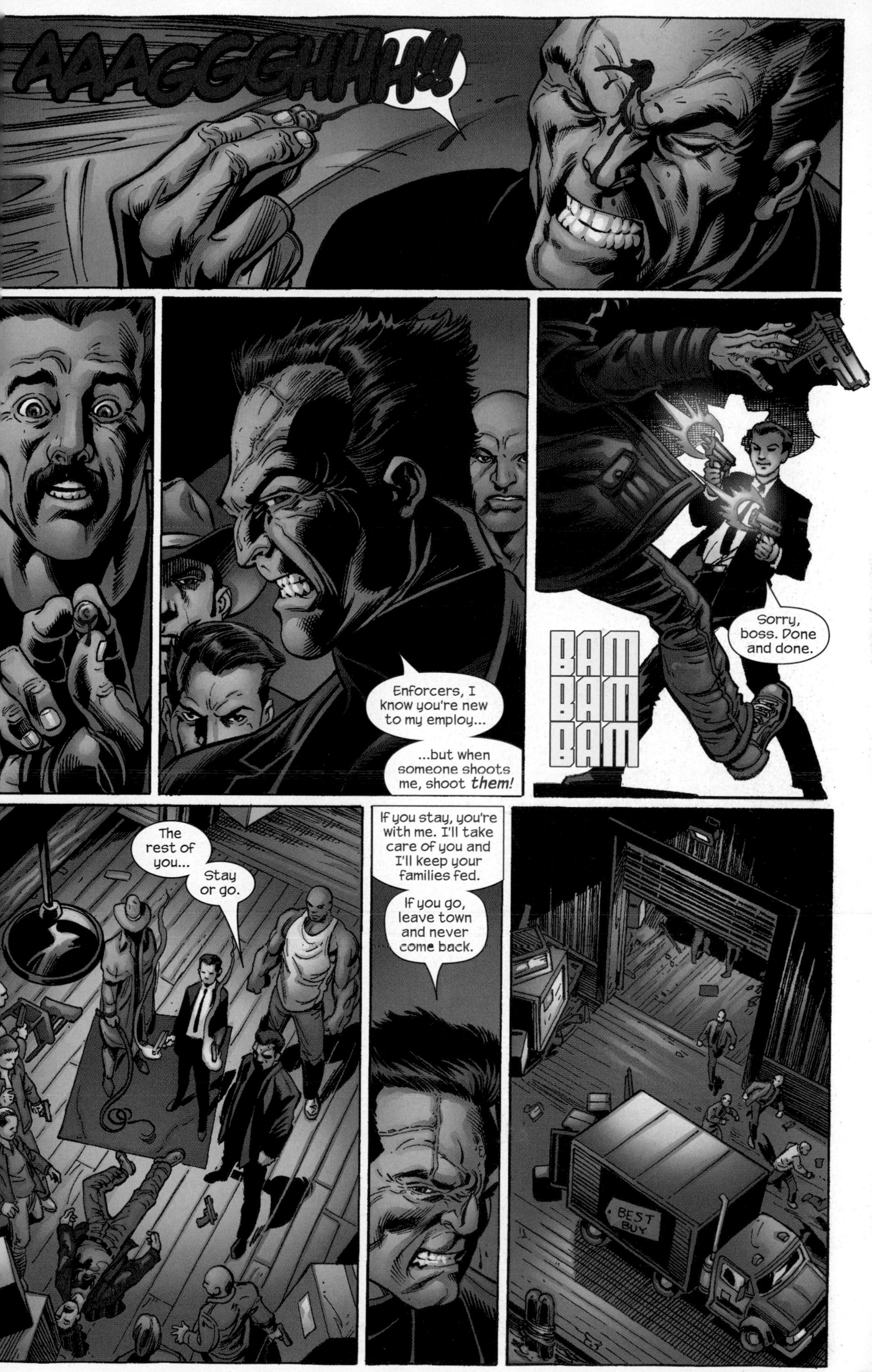
AAAGGGHHH!!!
Enforcers, I know you're new to my employ...
...but when someone shoots me, shoot *them*!
BAM BAM BAM
Sorry, boss. Done and done.
The rest of you...
Stay or go.
If you stay, you're with me. I'll take care of you and I'll keep your families fed.
If you go, leave town and never come back.
BEST BUY

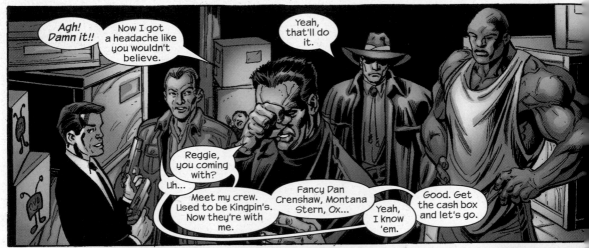

Agh! Damn it!!

Now I got a headache like you wouldn't believe.

Yeah, that'll do it.

Reggie, you coming with?

Uh...

Meet my crew. Used to be Kingpin's. Now they're with me.

Fancy Dan Crenshaw, Montana Stern, Ox...

Yeah, I know 'em.

Good. Get the cash box and let's go.

The hell is a Tivo?

It's pretty cool actually. It--

I don't care. Gimme.

What?

Gun.

Oh, uh... I don't really let anyone touch my--

We're going to have a problem this early on in our relationship?

Uh...

Dan... just...

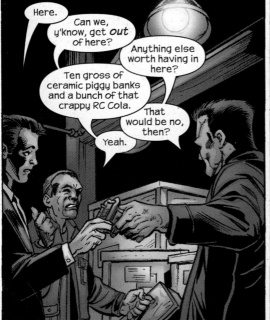

Here.

Can we, y'know, get out of here?

Anything else worth having in here?

Ten gross of ceramic piggy banks and a bunch of that crappy RC Cola.

That would be no, then?

Yeah.

Nickel-and-dime #$%@...

BAM

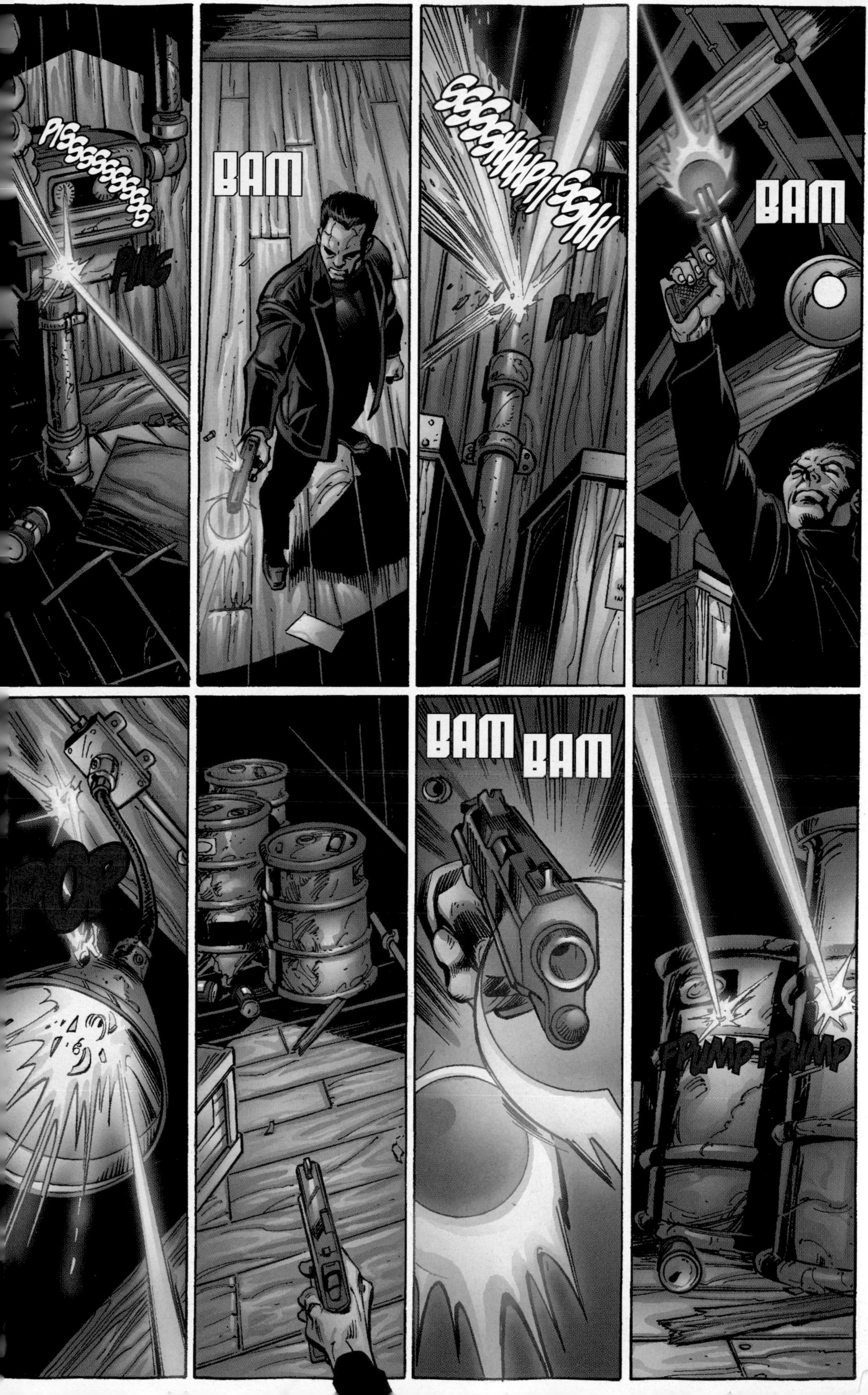
PISSSSSSSSSS
PING
BAM
SSSSSSHHH!!SSHH
PING
BAM
BAM
BAM
FRUMP FRUMP

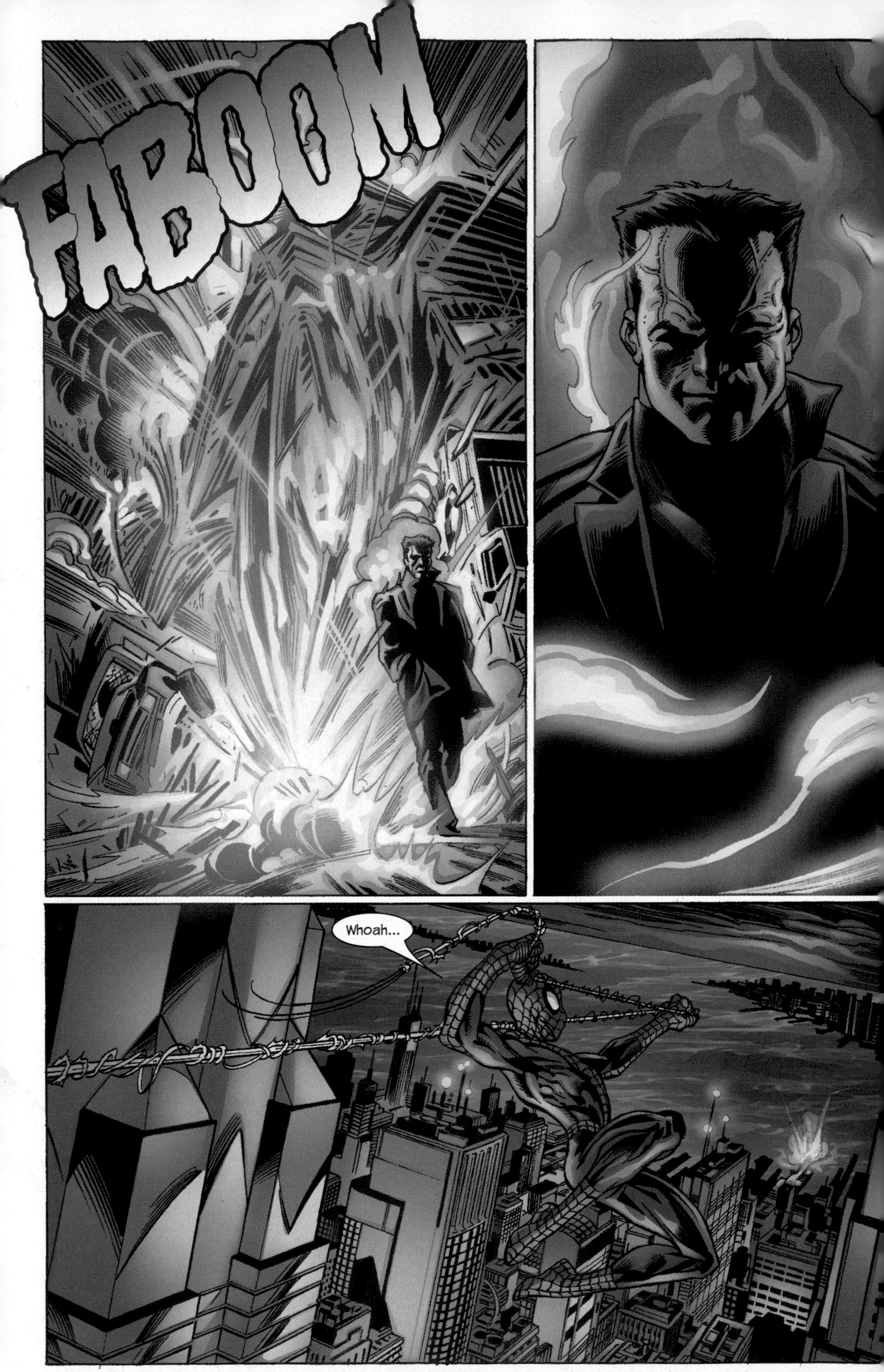
FABOOM
Whoah...

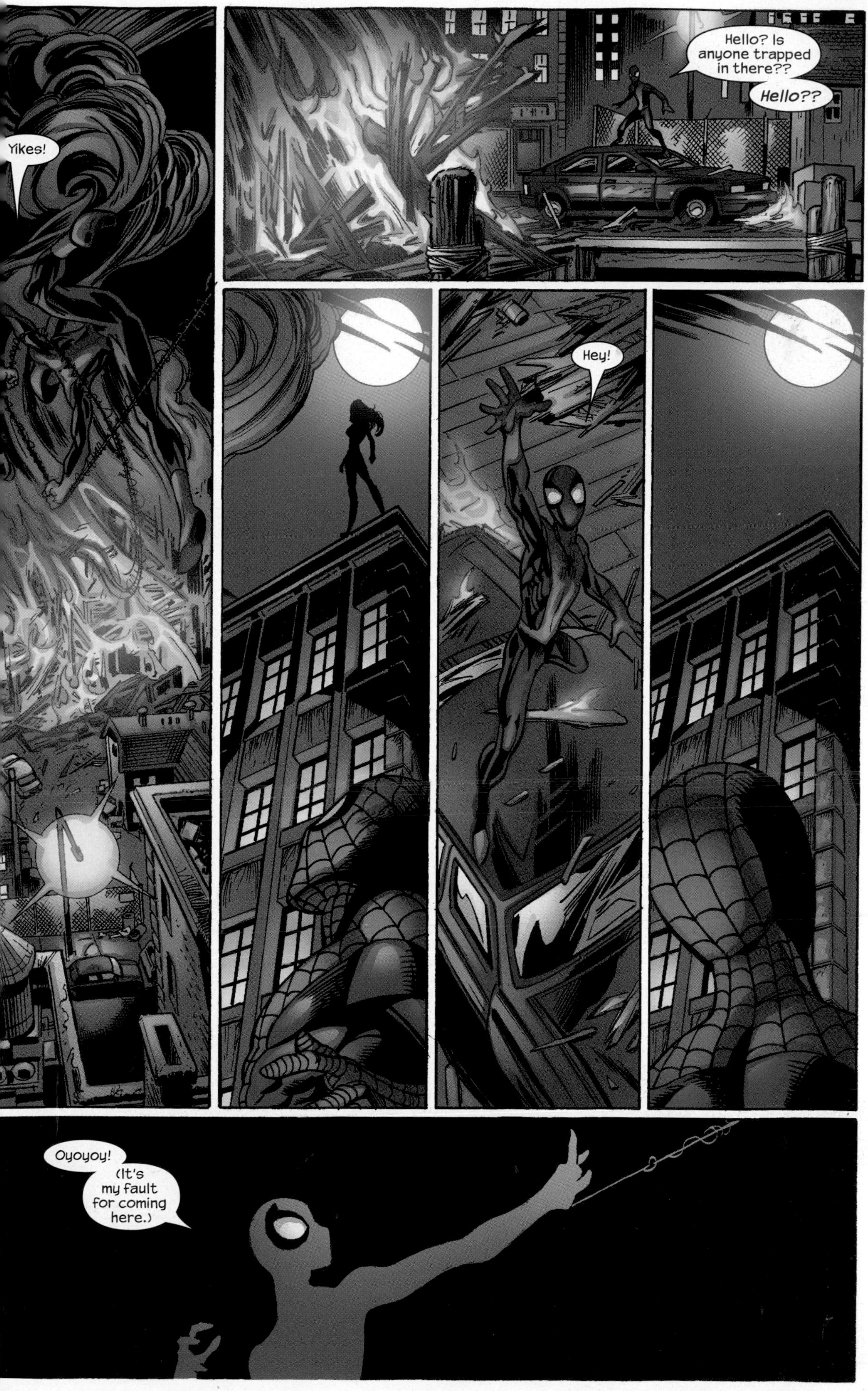
Yikes!
Hello? Is anyone trapped in there??
Hello??
Hey!
Oyoyoy!
(It's my fault for coming here.)

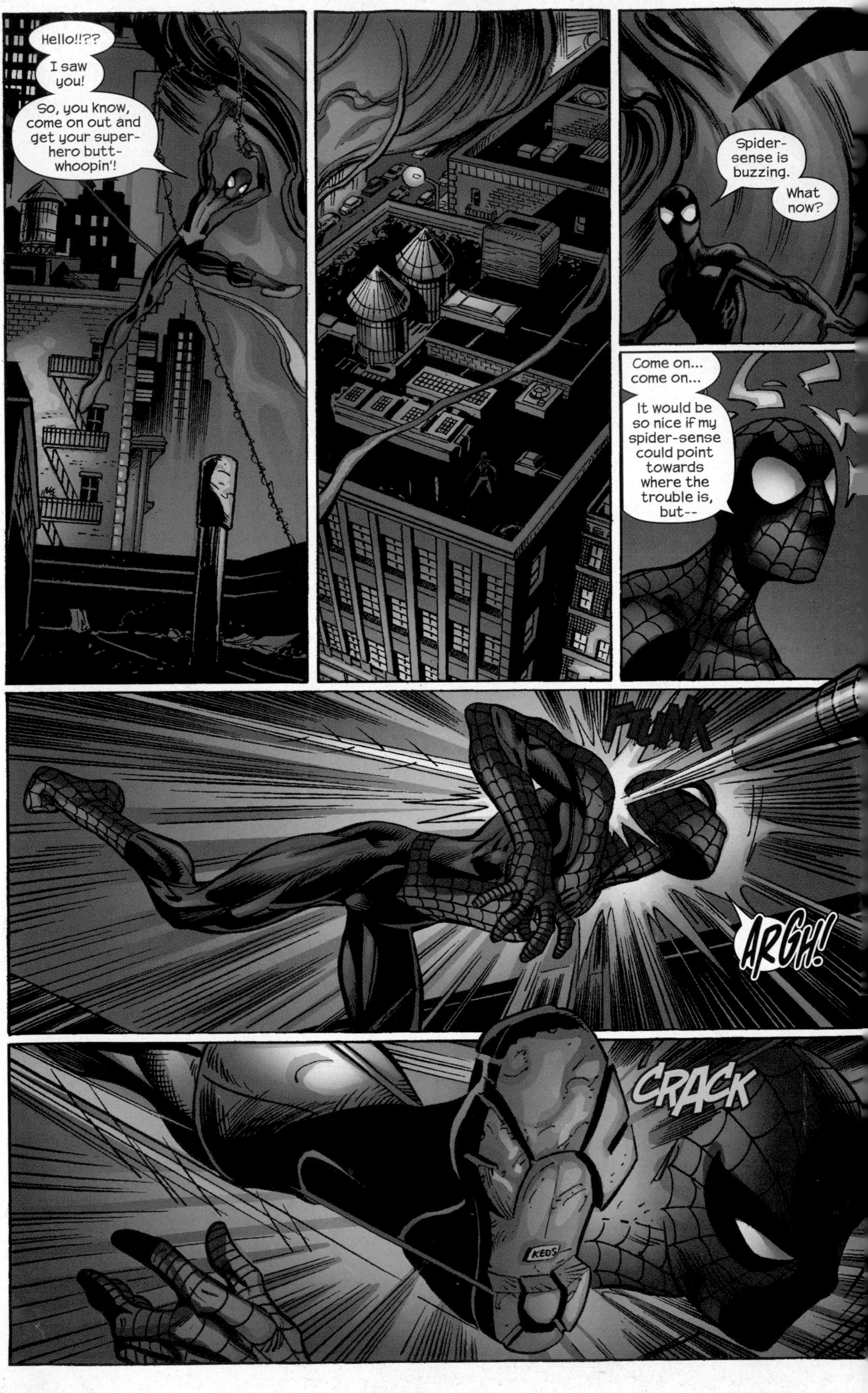
Hello!!??
I saw you!
So, you know, come on out and get your super-hero butt-whoopin'!
Spider-sense is buzzing.
What now?
Come on... come on...
It would be so nice if my spider-sense could point towards where the trouble is, but--
FTUNK
ARGH!
CRACK

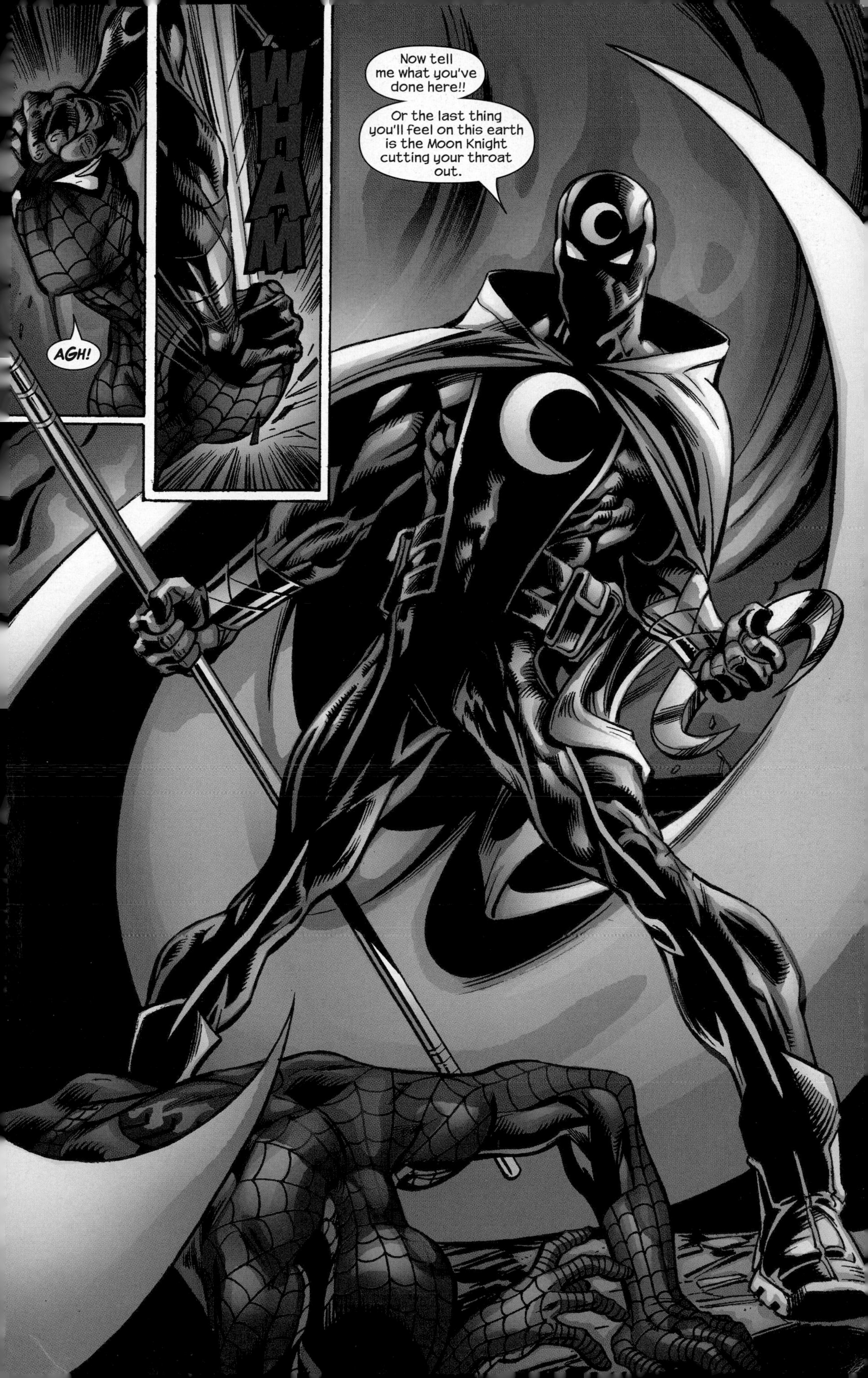
WHAM
AGH!
Now tell me what you've done here!!
Or the last thing you'll feel on this earth is the Moon Knight cutting your throat out.

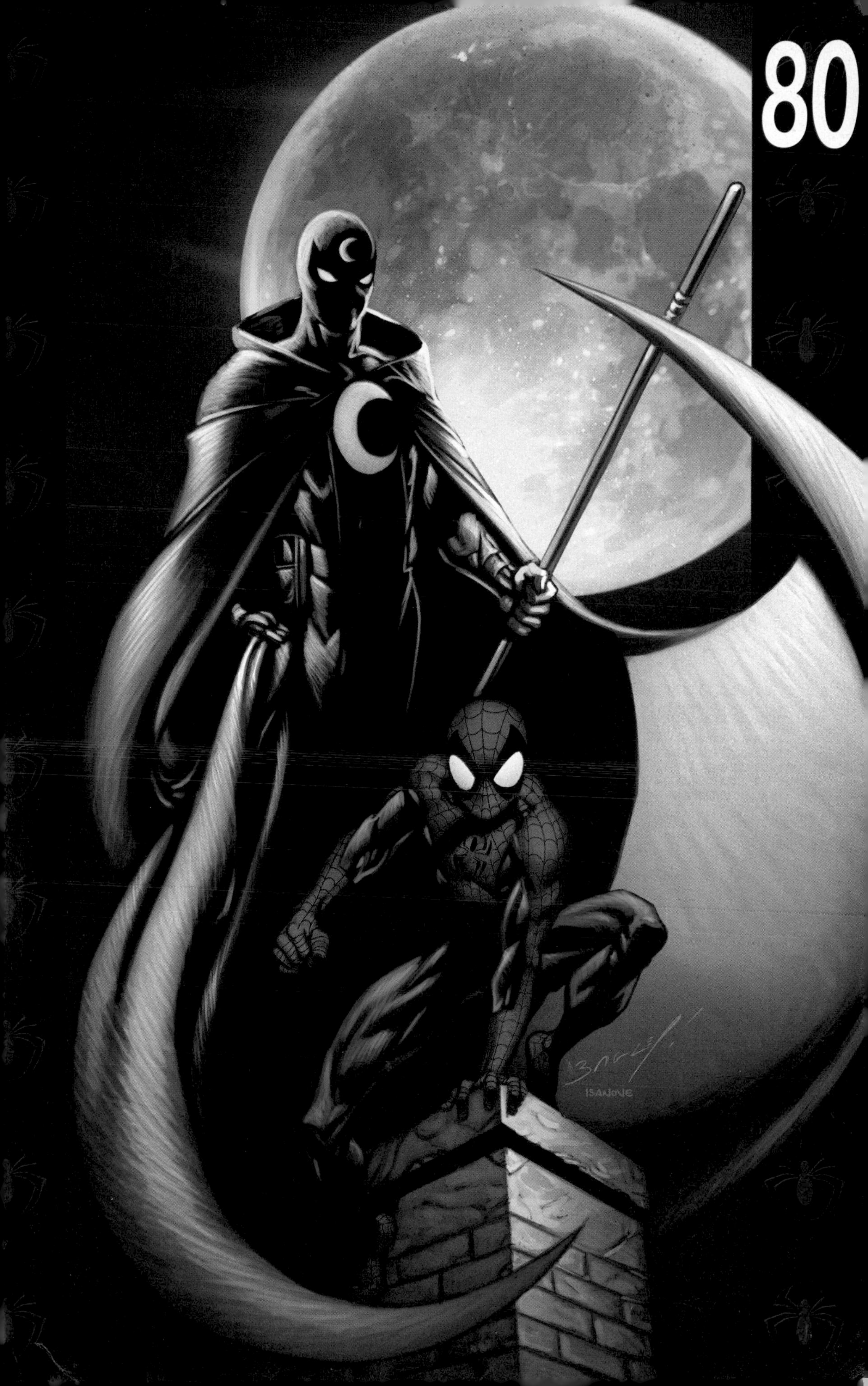
80

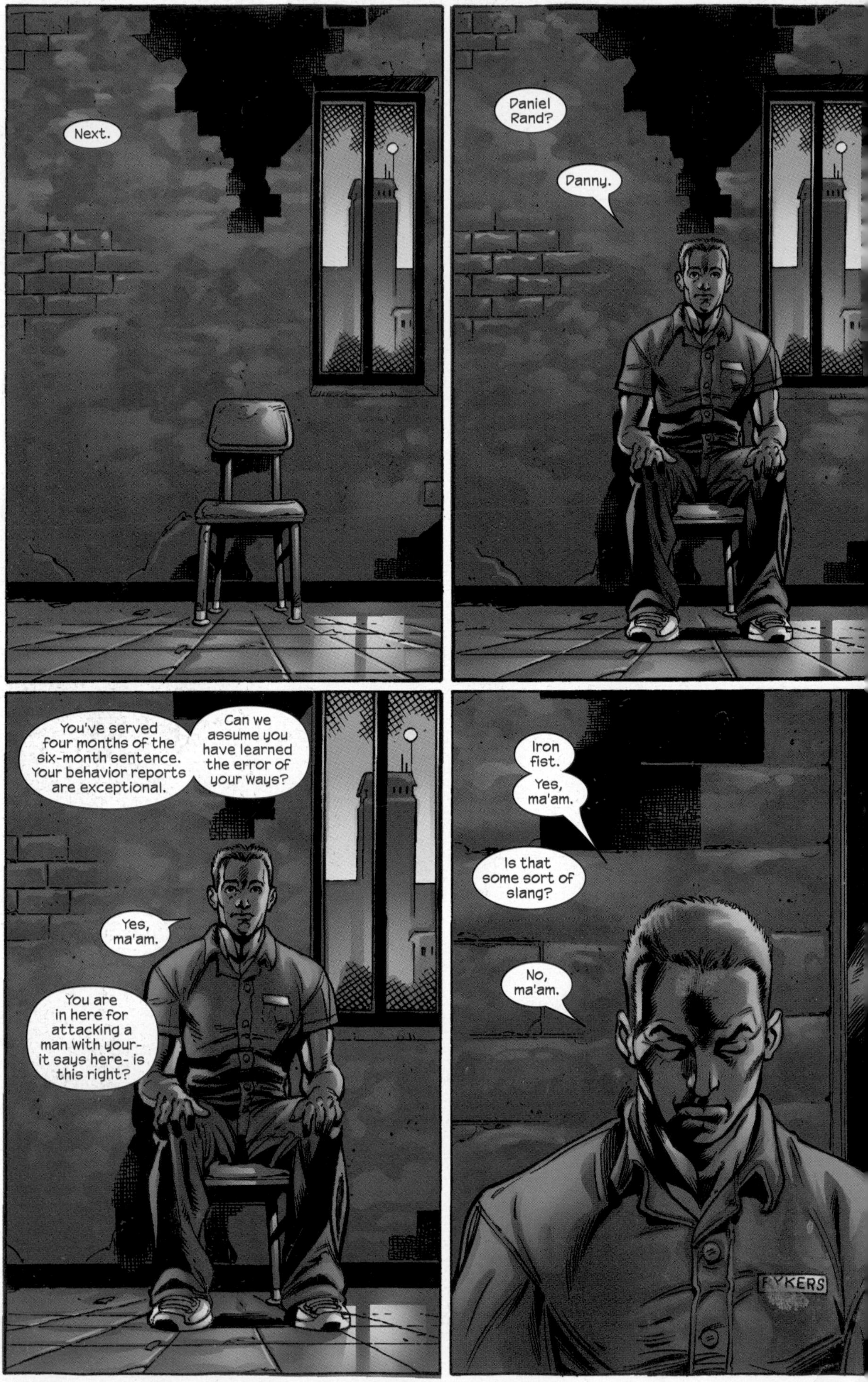
Next.
Daniel Rand?
Danny.
You've served four months of the six-month sentence. Your behavior reports are exceptional.
Can we assume you have learned the error of your ways?
Yes, ma'am.
You are in here for attacking a man with your- it says here- is this right?
Iron fist.
Yes, ma'am.
Is that some sort of slang?
No, ma'am.
RYKERS

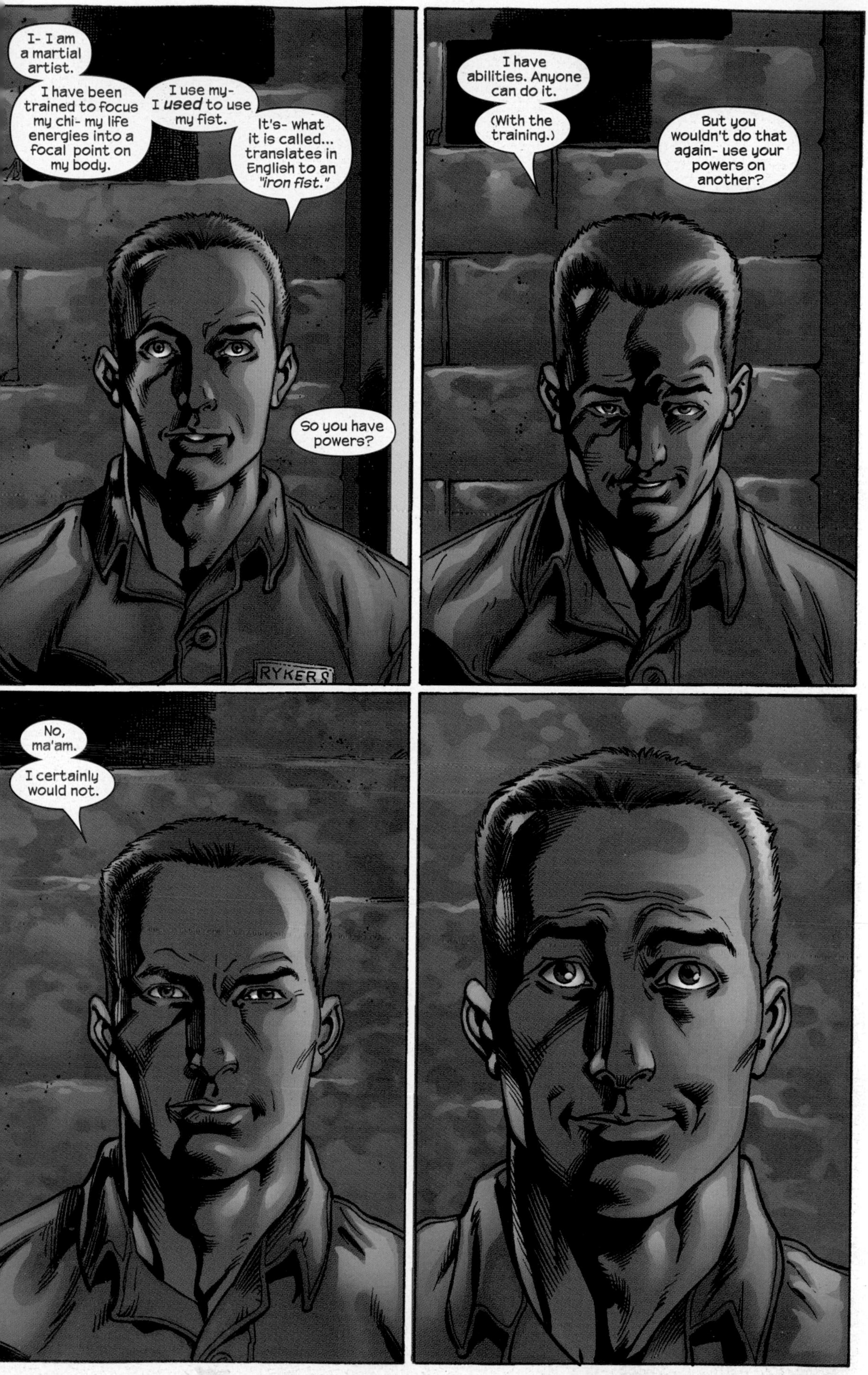

I- I am a martial artist.
I have been trained to focus my chi- my life energies into a focal point on my body.
I use my- I *used* to use my fist.
It's- what it is called... translates in English to an *"iron fist."*
So you have powers?
RYKERS
I have abilities. Anyone can do it.
(With the training.)
But you wouldn't do that again- use your powers on another?
No, ma'am.
I certainly would not.

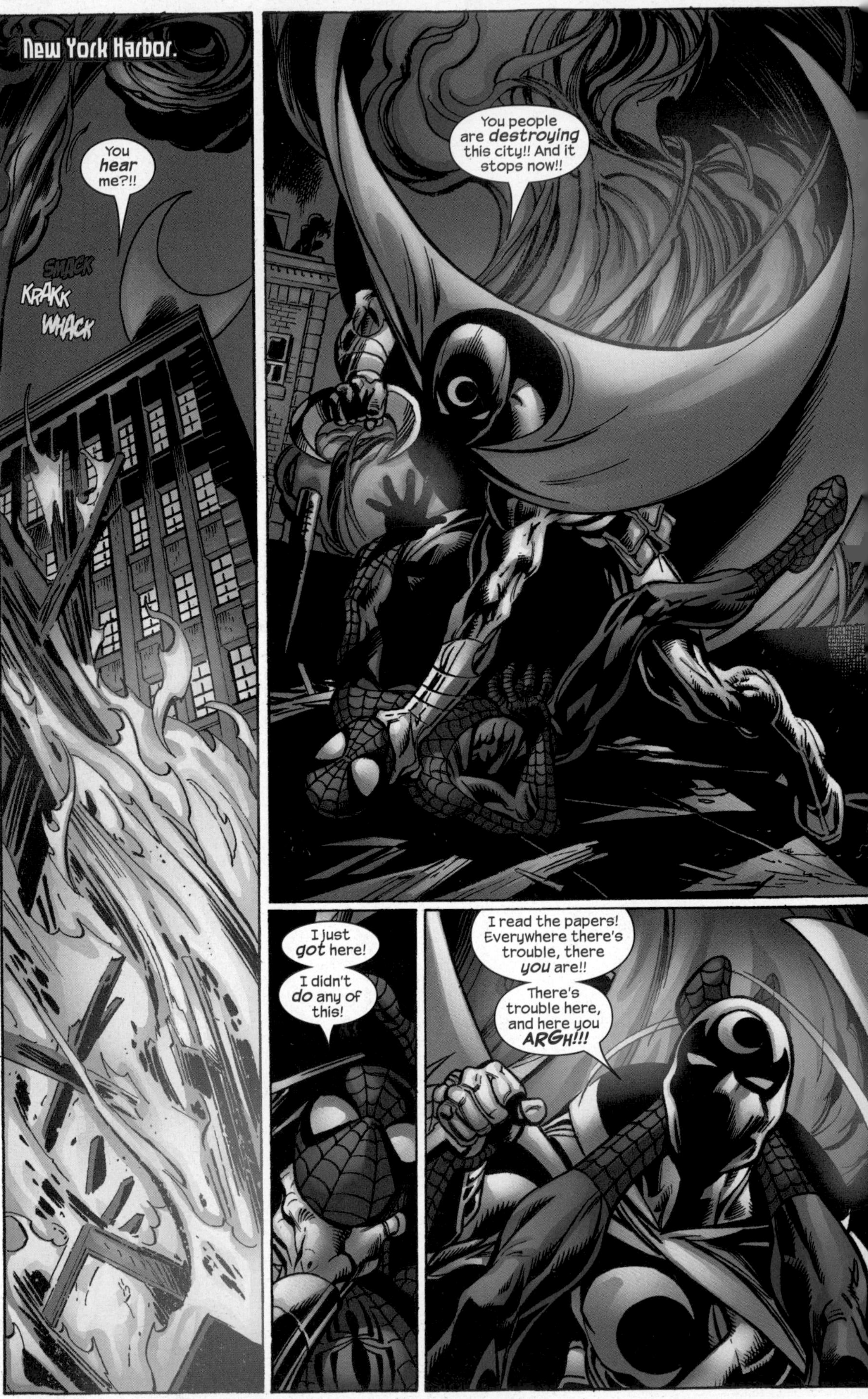
New York Harbor.
You *hear* me?!!
SMACK
KRAKK
WHACK
You people are *destroying* this city!! And it stops now!!
I just *got* here!
I didn't *do* any of this!
I read the papers! Everywhere there's trouble, there *you* are!!
There's trouble here, and here you *ARGH!!!*

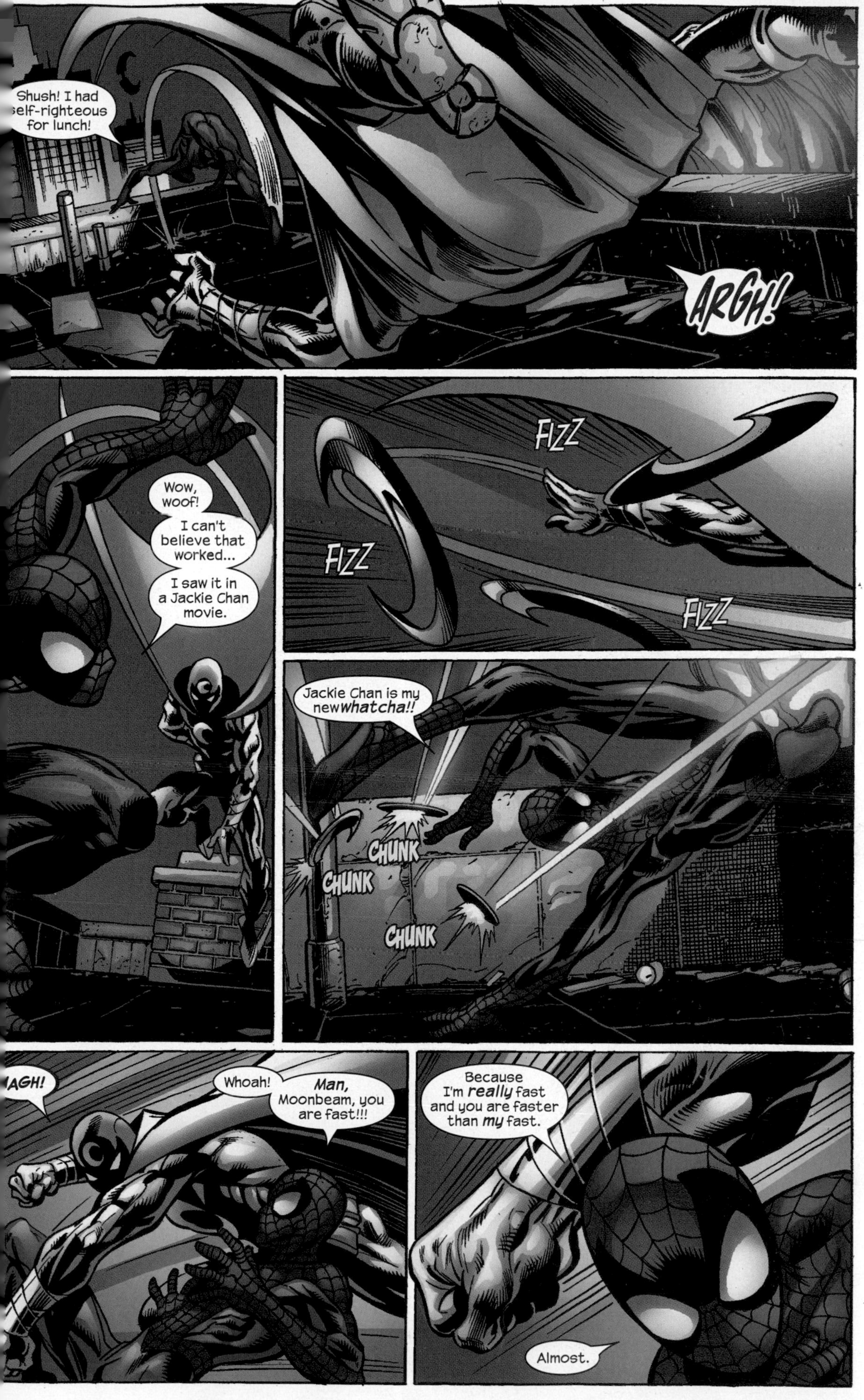

Shush! I had self-righteous for lunch!
ARGH!
Wow, woof!
I can't believe that worked...
I saw it in a Jackie Chan movie.
FIZZ
FIZZ
FIZZ
Jackie Chan is my new whatcha!!
CHUNK
CHUNK
CHUNK
AGH!
Whoah!
Man, Moonbeam, you are fast!!!
Because I'm really fast and you are faster than my fast.
Almost.

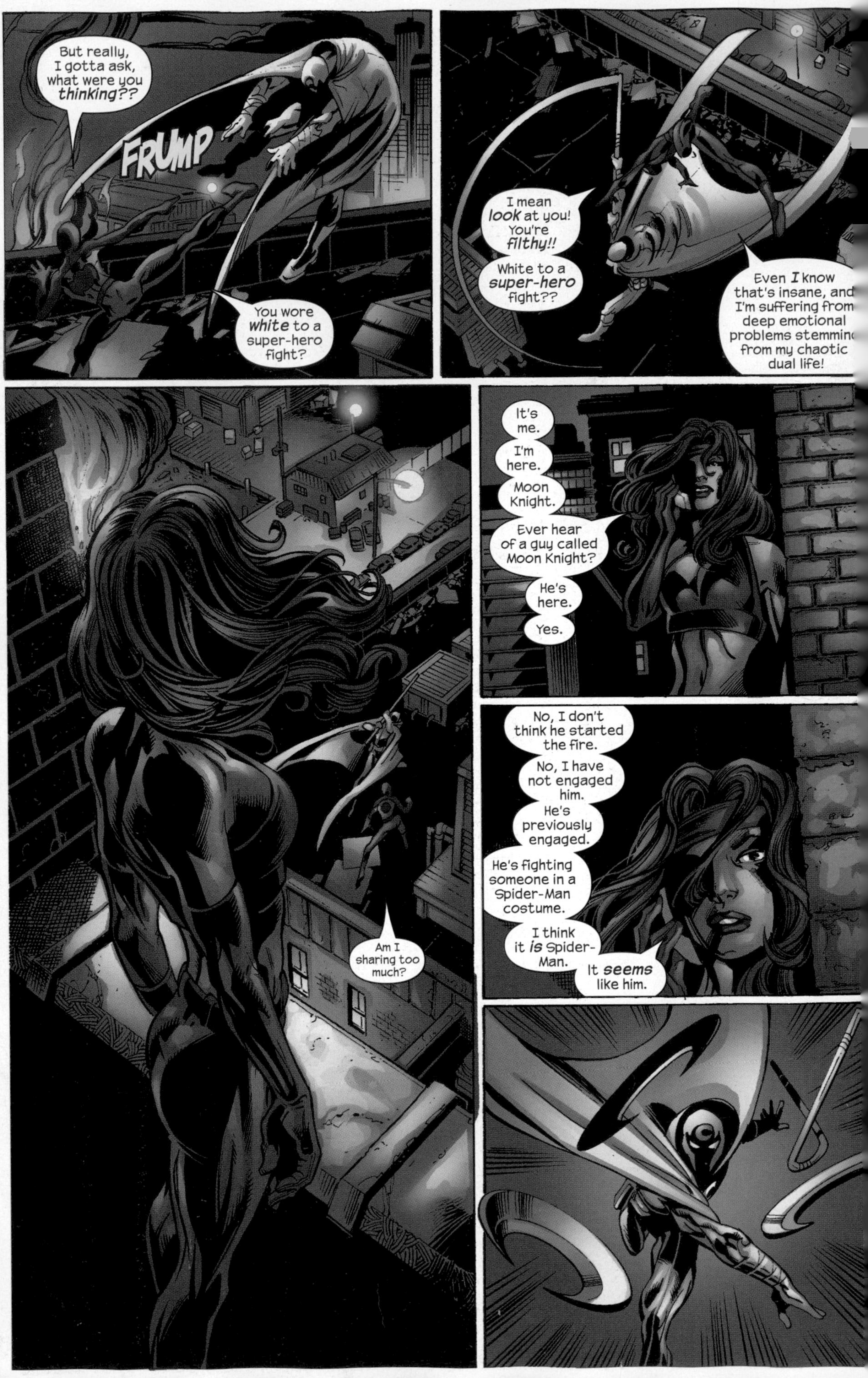

But really, I gotta ask, what were you *thinking??*
FRUMP
You wore *white* to a super-hero fight?
I mean *look* at you! You're *filthy!!*
White to a *super-hero* fight??
Even *I* know that's insane, and I'm suffering from deep emotional problems stemming from my chaotic dual life!
Am I sharing too much?
It's me.
I'm here.
Moon Knight.
Ever hear of a guy called Moon Knight?
He's here.
Yes.
No, I don't think he started the fire.
No, I have not engaged him.
He's previously engaged.
He's fighting someone in a Spider-Man costume.
I think it *is* Spider-Man.
It *seems* like him.

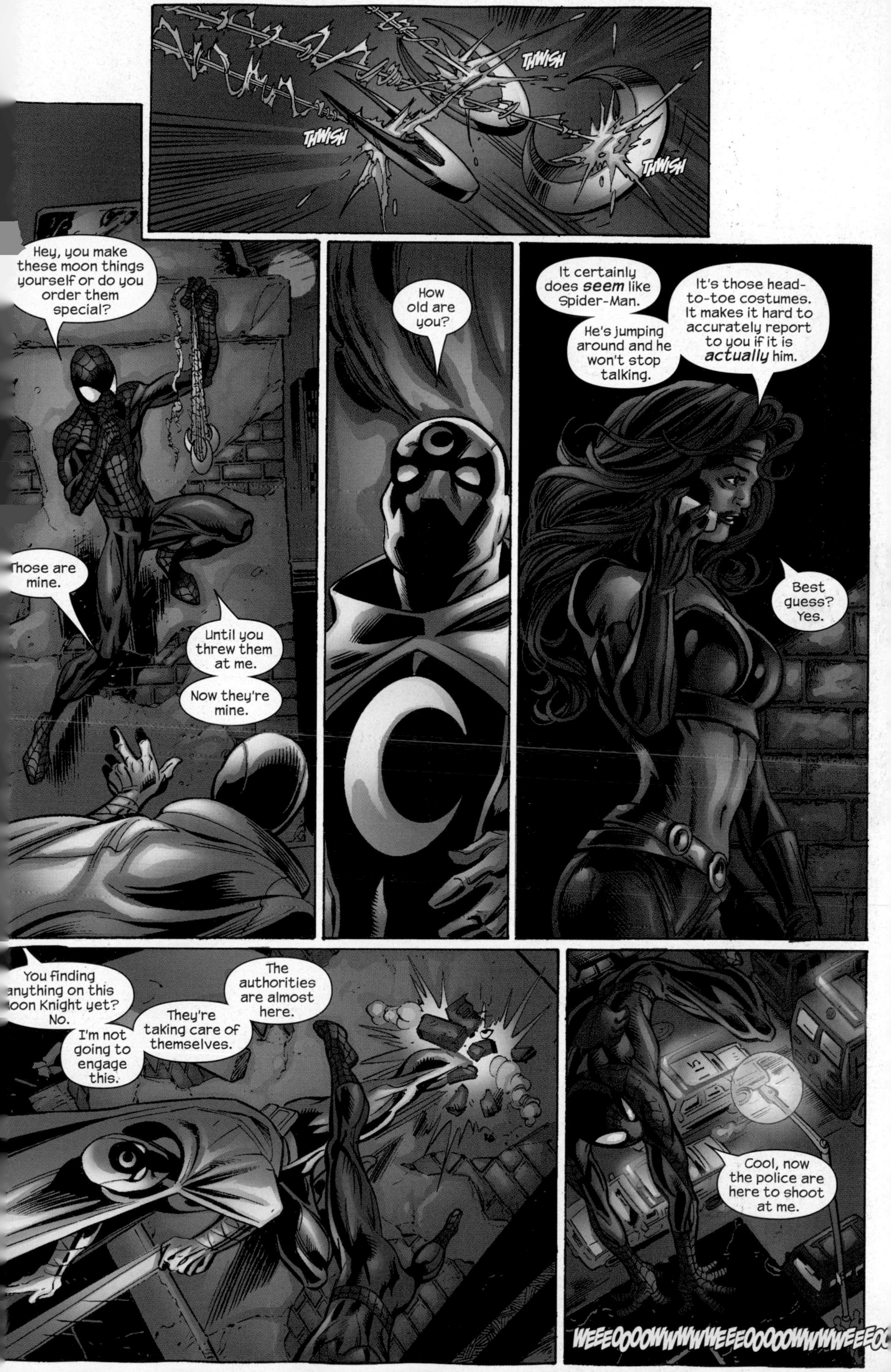
THWISH
THWISH
THWISH
Hey, you make these moon things yourself or do you order them special?
Those are mine.
Until you threw them at me.
Now they're mine.
How old are you?
It certainly does *seem* like Spider-Man.
He's jumping around and he won't stop talking.
It's those head-to-toe costumes. It makes it hard to accurately report to you if it is *actually* him.
Best guess? Yes.
You finding anything on this Moon Knight yet? No.
I'm not going to engage this.
They're taking care of themselves.
The authorities are almost here.
Cool, now the police are here to shoot at me.
WEEEOOOOWWWWWEEEOOOOOWWWWEEEO

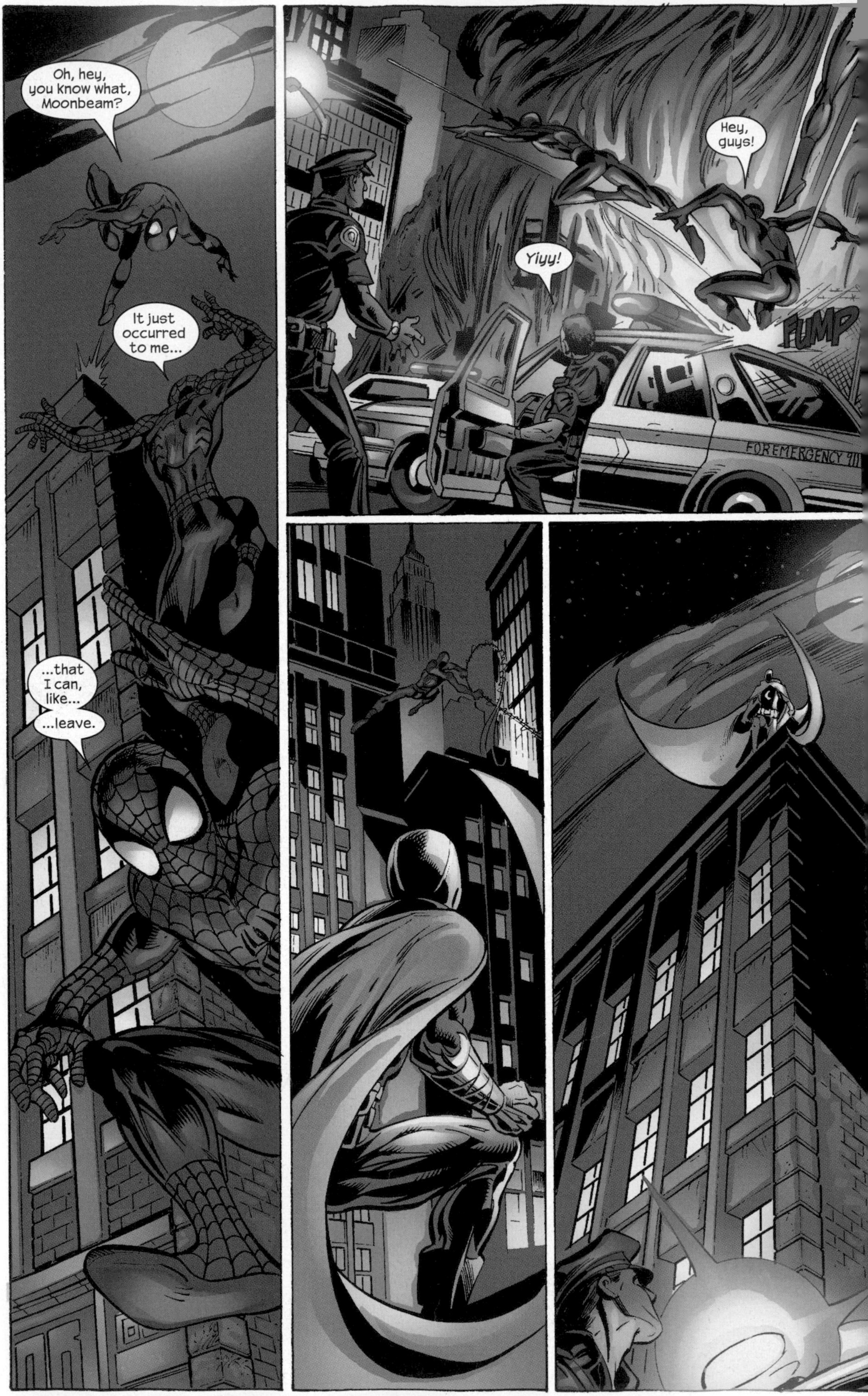
Oh, hey, you know what, Moonbeam?
It just occurred to me...
...that I can, like...
...leave.
Hey, guys!
Yiyy!
FUMP
FOR EMERGENCY 911

DAILY BUGLE

MOONMAN COMETH

Allan Silverman

Cetetuer adipiscing elit,
dunt ut laoreet dolore
isi enim ad minim
ullamcorper suscipit
odo consequat. Duis
it in vulputate velit
feugiat nulla
ore eu feugiat nulla
o odio dignissim qui
ugue duis dolore te

strud exerci tation
ip ex ea commodo
lor in hendrerit in
el illum dolore eu
san et iusto odio
ril delenit augue
ipsum dolor sit
o nonummy nibh
na aliquam erat

rit in vulputate
lore eu feugiat
et iusto odio
delenit augue
osum dolor sit
onummy nibh
aliquam erat
quis nostrud
ut aliquip ex

piscing elit,
oreet dolore
ad minim
er suscipit
quat. Duis
utate velit
egiat nulla
nissim qui
dolore te

rci tation
ommodo
drerit in
olore eu
sto odio
augue
olor sit
y nibh
m erat

utate
eugiat
odio
augue
or sit
nibh
erat
crud
ex

lit,
ore
m
it
is
it

Duis autem vel eum iriure
velit esse molestie conseq
nulla facilisis at vero er
dignissim qui blandit praes
duis dolore te feugait nulla
amet, consectetuer adipiscin
euismod tincidunt ut laoree
volutpat. Ut wisi enim ad
exerci tation ullamcorper sus
ea commodo consequat.

SILVER
DEAD

Ut wisi enim ad minim veniam, quis
ullamcorper suscipit lobortis nisl ut ali
consequat. Duis autem vel eum iriure do
vulputate velit esse molestie consequat
feugiat nulla facilisis at vero eros et acc
dignissim qui blandit praesent luptatum
duis dolore te feugait nulla facilisi. Lor
amet, consectetuer adipiscing elit, sed di
euismod tincidunt ut laoreet dolore ma
volutpat.

Duis autem vel eum iriure dolor in hen
velit esse molestie consequat, vel illum
nulla facilisis at vero eros et accumsan
dignissim qui blandit praesent luptatum
duis dolore te feugait nulla facilisi. Lore
amet, consectetuer adipiscing elit, sed diam
euismod tincidunt ut laoreet dolore magn
volutpat. Ut wisi enim ad minim veniam
exerci tation ullamcorper suscipit lobortis n
ea commodo consequat.

Lorem ipsum dolor sit amet, consectetuer a
sed diam nonummy nibh euismod tincidunt a
magna aliquam erat volutpat. Ut wisi eni
veniam, quis nostrud exerci tation ullamco
loboris nisl ut aliquip ex ea commodo con
autem vel eum iriure dolor in hendrerit in v
esse molestie consequat, vel illum dolore eu
facilisis at vero eros et accumsan et iusto odi
blandit praesent luptatum zzril delenit augue
feugiat nulla facilisi.

Ut wisi enim ad minim veniam, quis nostrud exerci tation
ullamcorper suscipit lobortis nisl ut aliquip ex ea commodo
consequat. Duis autem vel eum iriure dolor in hendrerit in
vulputate velit esse molestie consequat, vel illum dolore eu
dignissim qui blandit praesent luptatum zzril delenit augue
duis dolore te feugait nulla facilisi. Lorem ipsum dolor sit
amet, consectetuer adipiscing elit, sed diam nonummy nibh
euismod tincidunt ut laoreet dolore magna aliquam erat
volutpat.

Duis autem vel eum iriure dolor in hendrerit in
velit esse molestie conseq

Lorem ipsum dolor sit amet, consectetuer adipiscing elit,
sed diam nonummy nibh euismod tincidunt ut laoreet dolore
magna aliquam erat volutpat. Ut wisi enim ad minim
veniam, quis nostrud exerci tation ullamcorper suscipit
loboris nisl ut aliquip ex ea commodo consequat. Duis
autem vel eum iriure dolor in hendrerit in vulputate velit
esse molestie consequat, vel illum dolore eu feugiat nulla
facilisis at vero eros et accumsan et iusto odio dignissim qui
blandit praesent luptatum zzril delenit augue duis dolore te
feugait nulla facilisi.

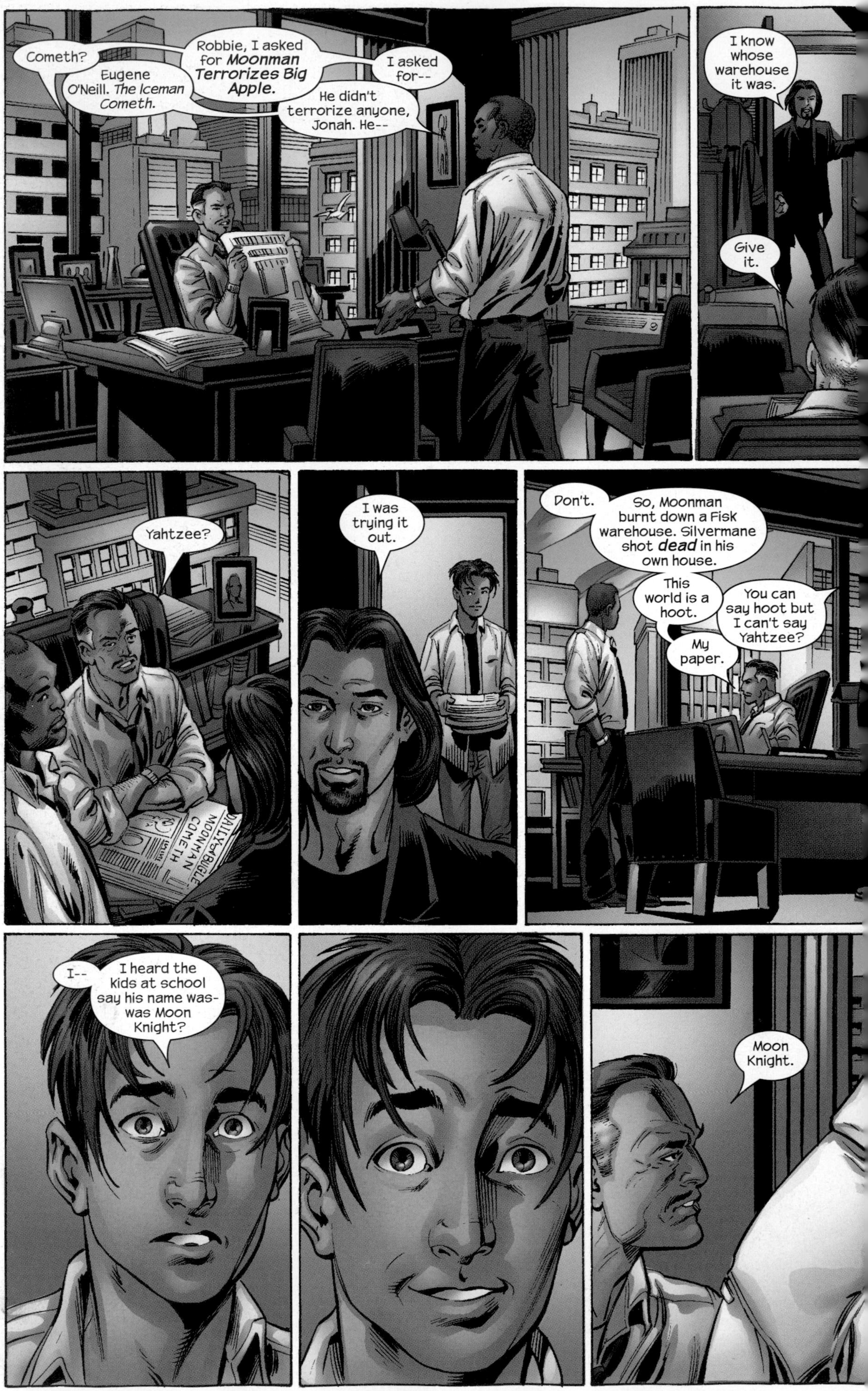
Cometh?
Robbie, I asked for **Moonman Terrorizes Big Apple.**
Eugene O'Neill. *The Iceman Cometh.*
I asked for--
He didn't terrorize anyone, Jonah. He--
I know whose warehouse it was.
Give it.
Yahtzee?
DAILY BUGLE
MOONMAN COMETH
I was trying it out.
Don't.
So, Moonman burnt down a Fisk warehouse. Silvermane shot **dead** in his own house.
This world is a hoot.
You can say hoot but I can't say Yahtzee?
My paper.
I--
I heard the kids at school say his name was-was Moon Knight?
Moon Knight.

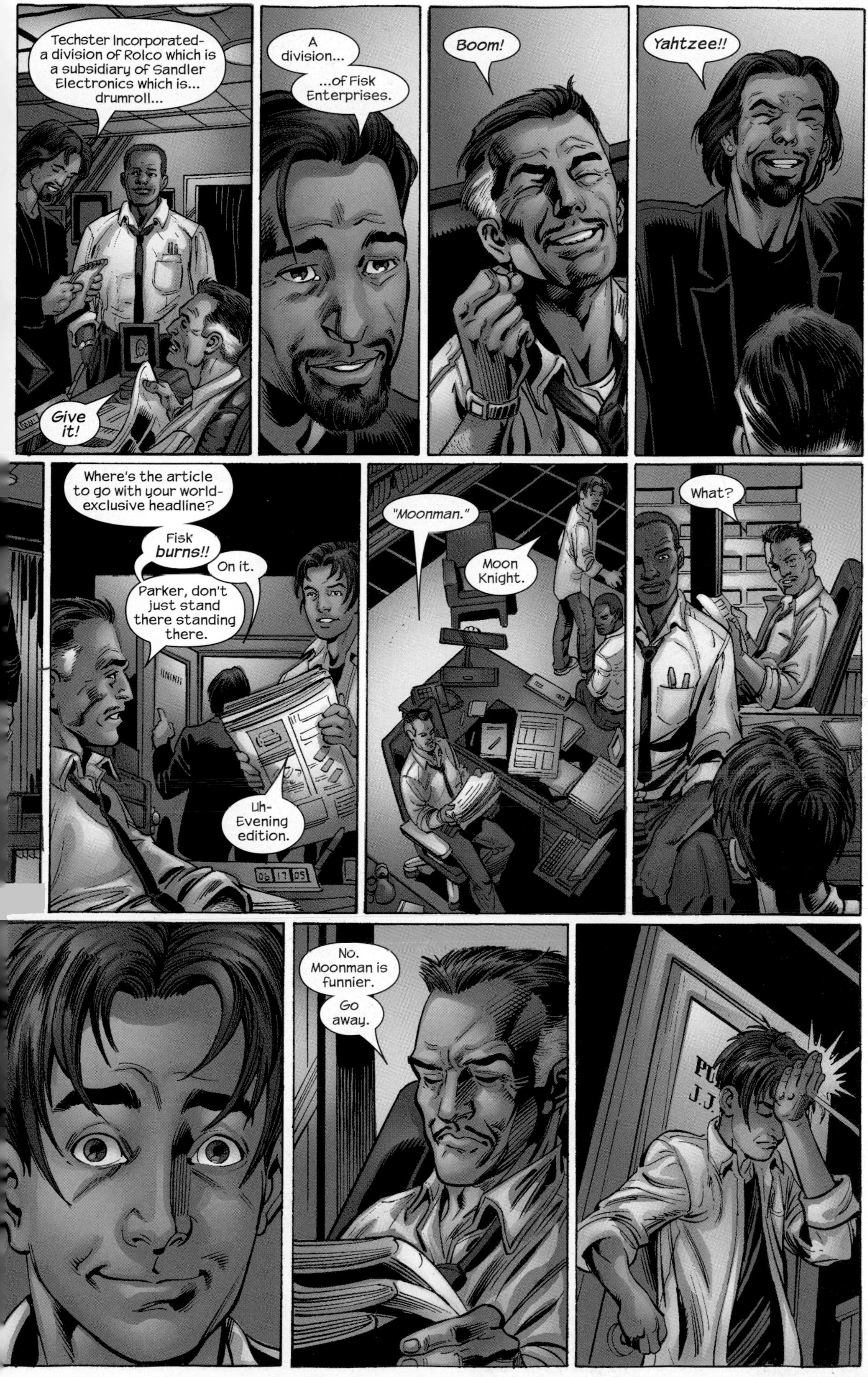
Techster Incorporated- a division of Rolco which is a subsidiary of Sandler Electronics which is... drumroll...
Give it!
A division...
...of Fisk Enterprises.
Boom!
Yahtzee!!
Where's the article to go with your world-exclusive headline?
Fisk burns!!
On it.
Parker, don't just stand there standing there.
Uh- Evening edition.
"Moonman."
Moon Knight.
What?
No. Moonman is funnier.
Go away.

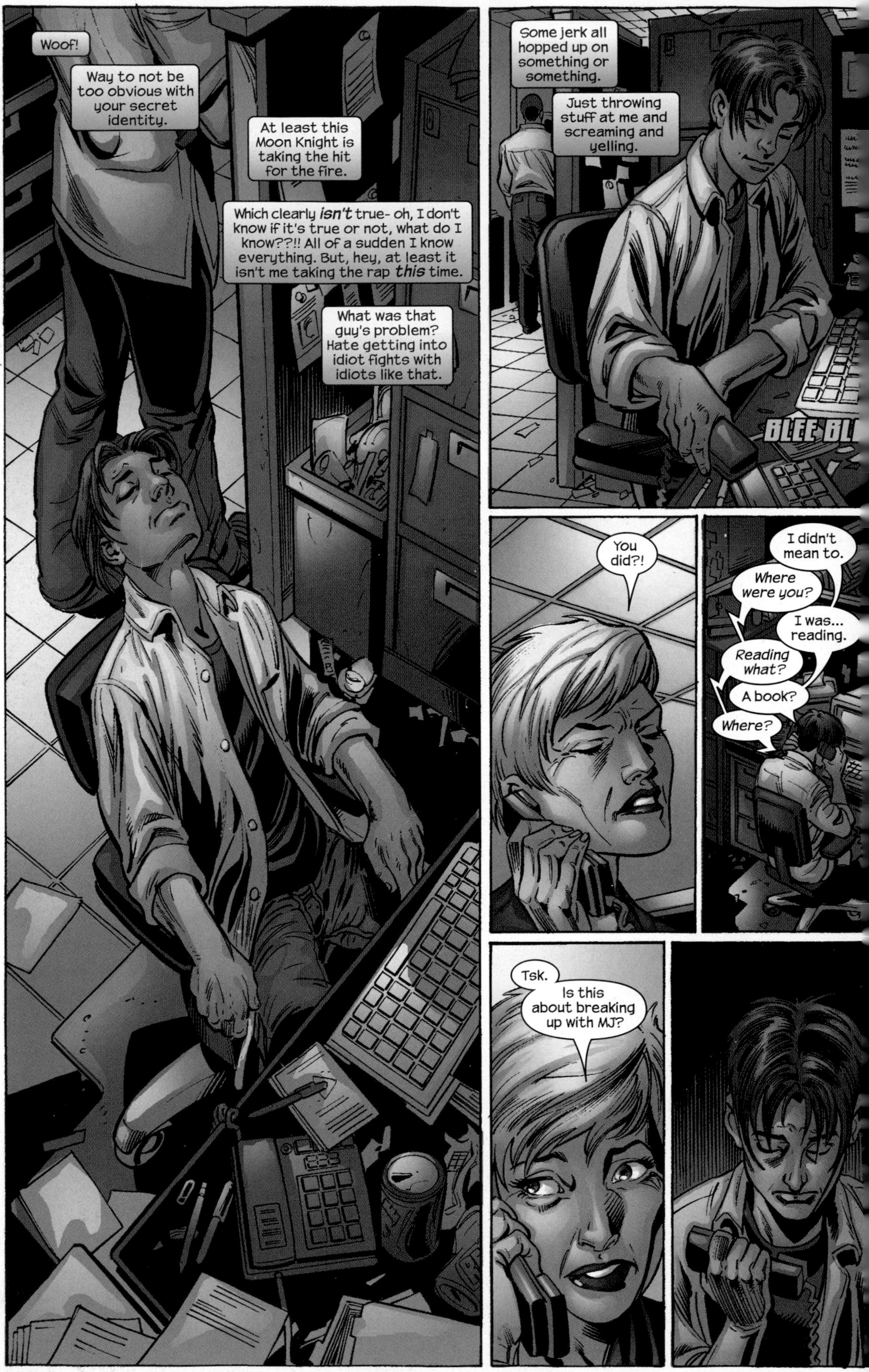

Woof!
Way to not be too obvious with your secret identity.
At least this Moon Knight is taking the hit for the fire.
Which clearly *isn't* true- oh, I don't know if it's true or not, what do I know??!! All of a sudden I know everything. But, hey, at least it isn't me taking the rap *this* time.
What was that guy's problem? Hate getting into idiot fights with idiots like that.
Some jerk all hopped up on something or something.
Just throwing stuff at me and screaming and yelling.
You did?!
I didn't mean to.
Where were you?
I was... reading.
Reading what?
A book?
Where?
Tsk.
Is this about breaking up with MJ?

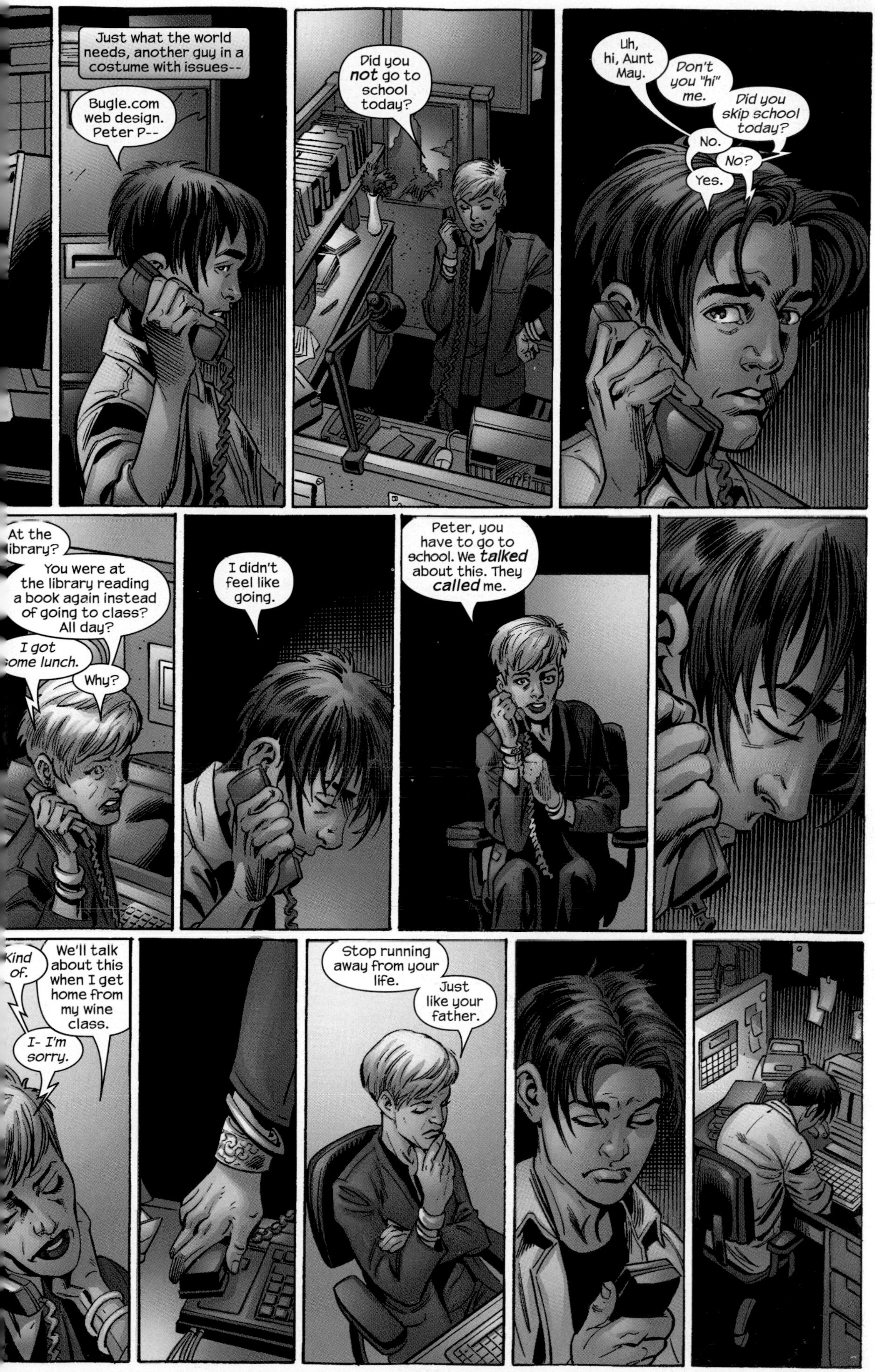

Just what the world needs, another guy in a costume with issues--
Bugle.com web design. Peter P--
Did you **not** go to school today?
Uh, hi, Aunt May.
Don't you "hi" me.
Did you skip school today?
No.
No?
Yes.
At the library?
You were at the library reading a book again instead of going to class? All day?
I got some lunch.
Why?
I didn't feel like going.
Peter, you have to go to school. We **talked** about this. They **called** me.
Kind of.
We'll talk about this when I get home from my wine class.
I- I'm sorry.
Stop running away from your life.
Just like your father.

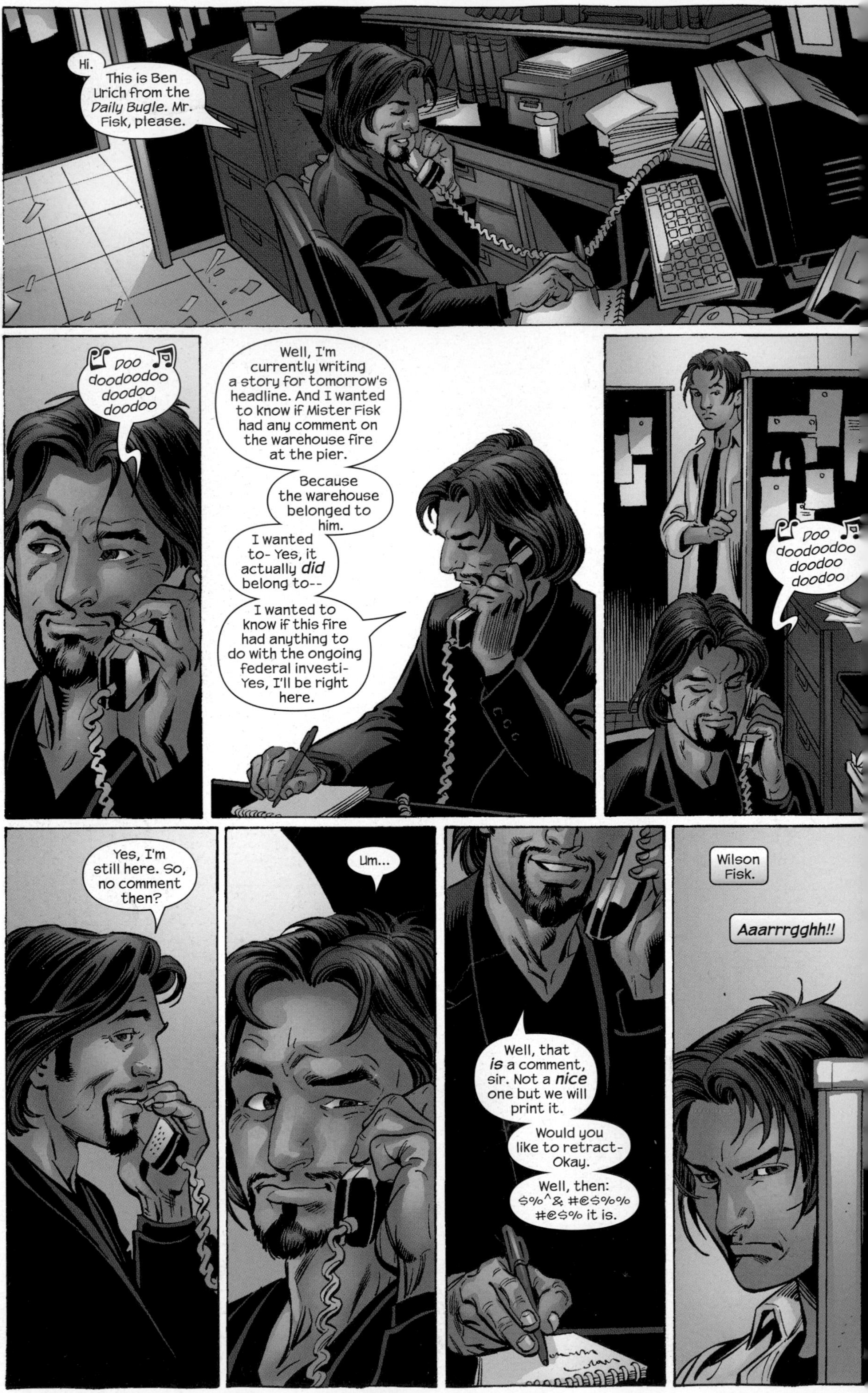
Hi.
This is Ben Urich from the *Daily Bugle*. Mr. Fisk, please.
Doo doodoodoo doodoo doodoo
Well, I'm currently writing a story for tomorrow's headline. And I wanted to know if Mister Fisk had any comment on the warehouse fire at the pier.
Because the warehouse belonged to him.
I wanted to- Yes, it actually *did* belong to--
I wanted to know if this fire had anything to do with the ongoing federal investi- Yes, I'll be right here.
Doo doodoodoo doodoo doodoo
Yes, I'm still here. So, no comment then?
Um...
Well, that *is* a comment, sir. Not a *nice* one but we will print it.
Would you like to retract- Okay.
Well, then: $%^& #@$%% #@$% it is.
Wilson Fisk.
Aaarrrgghh!!

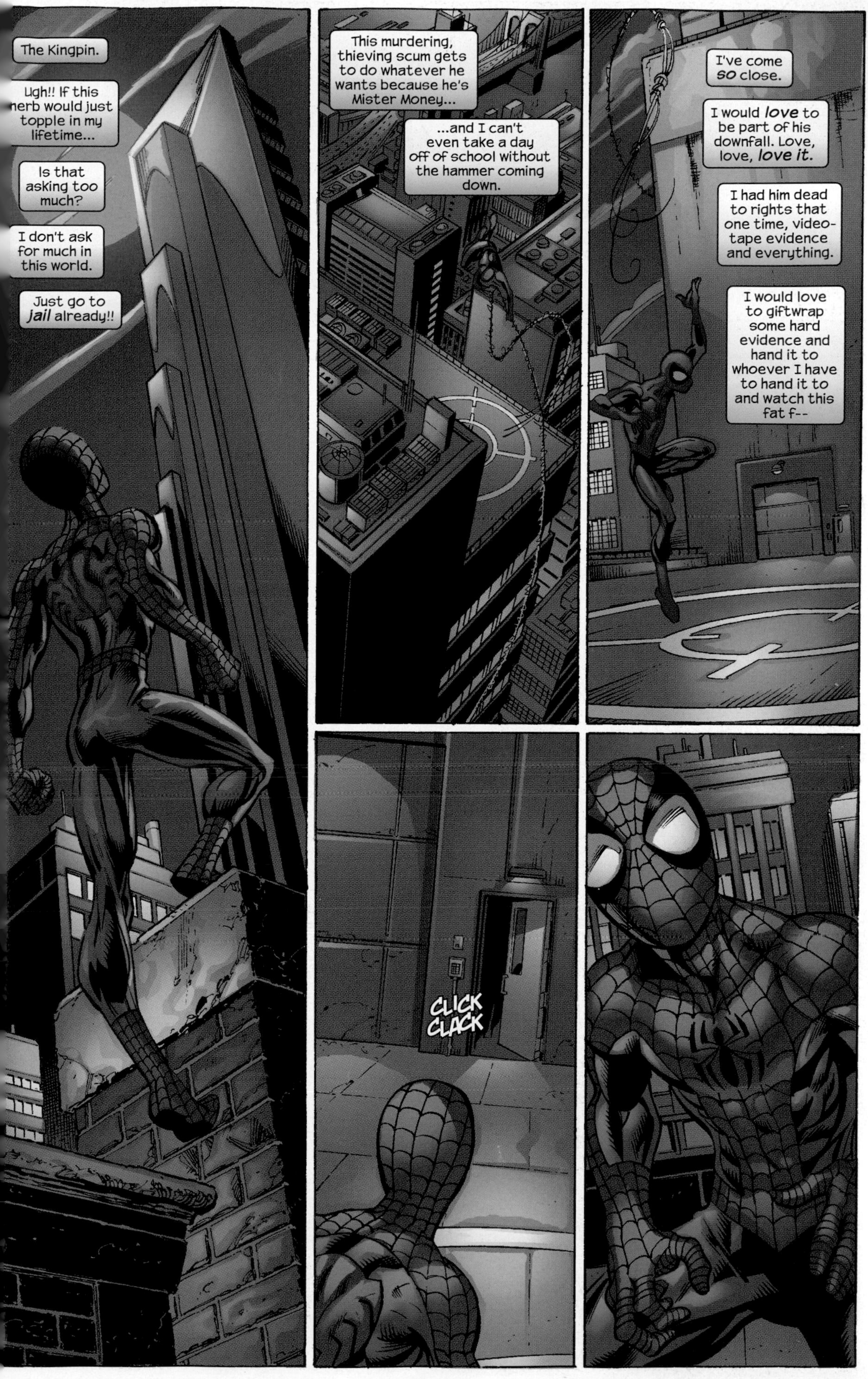
The Kingpin.
Ugh!! If this herb would just topple in my lifetime...
Is that asking too much?
I don't ask for much in this world.
Just go to *jail* already!!
This murdering, thieving scum gets to do whatever he wants because he's Mister Money...
...and I can't even take a day off of school without the hammer coming down.
I've come *so* close.
I would *love* to be part of his downfall. Love, love, *love it.*
I had him dead to rights that one time, video-tape evidence and everything.
I would love to giftwrap some hard evidence and hand it to whoever I have to hand it to and watch this fat f--
CLICK CLACK

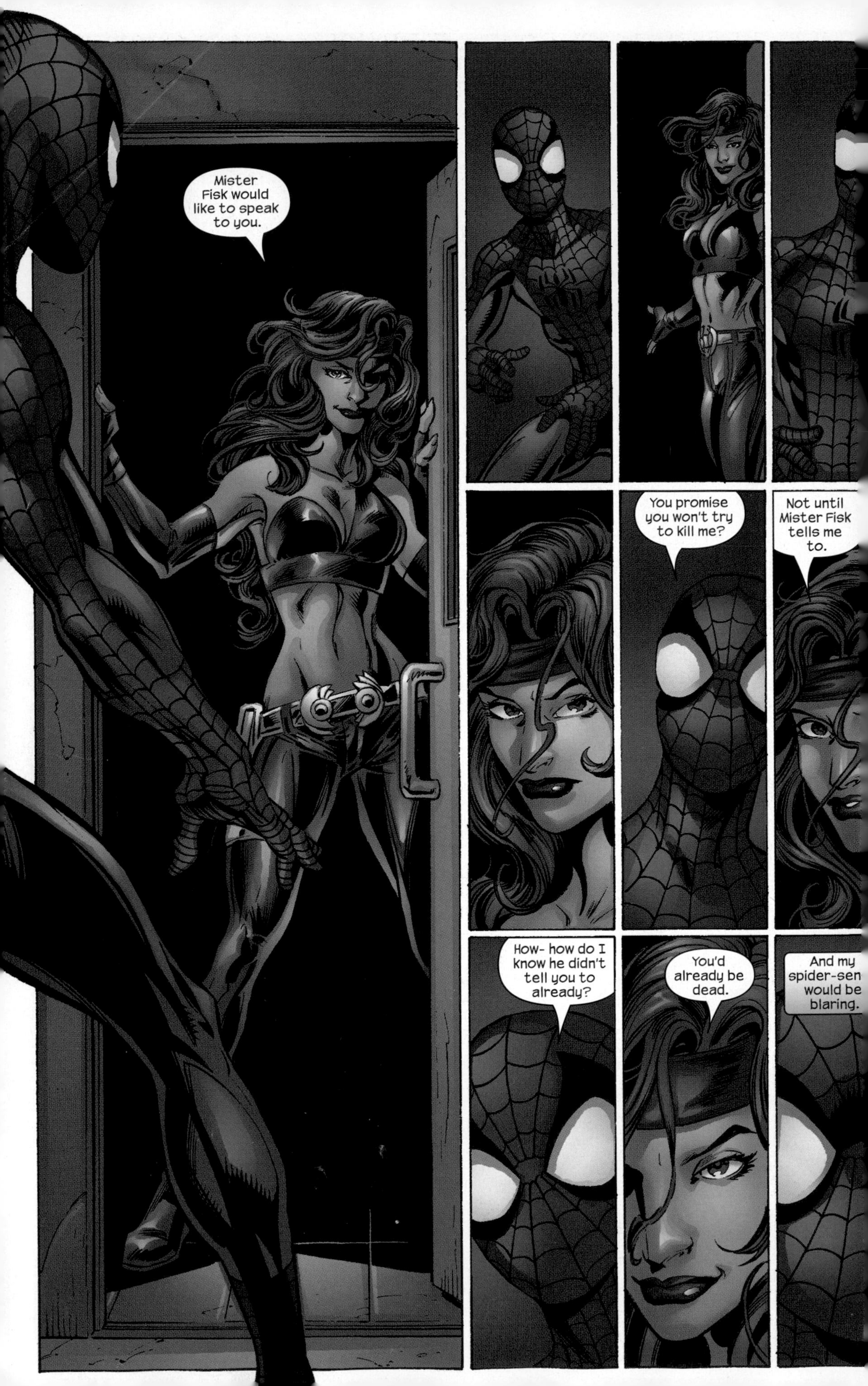
Mister Fisk would like to speak to you.
You promise you won't try to kill me?
Not until Mister Fisk tells me to.
How- how do I know he didn't tell you to already?
You'd already be dead.
And my spider-sen would be blaring.

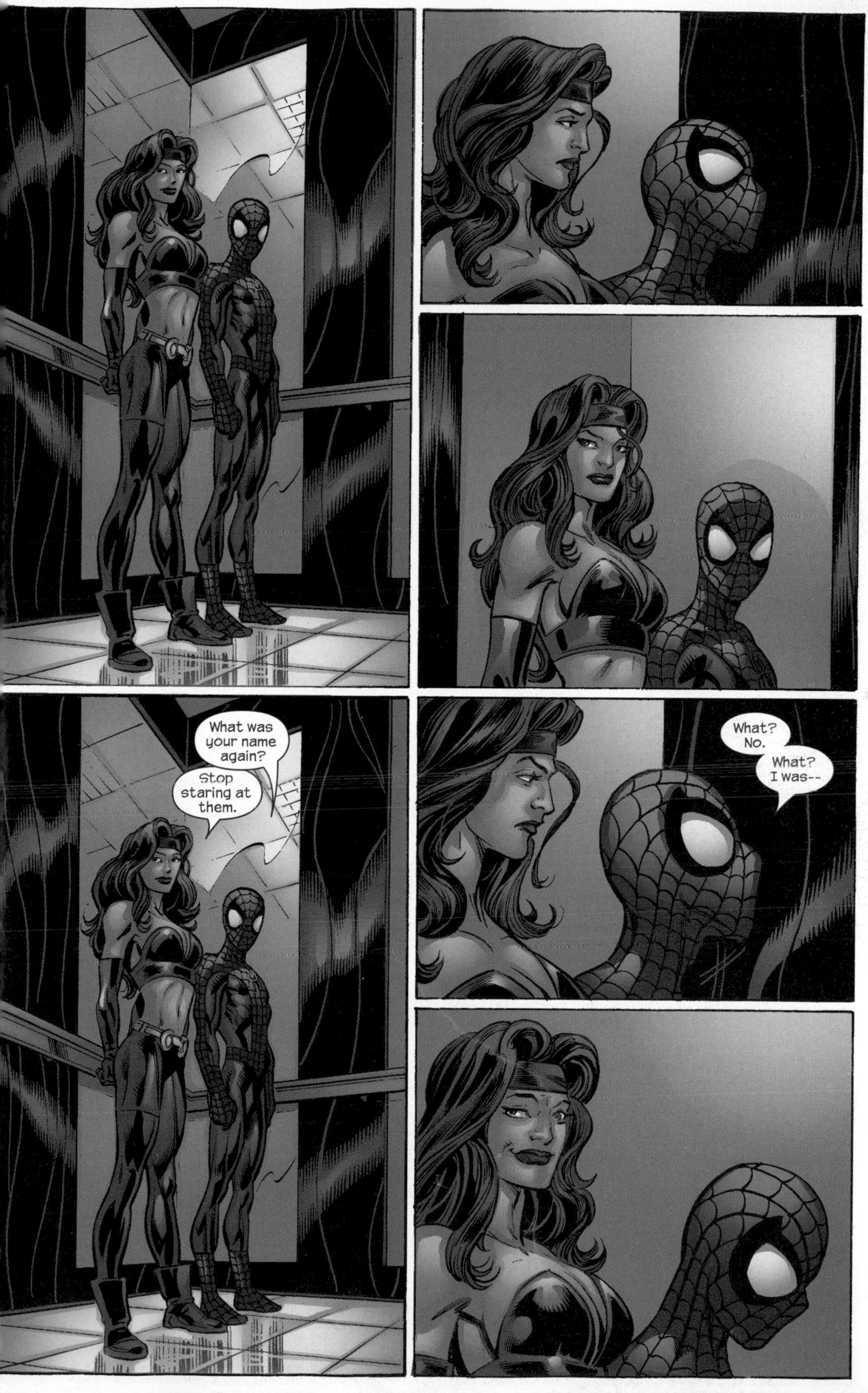
What was your name again?
Stop staring at them.
What? No.
What? I was--

I was just going to have a bite.

Have some pizza with me. Let's talk like men.

How did you know I was coming? I didn't even know I was coming.

Oh, I didn't.

I have cameras on the roof. Got them just because of you.

I told my men to tell me if you ever stopped by again.

I've been looking forward to the opportunity to talk to you in a less hostile environment.

Sit. Eat.

Ha!

I own the parlor.

I bought it after I tasted a slice actually.

It's the best in New York.

I know a lot of people claim that, but...

What do you want to *talk* about?

Many things. I have many questions. Many topics.

I *am* an enigma.

So...

Why do you think they hate you?

Who? You?

DAILY BUG

SPIDER-M MENAC

FISK B OUT LIB

FISK BAILS OUT LIBRARY

People.

The people who you risk your life for everyday.

Why do you they think they *hate* you?

The costume?

They--

Oh wait, I know why.

It's because I run a criminal empire and cloak it in charity work and quote unquote legitimate businesses and try to sell myself as something I'm not.

No wait, that's you.

They, society, *hate* you because they don't *want* your help.

You remind them of how weak-willed and *sheep*-like and *un*special they are.

How gleeful they are, deep down, to be ordinary.

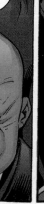

They don't want heroes. They don't want special people around them.

Because if there *are* special people and *they* aren't one of them- well who wants that?

Who wants a constant reminder that they *aren't* even trying to be special?

Hmmm. Thing is. If that's true or not...

(And I think it's simplistic and stuff...)

But if it *is* true...

I--

I guess I don't care.

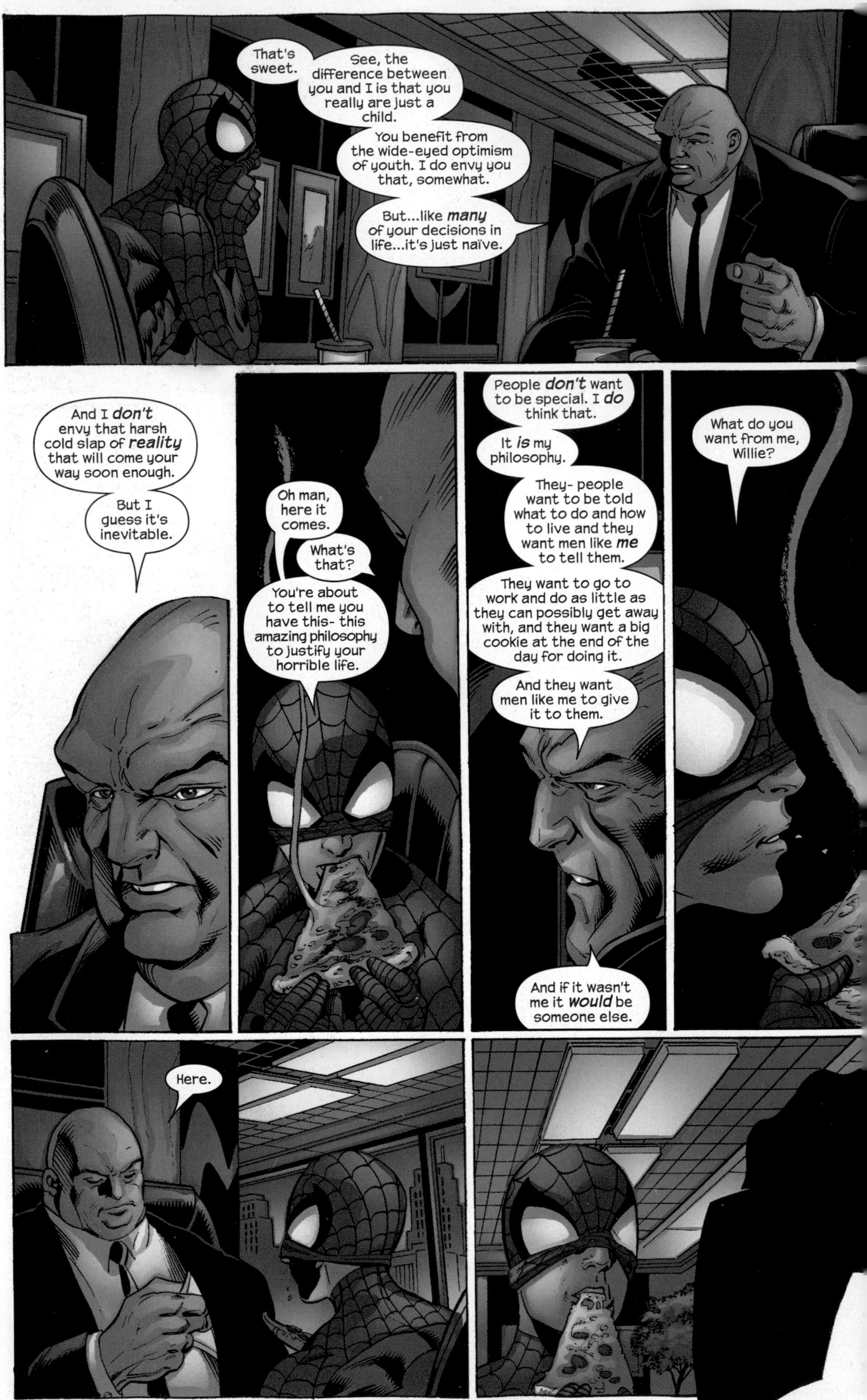
That's sweet.
See, the difference between you and I is that you really are just a child.
You benefit from the wide-eyed optimism of youth. I do envy you that, somewhat.
But...like *many* of your decisions in life...it's just naïve.
And I *don't* envy that harsh cold slap of *reality* that will come your way soon enough.
But I guess it's inevitable.
Oh man, here it comes.
What's that?
You're about to tell me you have this- this amazing philosophy to justify your horrible life.
People *don't* want to be special. I *do* think that.
It *is* my philosophy.
They- people want to be told what to do and how to live and they want men like *me* to tell them.
They want to go to work and do as little as they can possibly get away with, and they want a big cookie at the end of the day for doing it.
And they want men like me to give it to them.
And if it wasn't me it *would* be someone else.
What do you want from me, Willie?
Here.

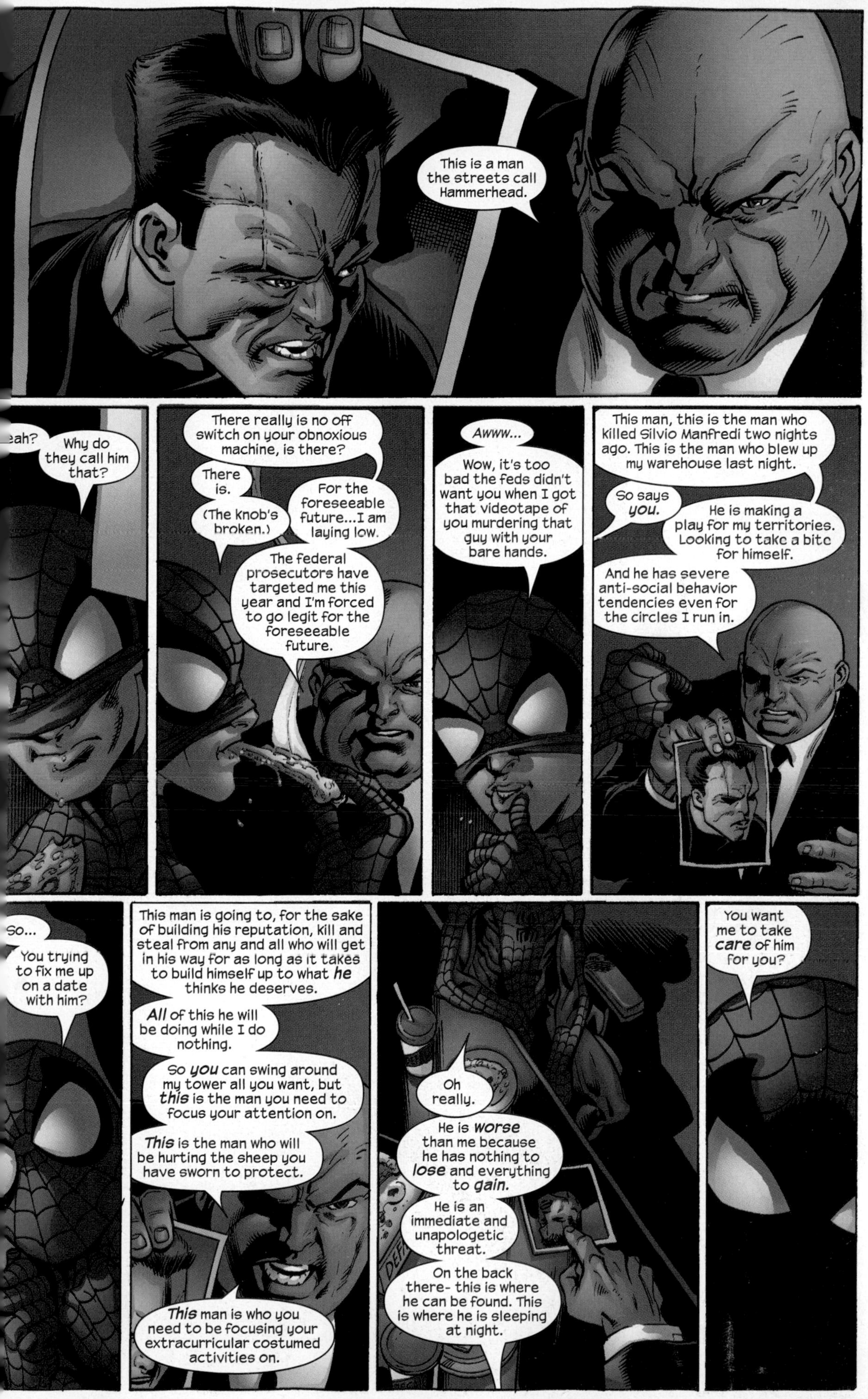
This is a man the streets call Hammerhead.
eah?
Why do they call him that?
There really is no off switch on your obnoxious machine, is there?
There is.
(The knob's broken.)
For the foreseeable future...I am laying low.
The federal prosecutors have targeted me this year and I'm forced to go legit for the foreseeable future.
Awww...
Wow, it's too bad the feds didn't want you when I got that videotape of you murdering that guy with your bare hands.
This man, this is the man who killed Silvio Manfredi two nights ago. This is the man who blew up my warehouse last night.
So says you.
He is making a play for my territories. Looking to take a bite for himself.
And he has severe anti-social behavior tendencies even for the circles I run in.
So...
You trying to fix me up on a date with him?
This man is going to, for the sake of building his reputation, kill and steal from any and all who will get in his way for as long as it takes to build himself up to what he thinks he deserves.
All of this he will be doing while I do nothing.
So you can swing around my tower all you want, but this is the man you need to focus your attention on.
This is the man who will be hurting the sheep you have sworn to protect.
This man is who you need to be focusing your extracurricular costumed activities on.
Oh really.
He is worse than me because he has nothing to lose and everything to gain.
He is an immediate and unapologetic threat.
On the back there- this is where he can be found. This is where he is sleeping at night.
You want me to take care of him for you?

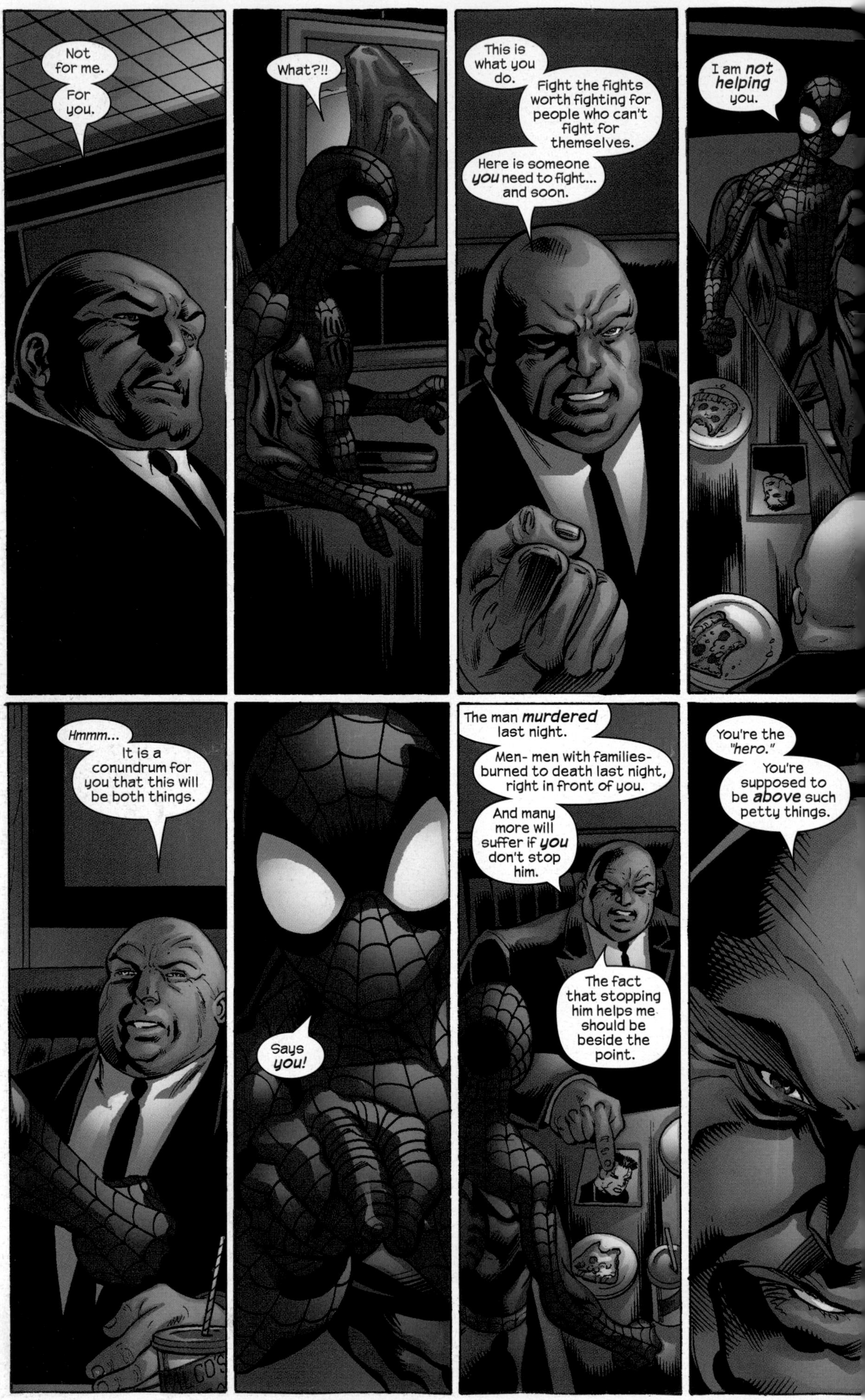
Not for me.
For you.
What?!!
This is what you do.
Fight the fights worth fighting for people who can't fight for themselves.
Here is someone *you* need to fight... and soon.
I am ***not helping*** you.
Hmmm...
It is a conundrum for you that this will be both things.
Says *you!*
The man ***murdered*** last night.
Men- men with families- burned to death last night, right in front of you.
And many more will suffer if ***you*** don't stop him.
The fact that stopping him helps me should be beside the point.
You're the *"hero."*
You're supposed to be ***above*** such petty things.

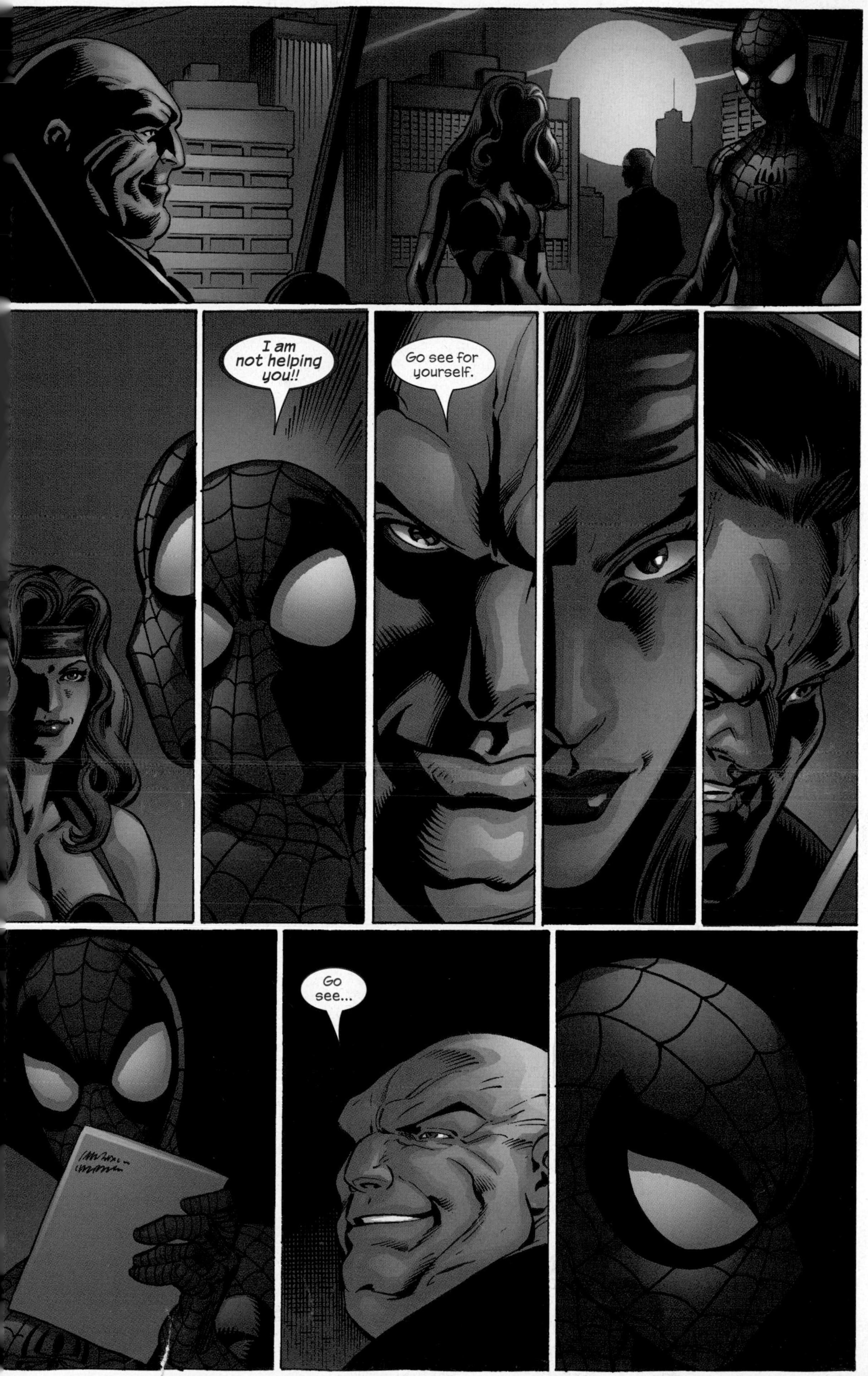
I am not helping you!!
Go see for yourself.
Go see...

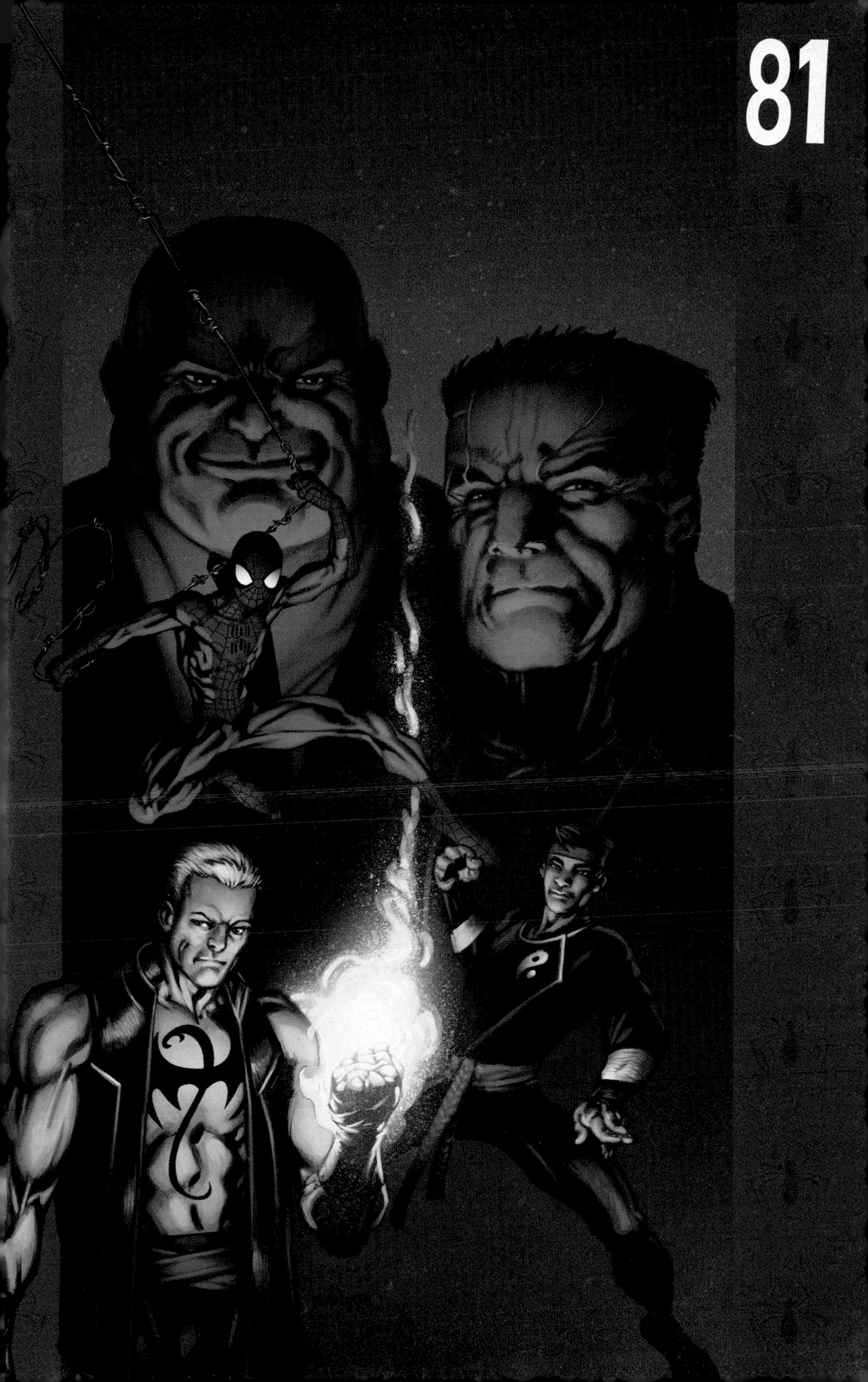

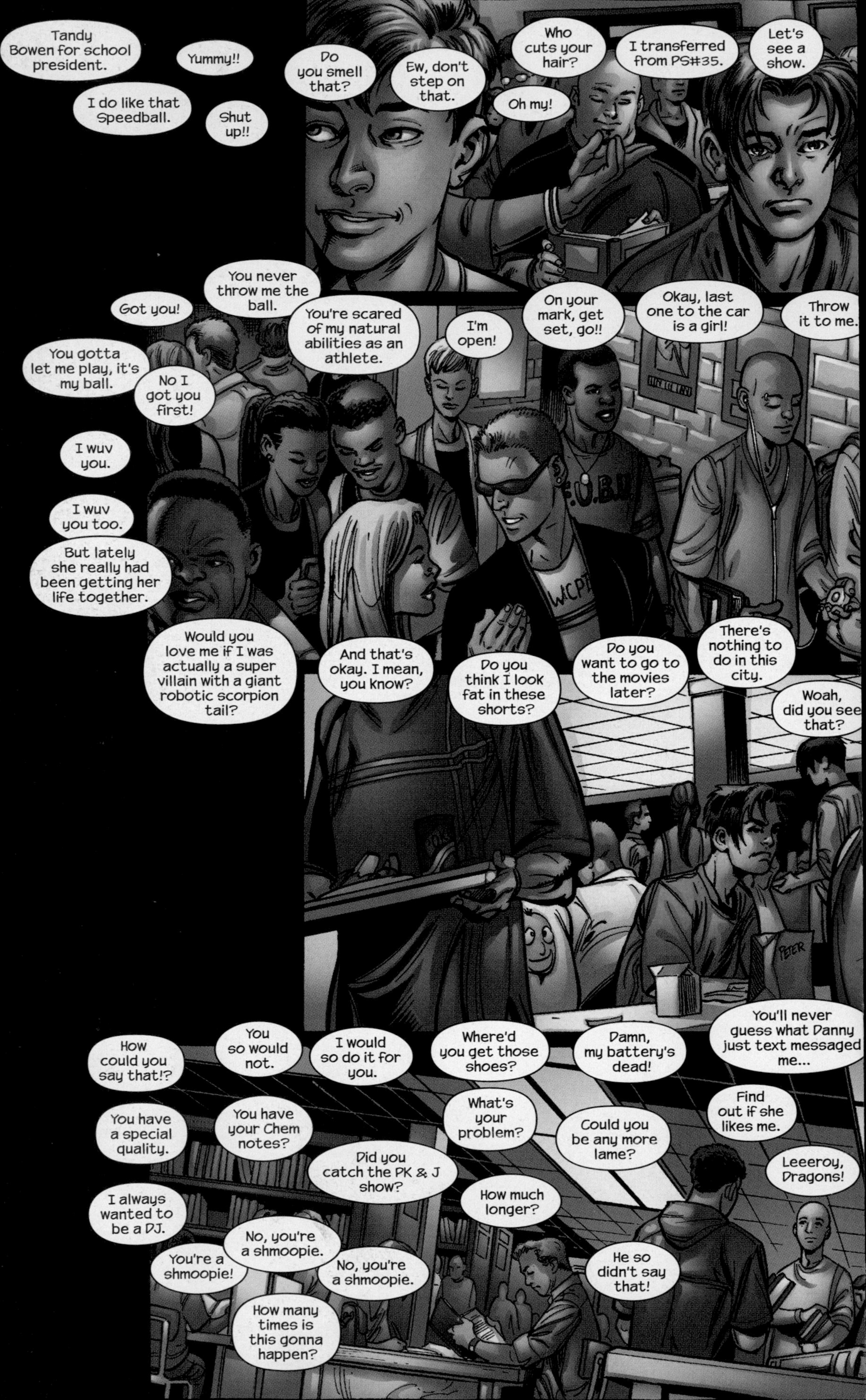
Tandy Bowen for school president.
Yummy!!
I do like that Speedball.
Shut up!!
Do you smell that?
Ew, don't step on that.
Who cuts your hair?
Oh my!
I transferred from PS#35.
Let's see a show.
Got you!
You never throw me the ball.
You gotta let me play, it's my ball.
No I got you first!
You're scared of my natural abilities as an athlete.
I'm open!
On your mark, get set, go!!
Okay, last one to the car is a girl!
Throw it to me.
I wuv you.
I wuv you too.
But lately she really had been getting her life together.
Would you love me if I was actually a super villain with a giant robotic scorpion tail?
And that's okay. I mean, you know?
Do you think I look fat in these shorts?
Do you want to go to the movies later?
There's nothing to do in this city.
Woah, did you see that?
How could you say that!?
You so would not.
I would so do it for you.
Where'd you get those shoes?
Damn, my battery's dead!
You'll never guess what Danny just text messaged me...
You have a special quality.
You have your Chem notes?
What's your problem?
Could you be any more lame?
Find out if she likes me.
Did you catch the PK & J show?
Leeeroy, Dragons!
I always wanted to be a DJ.
How much longer?
You're a shmoopie!
No, you're a shmoopie.
No, you're a shmoopie.
He so didn't say that!
How many times is this gonna happen?

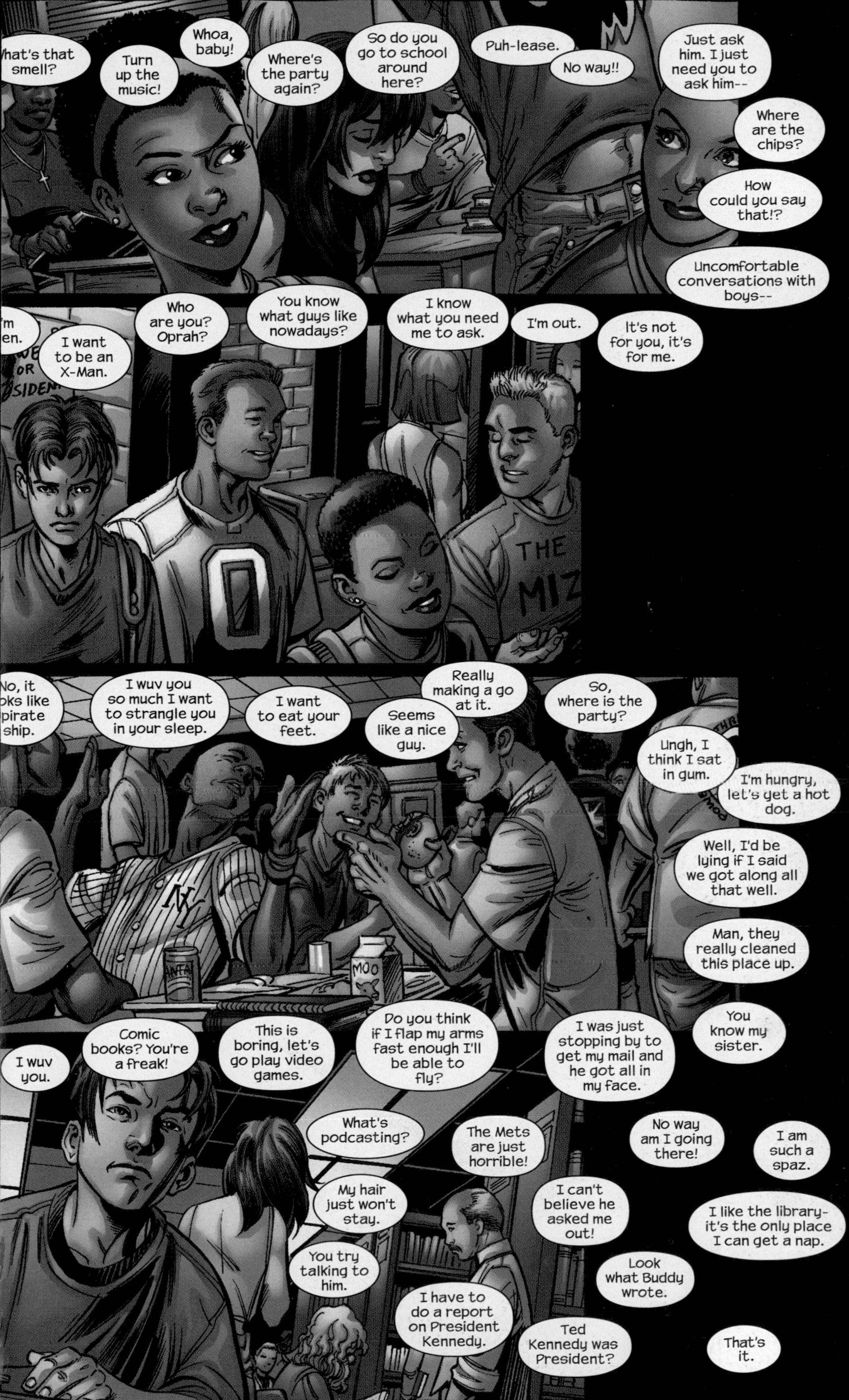
hat's that smell?
Turn up the music!
Whoa, baby!
Where's the party again?
So do you go to school around here?
Puh-lease.
No way!!
Just ask him. I just need you to ask him--
Where are the chips?
How could you say that!?
Uncomfortable conversations with boys--
'm en.
I want to be an X-Man.
Who are you? Oprah?
You know what guys like nowadays?
I know what you need me to ask.
I'm out.
It's not for you, it's for me.
THE MIZ
o, it oks like pirate ship.
I wuv you so much I want to strangle you in your sleep.
I want to eat your feet.
Seems like a nice guy.
Really making a go at it.
So, where is the party?
Ungh, I think I sat in gum.
I'm hungry, let's get a hot dog.
Well, I'd be lying if I said we got along all that well.
Man, they really cleaned this place up.
MOO
You know my sister.
I wuv you.
Comic books? You're a freak!
This is boring, let's go play video games.
Do you think if I flap my arms fast enough I'll be able to fly?
I was just stopping by to get my mail and he got all in my face.
What's podcasting?
The Mets are just horrible!
No way am I going there!
I am such a spaz.
My hair just won't stay.
I can't believe he asked me out!
I like the library- it's the only place I can get a nap.
You try talking to him.
Look what Buddy wrote.
I have to do a report on President Kennedy.
Ted Kennedy was President?
That's it.

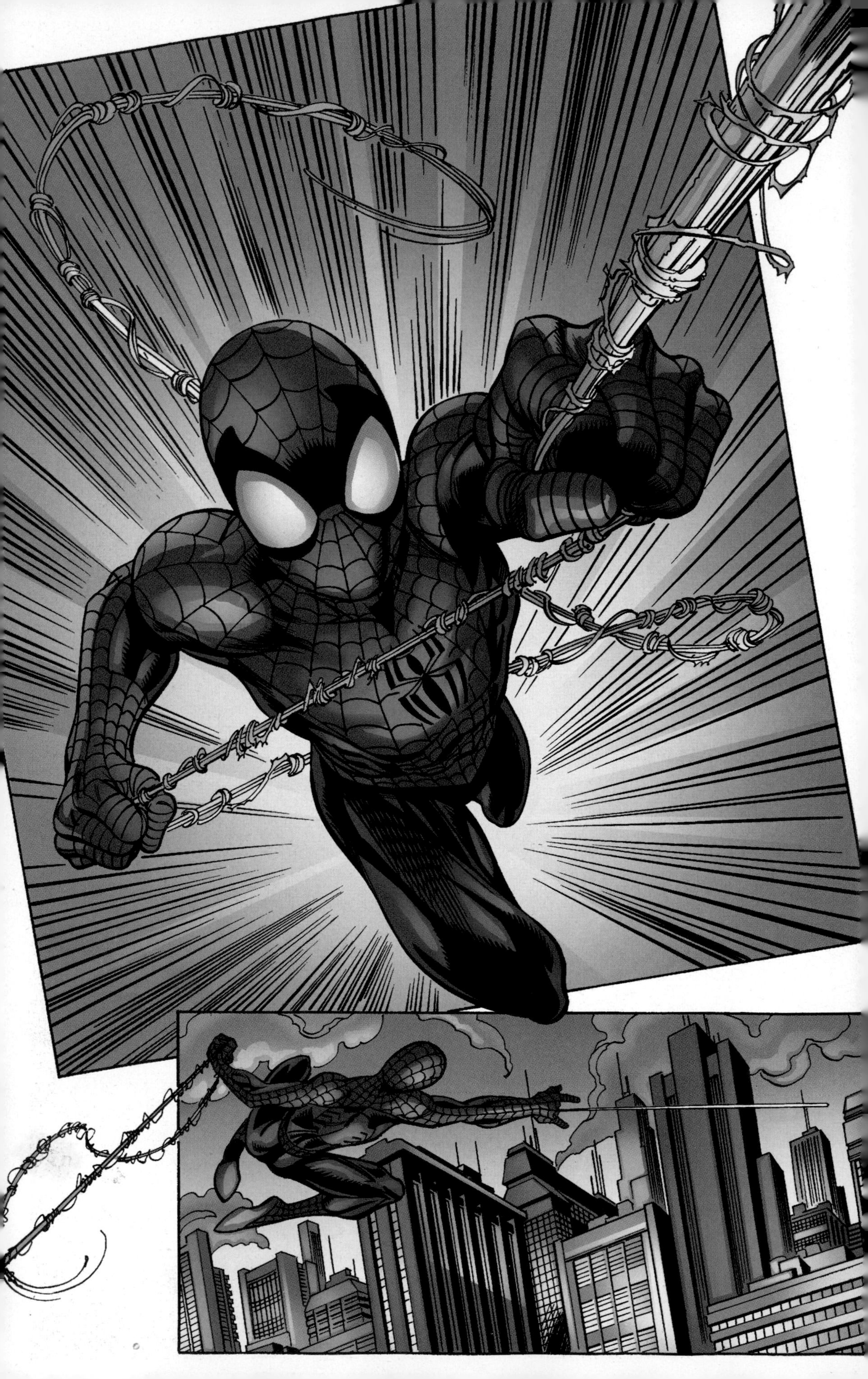

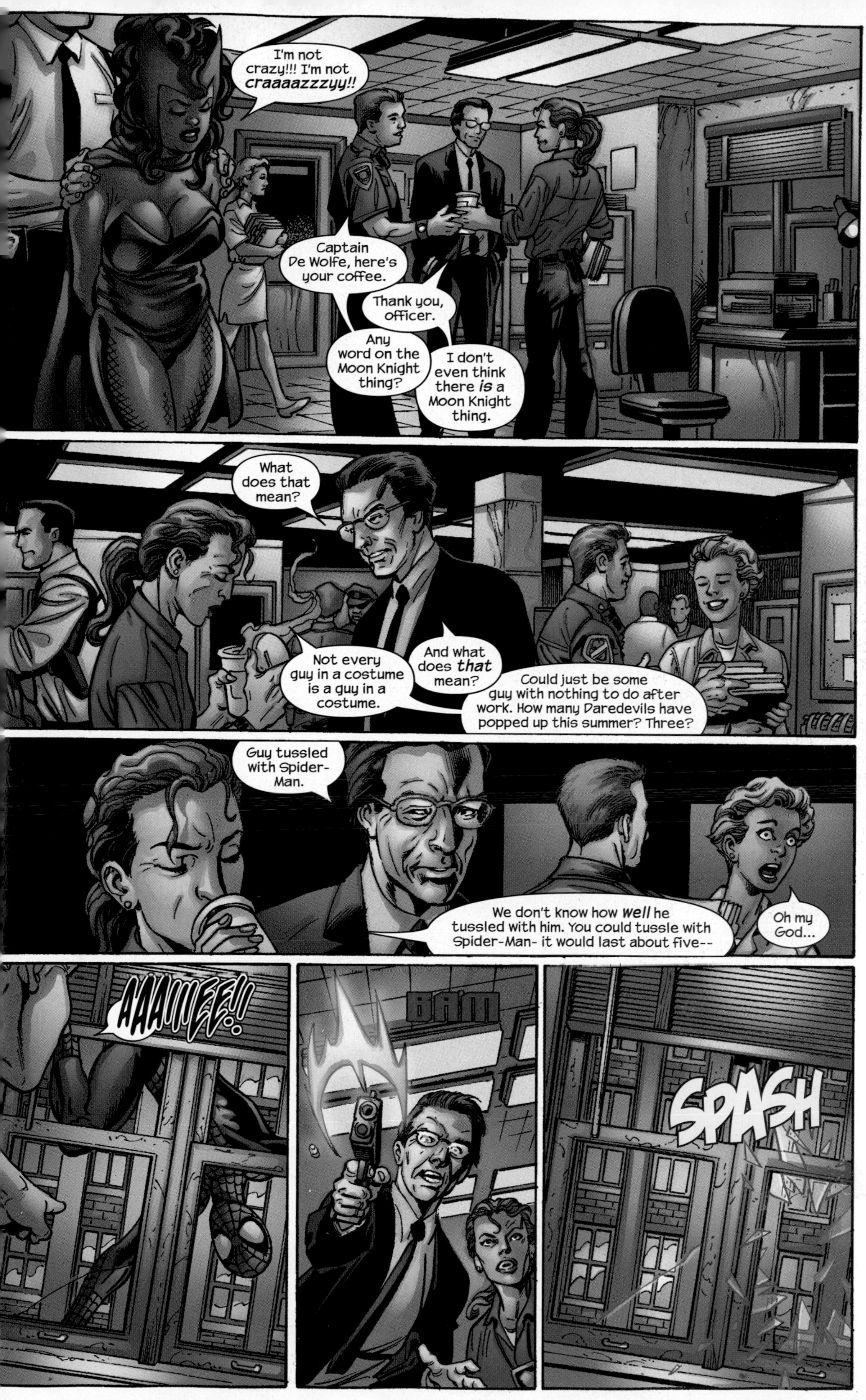

I'm not crazy!!! I'm not craaaazzzzyy!!
Captain De Wolfe, here's your coffee.
Thank you, officer.
Any word on the Moon Knight thing?
I don't even think there *is* a Moon Knight thing.
What does that mean?
Not every guy in a costume is a guy in a costume.
And what does *that* mean?
Could just be some guy with nothing to do after work. How many Daredevils have popped up this summer? Three?
Guy tussled with Spider-Man.
We don't know how *well* he tussled with him. You could tussle with Spider-Man- it would last about five--
Oh my God...
AAAIIIEE!!
BAM
SPASH

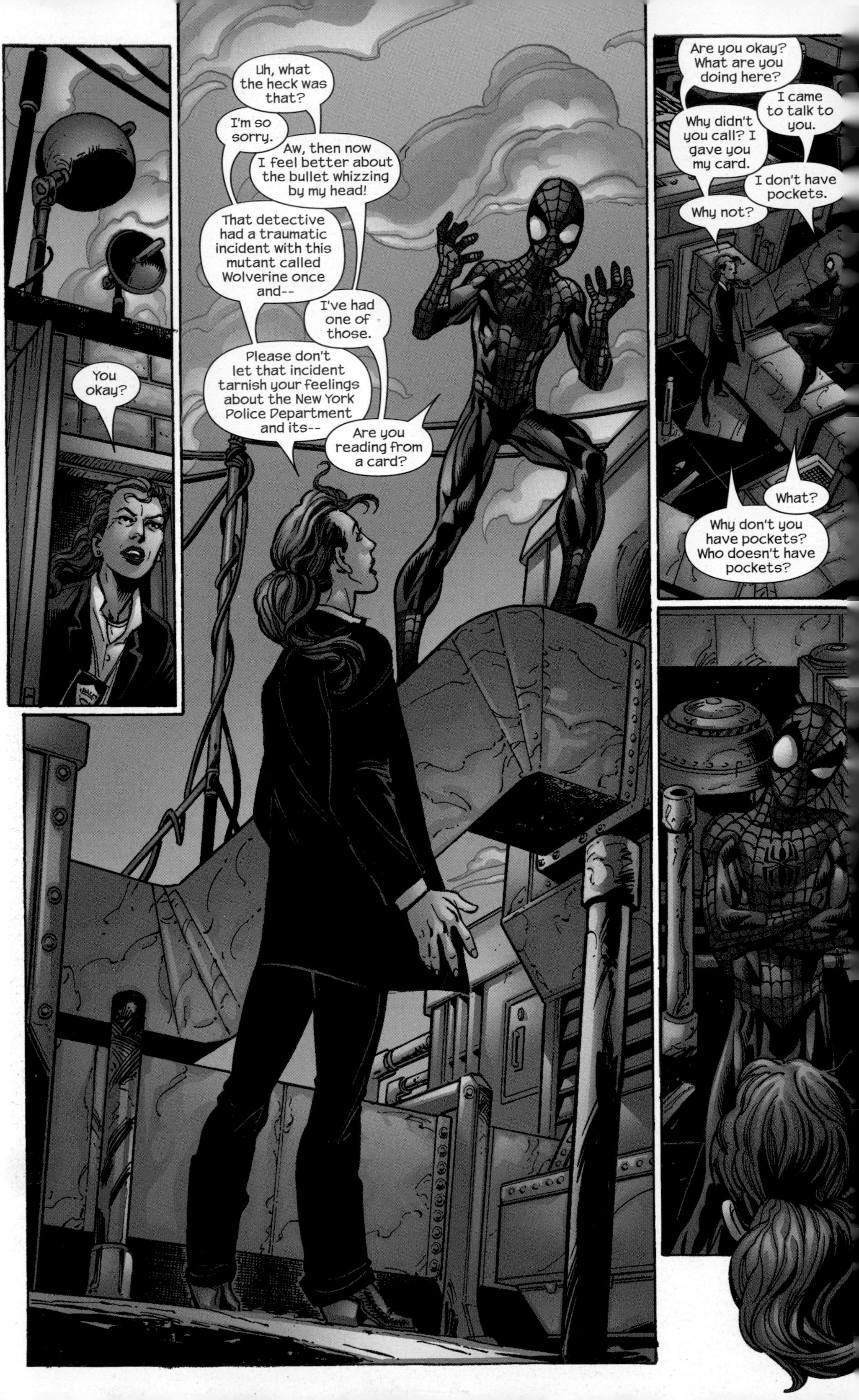
You okay?
Uh, what the heck was that?
I'm so sorry.
Aw, then now I feel better about the bullet whizzing by my head!
That detective had a traumatic incident with this mutant called Wolverine once and--
I've had one of those.
Please don't let that incident tarnish your feelings about the New York Police Department and its--
Are you reading from a card?
Are you okay? What are you doing here?
I came to talk to you.
Why didn't you call? I gave you my card.
I don't have pockets.
Why not?
What?
Why don't you have pockets? Who doesn't have pockets?

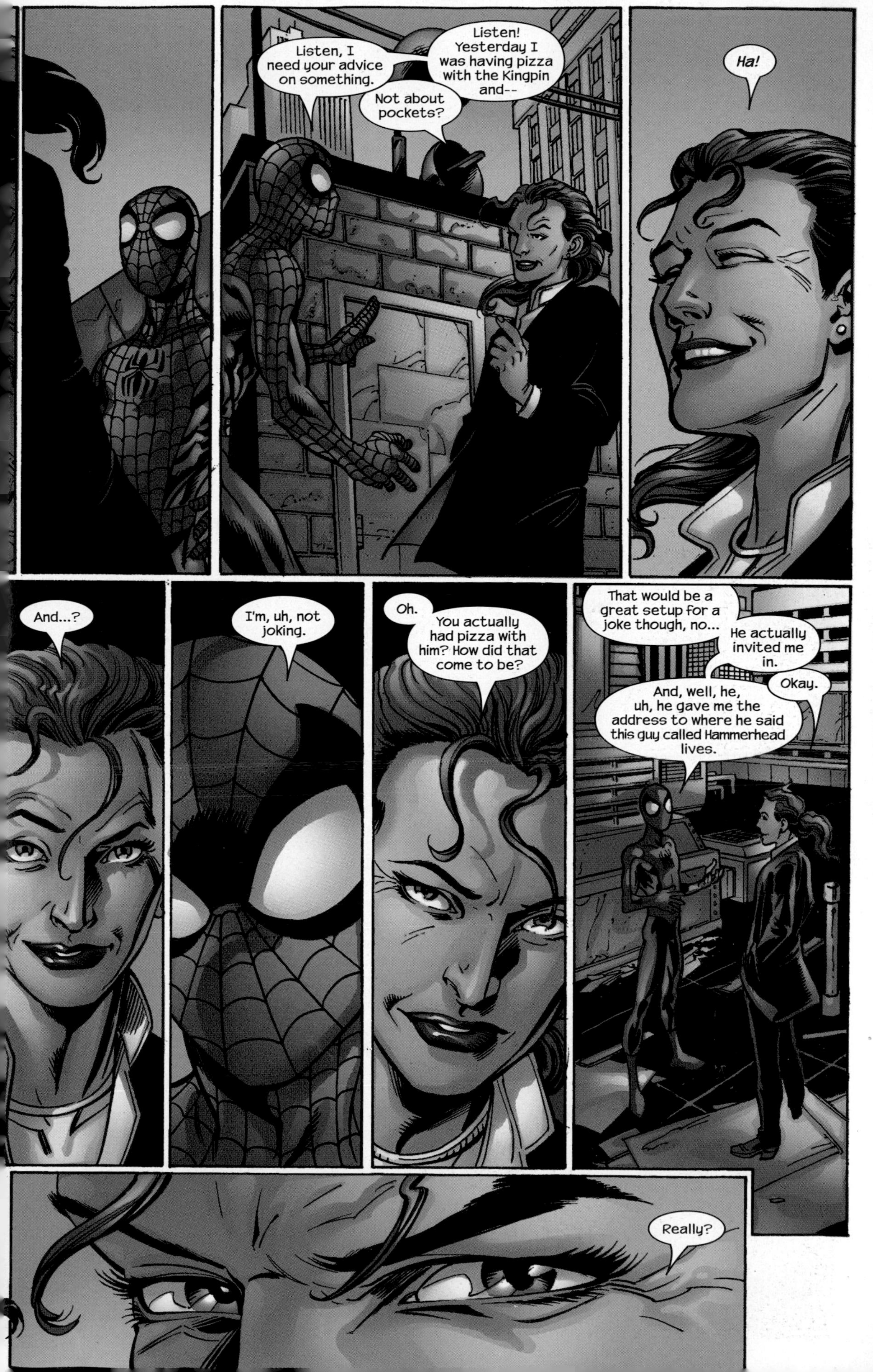
Listen, I need your advice on something.
Listen! Yesterday I was having pizza with the Kingpin and--
Not about pockets?
Ha!
And...?
I'm, uh, not joking.
Oh.
You actually had pizza with him? How did that come to be?
That would be a great setup for a joke though, no...
He actually invited me in.
Okay.
And, well, he, uh, he gave me the address to where he said this guy called Hammerhead lives.
Really?

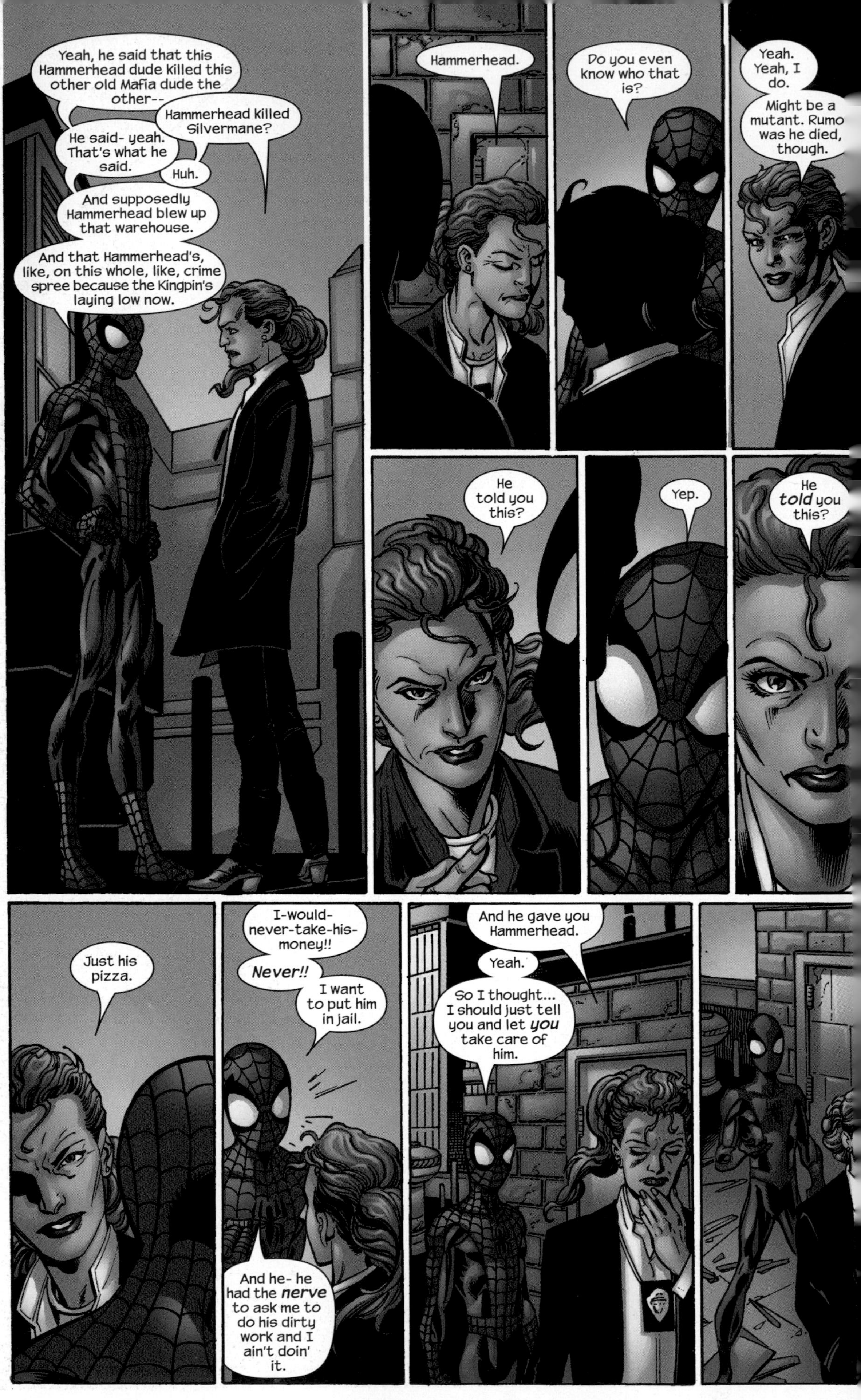
Yeah, he said that this Hammerhead dude killed this other old Mafia dude the other--
Hammerhead killed Silvermane?
He said- yeah. That's what he said.
Huh.
And supposedly Hammerhead blew up that warehouse.
And that Hammerhead's, like, on this whole, like, crime spree because the Kingpin's laying low now.
Hammerhead.
Do you even know who that is?
Yeah. Yeah, I do.
Might be a mutant. Rumo was he died, though.
He told you this?
Yep.
He *told* you this?
Just his pizza.
I-would-never-take-his-money!!
Never!!
I want to put him in jail.
And he- he had the *nerve* to ask me to do his dirty work and I ain't doin' it.
And he gave you Hammerhead.
Yeah.
So I thought... I should just tell you and let *you* take care of him.

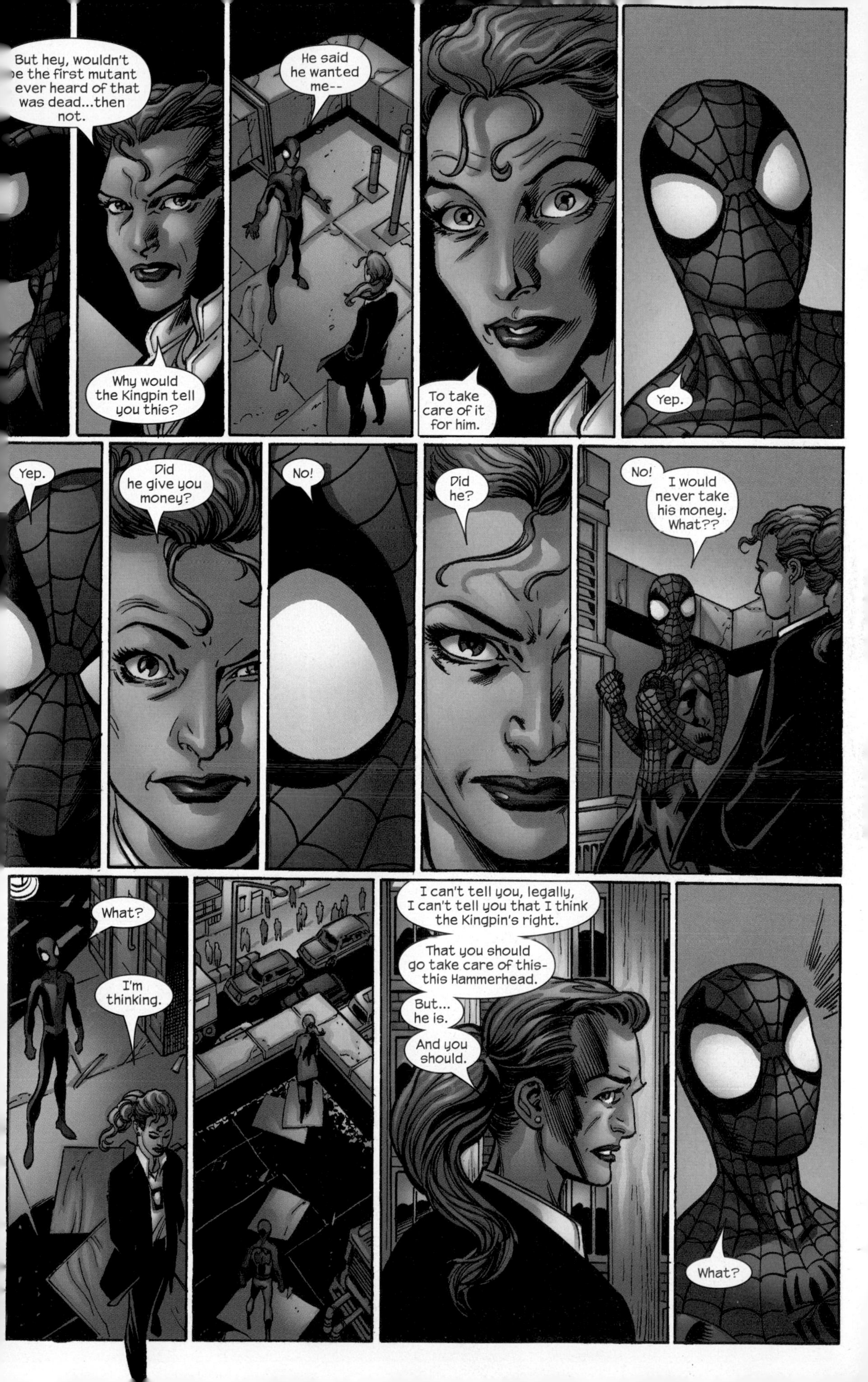
But hey, wouldn't be the first mutant ever heard of that was dead...then not.
Why would the Kingpin tell you this?
He said he wanted me--
To take care of it for him.
Yep.
Yep.
Did he give you money?
No!
Did he?
No!
I would never take his money. What??
What?
I'm thinking.
I can't tell you, legally, I can't tell you that I think the Kingpin's right.
That you should go take care of this- this Hammerhead.
But... he is.
And you should.
What?

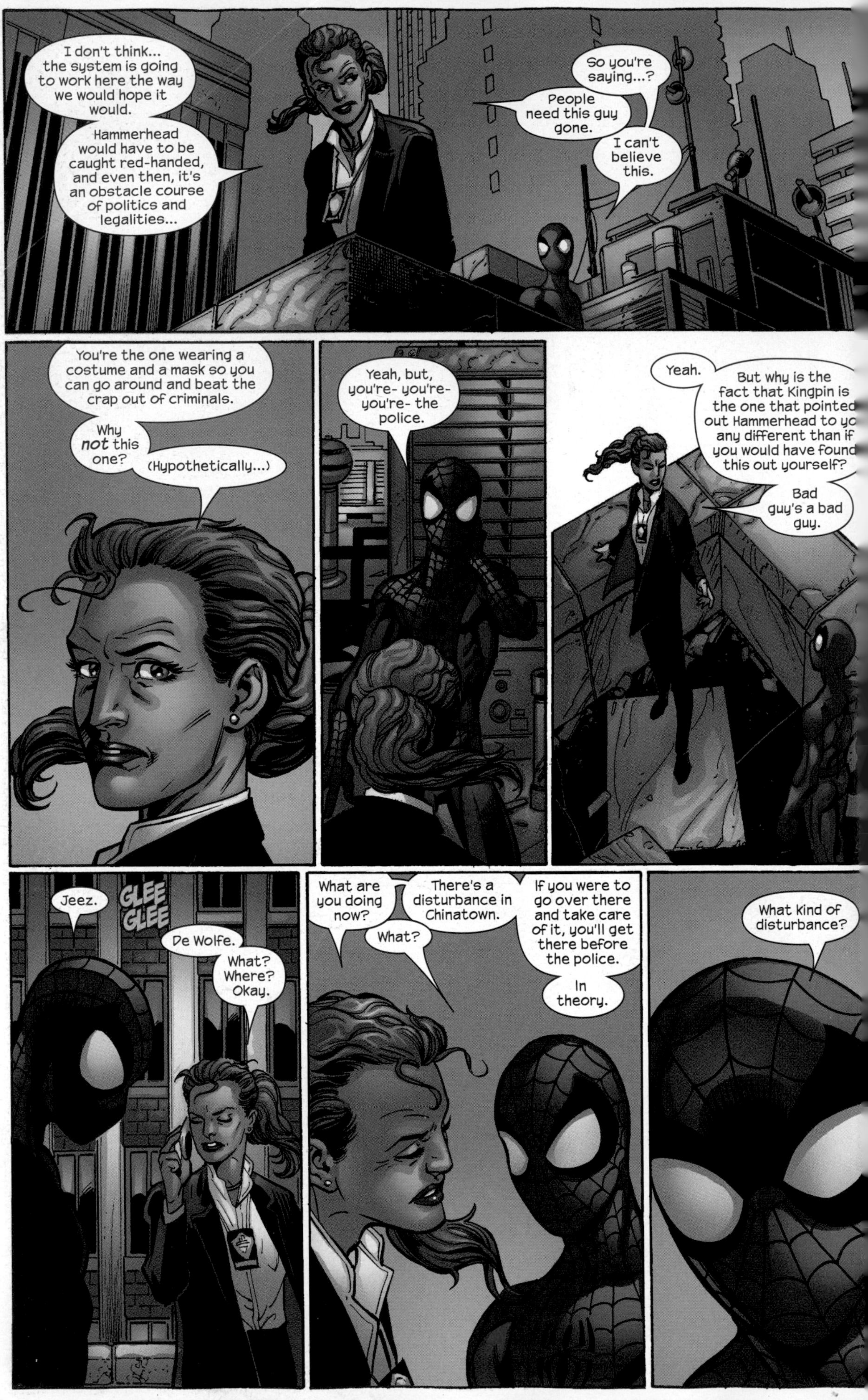
I don't think... the system is going to work here the way we would hope it would.
Hammerhead would have to be caught red-handed, and even then, it's an obstacle course of politics and legalities...
So you're saying...?
People need this guy gone.
I can't believe this.
You're the one wearing a costume and a mask so you can go around and beat the crap out of criminals.
Why not this one?
(Hypothetically...)
Yeah, but, you're- you're- you're- the police.
Yeah.
But why is the fact that Kingpin is the one that pointed out Hammerhead to yo any different than if you would have found this out yourself?
Bad guy's a bad guy.
Jeez.
GLEE GLEE
De Wolfe.
What? Where? Okay.
What are you doing now?
There's a disturbance in Chinatown.
What?
If you were to go over there and take care of it, you'll get there before the police.
In theory.
What kind of disturbance?

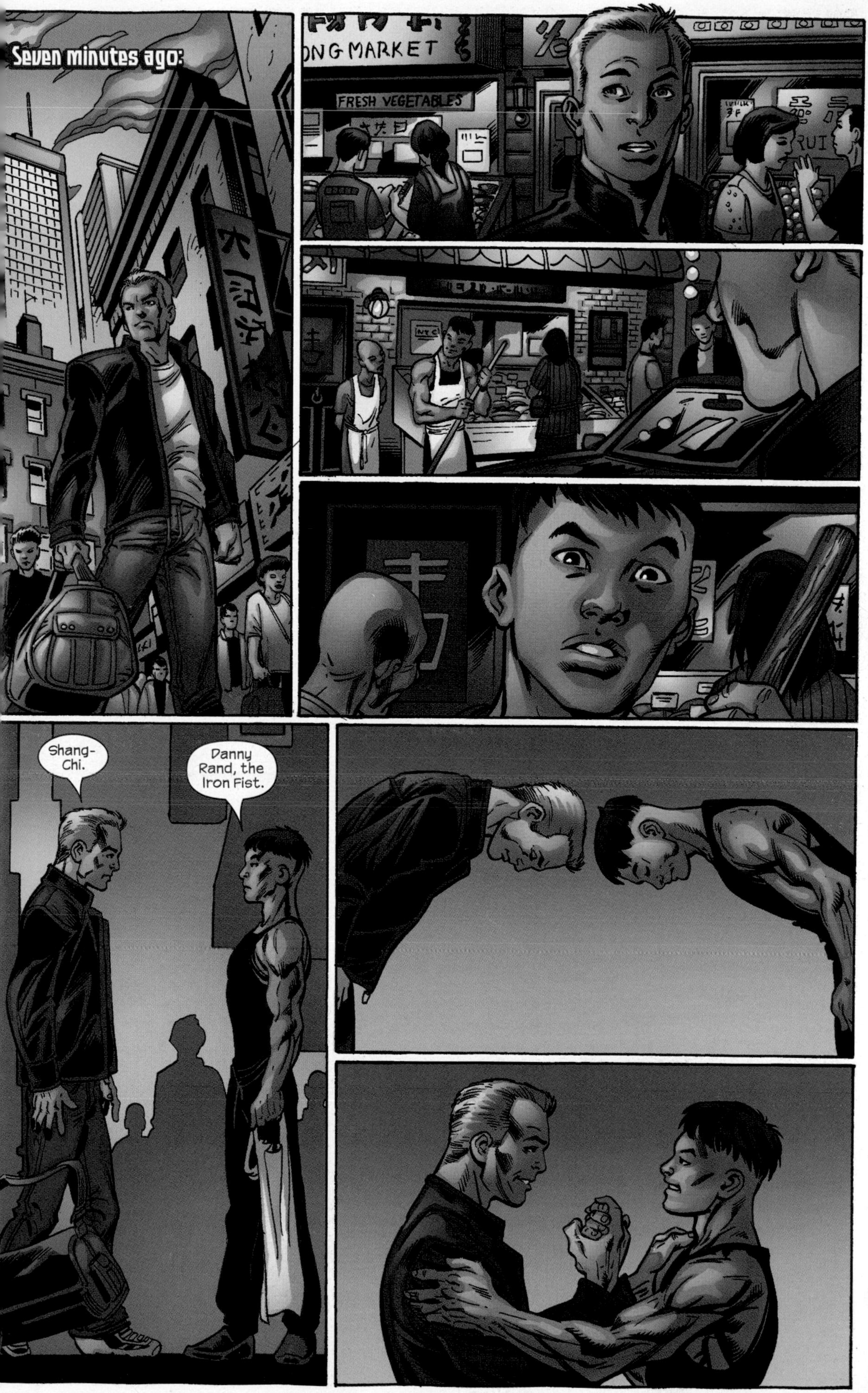
Seven minutes ago:
ONG MARKET
FRESH VEGETABLES
Shang-Chi.
Danny Rand, the Iron Fist.

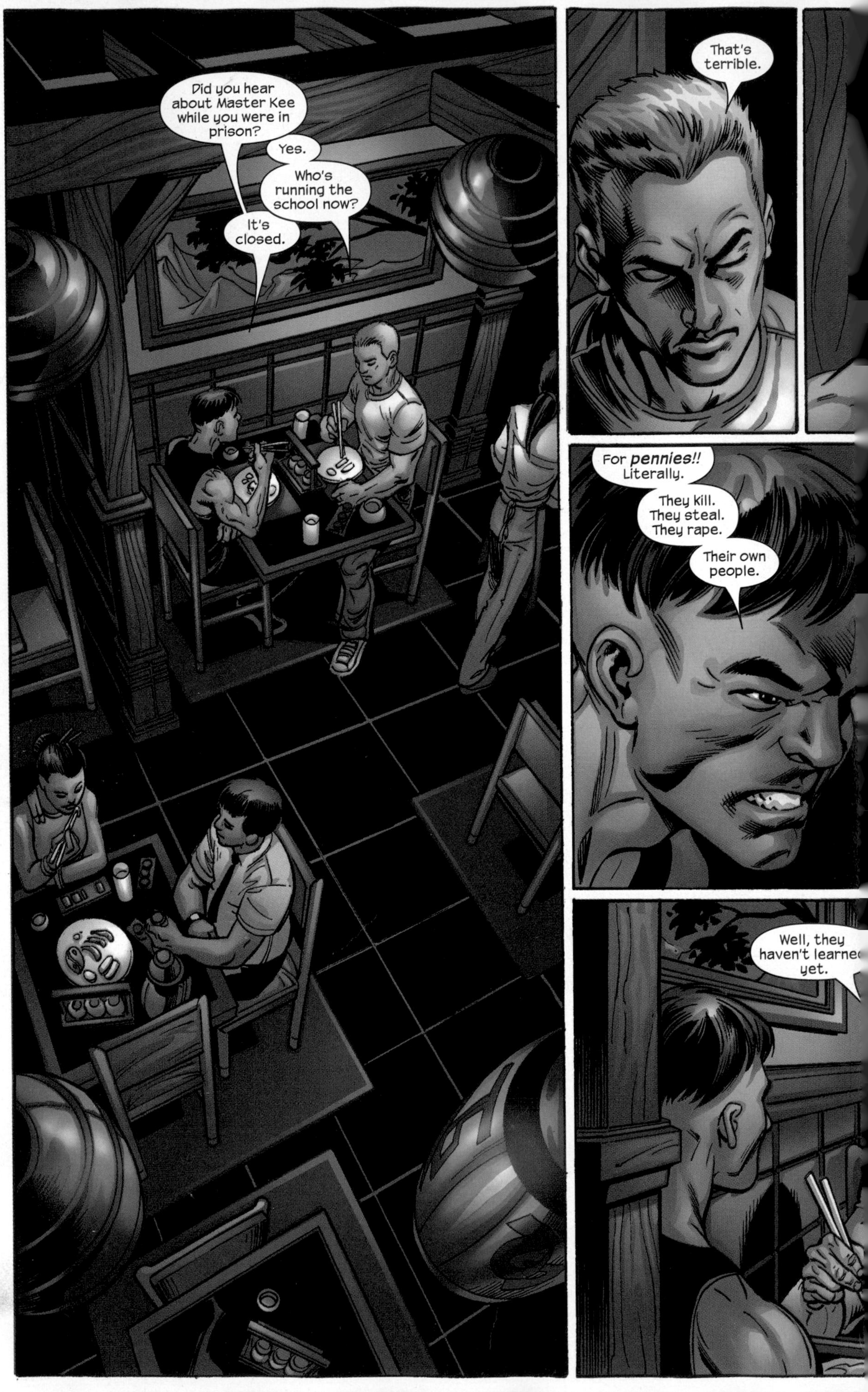
Did you hear about Master Kee while you were in prison?
Yes.
Who's running the school now?
It's closed.
That's terrible.
For *pennies!!* Literally.
They kill. They steal. They rape.
Their own people.
Well, they haven't learned yet.

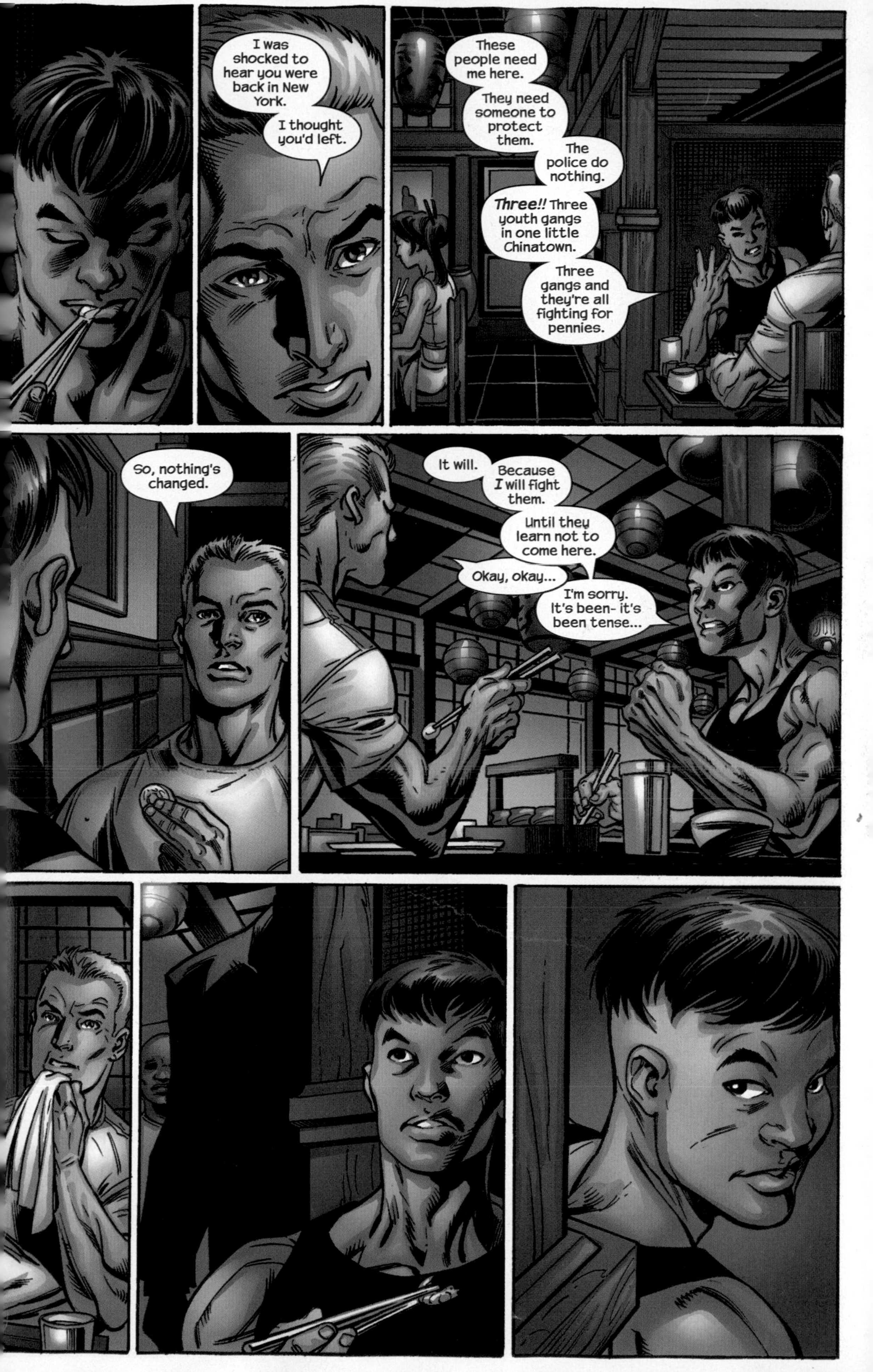
I was shocked to hear you were back in New York.
I thought you'd left.
These people need me here.
They need someone to protect them.
The police do nothing.
Three!! Three youth gangs in one little Chinatown.
Three gangs and they're all fighting for pennies.
So, nothing's changed.
It will.
Because *I* will fight them.
Until they learn not to come here.
Okay, okay...
I'm sorry. It's been- it's been tense...

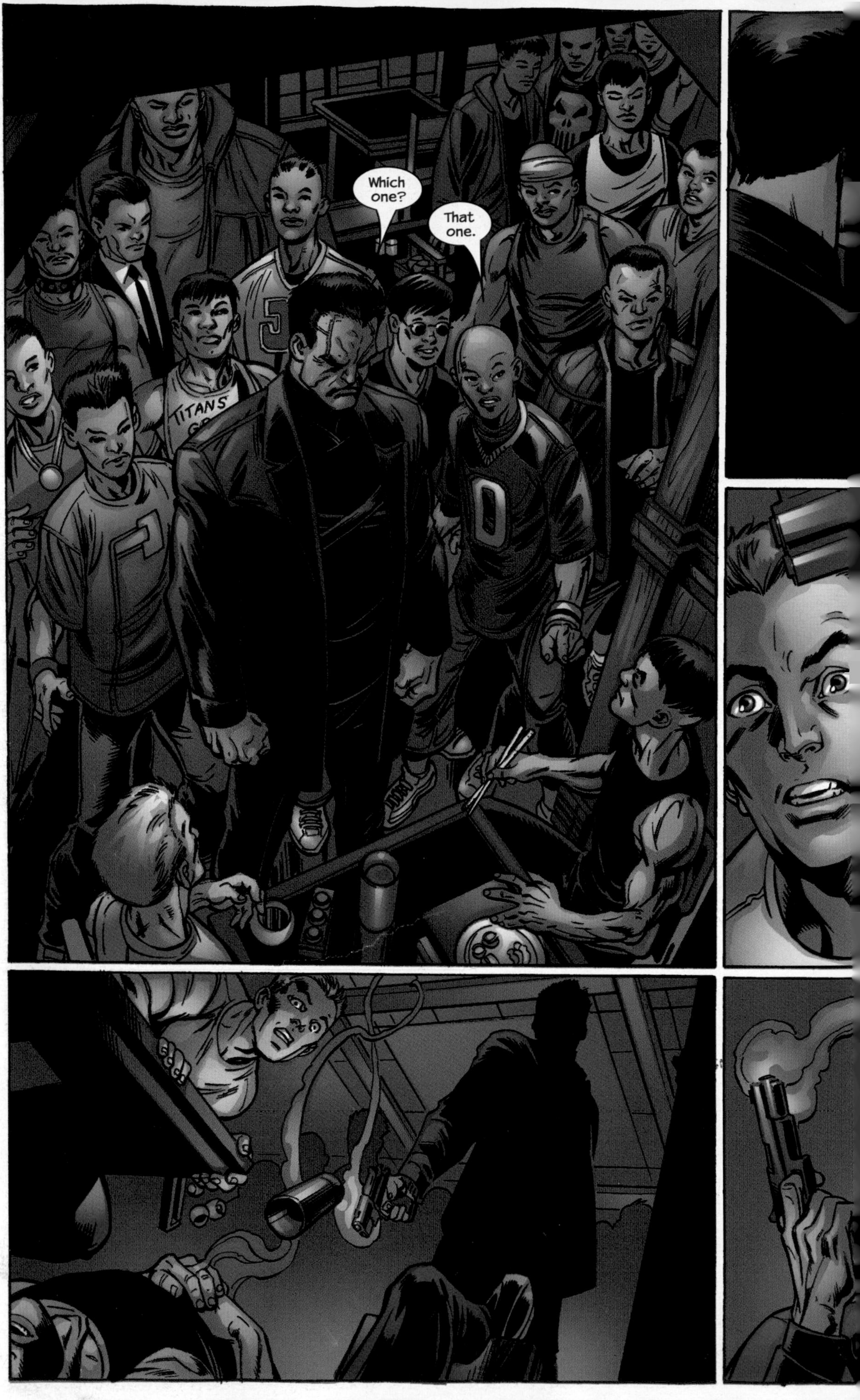
Which one?
That one.

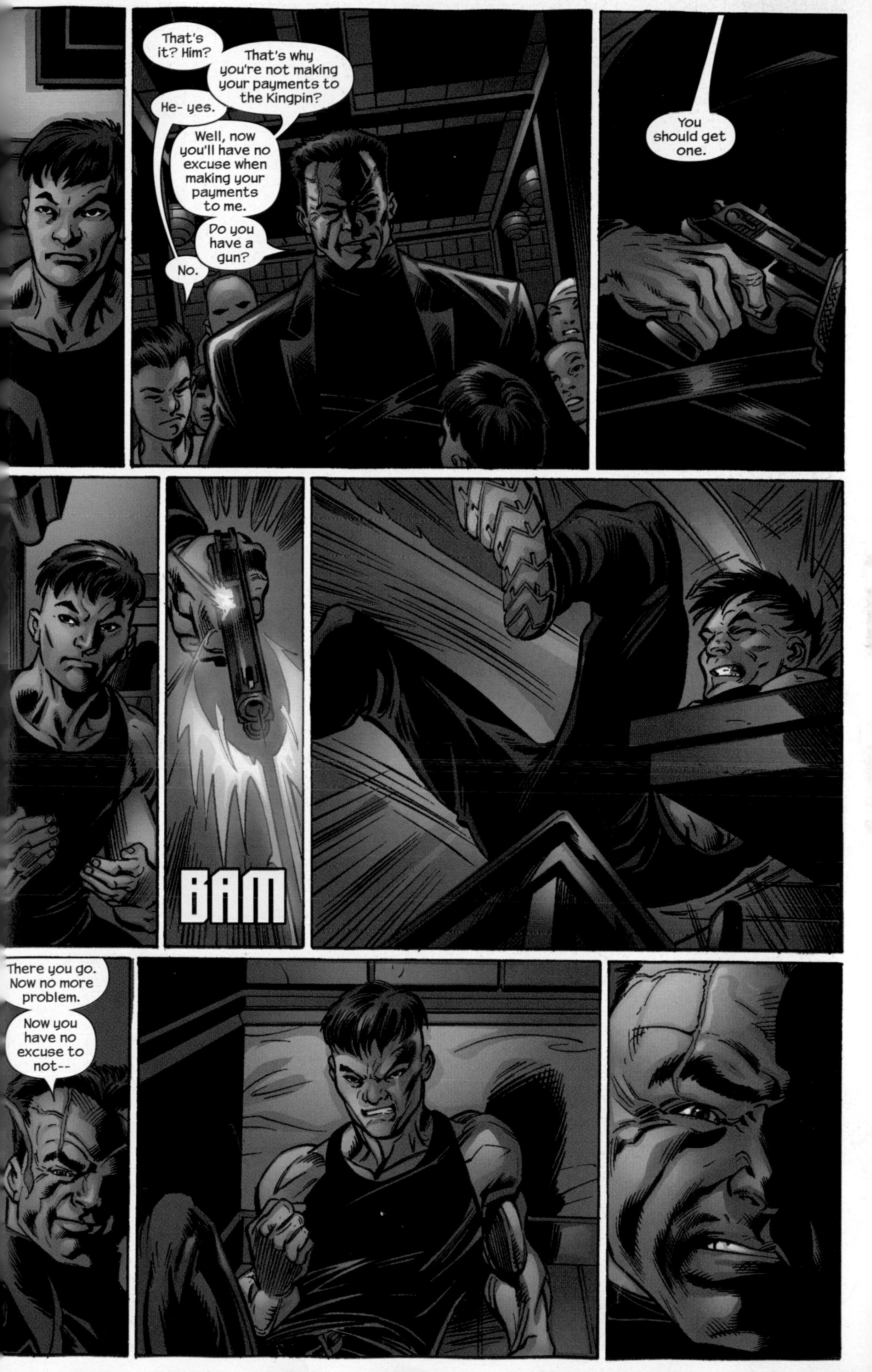
That's it? Him?
That's why you're not making your payments to the Kingpin?
He- yes.
Well, now you'll have no excuse when making your payments to me.
Do you have a gun?
No.
You should get one.
BAM
There you go. Now no more problem.
Now you have no excuse to not--

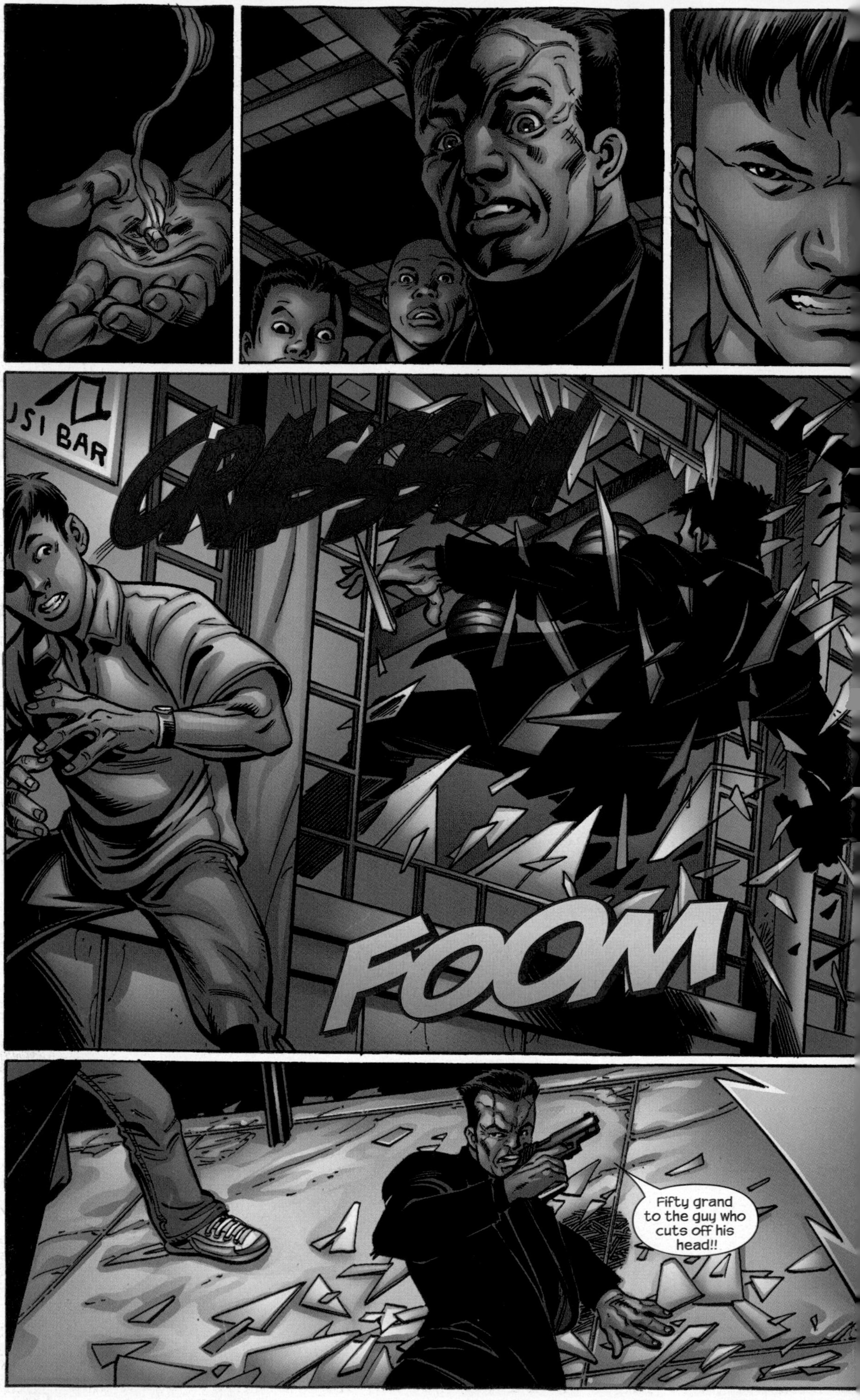
BAR
FOOM
Fifty grand to the guy who cuts off his head!!

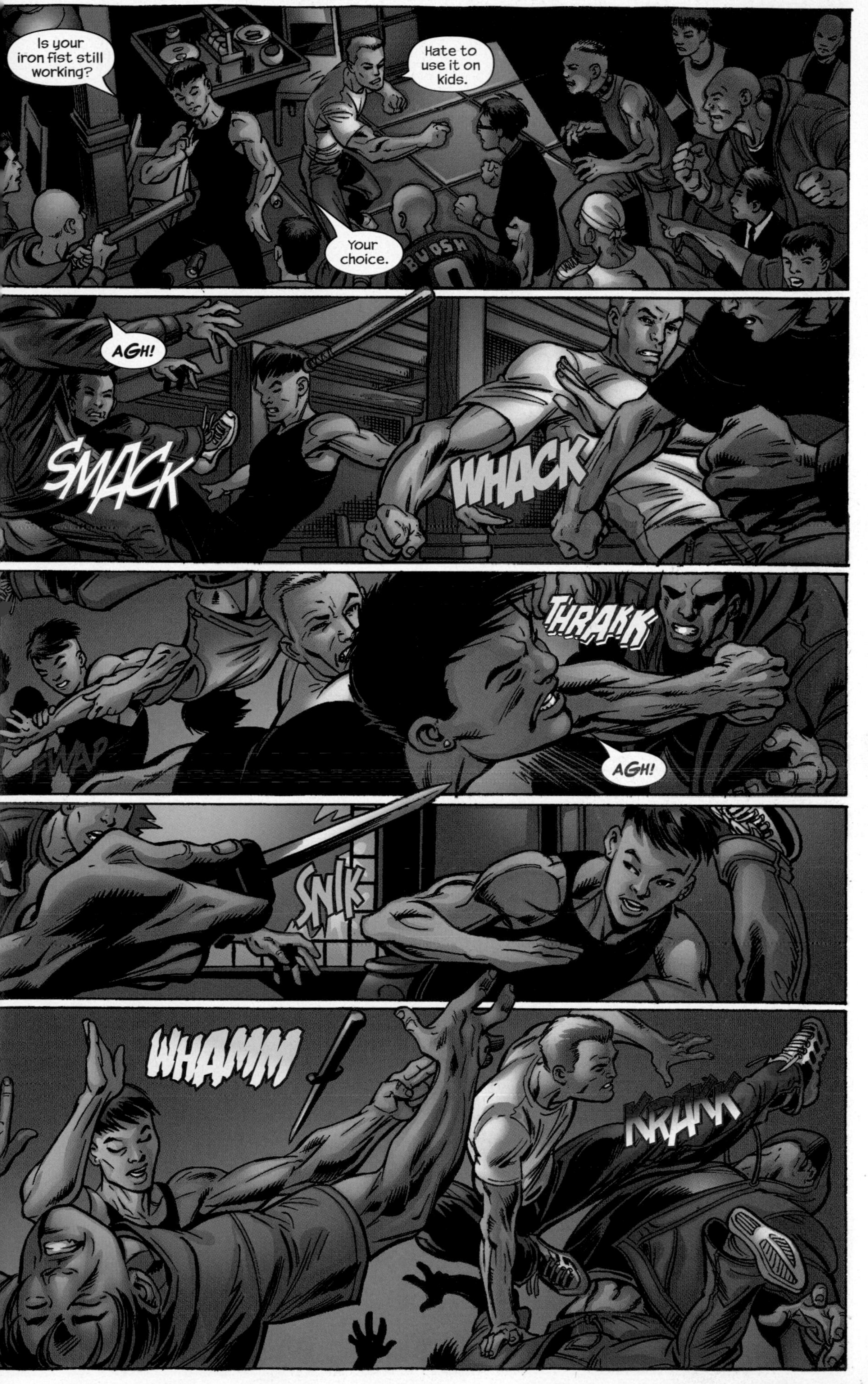
Is your iron fist still working?
Hate to use it on kids.
Your choice.
AGH!
SMACK
WHACK
THRAKK
AGH!
SNIK
WHAMM
KRAM

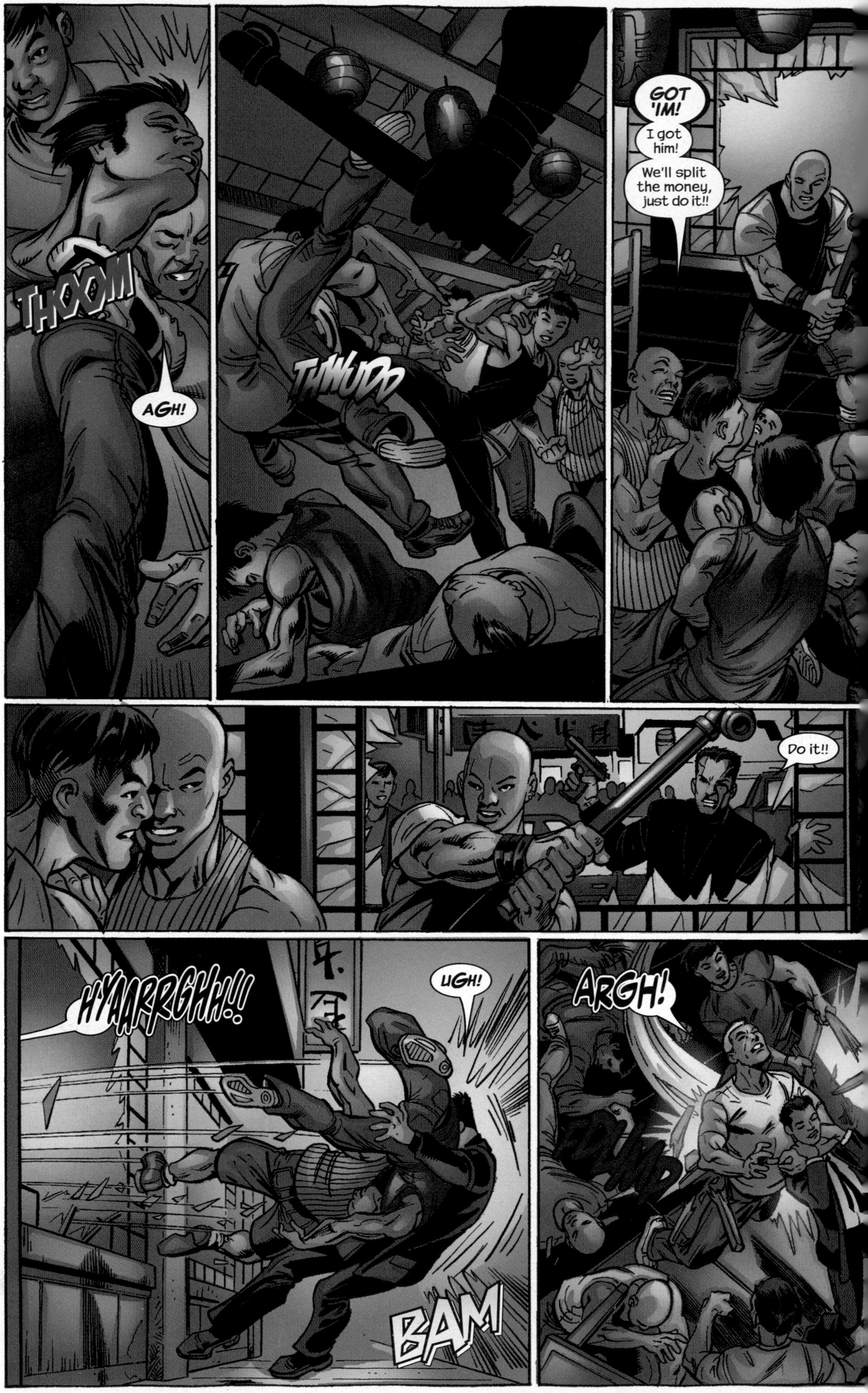
THOOM
AGH!
THWUDD
GOT 'IM!
I got him!
We'll split the money, just do it!!
Do it!!
HYAARRGHH!!
UGH!
BAM
ARGH!
THWUDD

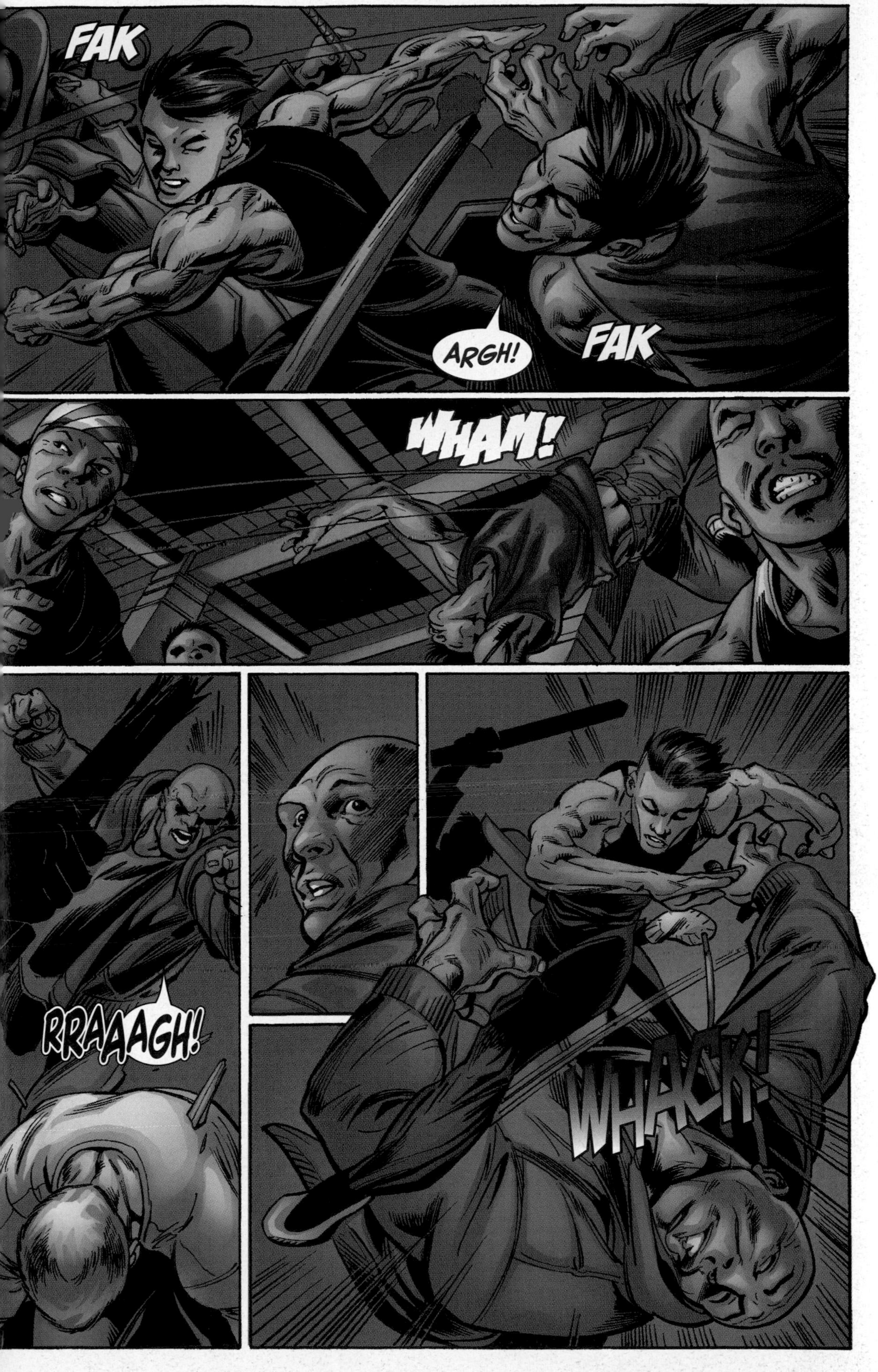
FAK
ARGH!
FAK
WHAM!
RRAAAGH!
WHACK!

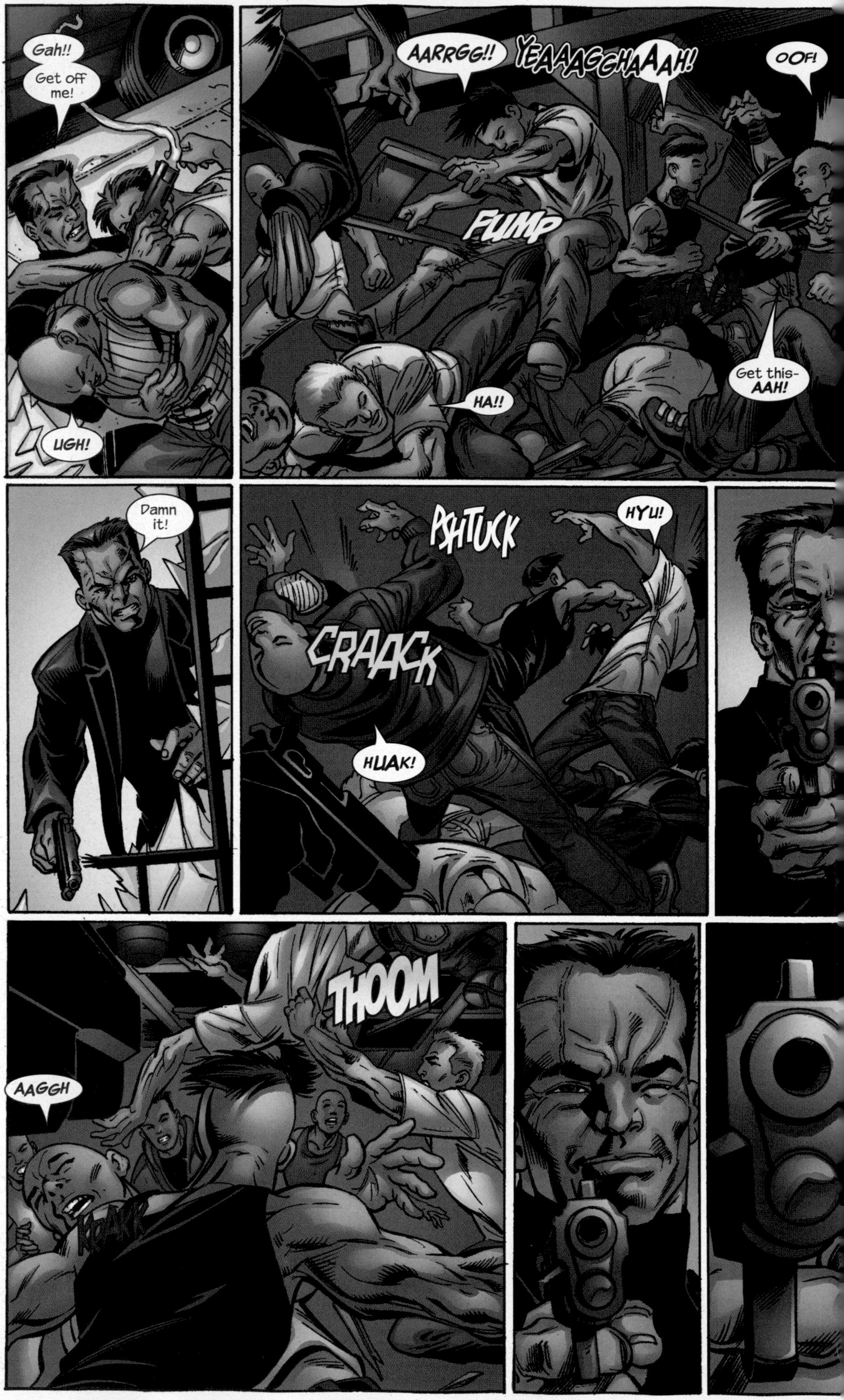
Gah!!
Get off me!
UGH!
AARRGG!!
YEAAAGGHAAAH!
OOF!
FUMP
HA!!
Get this-AAH!
Damn it!
PSHTUCK
HYU!
CRAACK
HUAK!
THOOM
AAGGH

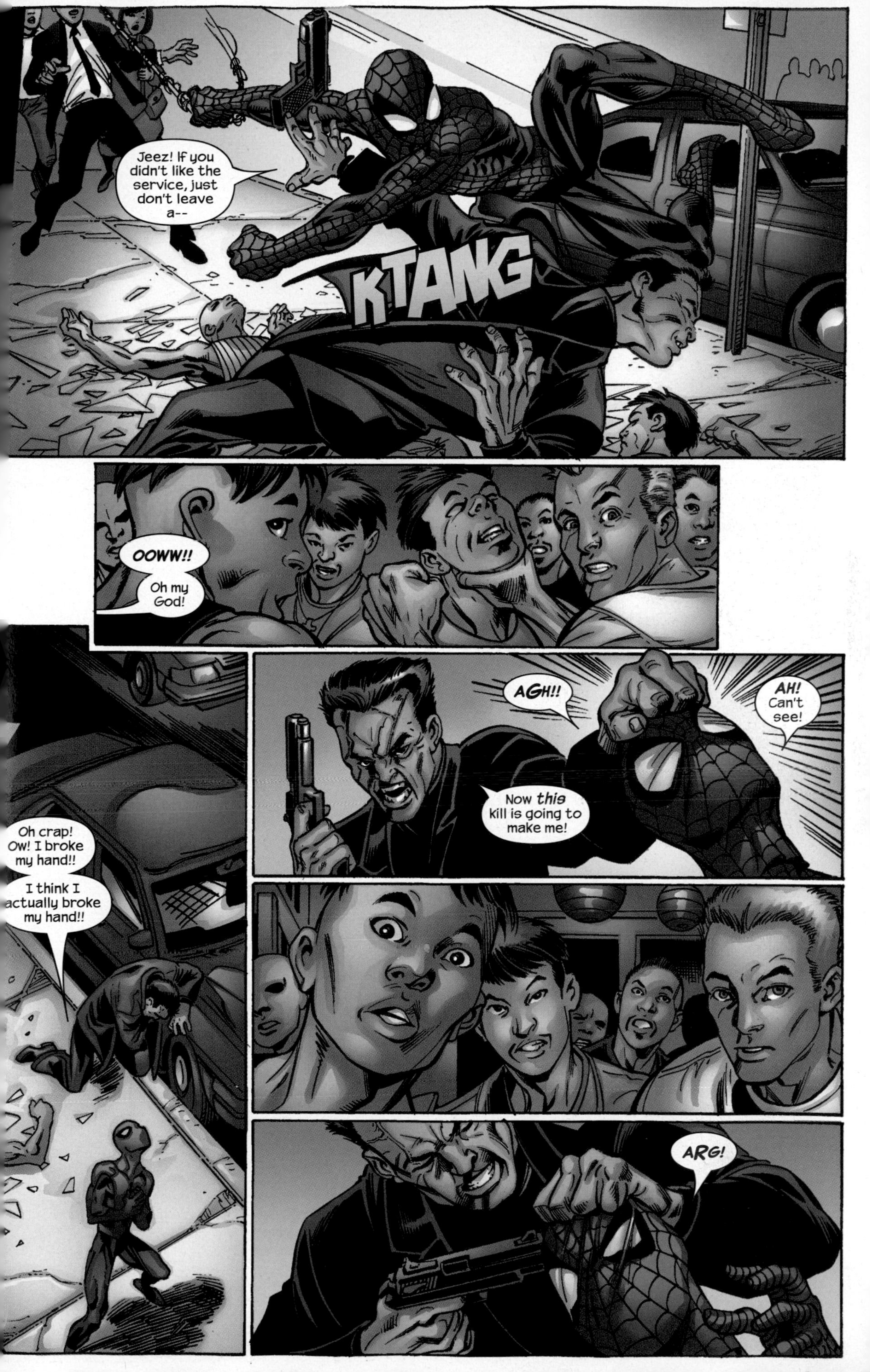
Jeez! If you didn't like the service, just don't leave a--
KTANG
OOWW!!
Oh my God!
AGH!!
AH! Can't see!
Now *this* kill is going to make me!
Oh crap! Ow! I broke my hand!!
I think I actually broke my hand!!
ARG!

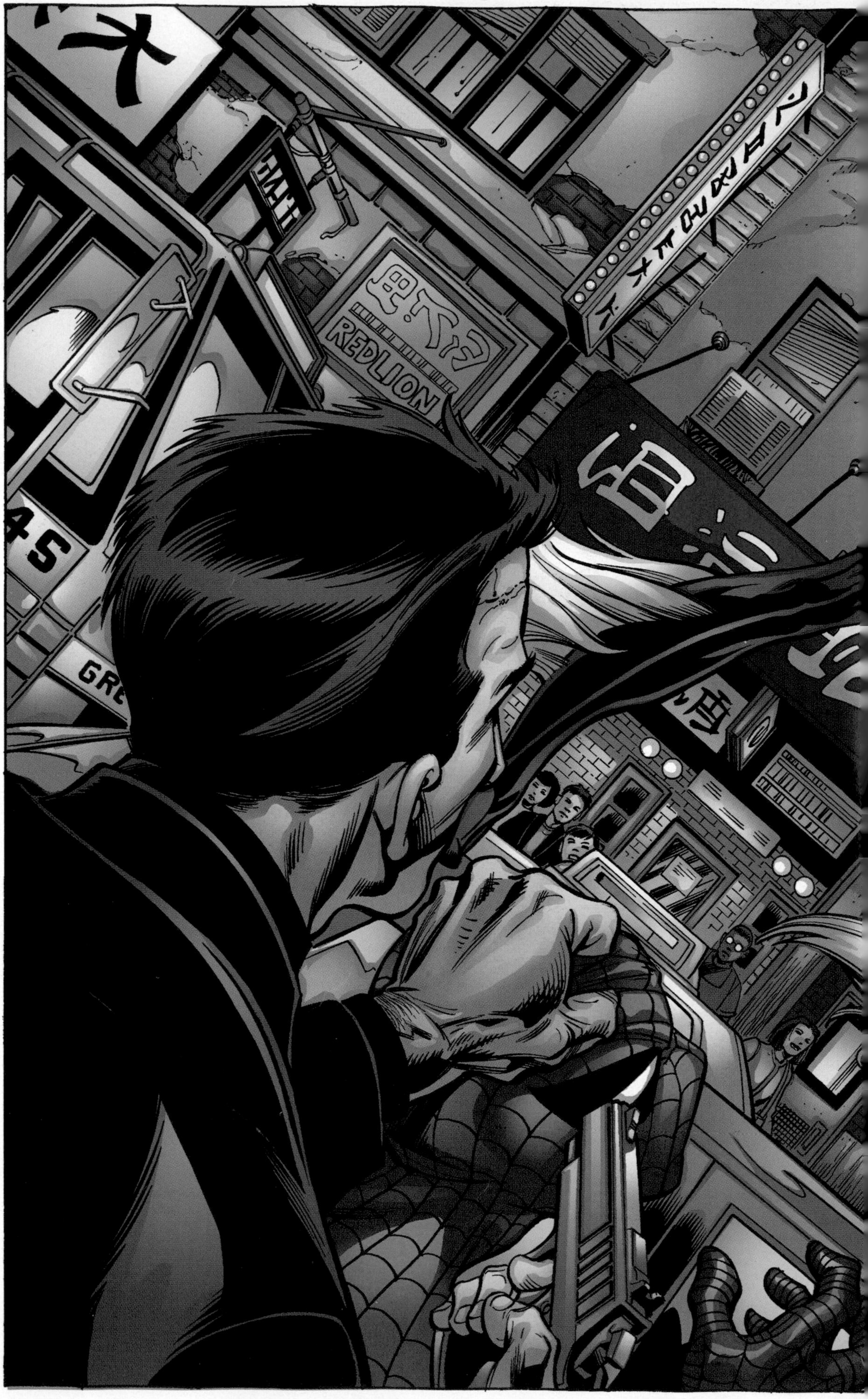
REDLION
45

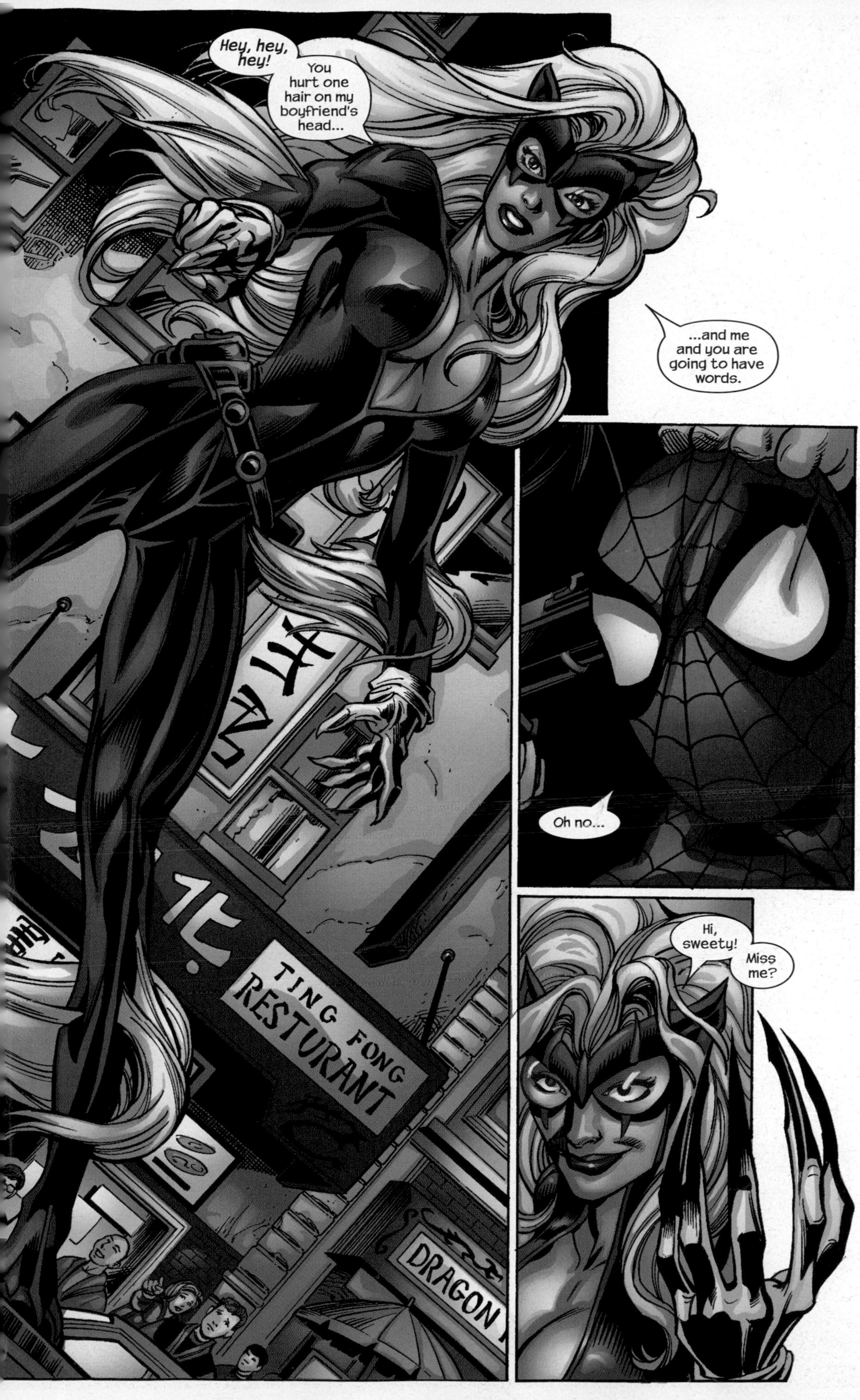
Hey, hey, hey!
You hurt one hair on my boyfriend's head...
...and me and you are going to have words.
Oh no...
Hi, sweety!
Miss me?
TING FONG RESTURANT
DRAGON

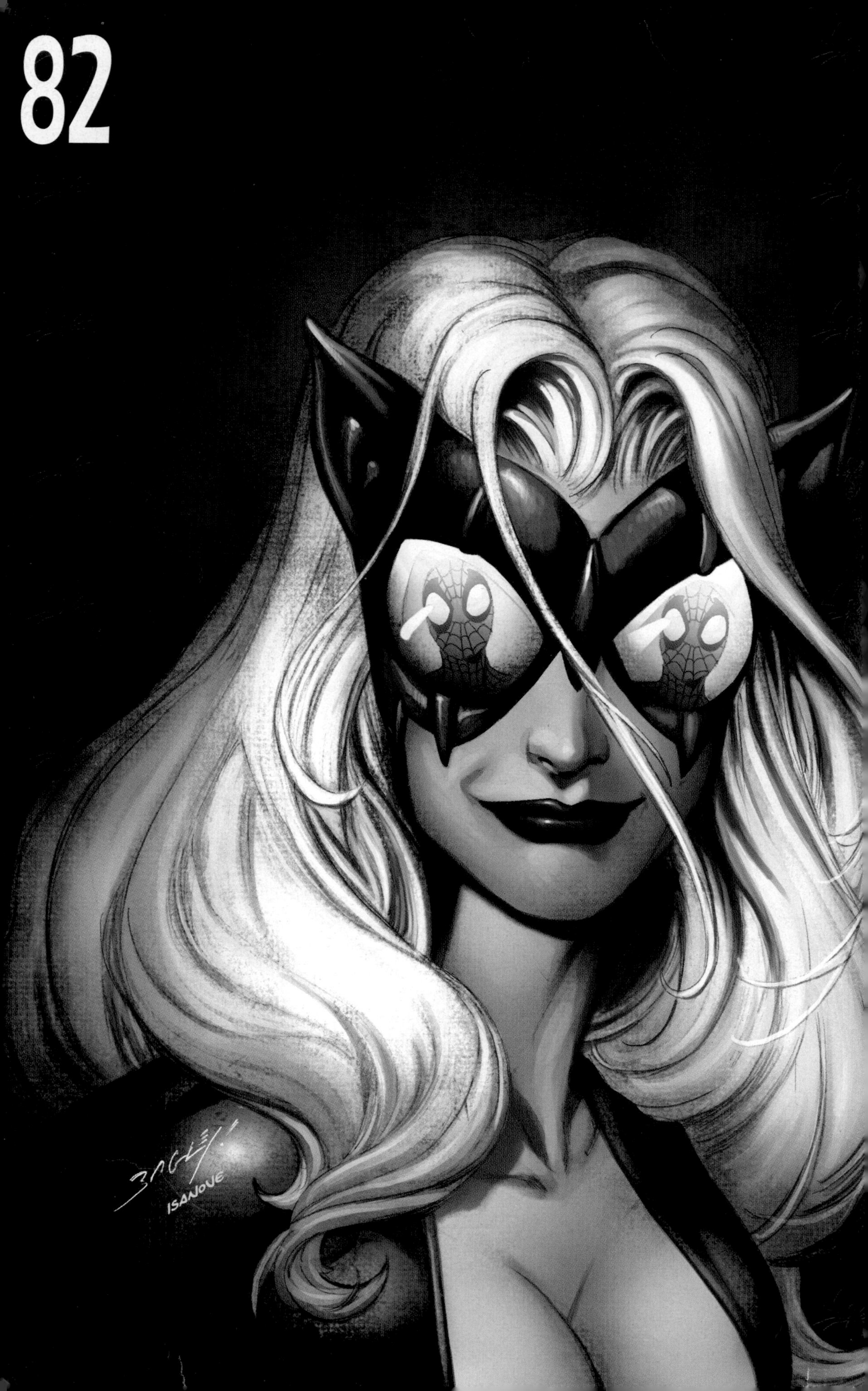

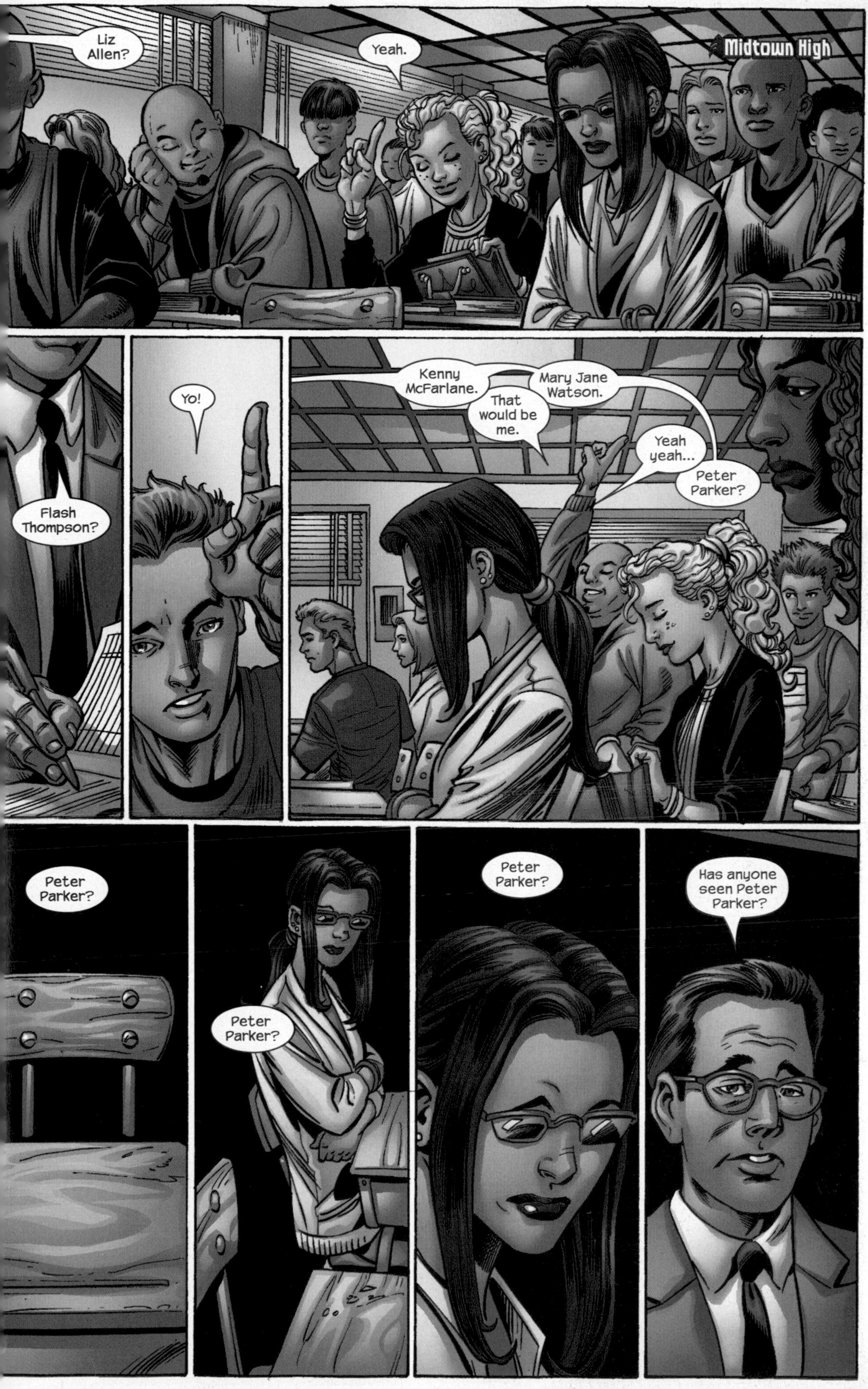
Midtown High
Liz Allen?
Yeah.
Flash Thompson?
Yo!
Kenny McFarlane.
That would be me.
Mary Jane Watson.
Yeah yeah...
Peter Parker?
Peter Parker?
Peter Parker?
Peter Parker?
Has anyone seen Peter Parker?

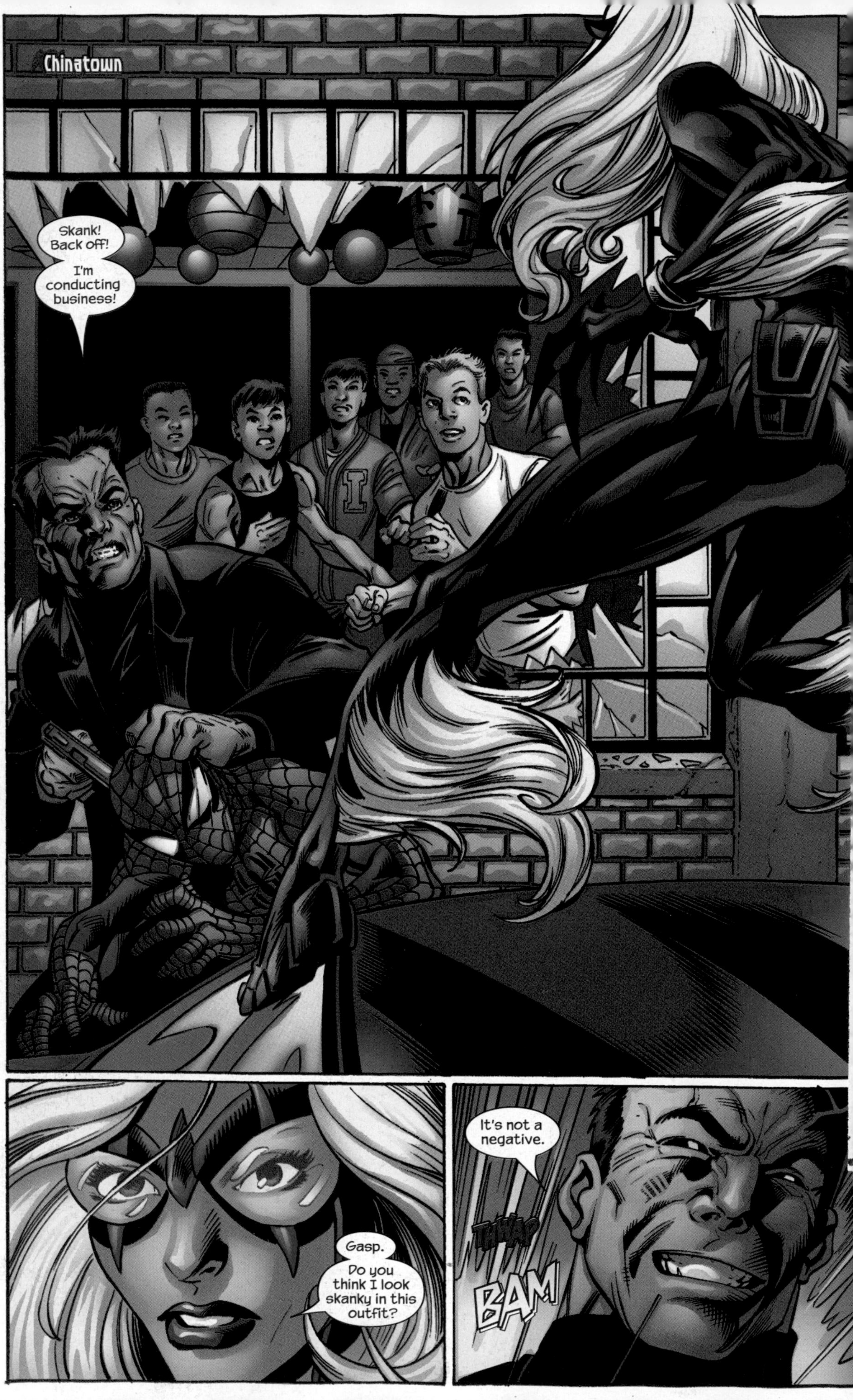
Chinatown
Skank! Back off!
I'm conducting business!
Gasp.
Do you think I look skanky in this outfit?
It's not a negative.
THWAP
BAM

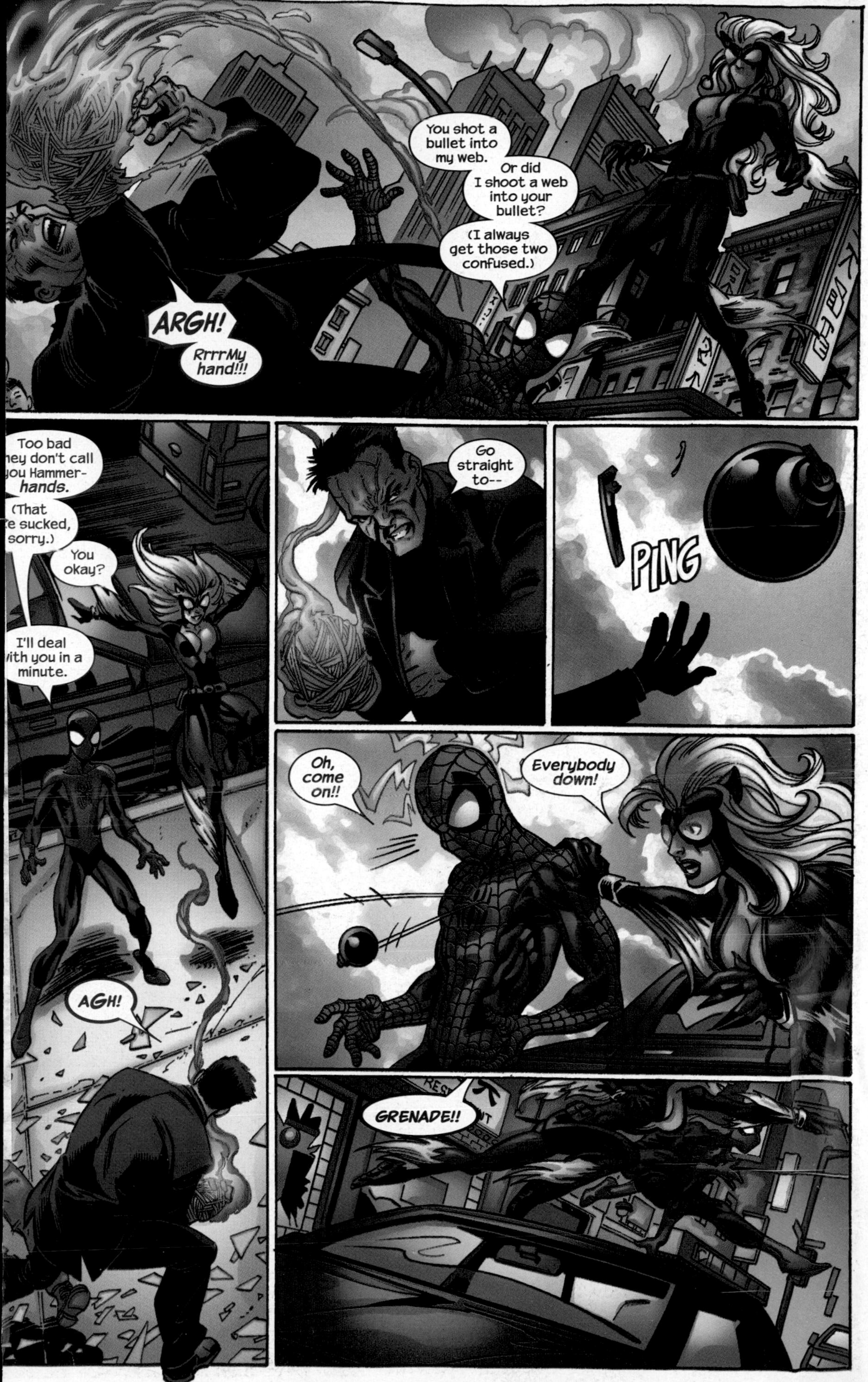
You shot a bullet into my web.
Or did I shoot a web into your bullet?
(I always get those two confused.)
ARGH!
RrrrMy hand!!!
Too bad hey don't call you Hammer-hands.
(That e sucked, sorry.)
You okay?
I'll deal with you in a minute.
AGH!
Go straight to--
PING
Oh, come on!!
Everybody down!
GRENADE!!

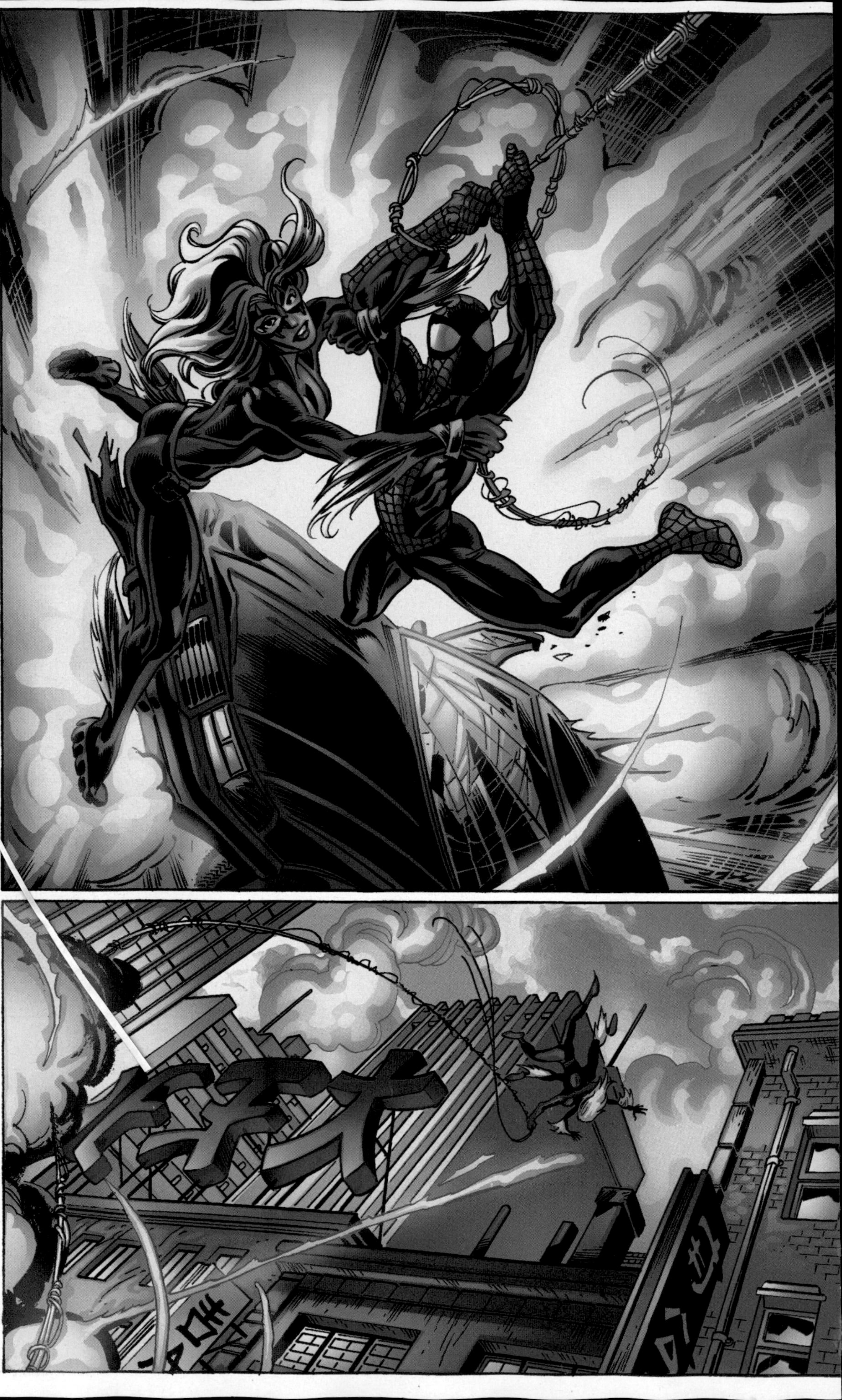

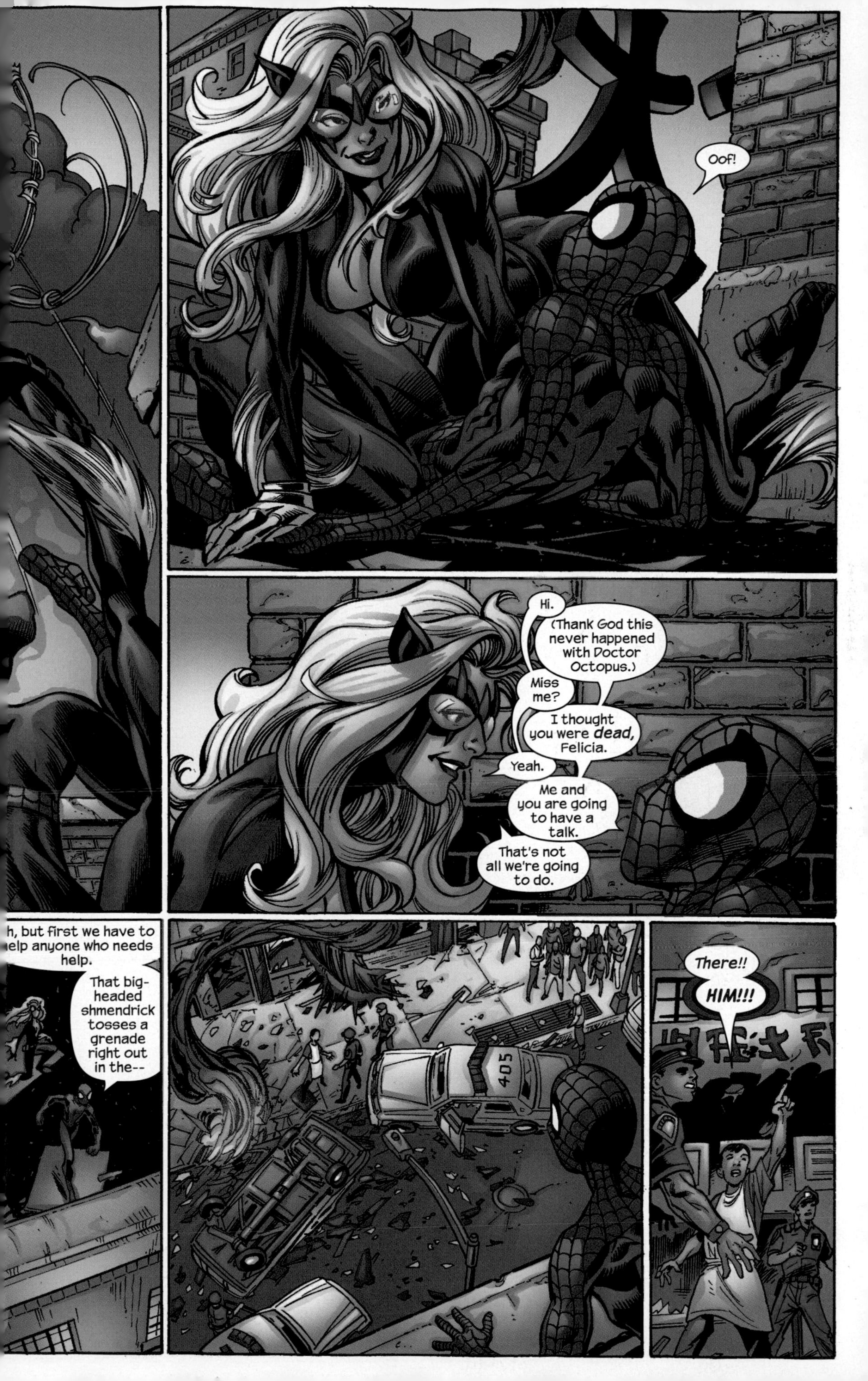
Oof!
Hi.
(Thank God this never happened with Doctor Octopus.)
Miss me?
I thought you were *dead,* Felicia.
Yeah.
Me and you are going to have a talk.
That's not all we're going to do.
h, but first we have to elp anyone who needs help.
That big-headed shmendrick tosses a grenade right out in the--
There!!
HIM!!!

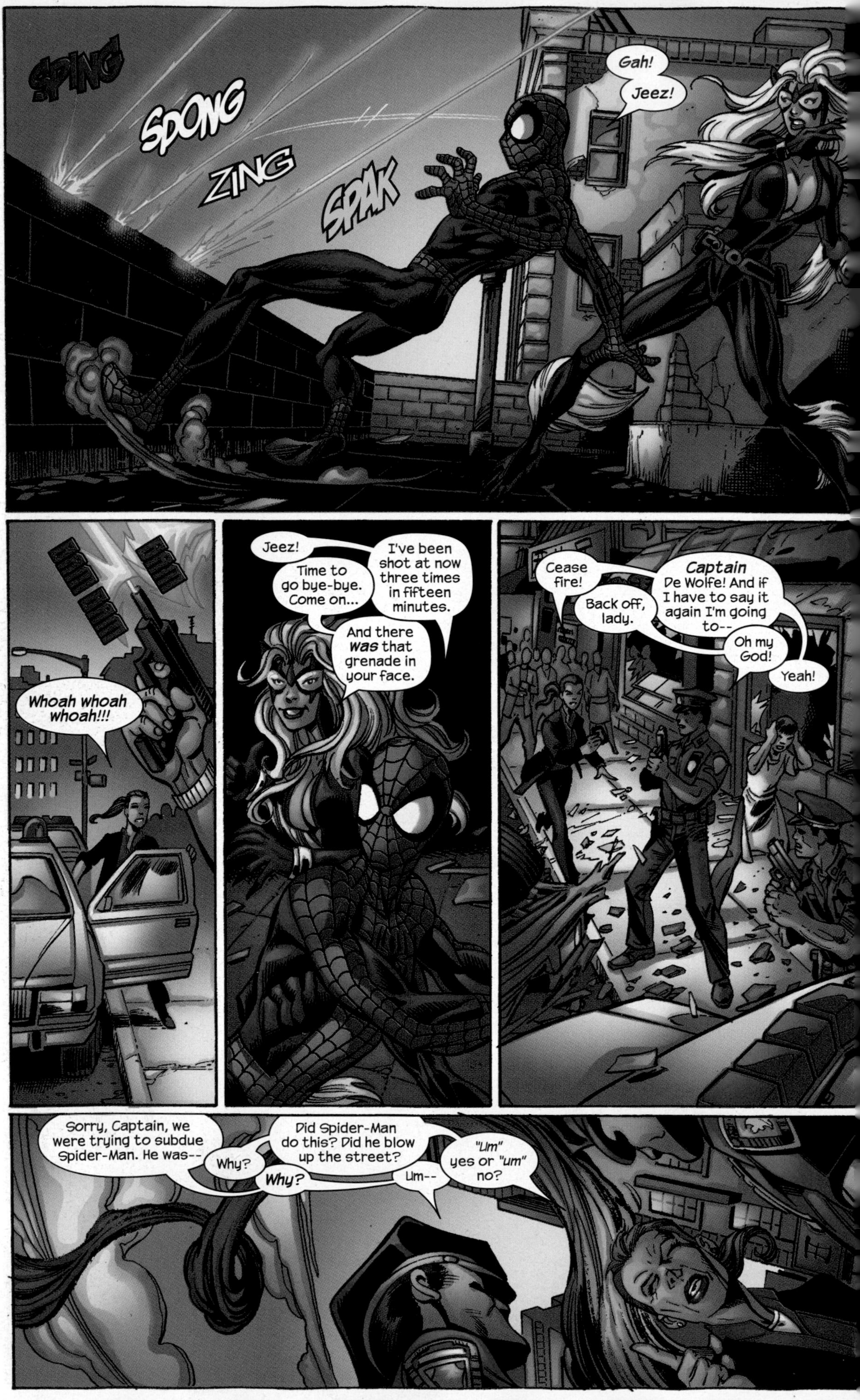
SPING
SPONG
ZING
SPAK
Gah!
Jeez!
Whoah whoah whoah!!!
Jeez!
Time to go bye-bye. Come on...
I've been shot at now three times in fifteen minutes.
And there *was* that grenade in your face.
Cease fire!
Back off, lady.
Captain De Wolfe! And if I have to say it again I'm going to--
Oh my God!
Yeah!
Sorry, Captain, we were trying to subdue Spider-Man. He was--
Why?
Why?
Did Spider-Man do this? Did he blow up the street?
Um--
"Um" yes or "um" no?

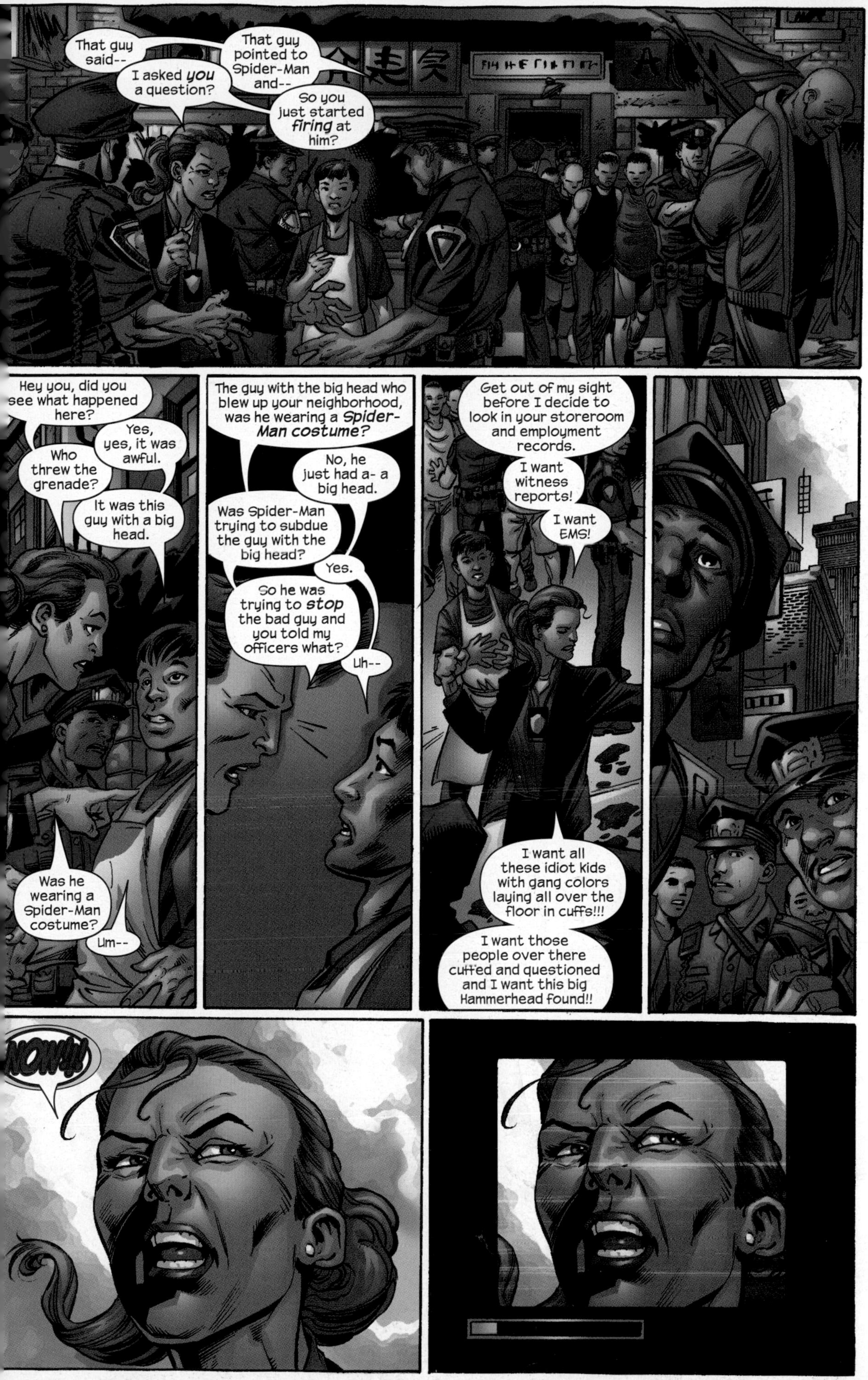
That guy said--
I asked you a question?
That guy pointed to Spider-Man and--
So you just started firing at him?
Hey you, did you see what happened here?
Yes, yes, it was awful.
Who threw the grenade?
It was this guy with a big head.
Was he wearing a Spider-Man costume?
Um--
The guy with the big head who blew up your neighborhood, was he wearing a Spider-Man costume?
No, he just had a- a big head.
Was Spider-Man trying to subdue the guy with the big head?
Yes.
So he was trying to stop the bad guy and you told my officers what?
Uh--
Get out of my sight before I decide to look in your storeroom and employment records.
I want witness reports!
I want EMS!
I want all these idiot kids with gang colors laying all over the floor in cuffs!!!
I want those people over there cuffed and questioned and I want this big Hammerhead found!!
NOW!!!

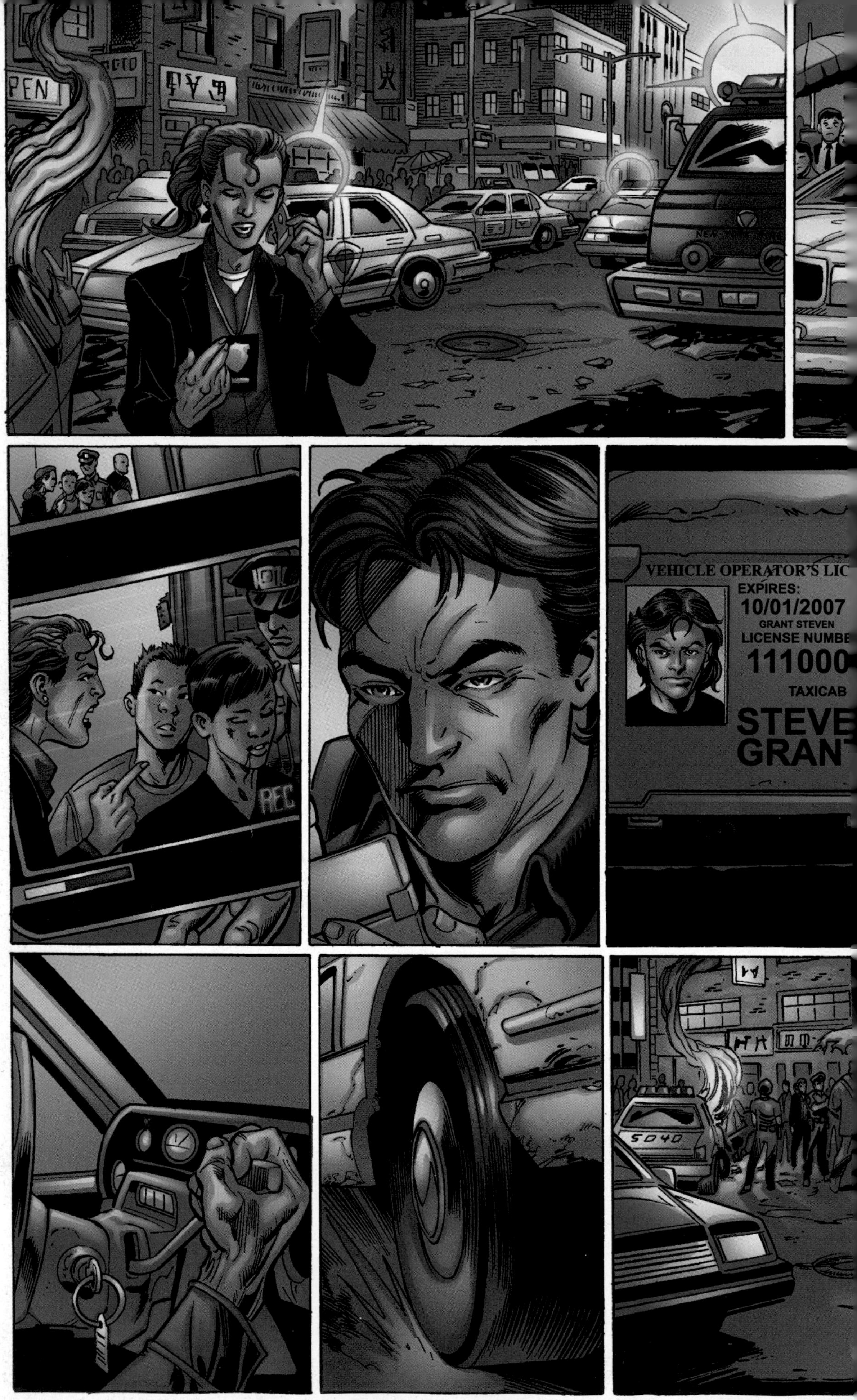

PEN
VEHICLE OPERATOR'S LIC
EXPIRES:
10/01/2007
GRANT STEVEN
LICENSE NUMBE
111000
TAXICAB
STEVE
GRANT
REC
5040

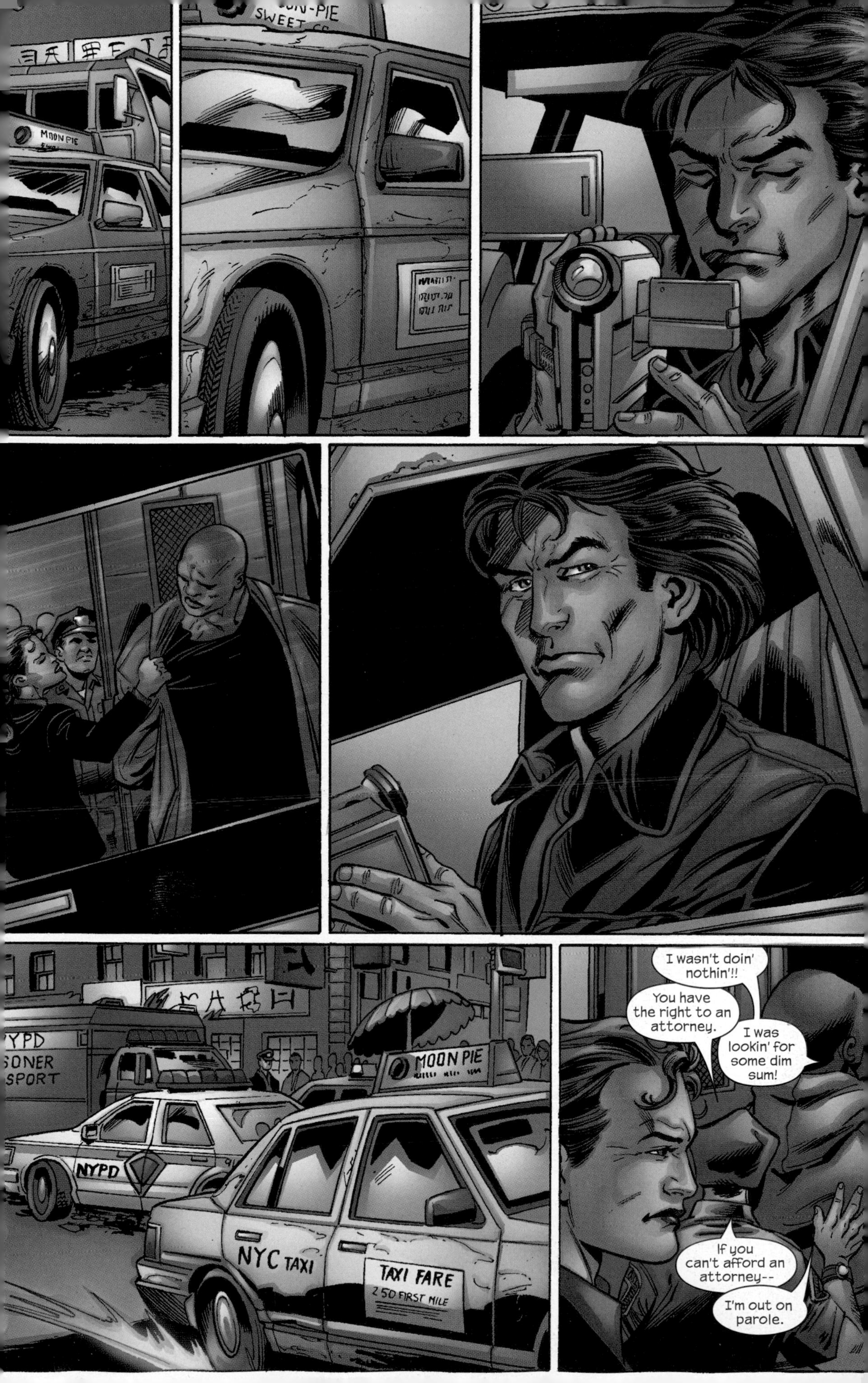
MOON PIE
MOON PIE
NYPD
NYC TAXI
TAXI FARE
2.50 FIRST MILE
I wasn't doin' nothin'!!
You have the right to an attorney.
I was lookin' for some dim sum!
If you can't afford an attorney--
I'm out on parole.

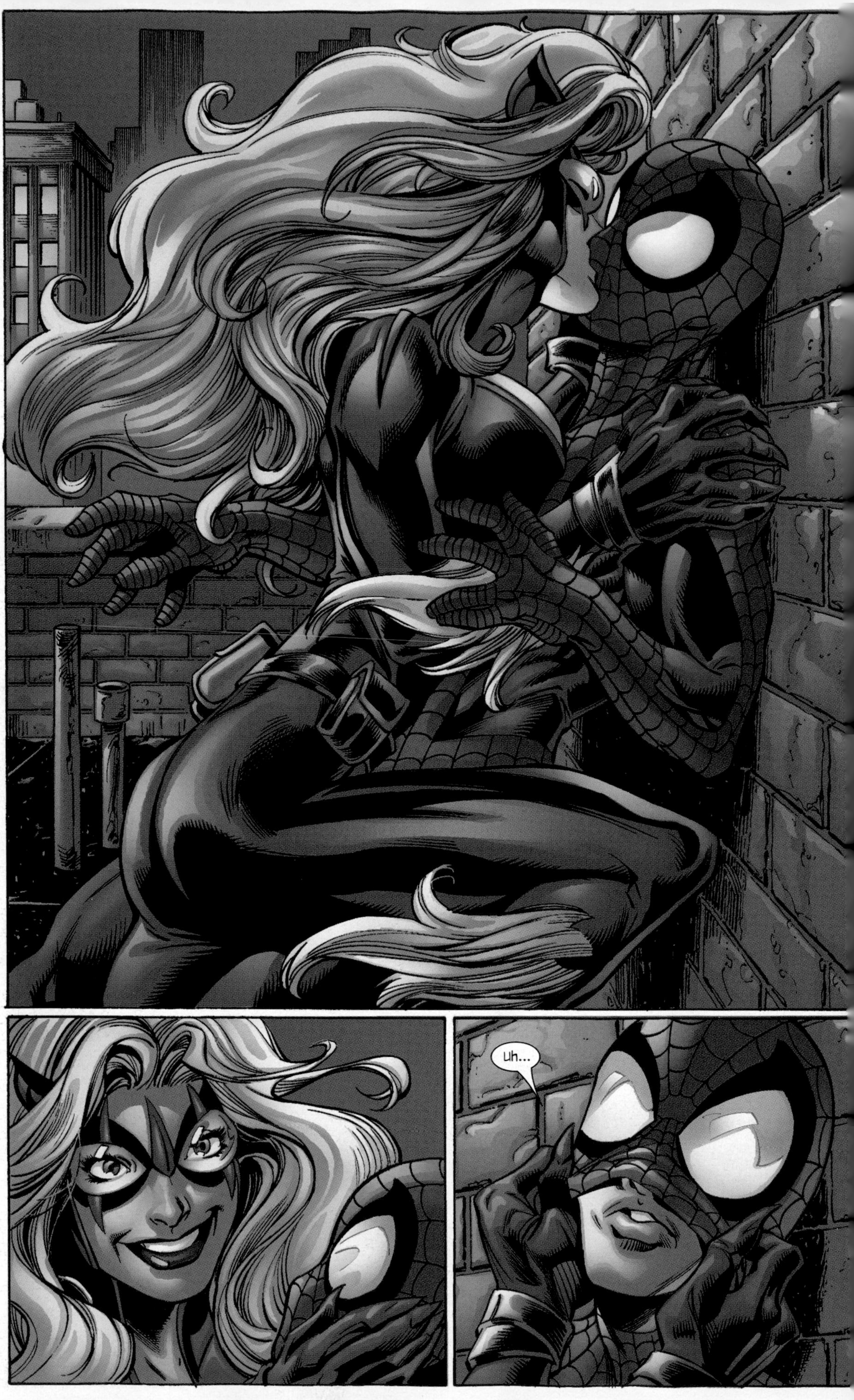
Uh...

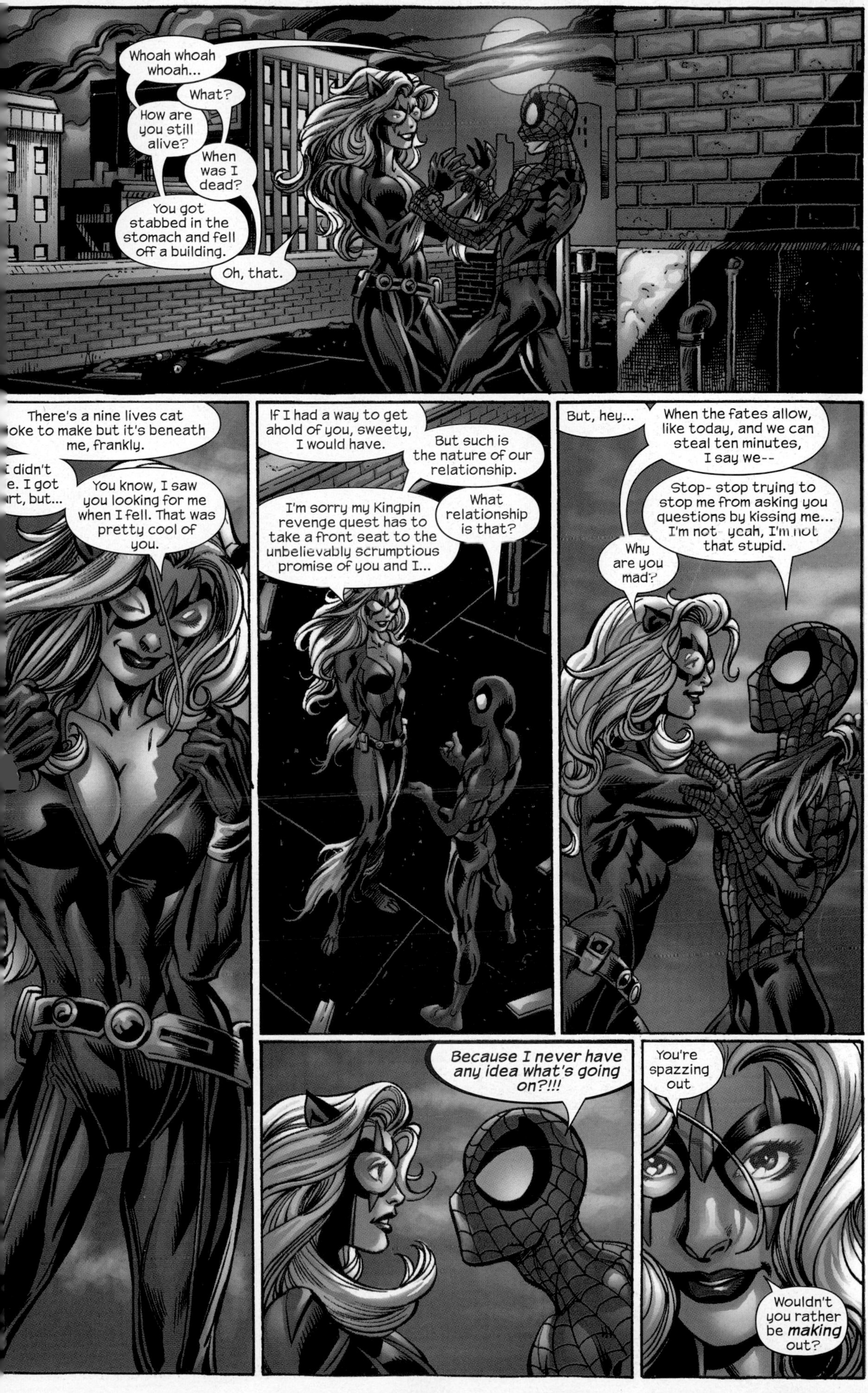
Whoah whoah whoah...
What?
How are you still alive?
When was I dead?
You got stabbed in the stomach and fell off a building.
Oh, that.
There's a nine lives cat joke to make but it's beneath me, frankly.
I didn't e. I got rt, but...
You know, I saw you looking for me when I fell. That was pretty cool of you.
If I had a way to get ahold of you, sweety, I would have.
But such is the nature of our relationship.
I'm sorry my Kingpin revenge quest has to take a front seat to the unbelievably scrumptious promise of you and I...
What relationship is that?
But, hey...
When the fates allow, like today, and we can steal ten minutes, I say we--
Stop- stop trying to stop me from asking you questions by kissing me... I'm not- yeah, I'm not that stupid.
Why are you mad?
Because I never have any idea what's going on?!!!
You're spazzing out
Wouldn't you rather be *making* out?

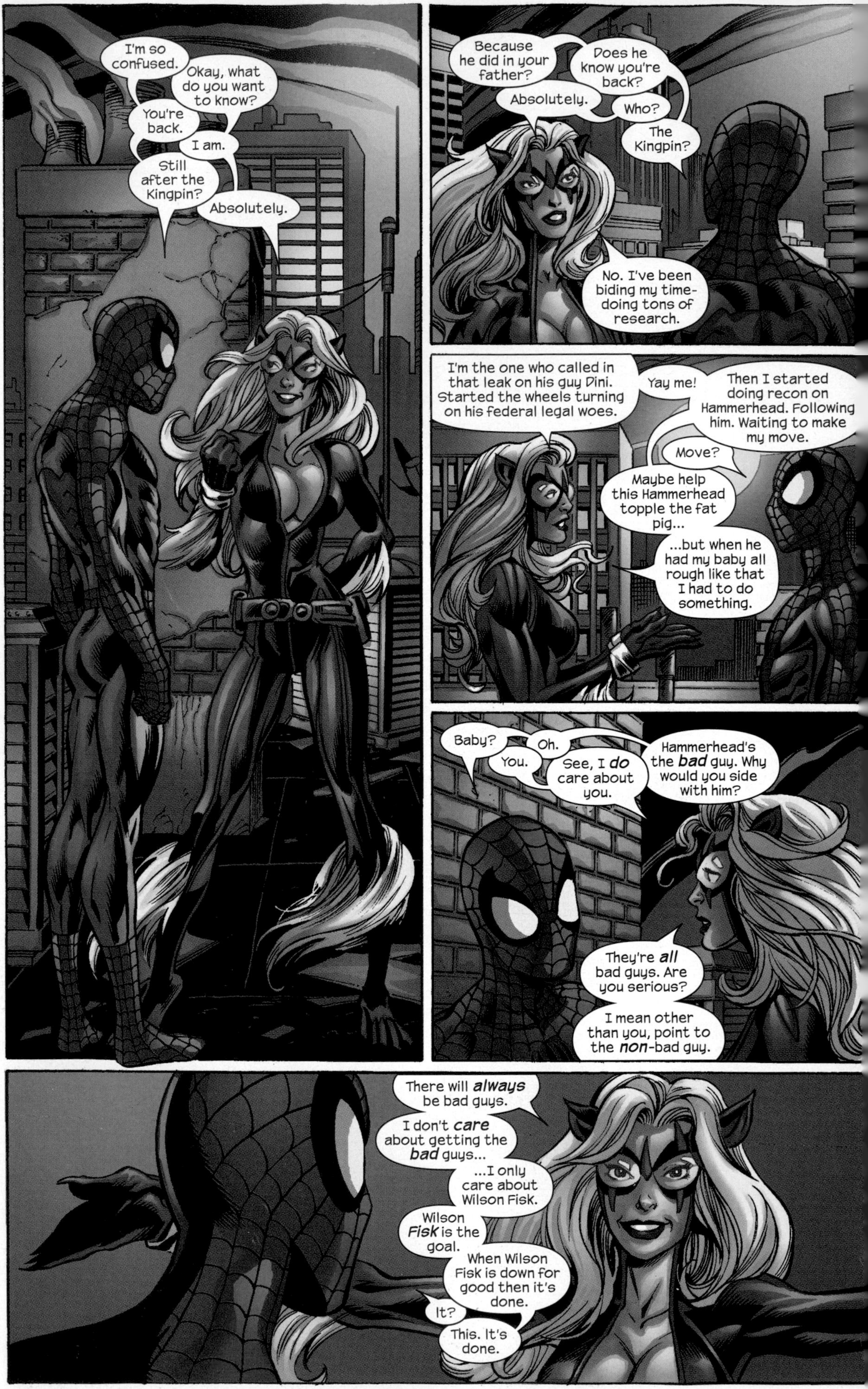

I'm so confused.
Okay, what do you want to know?
You're back.
I am.
Still after the Kingpin?
Absolutely.
Because he did in your father?
Does he know you're back?
Absolutely.
Who?
The Kingpin?
No. I've been biding my time- doing tons of research.
I'm the one who called in that leak on his guy Dini. Started the wheels turning on his federal legal woes.
Yay me!
Then I started doing recon on Hammerhead. Following him. Waiting to make my move.
Move?
Maybe help this Hammerhead topple the fat pig...
...but when he had my baby all rough like that I had to do something.
Baby?
Oh.
You.
See, I *do* care about you.
Hammerhead's the *bad* guy. Why would you side with him?
They're *all* bad guys. Are you serious?
I mean other than you, point to the *non*-bad guy.
There will *always* be bad guys.
I don't *care* about getting the *bad* guys...
...I only care about Wilson Fisk.
Wilson *Fisk* is the goal.
When Wilson Fisk is down for good then it's done.
It?
This. It's done.

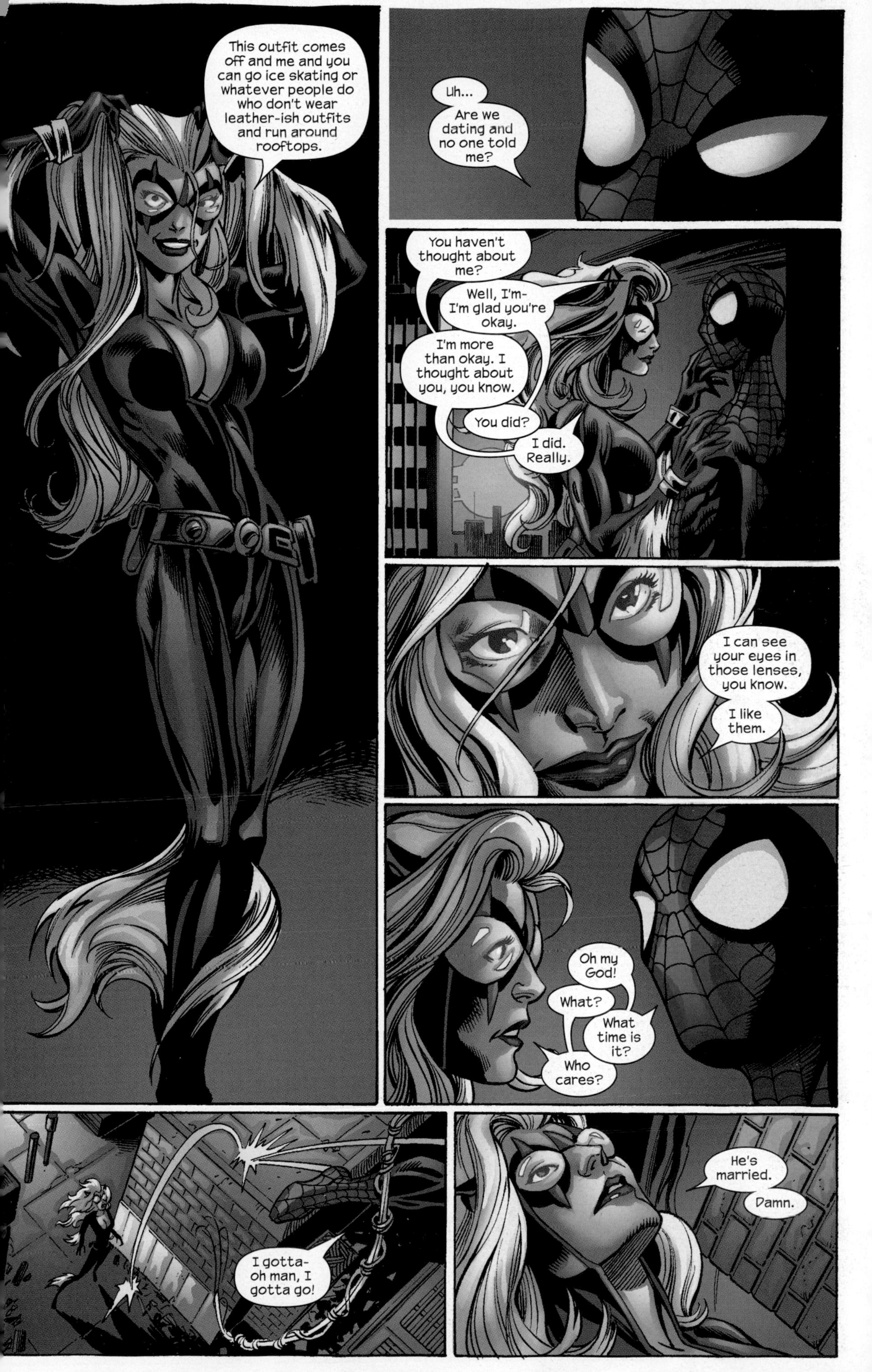
This outfit comes off and me and you can go ice skating or whatever people do who don't wear leather-ish outfits and run around rooftops.
Uh...
Are we dating and no one told me?
You haven't thought about me?
Well, I'm- I'm glad you're okay.
I'm more than okay. I thought about you, you know.
You did?
I did. Really.
I can see your eyes in those lenses, you know.
I like them.
Oh my God!
What?
What time is it?
Who cares?
I gotta- oh man, I gotta go!
He's married.
Damn.

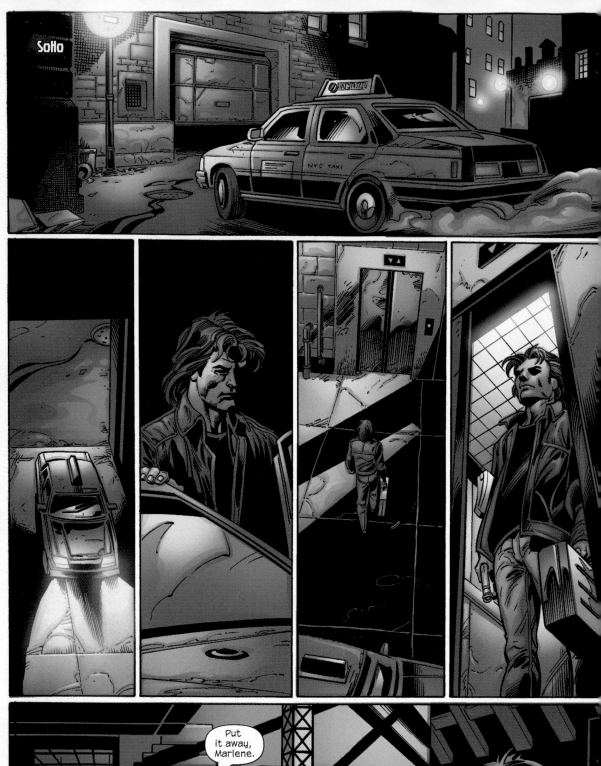

SoHo

Put it away, Marlene.

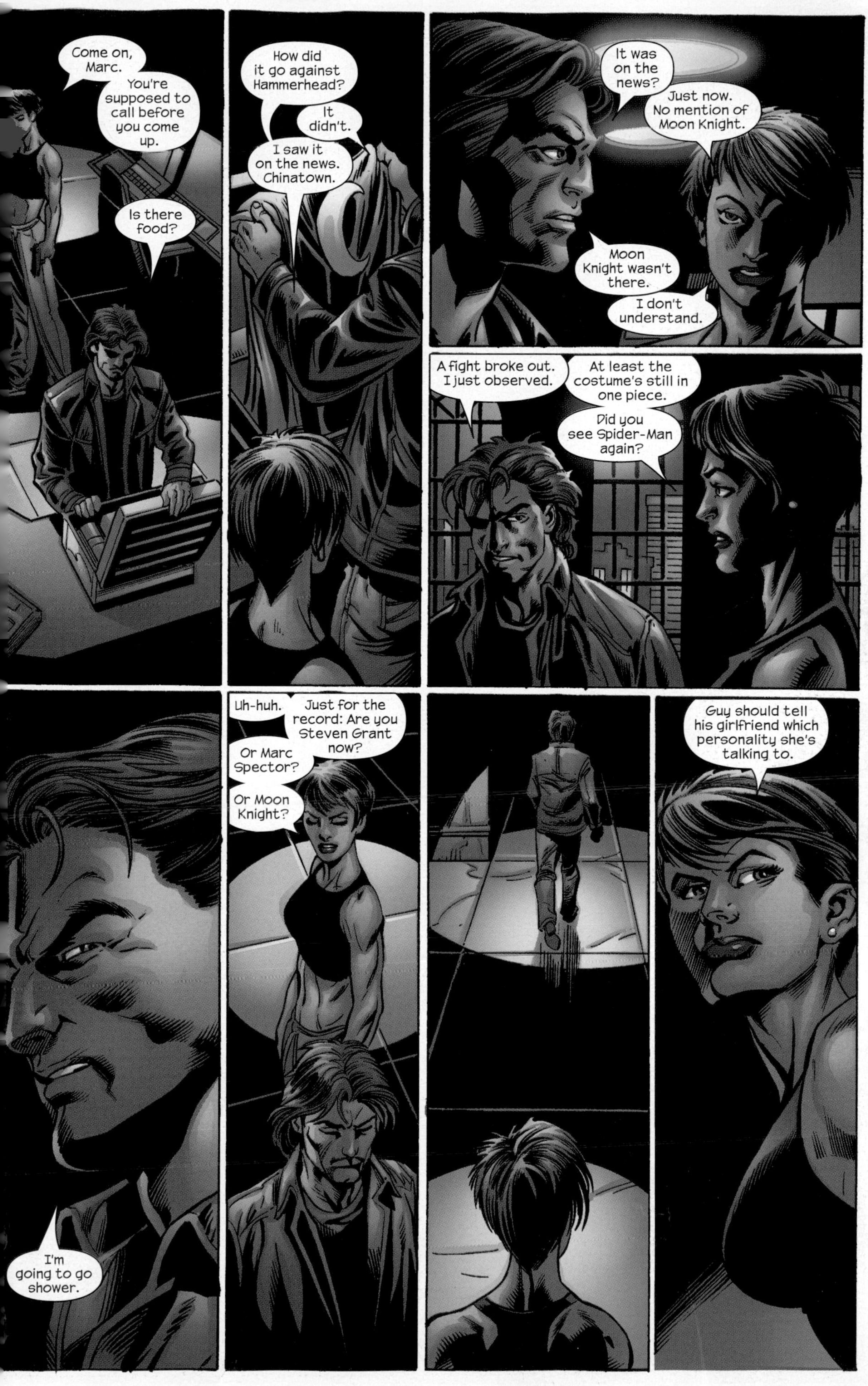
Come on, Marc.
You're supposed to call before you come up.
Is there food?
How did it go against Hammerhead?
It didn't.
I saw it on the news. Chinatown.
It was on the news?
Just now. No mention of Moon Knight.
Moon Knight wasn't there.
I don't understand.
A fight broke out. I just observed.
At least the costume's still in one piece.
Did you see Spider-Man again?
I'm going to go shower.
Uh-huh.
Just for the record: Are you Steven Grant now?
Or Marc Spector?
Or Moon Knight?
Guy should tell his girlfriend which personality she's talking to.

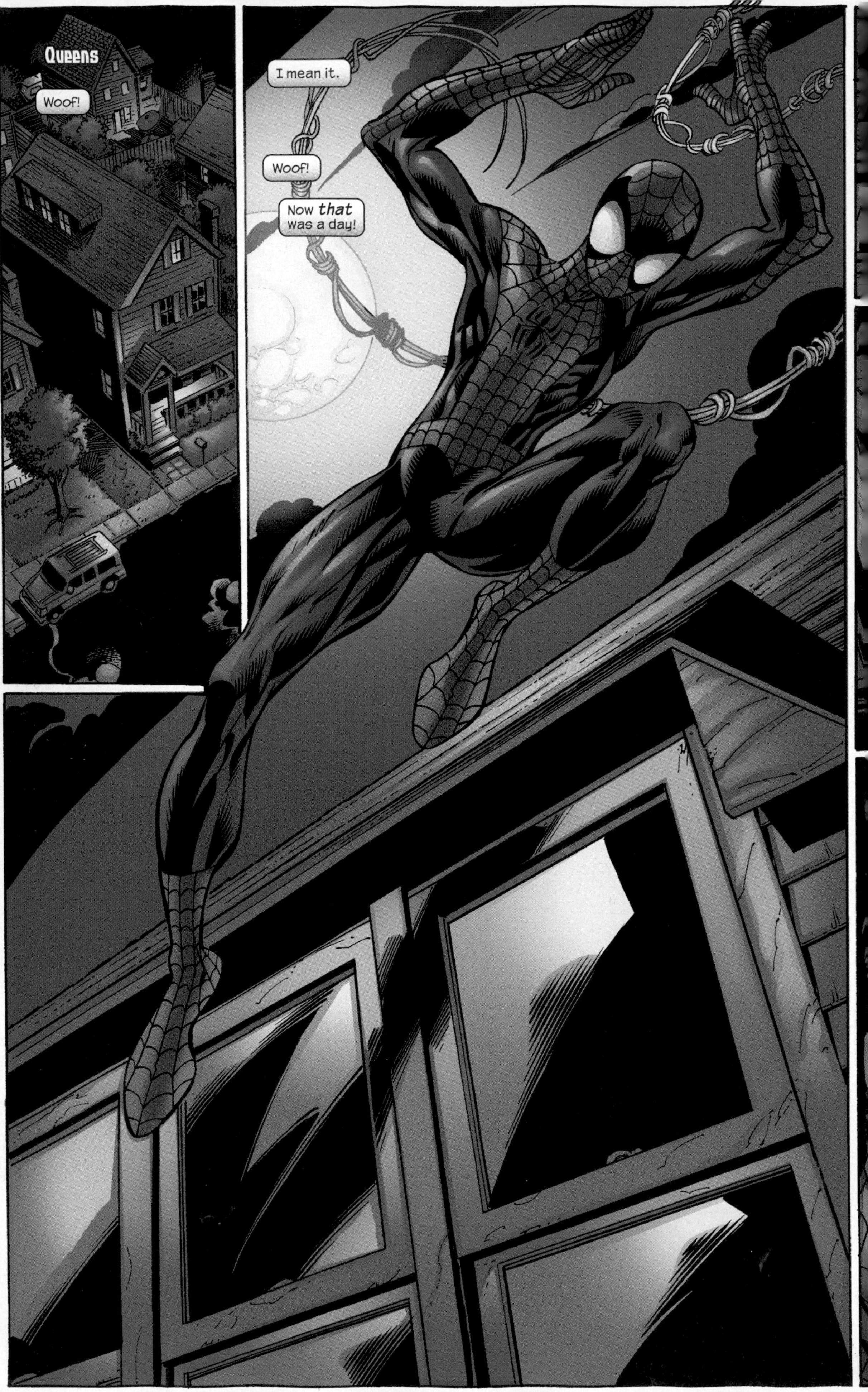
Queens
Woof!
I mean it.
Woof!
Now *that* was a day!

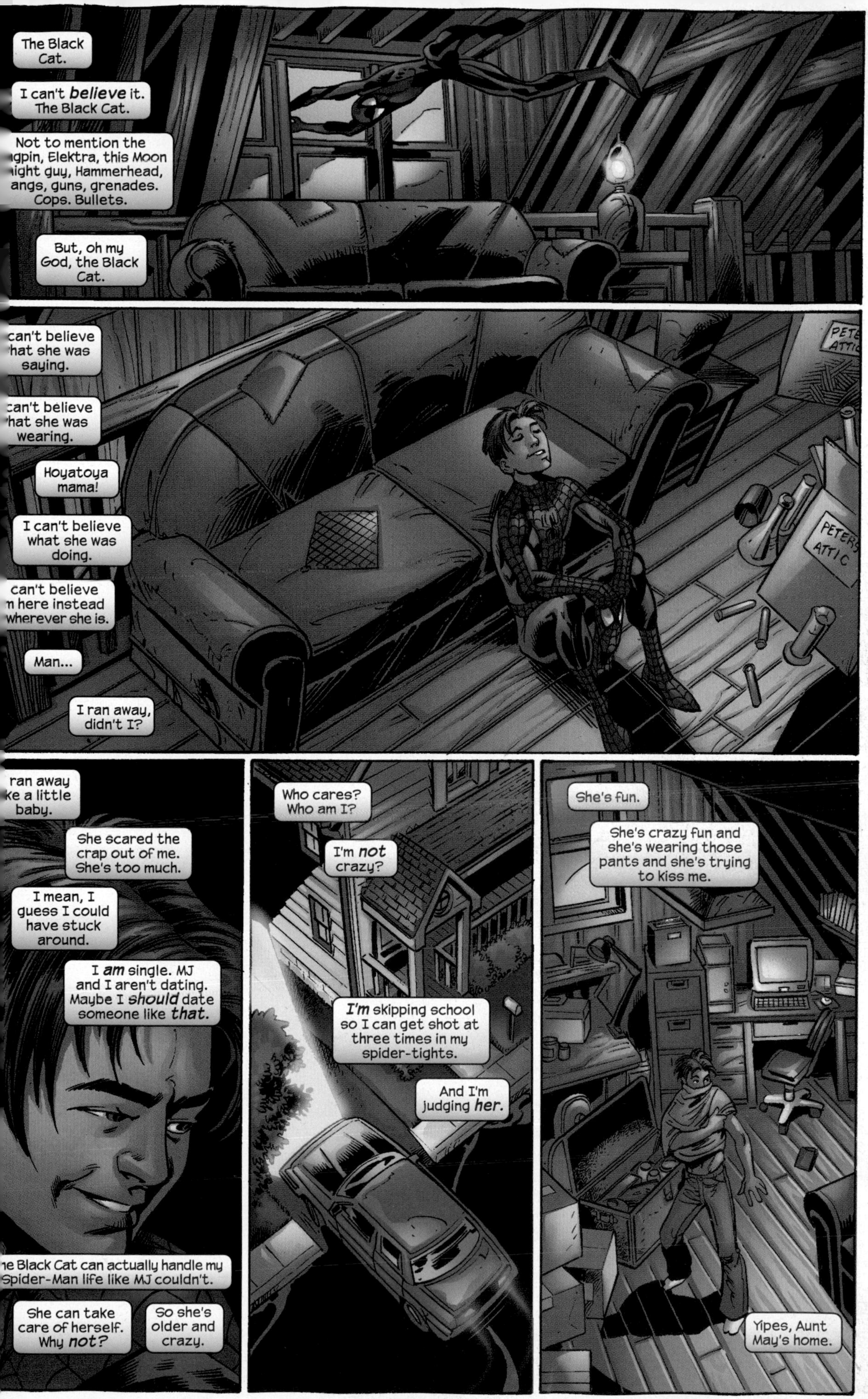

The Black Cat.
I can't *believe* it. The Black Cat.
Not to mention the
gpin, Elektra, this Moon
ight guy, Hammerhead,
angs, guns, grenades.
Cops. Bullets.
But, oh my God, the Black Cat.
can't believe
hat she was
saying.
can't believe
hat she was
wearing.
Hoyatoya mama!
I can't believe what she was doing.
can't believe
n here instead
wherever she is.
Man...
I ran away, didn't I?
PETE
ATTIC
PETERS ATTIC
ran away
ke a little
baby.
She scared the crap out of me. She's too much.
I mean, I guess I could have stuck around.
I *am* single. MJ and I aren't dating. Maybe I *should* date someone like *that*.
ne Black Cat can actually handle my
Spider-Man life like MJ couldn't.
She can take care of herself. Why *not?*
So she's older and crazy.
Who cares? Who am I?
I'm *not* crazy?
I'm skipping school so I can get shot at three times in my spider-tights.
And I'm judging *her*.
She's fun.
She's crazy fun and she's wearing those pants and she's trying to kiss me.
Yipes, Aunt May's home.

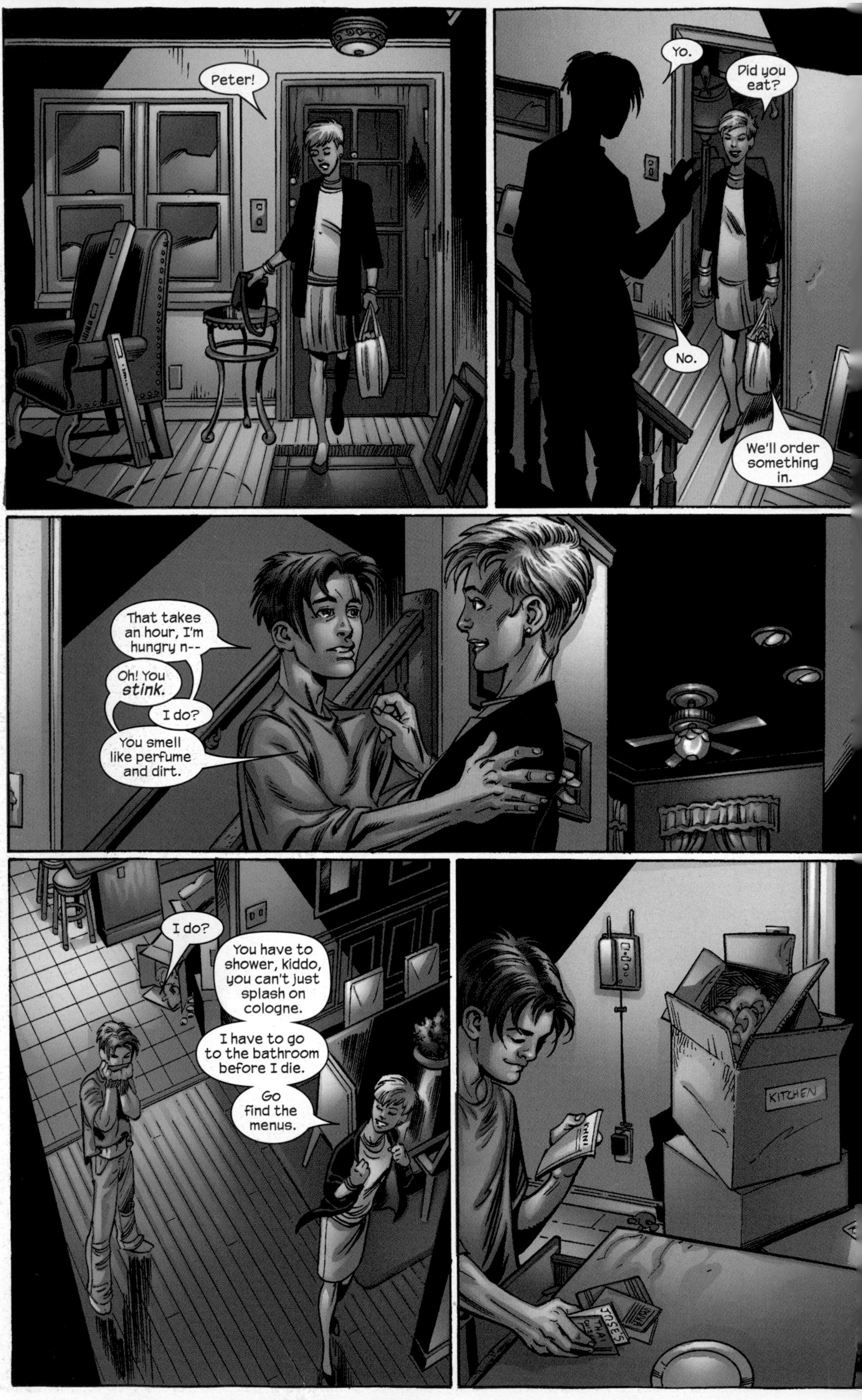
Peter!
Yo.
Did you eat?
No.
We'll order something in.
That takes an hour, I'm hungry n--
Oh! You *stink.*
I do?
You smell like perfume and dirt.
I do?
You have to shower, kiddo, you can't just splash on cologne.
I have to go to the bathroom before I die.
Go find the menus.
KITCHEN
JOSE'S

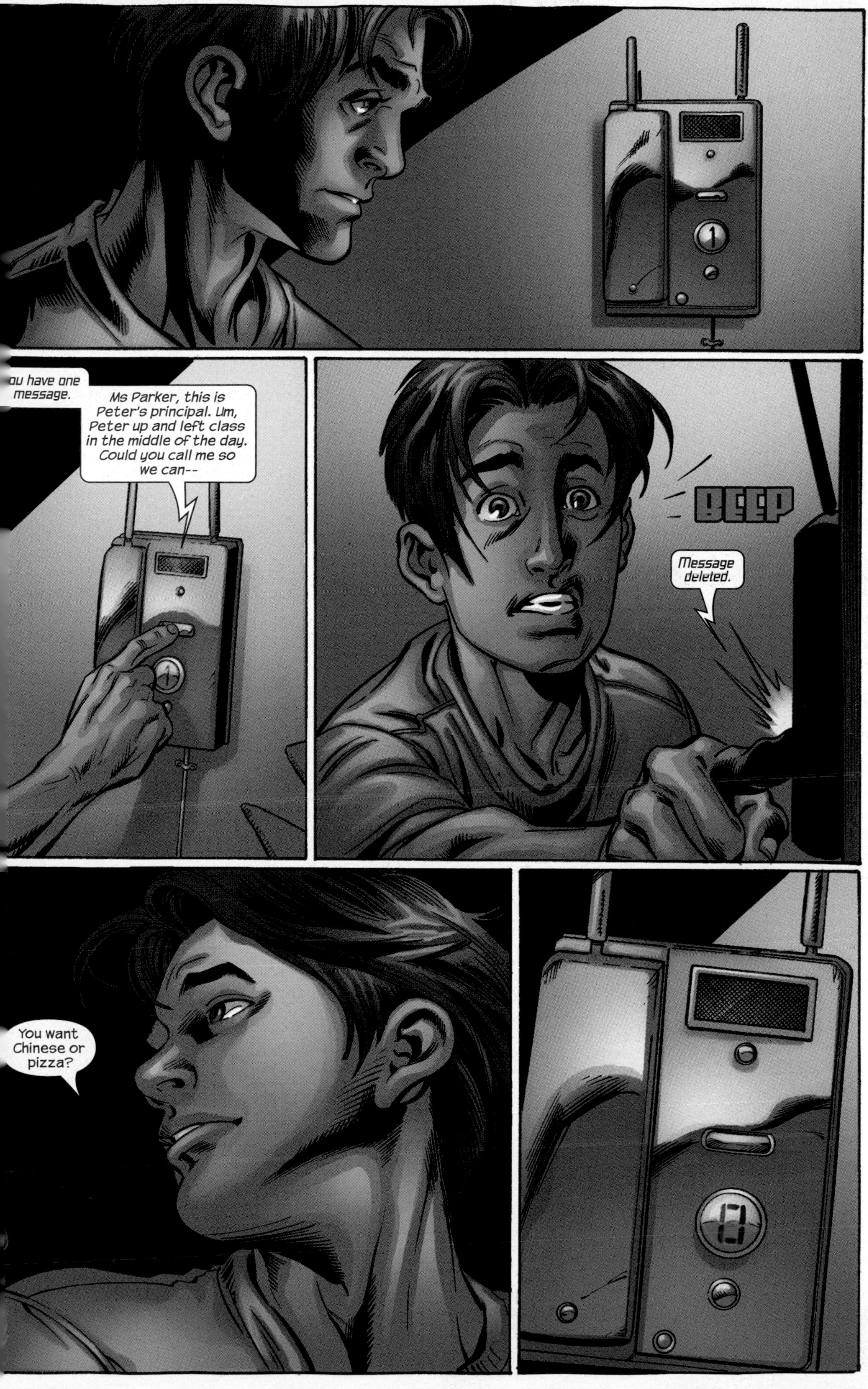

ou have one message.
Ms Parker, this is Peter's principal. Um, Peter up and left class in the middle of the day. Could you call me so we can--
BEEP
Message deleted.
You want Chinese or pizza?

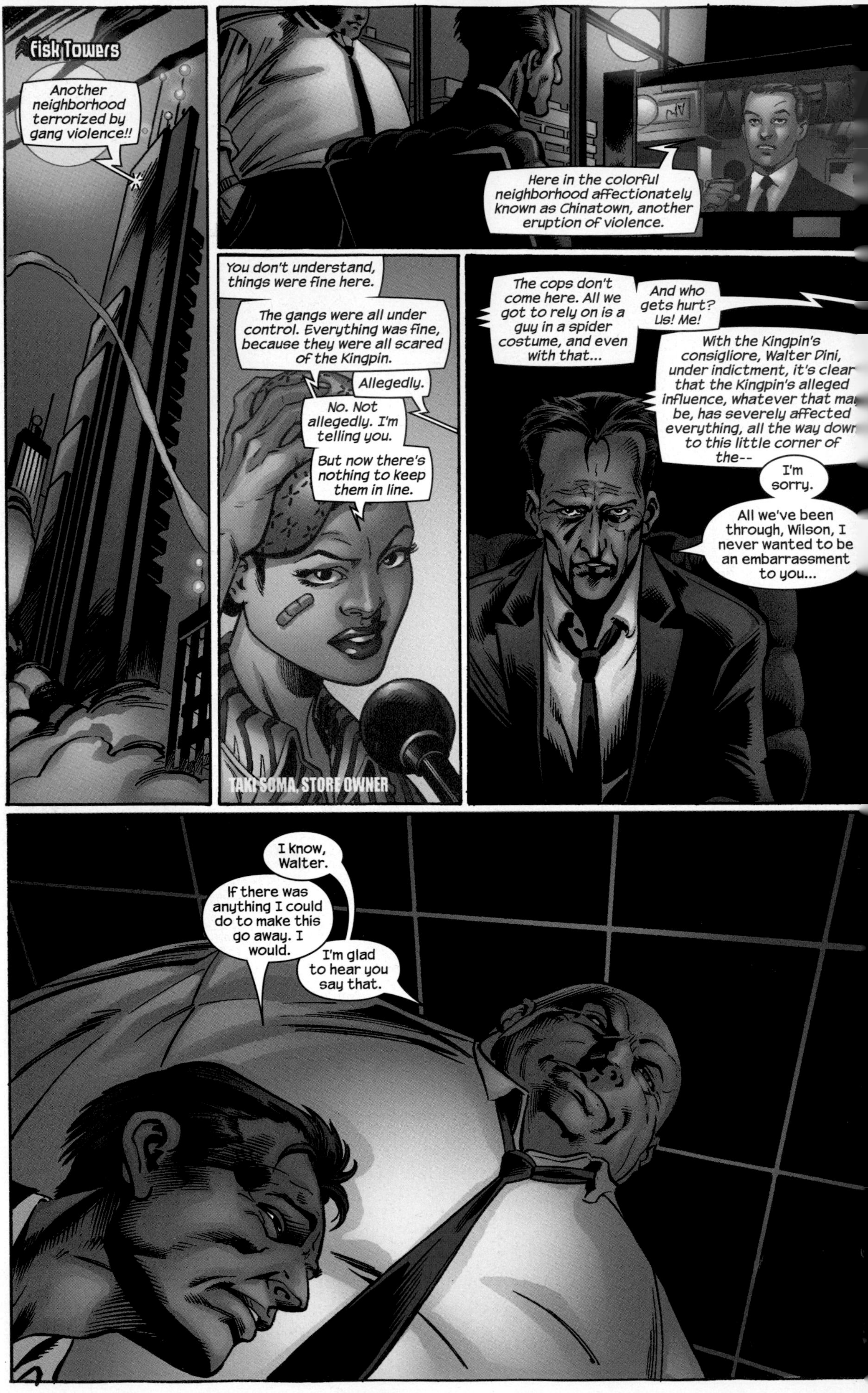
Fisk Towers
Another neighborhood terrorized by gang violence!!
Here in the colorful neighborhood affectionately known as Chinatown, another eruption of violence.
You don't understand, things were fine here.
The gangs were all under control. Everything was fine, because they were all scared of the Kingpin.
Allegedly.
No. Not allegedly. I'm telling you.
But now there's nothing to keep them in line.
TAKI SOMA, STORE OWNER
The cops don't come here. All we got to rely on is a guy in a spider costume, and even with that...
And who gets hurt? Us! Me!
With the Kingpin's consigliore, Walter Dini, under indictment, it's clear that the Kingpin's alleged influence, whatever that may be, has severely affected everything, all the way down to this little corner of the--
I'm sorry.
All we've been through, Wilson, I never wanted to be an embarrassment to you...
I know, Walter.
If there was anything I could do to make this go away. I would.
I'm glad to hear you say that.

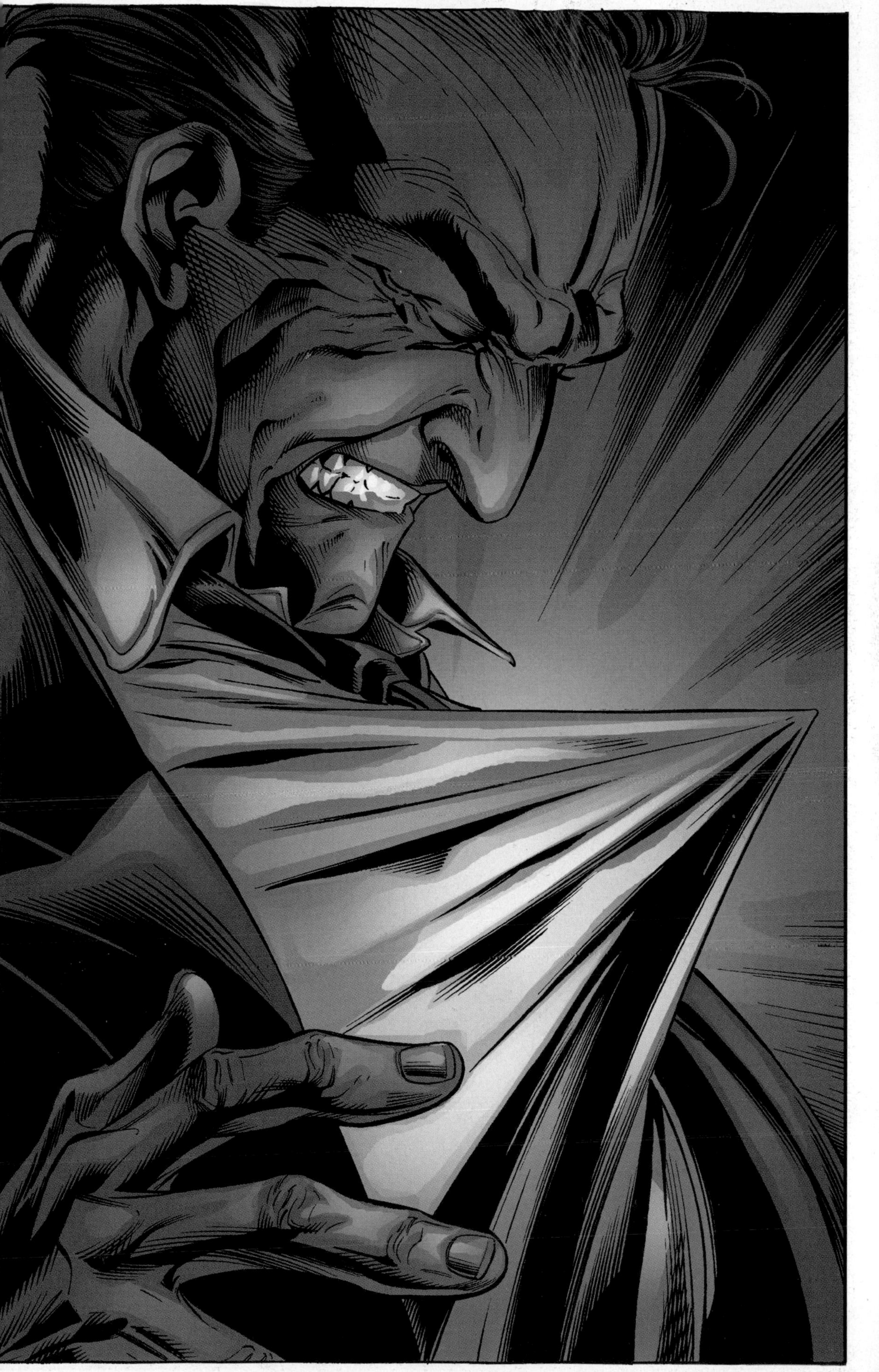

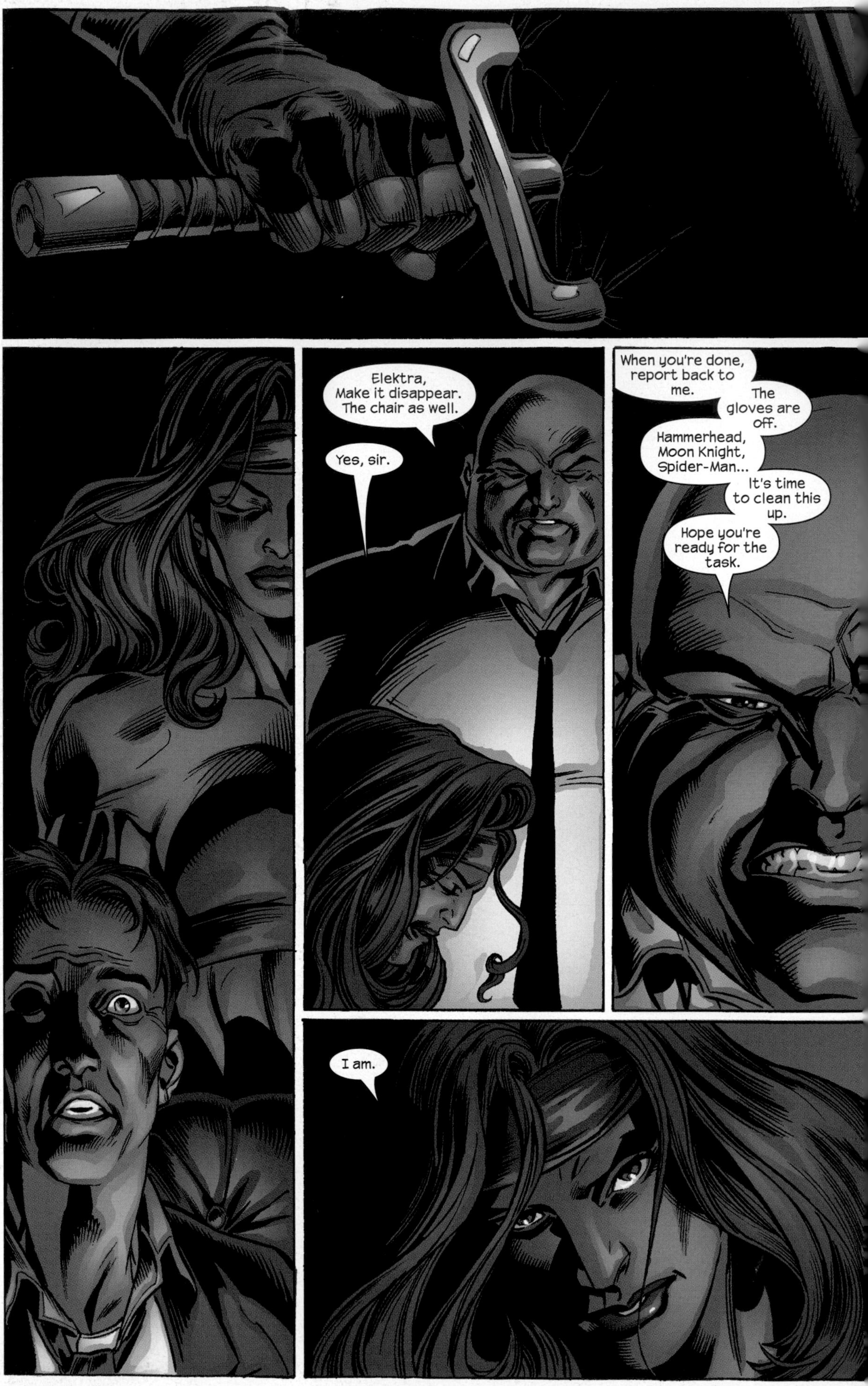
Elektra,
Make it disappear.
The chair as well.
Yes, sir.
When you're done, report back to me.
The gloves are off.
Hammerhead, Moon Knight, Spider-Man...
It's time to clean this up.
Hope you're ready for the task.
I am.

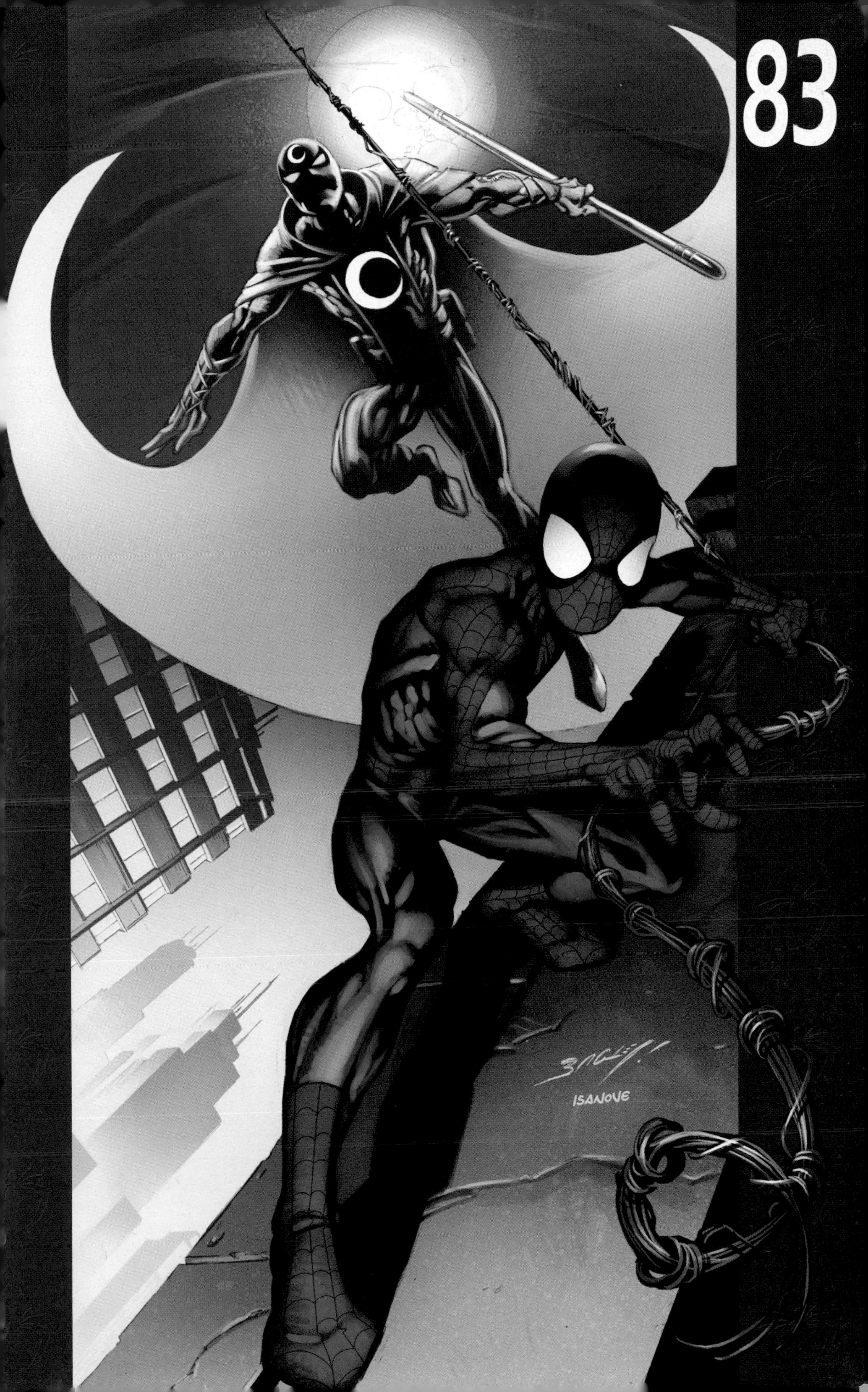
83
ISANOVE

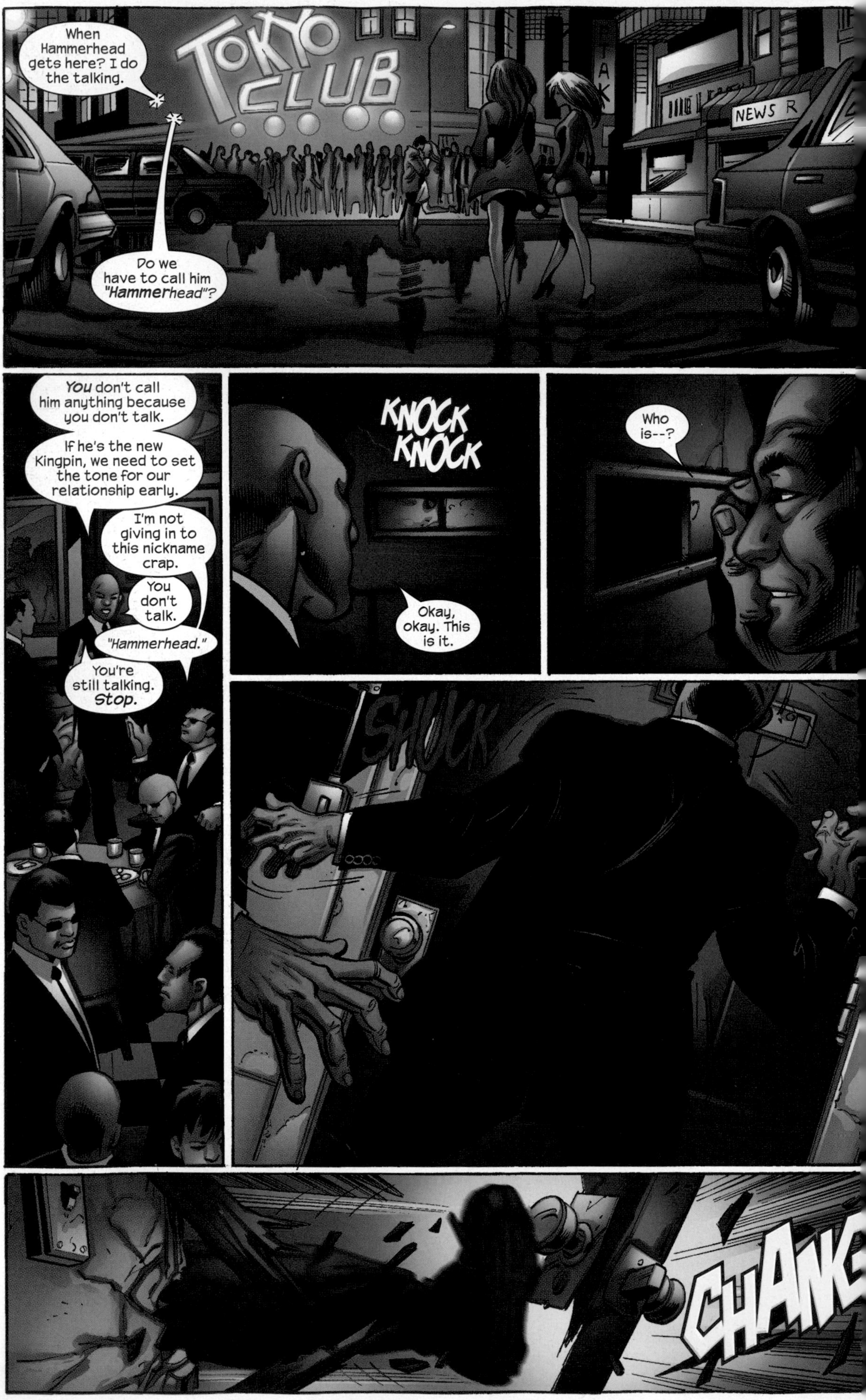
TOKYO CLUB
NEWS R
When Hammerhead gets here? I do the talking.
Do we have to call him "Hammerhead"?
You don't call him anything because you don't talk.
If he's the new Kingpin, we need to set the tone for our relationship early.
I'm not giving in to this nickname crap.
You don't talk.
"Hammerhead."
You're still talking. Stop.
KNOCK KNOCK
Okay, okay. This is it.
Who is--?
SHUCK
CHANG

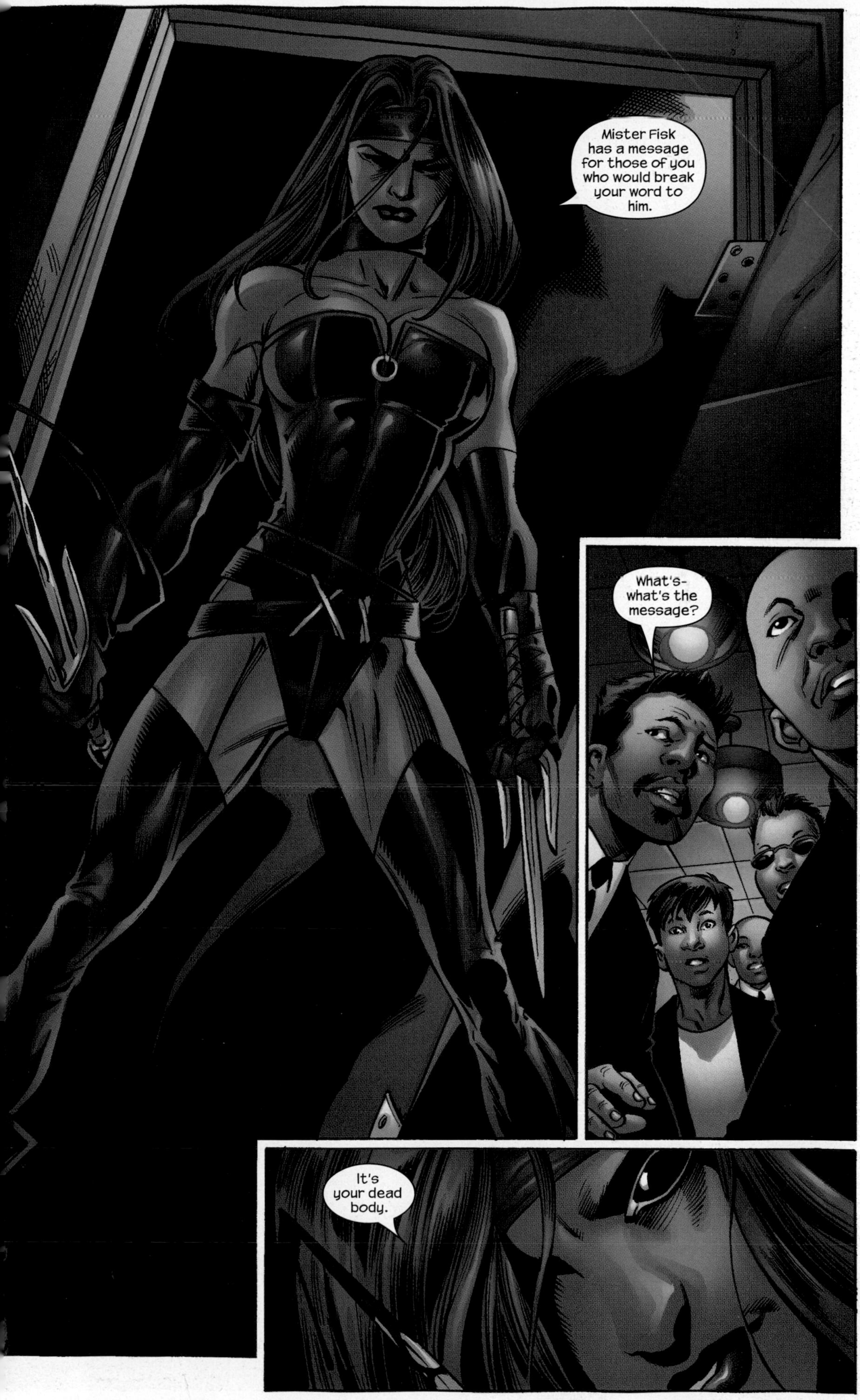
Mister Fisk has a message for those of you who would break your word to him.
What's- what's the message?
It's your dead body.

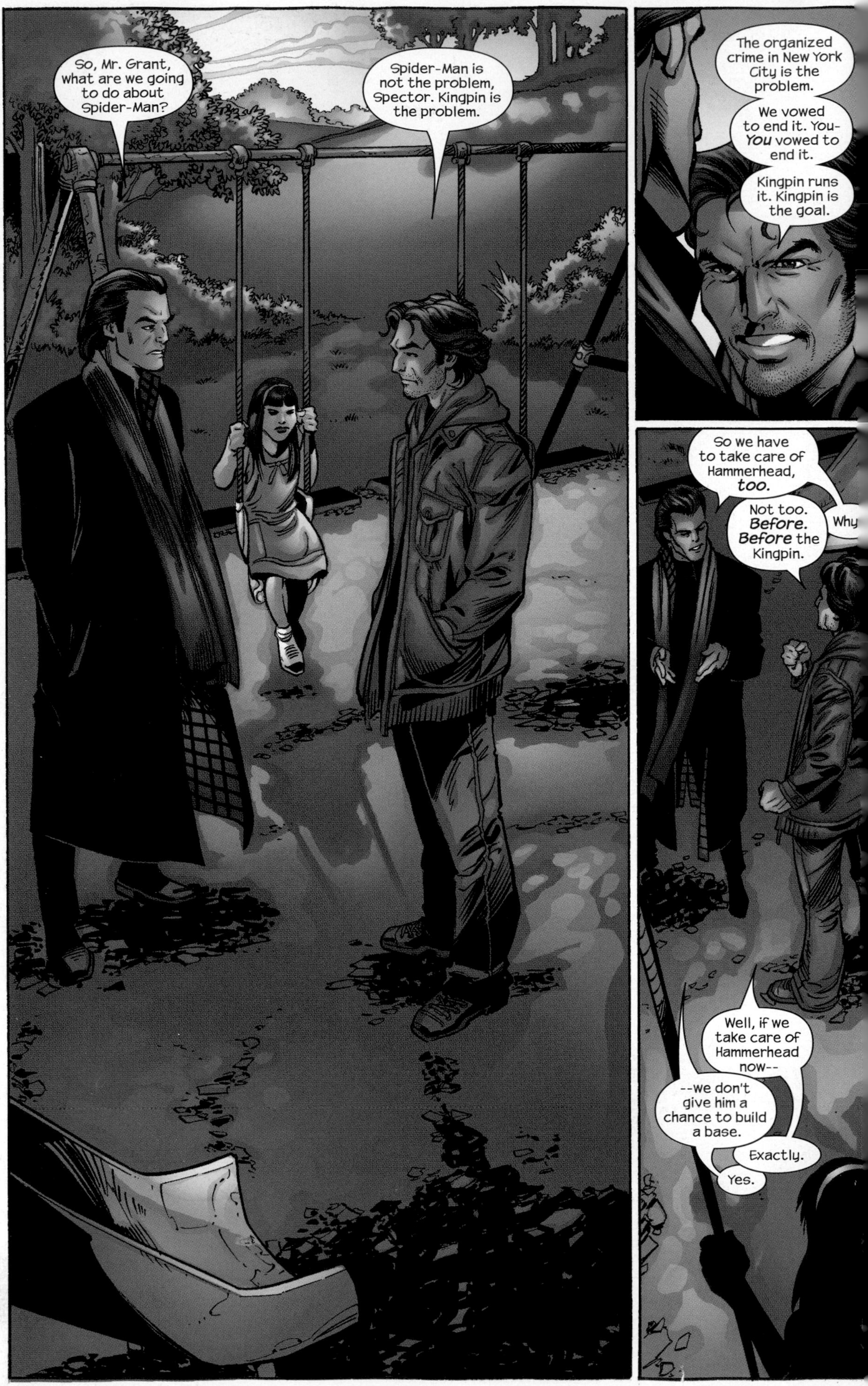
So, Mr. Grant, what are we going to do about Spider-Man?
Spider-Man is not the problem, Spector. Kingpin is the problem.
The organized crime in New York City is the problem.
We vowed to end it. You-*You* vowed to end it.
Kingpin runs it. Kingpin is the goal.
So we have to take care of Hammerhead, **too.**
Not too. ***Before.*** ***Before*** the Kingpin.
Why
Well, if we take care of Hammerhead now--
--we don't give him a chance to build a base.
Exactly.
Yes.

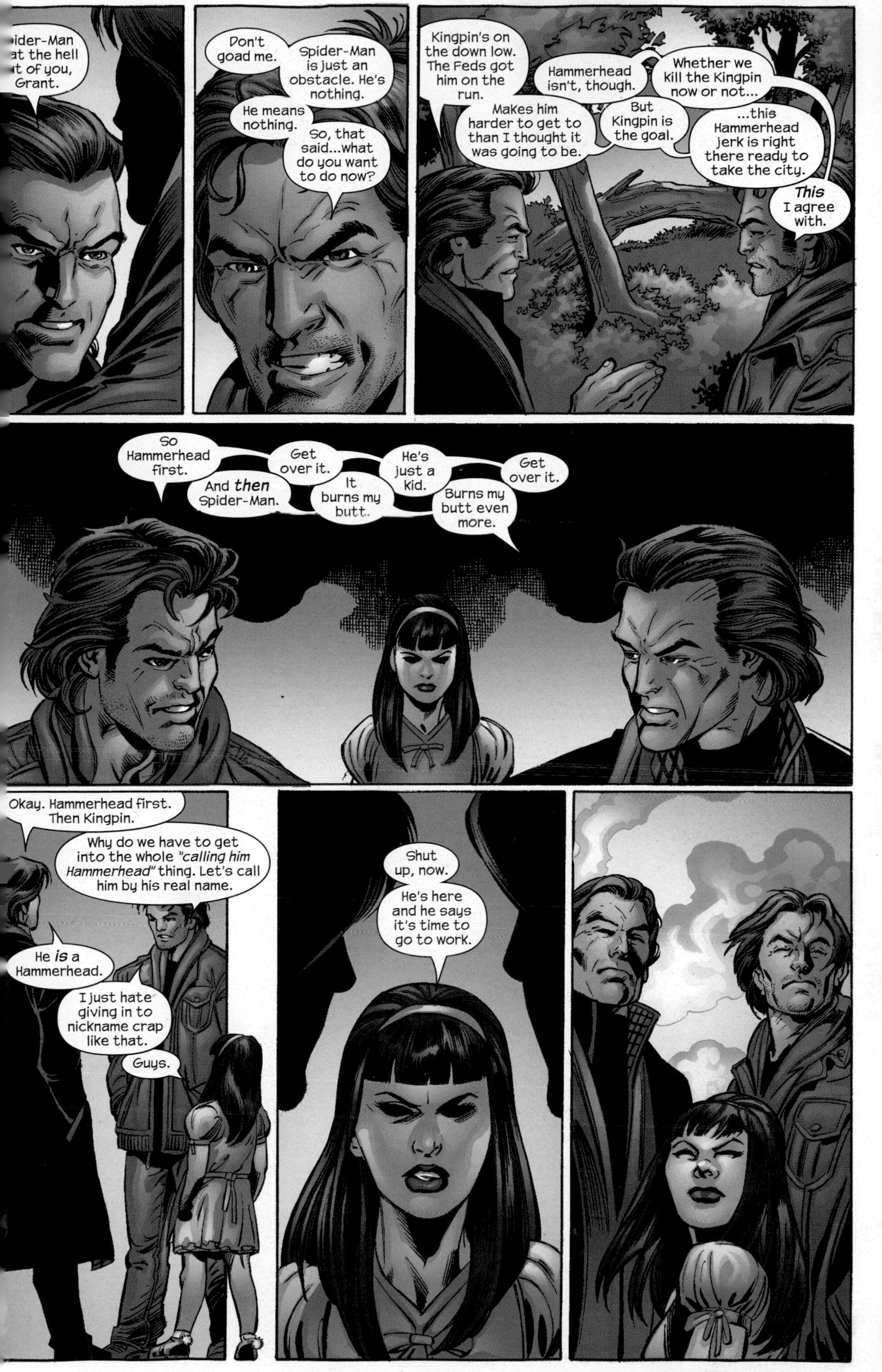
pider-Man
at the hell
t of you,
Grant.
Don't goad me.
Spider-Man is just an obstacle. He's nothing.
He means nothing.
So, that said...what do you want to do now?
Kingpin's on the down low. The Feds got him on the run.
Makes him harder to get to than I thought it was going to be.
Hammerhead isn't, though.
But Kingpin is the goal.
Whether we kill the Kingpin now or not...
...this Hammerhead jerk is right there ready to take the city.
This I agree with.
So Hammerhead first.
And *then* Spider-Man.
Get over it.
It burns my butt.
He's just a kid.
Burns my butt even more.
Get over it.
Okay. Hammerhead first. Then Kingpin.
Why do we have to get into the whole *"calling him Hammerhead"* thing. Let's call him by his real name.
He *is* a Hammerhead.
I just hate giving in to nickname crap like that.
Guys.
Shut up, now.
He's here and he says it's time to go to work.

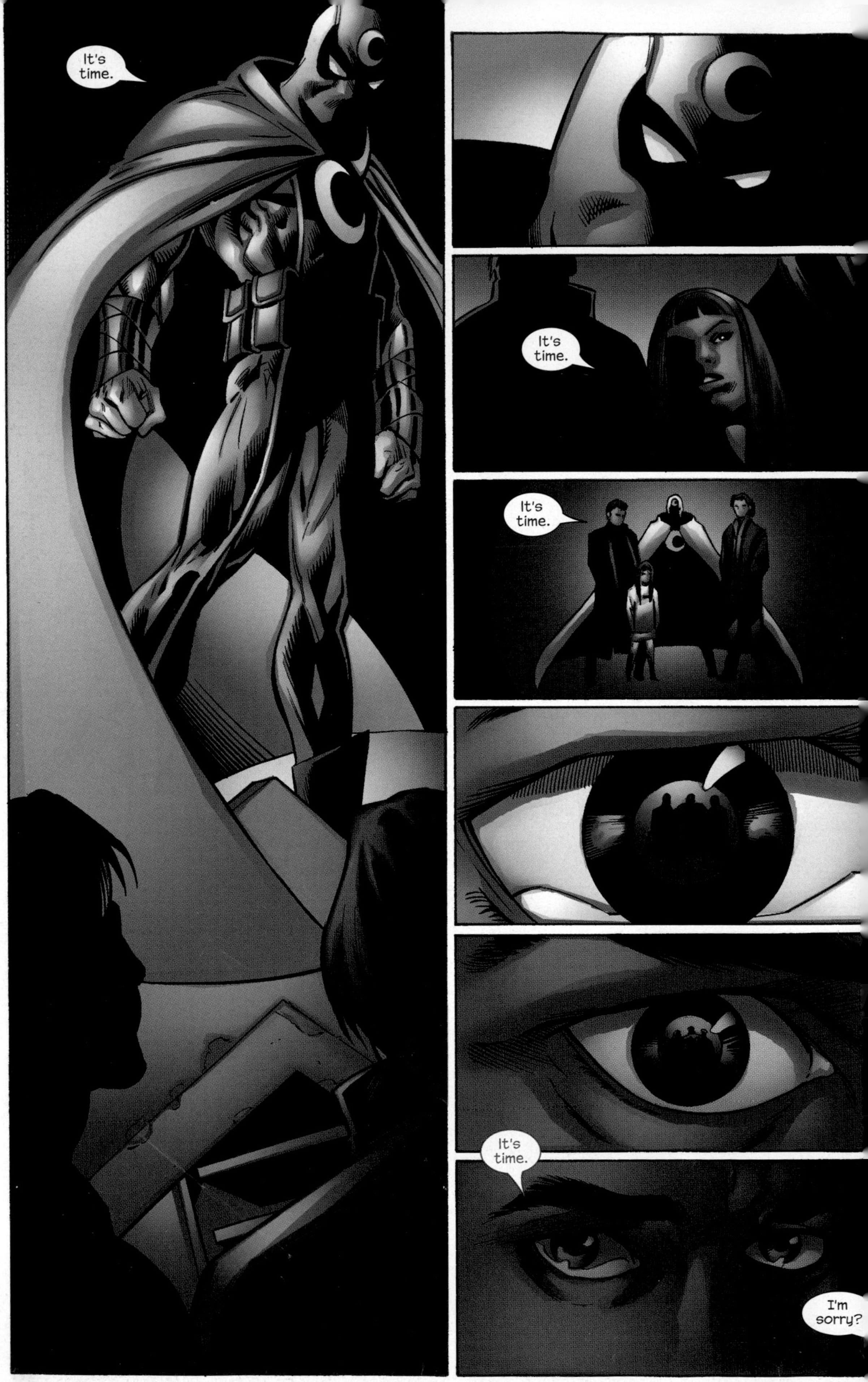
It's time.
It's time.
It's time.
It's time.
I'm sorry?

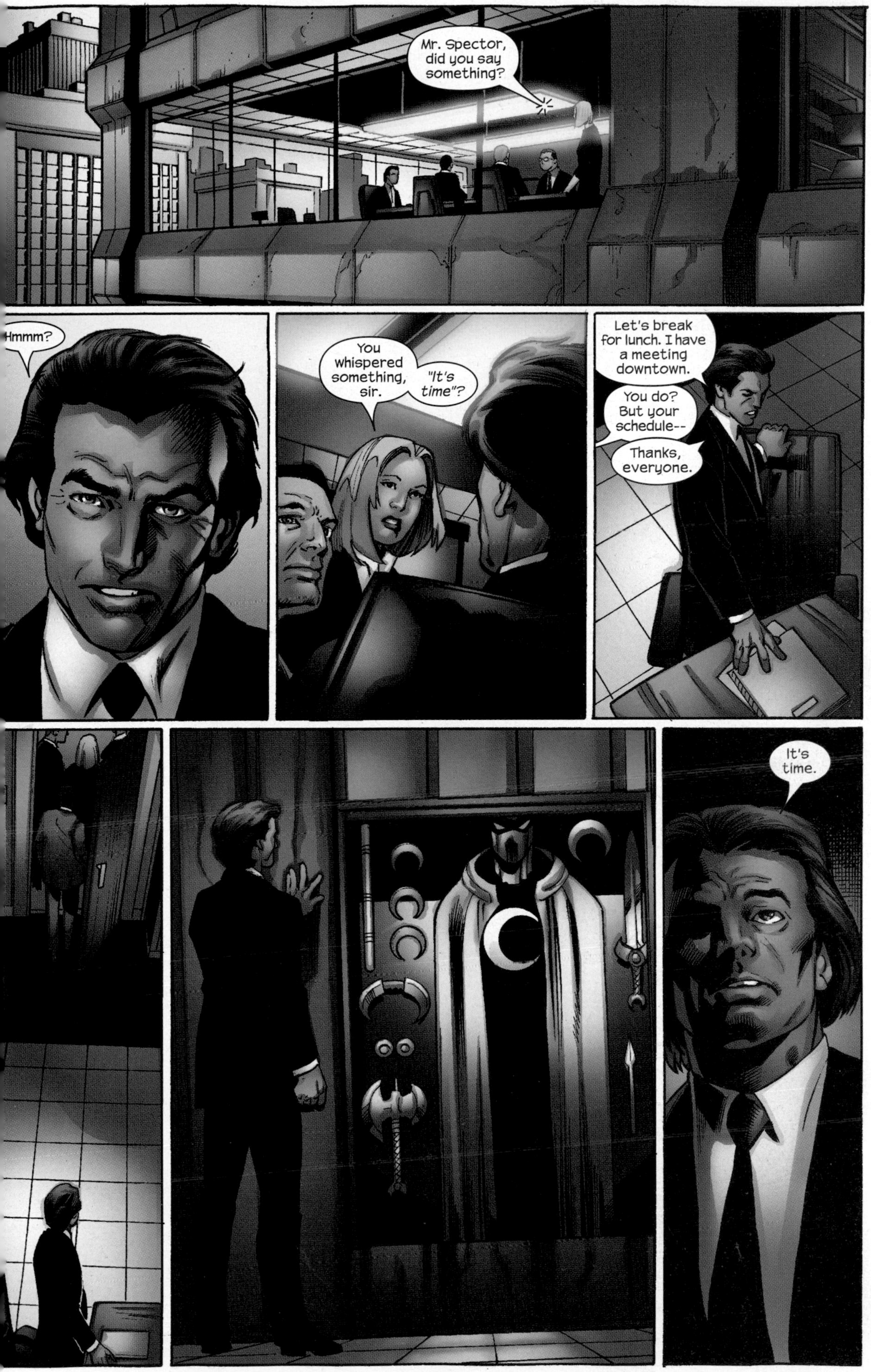

Mr. Spector, did you say something?
Hmmm?
You whispered something, sir.
"It's time"?
Let's break for lunch. I have a meeting downtown.
You do? But your schedule--
Thanks, everyone.
It's time.

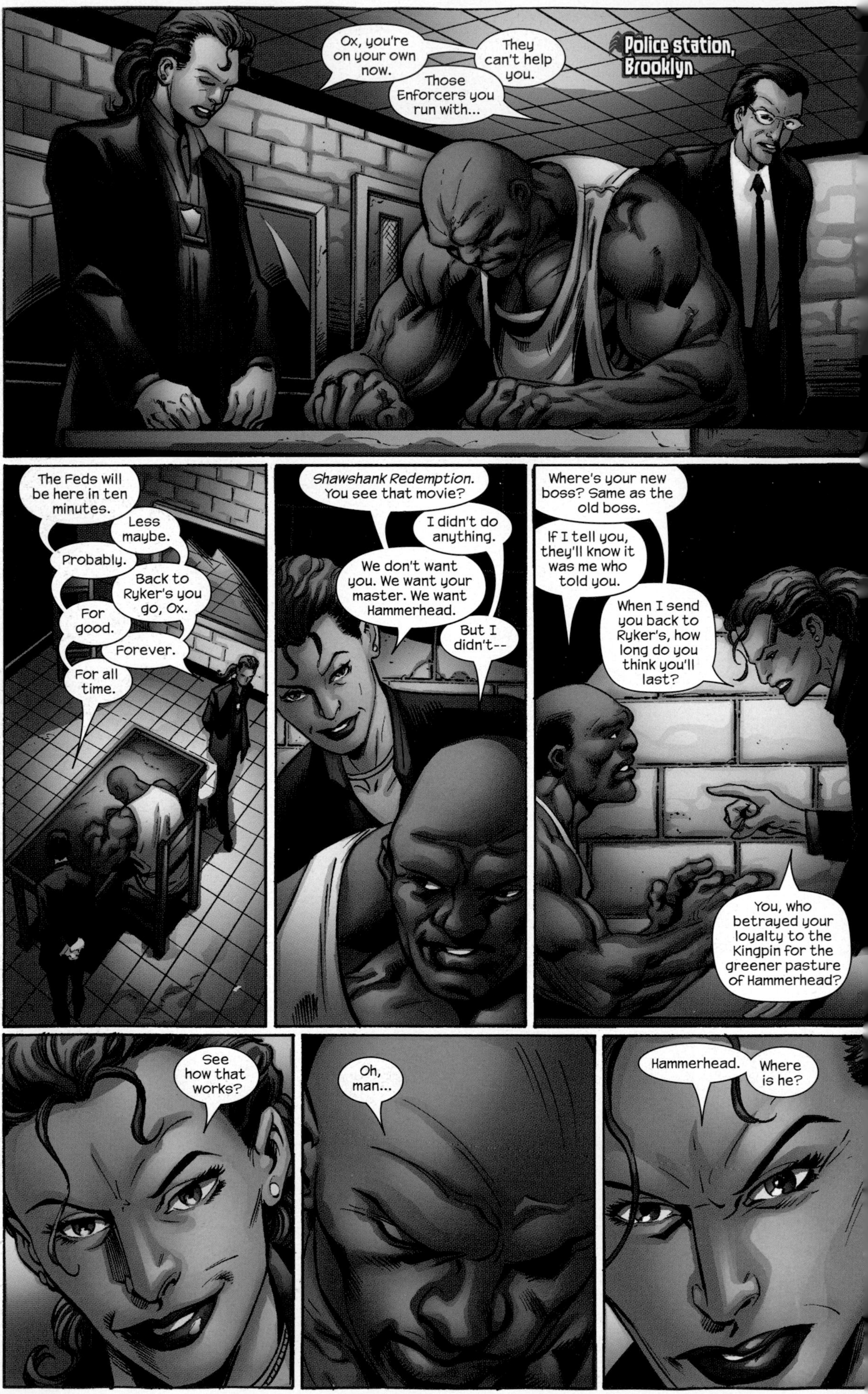
Police station, Brooklyn
Ox, you're on your own now.
They can't help you.
Those Enforcers you run with...
The Feds will be here in ten minutes.
Less maybe.
Probably.
Back to Ryker's you go, Ox.
For good.
Forever.
For all time.
Shawshank Redemption. You see that movie?
I didn't do anything.
We don't want you. We want your master. We want Hammerhead.
But I didn't--
Where's your new boss? Same as the old boss.
If I tell you, they'll know it was me who told you.
When I send you back to Ryker's, how long do you think you'll last?
You, who betrayed your loyalty to the Kingpin for the greener pasture of Hammerhead?
See how that works?
Oh, man...
Hammerhead.
Where is he?

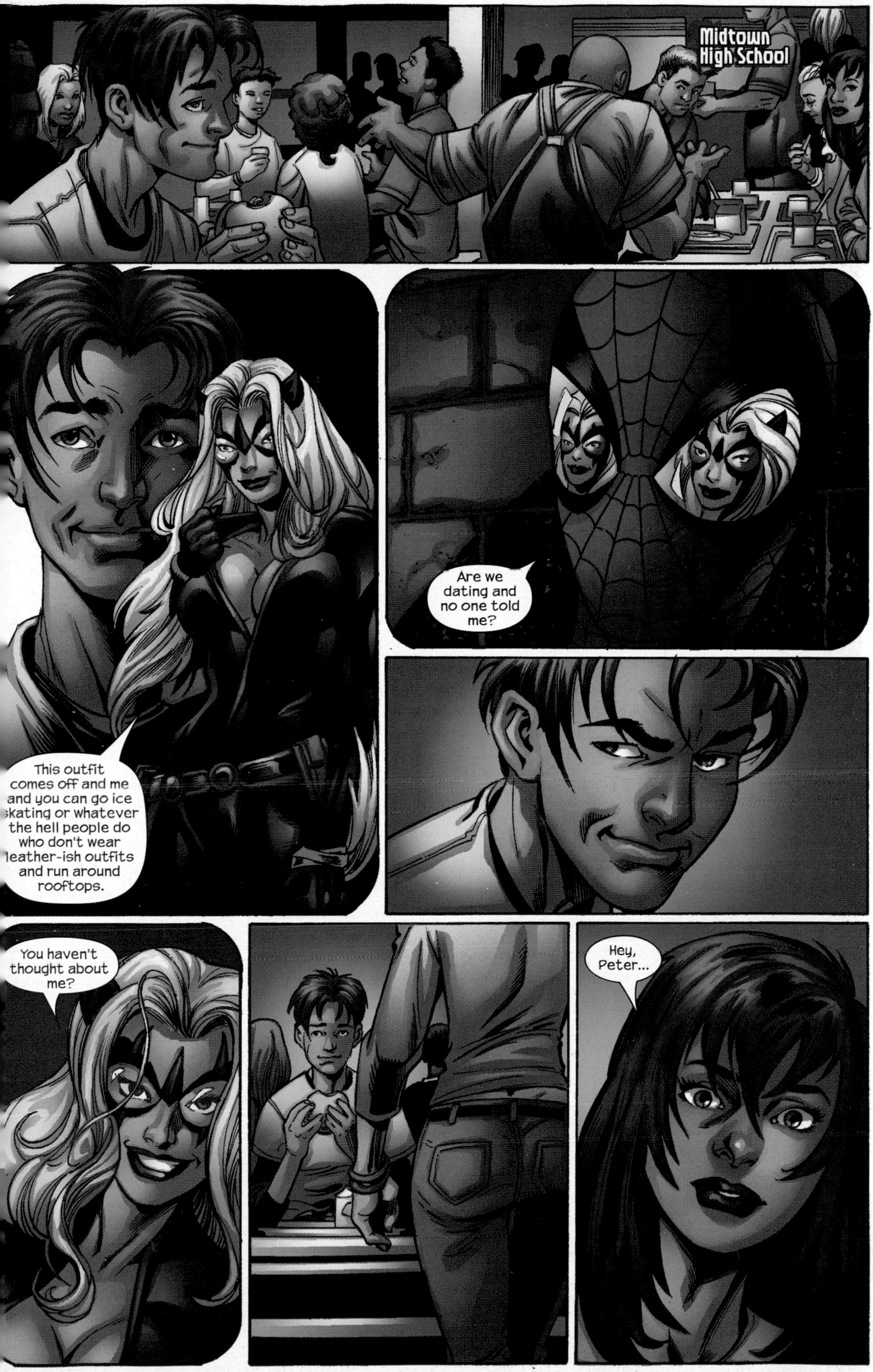
Midtown High School
This outfit comes off and me and you can go ice skating or whatever the hell people do who don't wear leather-ish outfits and run around rooftops.
Are we dating and no one told me?
You haven't thought about me?
Hey, Peter...

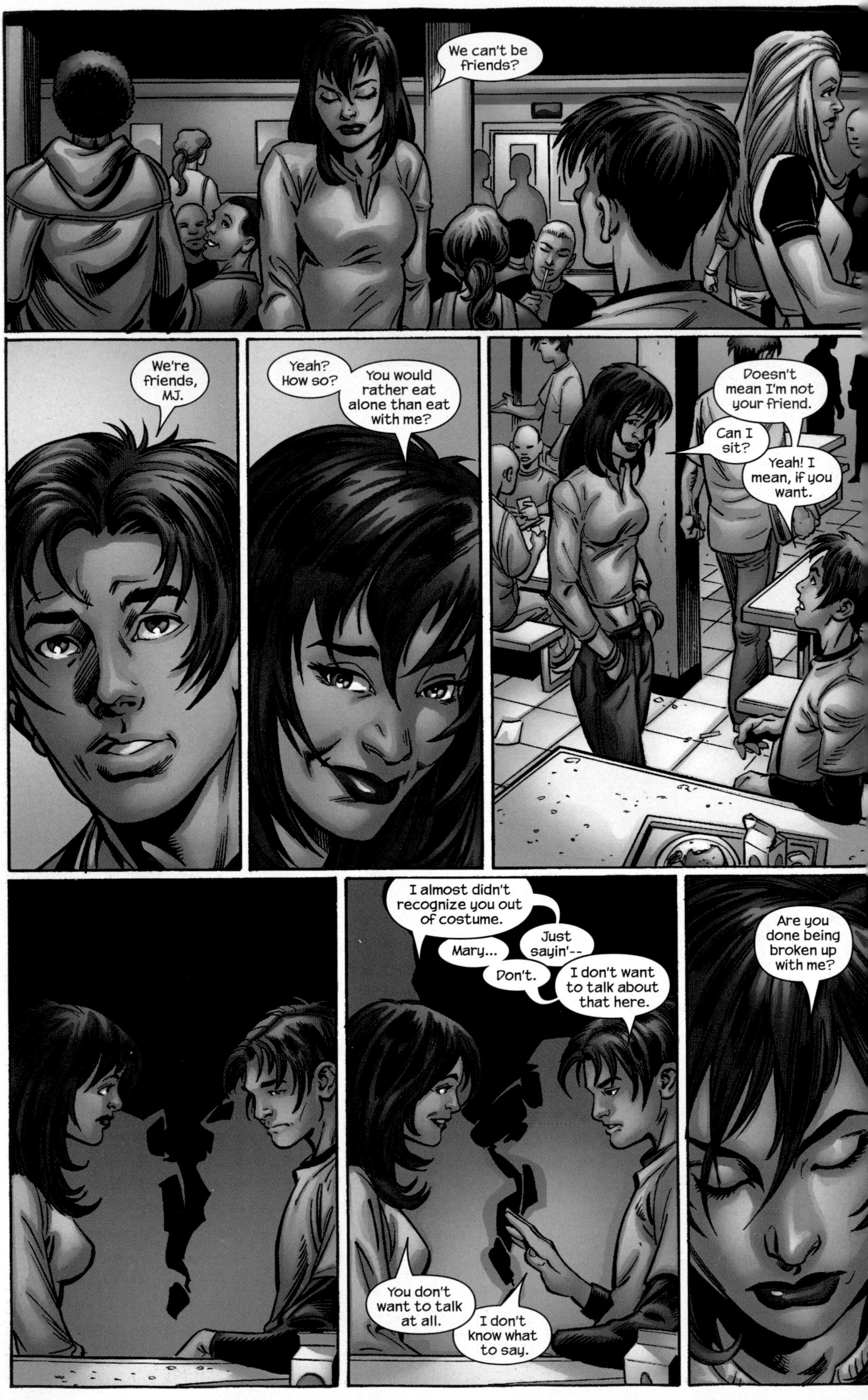
We can't be friends?
We're friends, MJ.
Yeah? How so?
You would rather eat alone than eat with me?
Doesn't mean I'm not your friend.
Can I sit?
Yeah! I mean, if you want.
I almost didn't recognize you out of costume.
Just sayin'--
Mary...
Don't.
I don't want to talk about that here.
You don't want to talk at all.
I don't know what to say.
Are you done being broken up with me?

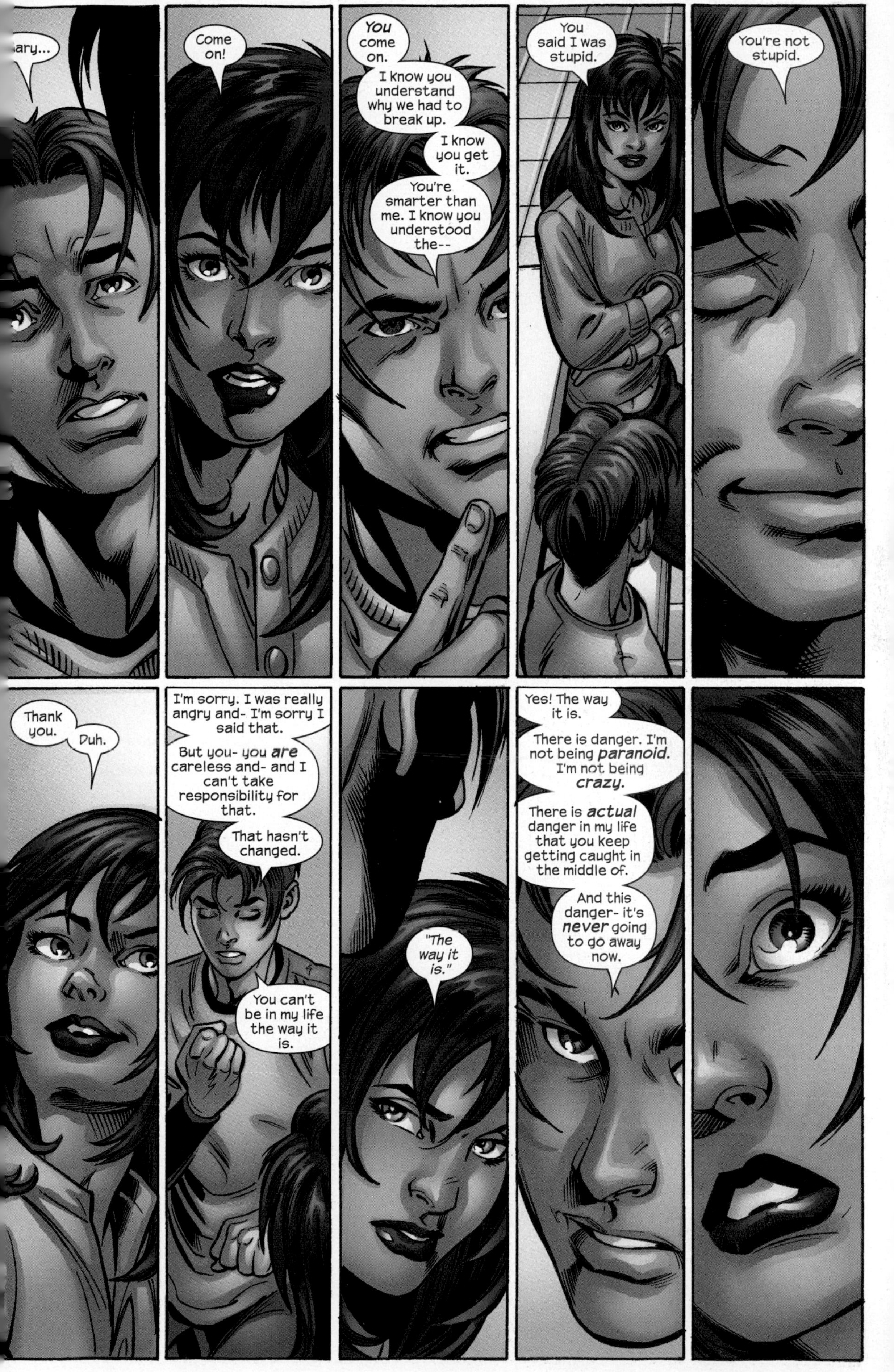

ary...
Come on!
You come on.
I know you understand why we had to break up.
I know you get it.
You're smarter than me. I know you understood the--
You said I was stupid.
You're not stupid.
Thank you.
Duh.
I'm sorry. I was really angry and- I'm sorry I said that.
But you- you are careless and- and I can't take responsibility for that.
That hasn't changed.
You can't be in my life the way it is.
"The way it is."
Yes! The way it is.
There is danger. I'm not being paranoid. I'm not being crazy.
There is actual danger in my life that you keep getting caught in the middle of.
And this danger- it's never going to go away now.

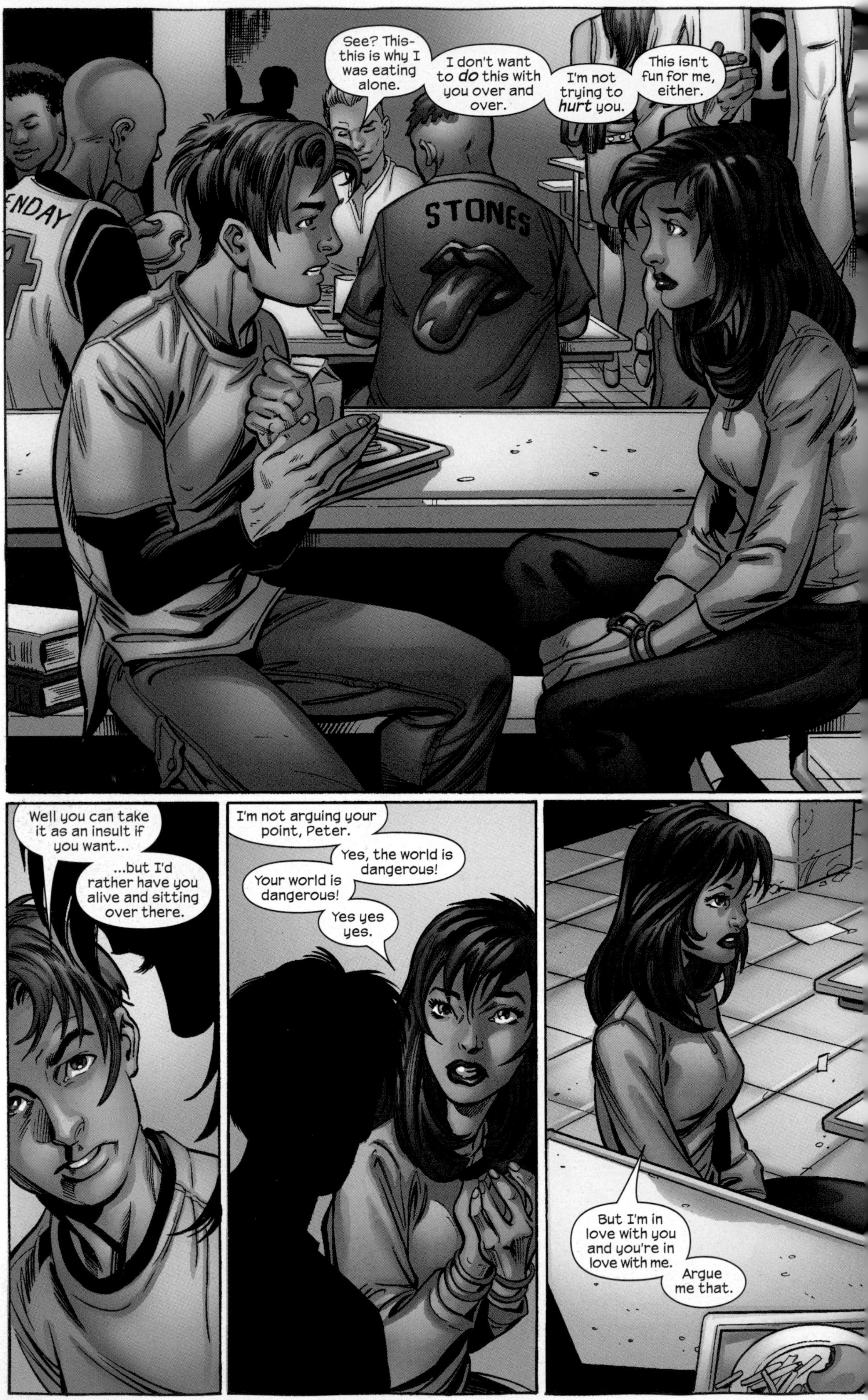
See? This- this is why I was eating alone.
I don't want to *do* this with you over and over.
I'm not trying to *hurt* you.
This isn't fun for me, either.
STONES
Well you can take it as an insult if you want...
...but I'd rather have you alive and sitting over there.
I'm not arguing your point, Peter.
Yes, the world is dangerous!
Your world is dangerous!
Yes yes yes.
But I'm in love with you and you're in love with me.
Argue me that.

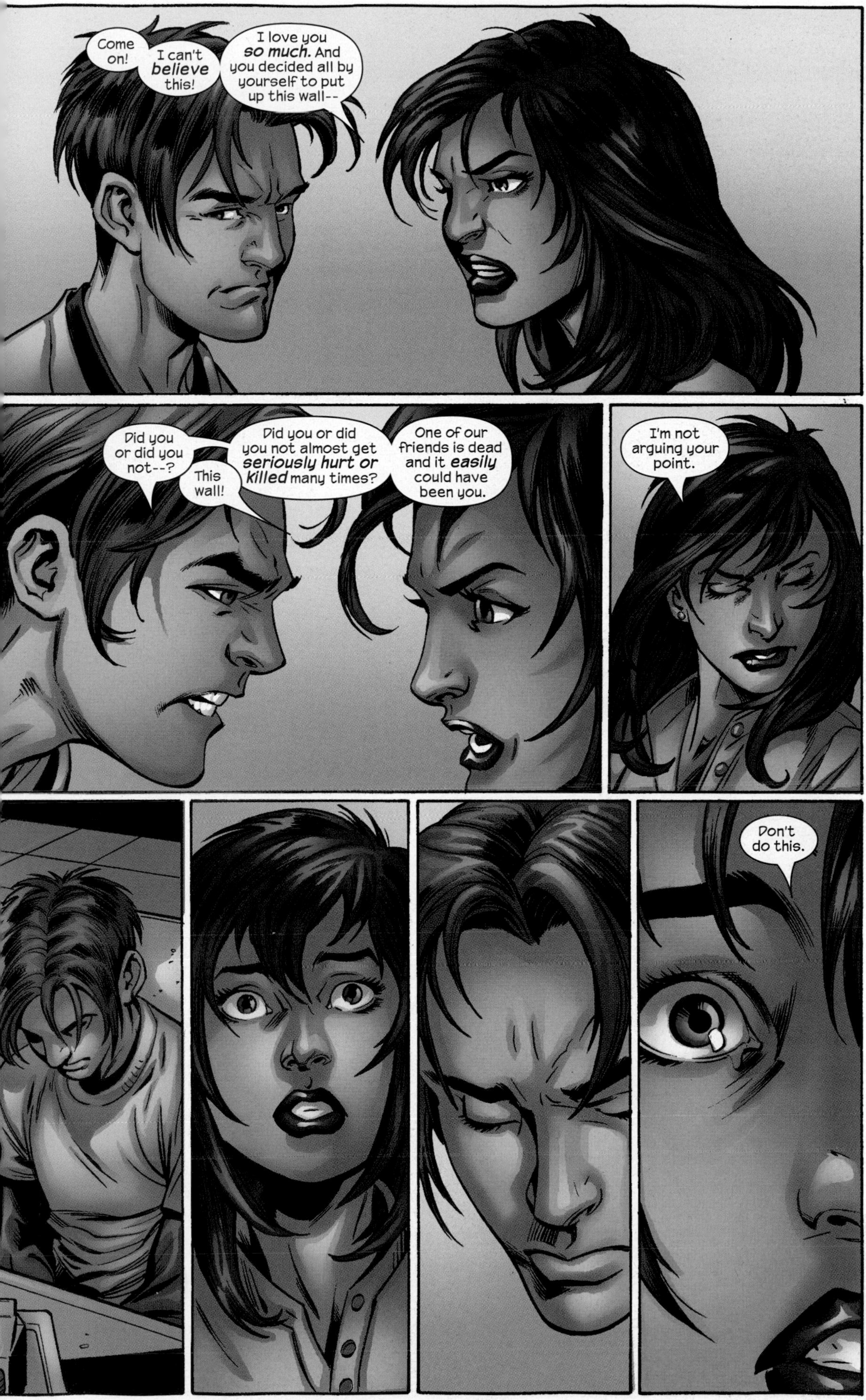
Come on!
I can't *believe* this!
I love you *so much.* And you decided all by yourself to put up this wall--
Did you or did you not--?
This wall!
Did you or did you not almost get *seriously hurt or killed* many times?
One of our friends is dead and it *easily* could have been you.
I'm not arguing your point.
Don't do this.

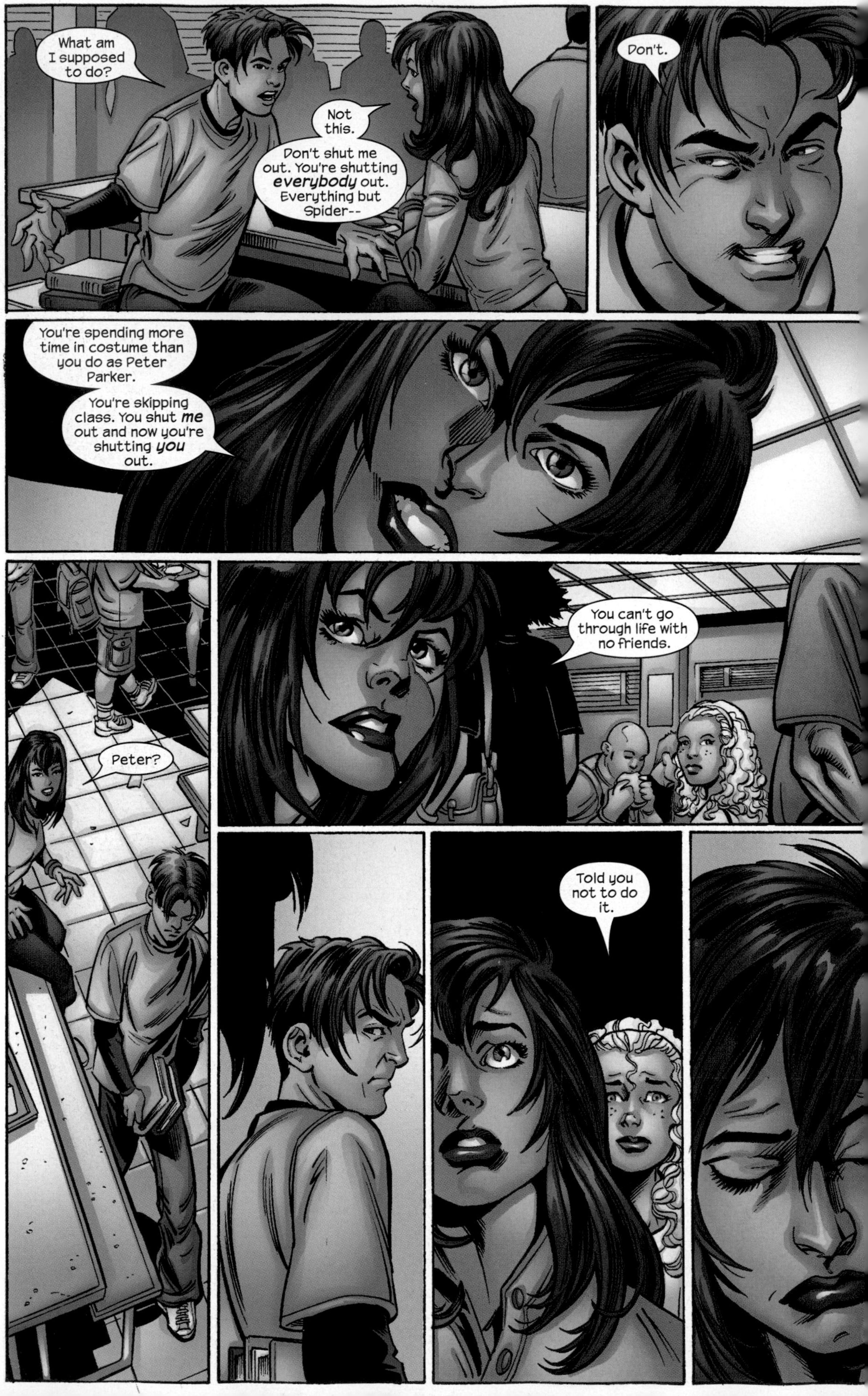
What am I supposed to do?
Not this.
Don't shut me out. You're shutting *everybody* out. Everything but Spider--
Don't.
You're spending more time in costume than you do as Peter Parker.
You're skipping class. You shut *me* out and now you're shutting *you* out.
Peter?
You can't go through life with no friends.
Told you not to do it.

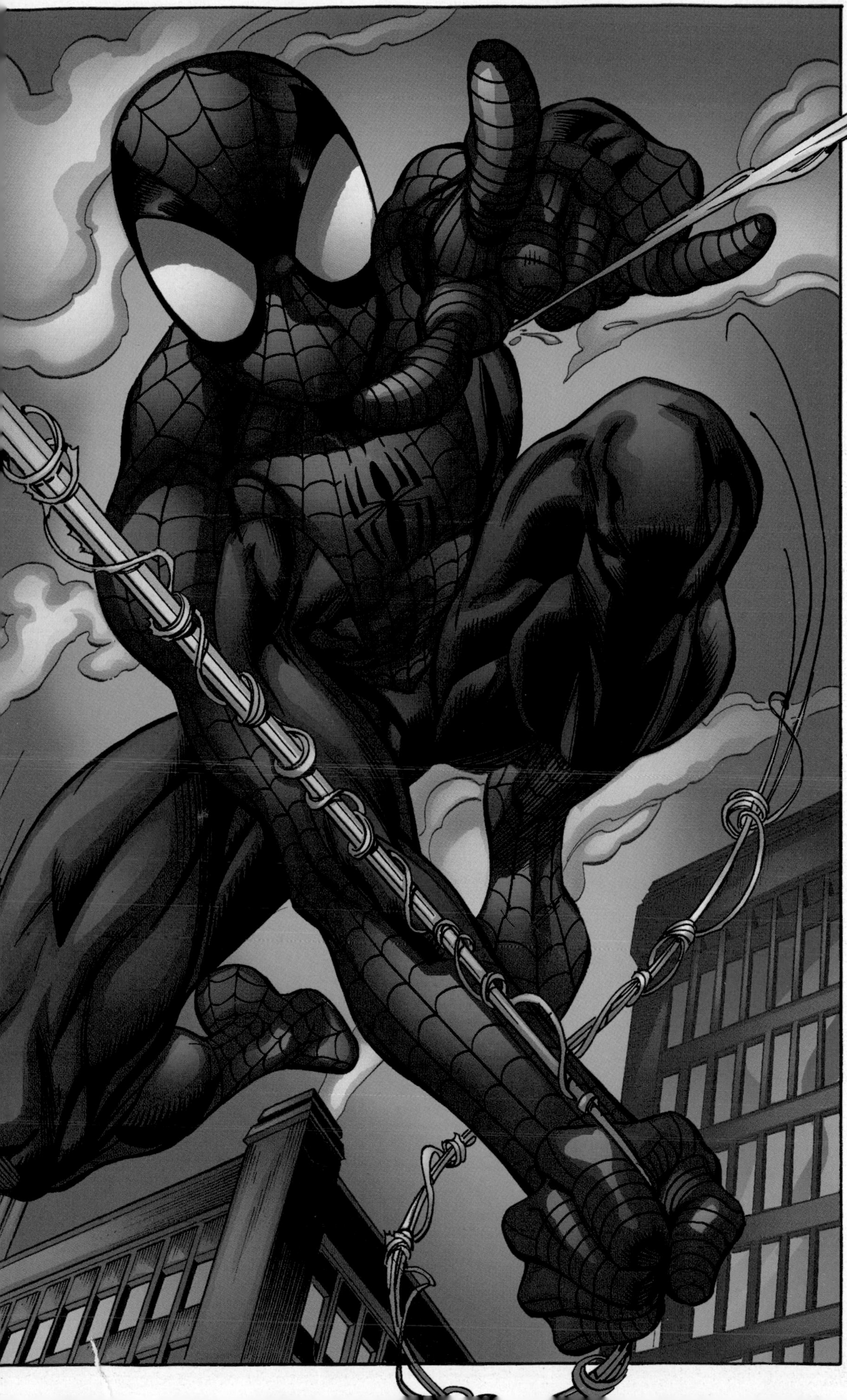

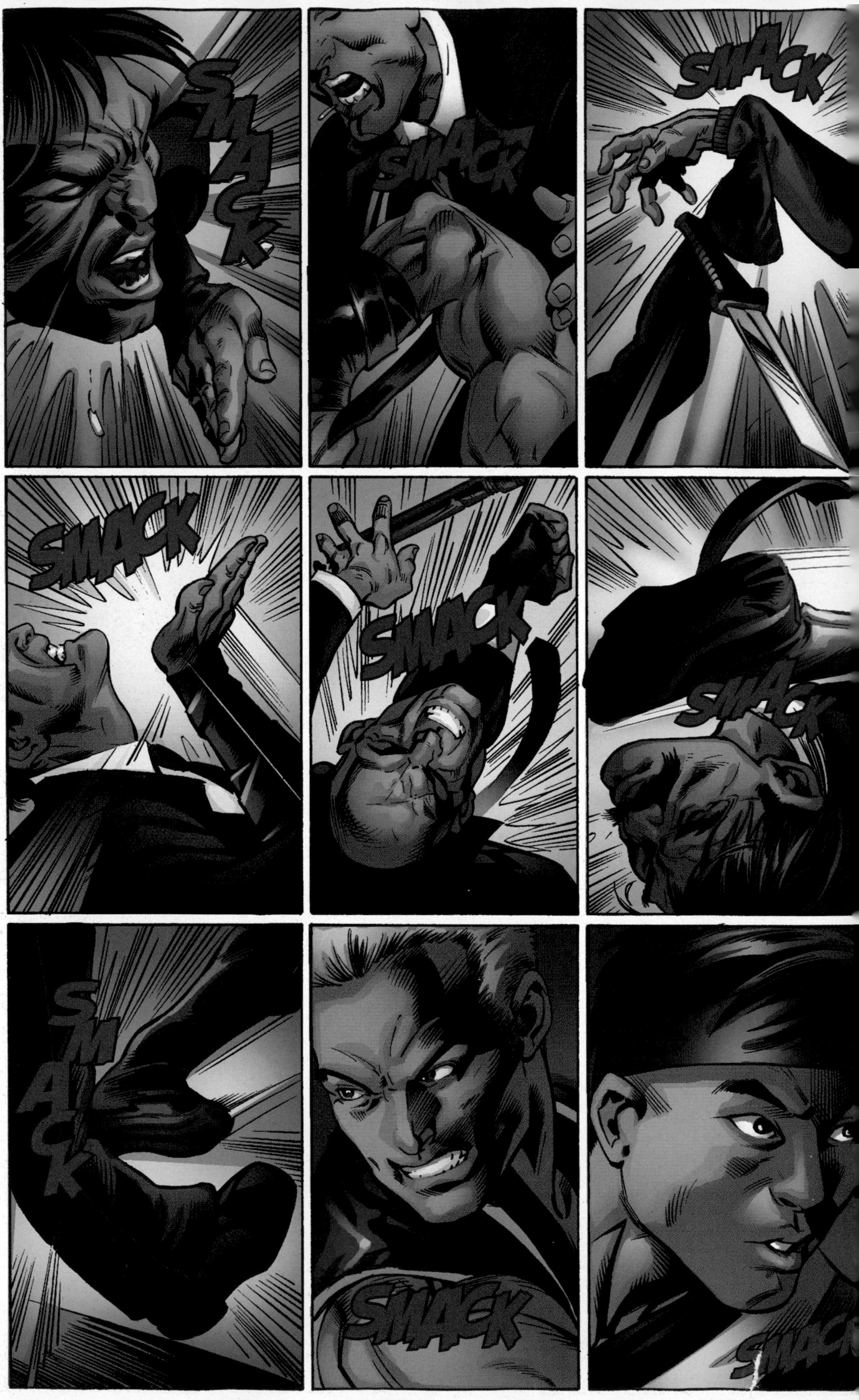
SMACK
SMACK
SMACK
SMACK
SMACK
SMACK
SMACK
SMACK
SMACK

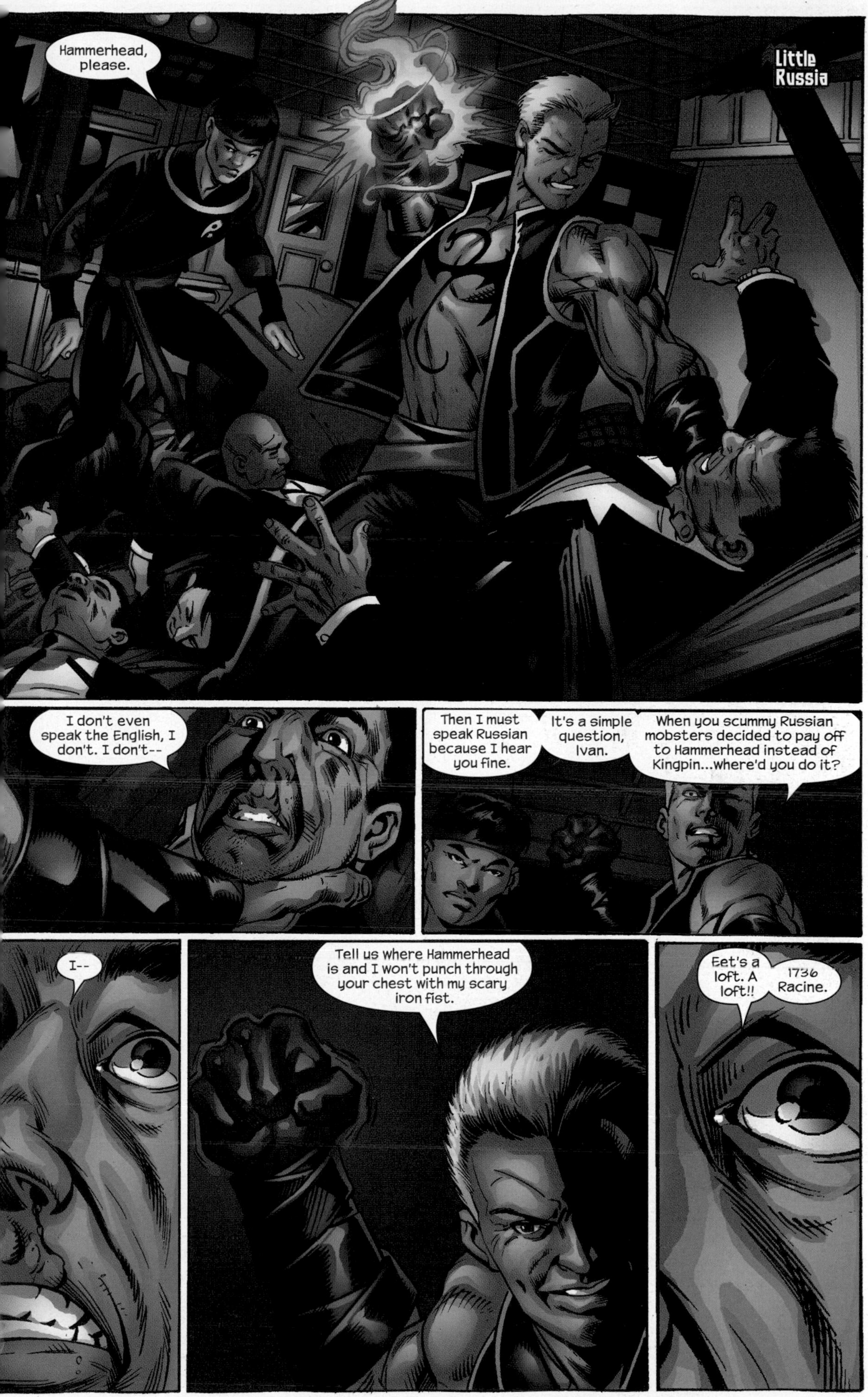
Hammerhead, please.
Little Russia
I don't even speak the English, I don't. I don't--
Then I must speak Russian because I hear you fine.
It's a simple question, Ivan.
When you scummy Russian mobsters decided to pay off to Hammerhead instead of Kingpin...where'd you do it?
I--
Tell us where Hammerhead is and I won't punch through your chest with my scary iron fist.
Eet's a loft. A loft!!
1736 Racine.

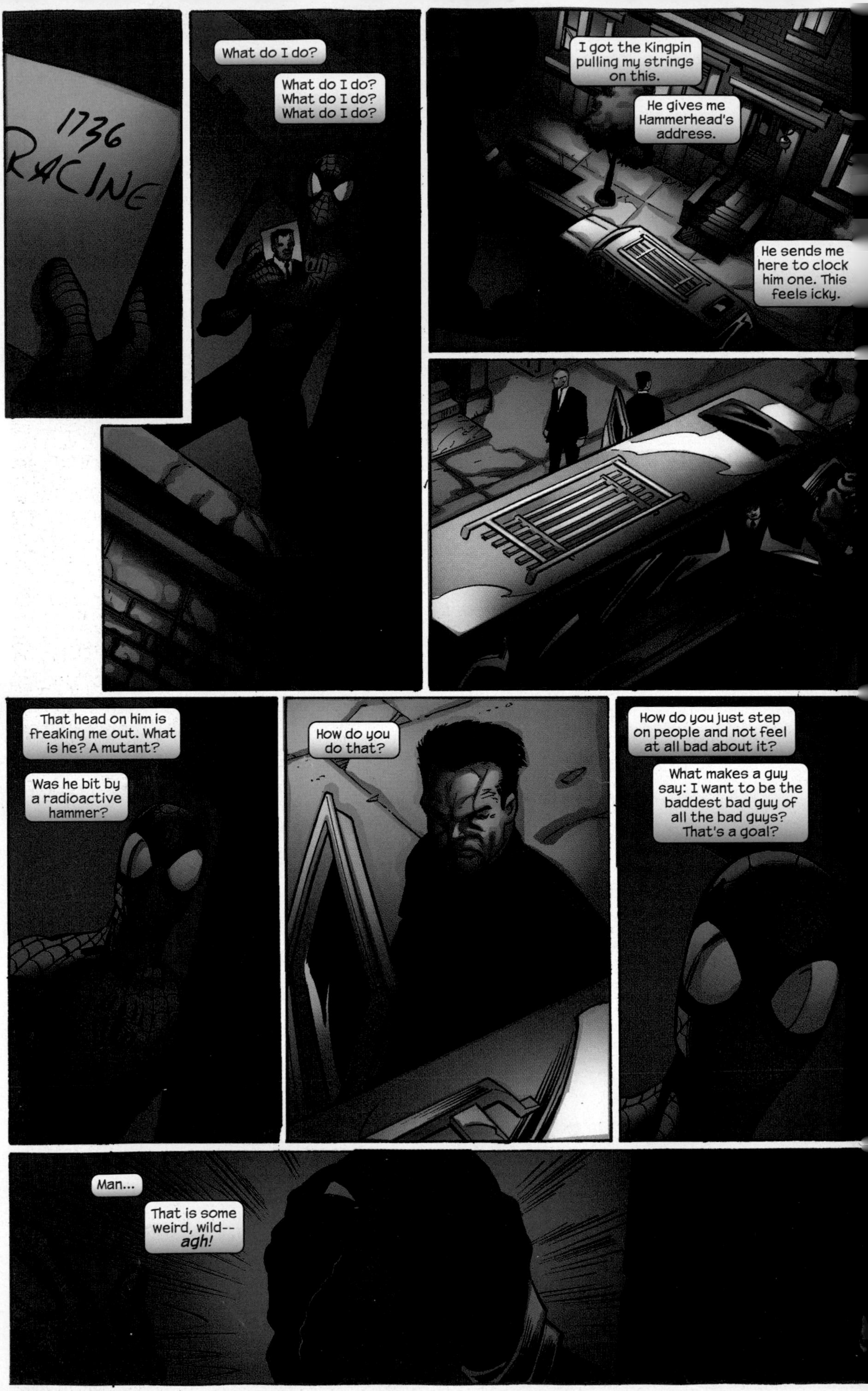
1736
RACINE
What do I do?
What do I do?
What do I do?
What do I do?
I got the Kingpin pulling my strings on this.
He gives me Hammerhead's address.
He sends me here to clock him one. This feels icky.
That head on him is freaking me out. What is he? A mutant?
Was he bit by a radioactive hammer?
How do you do that?
How do you just step on people and not feel at all bad about it?
What makes a guy say: I want to be the baddest bad guy of all the bad guys? That's a goal?
Man...
That is some weird, wild-- *agh!*

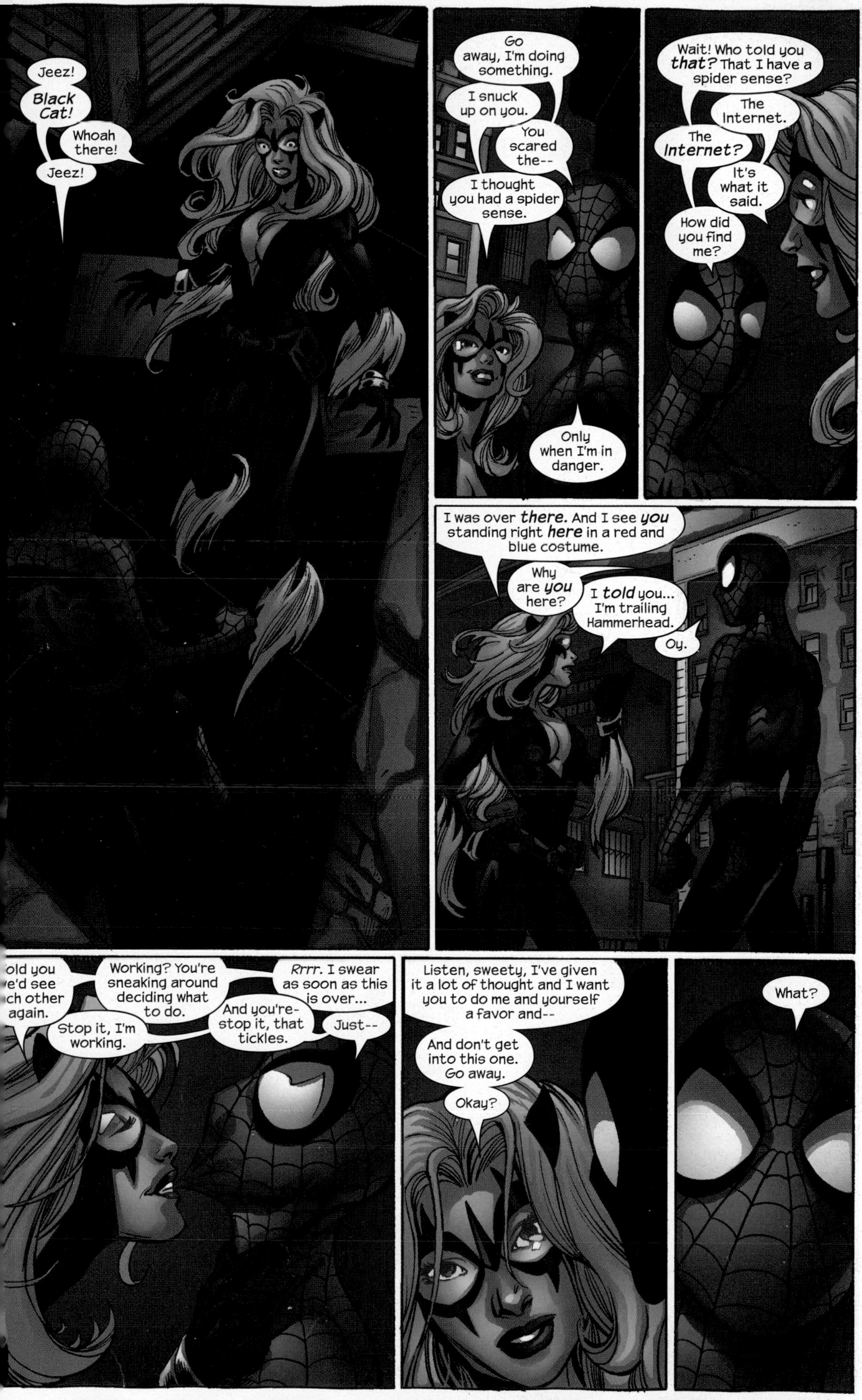

Jeez!
Black Cat!
Whoah there!
Jeez!
Go away, I'm doing something.
I snuck up on you.
You scared the--
I thought you had a spider sense.
Only when I'm in danger.
Wait! Who told you that? That I have a spider sense?
The Internet.
The Internet?
It's what it said.
How did you find me?
I was over there. And I see you standing right here in a red and blue costume.
Why are you here?
I told you... I'm trailing Hammerhead.
Oy.
old you e'd see ch other again.
Stop it, I'm working.
Working? You're sneaking around deciding what to do.
And you're- stop it, that tickles.
Rrrr. I swear as soon as this is over...
Just--
Listen, sweety, I've given it a lot of thought and I want you to do me and yourself a favor and--
And don't get into this one. Go away.
Okay?
What?

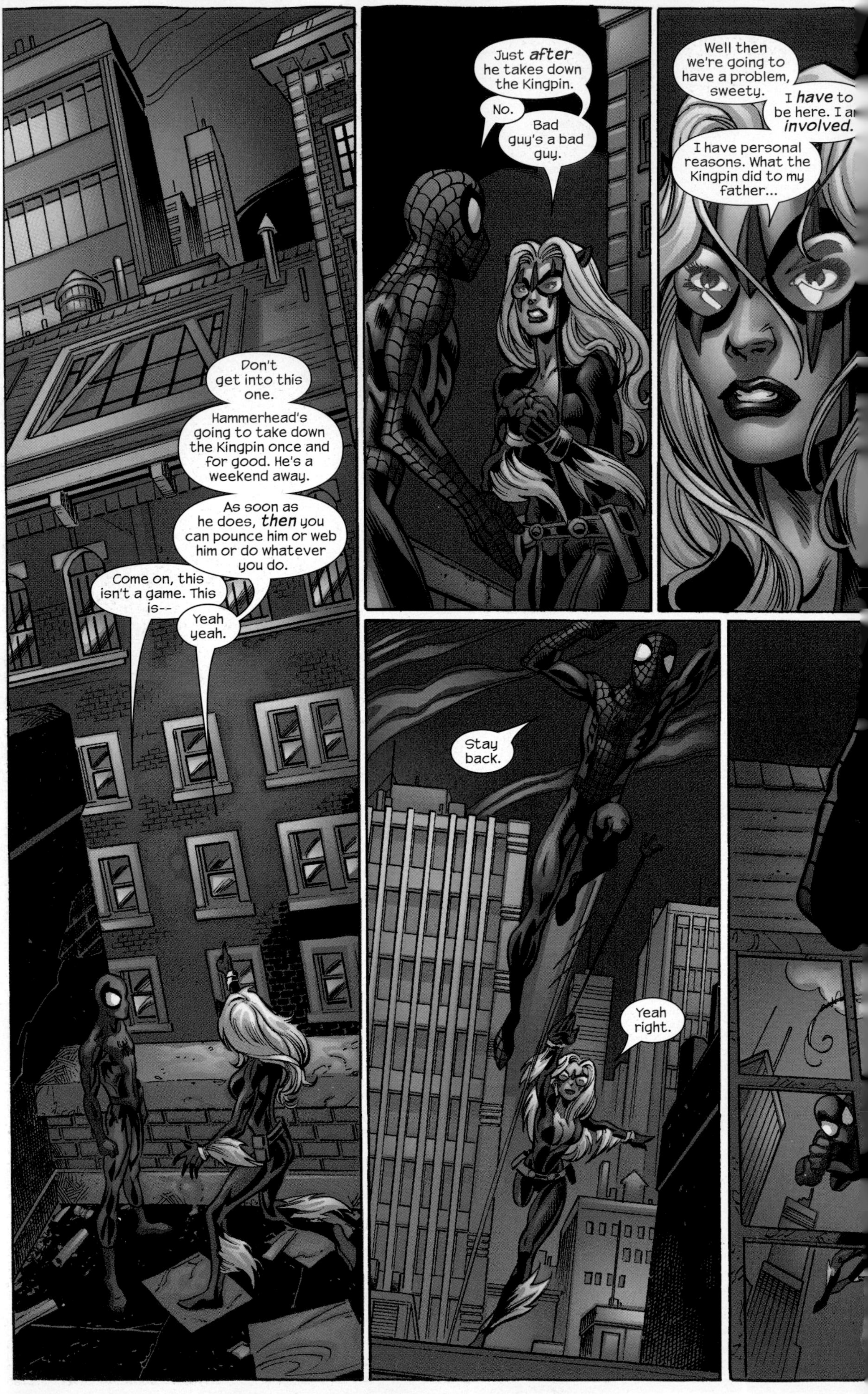
Don't get into this one.
Hammerhead's going to take down the Kingpin once and for good. He's a weekend away.
As soon as he does, *then* you can pounce him or web him or do whatever you do.
Come on, this isn't a game. This is--
Yeah yeah.
Just *after* he takes down the Kingpin.
No.
Bad guy's a bad guy.
Well then we're going to have a problem, sweety.
I *have* to be here. I a
involved.
I have personal reasons. What the Kingpin did to my father...
Stay back.
Yeah right.

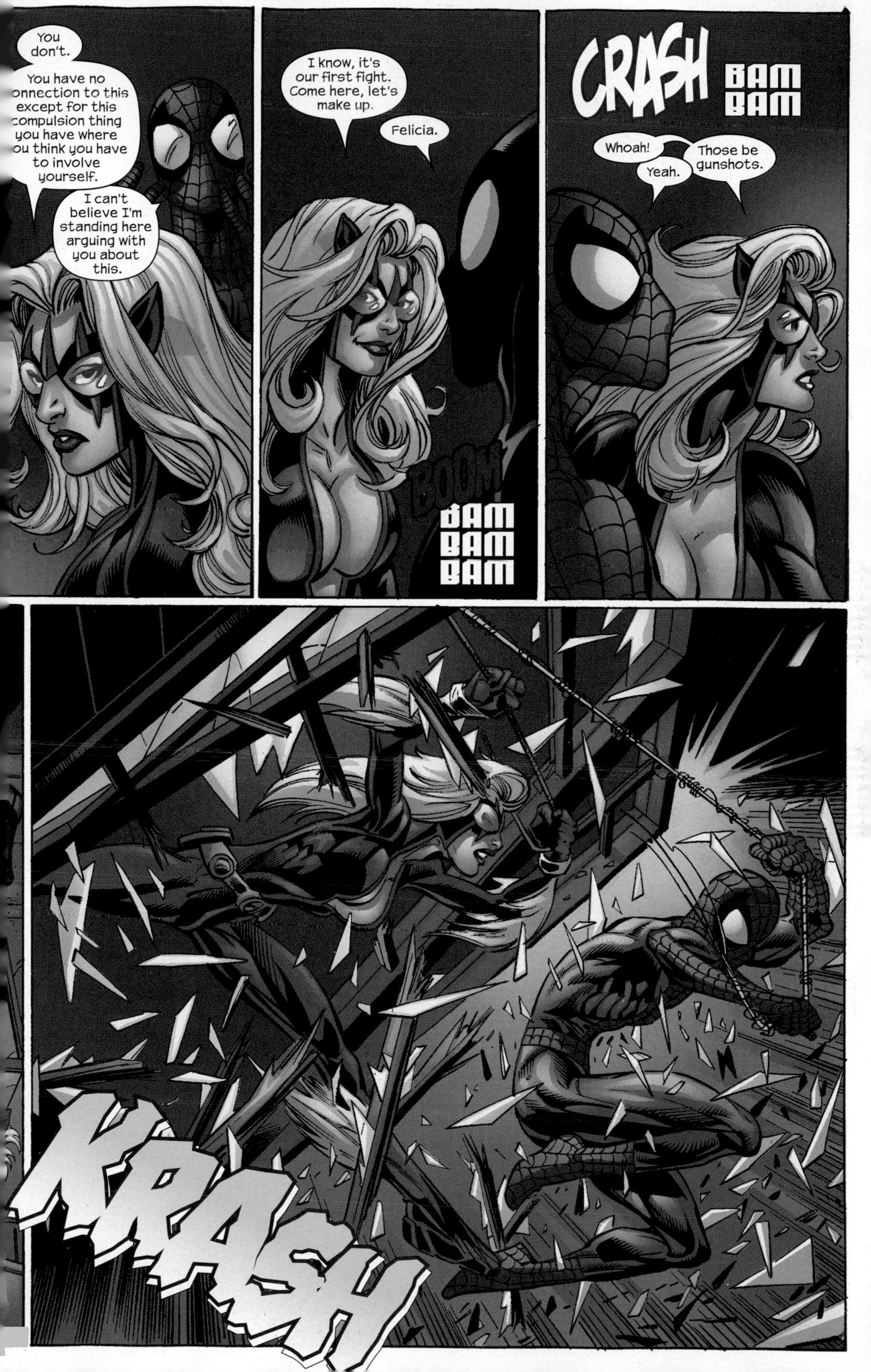

You don't.
You have no connection to this except for this compulsion thing you have where you think you have to involve yourself.
I can't believe I'm standing here arguing with you about this.
I know, it's our first fight. Come here, let's make up.
Felicia.
BOOM
BAM BAM BAM
CRASH
BAM BAM
Whoah!
Yeah.
Those be gunshots.
KRASH

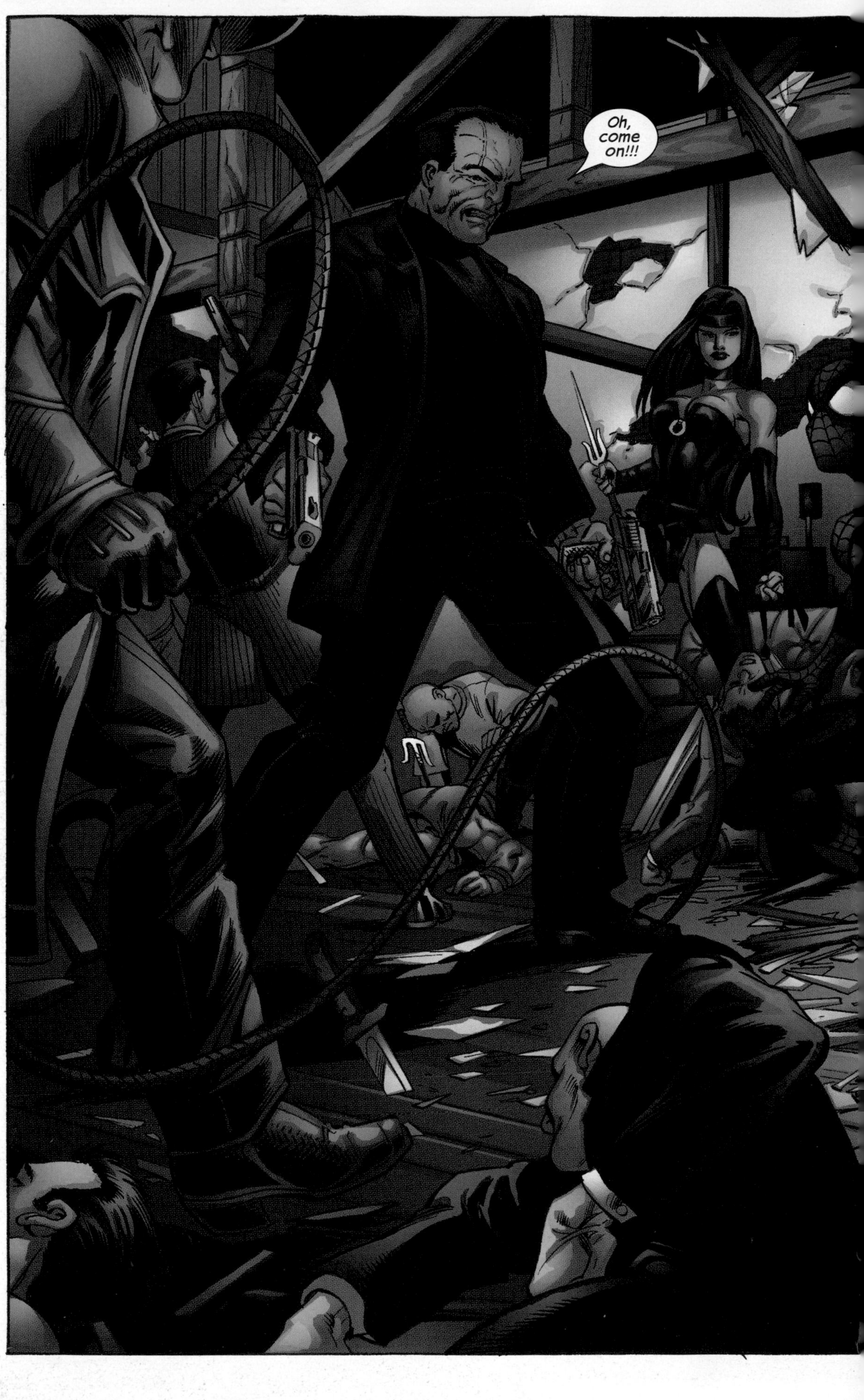
Oh, come on!!!

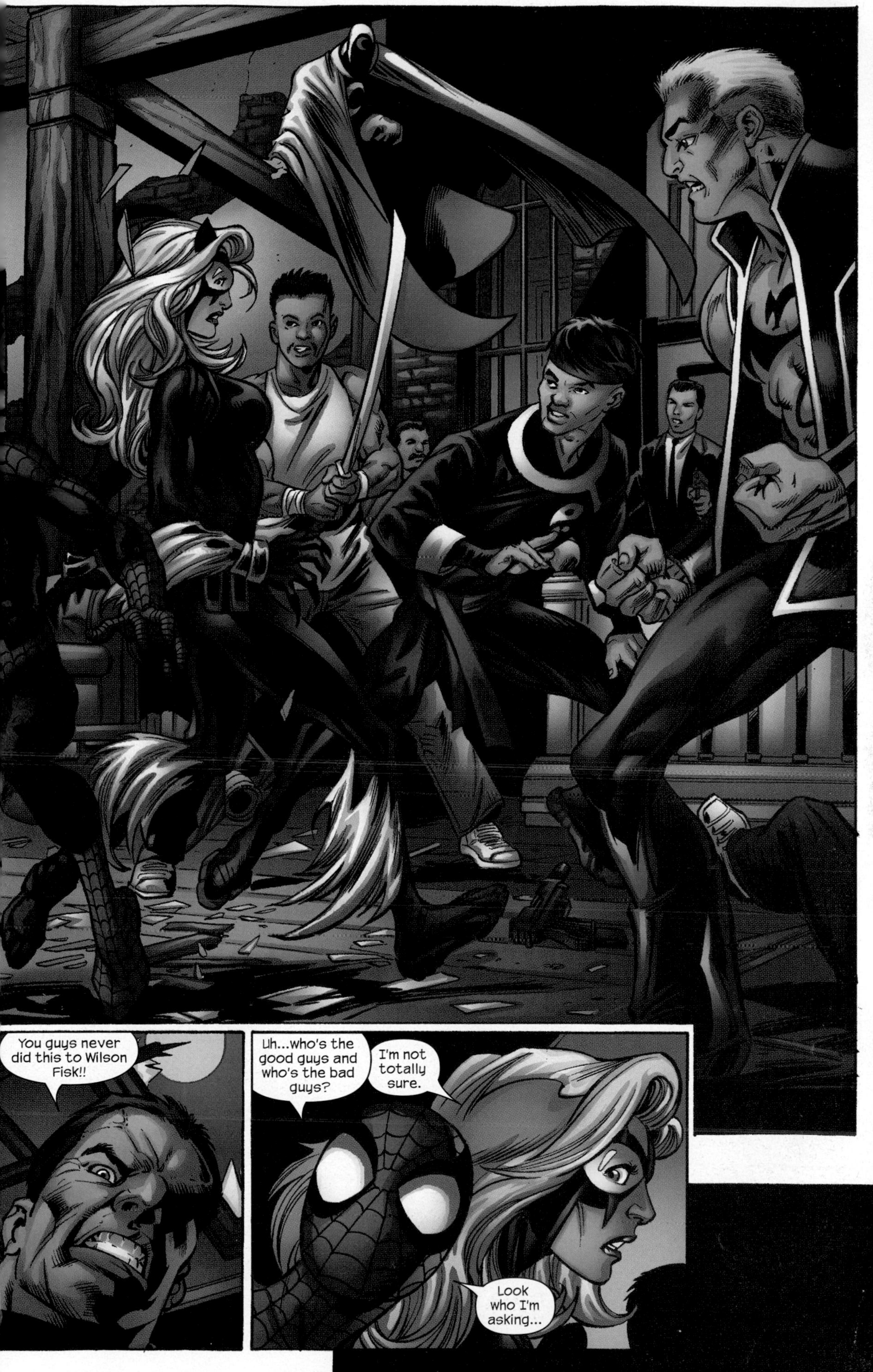
You guys never did this to Wilson Fisk!!
Uh...who's the good guys and who's the bad guys?
I'm not totally sure.
Look who I'm asking...

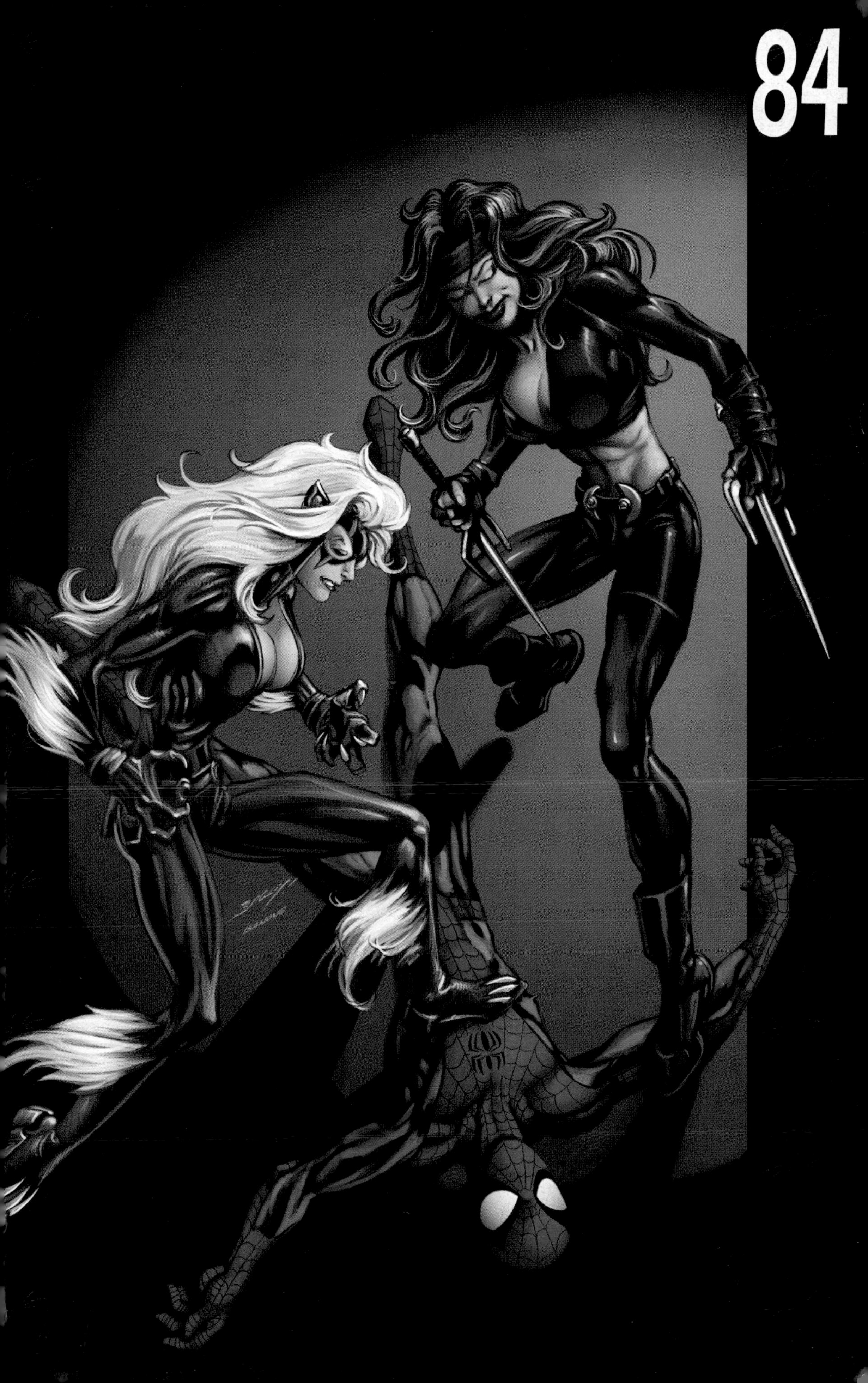
84

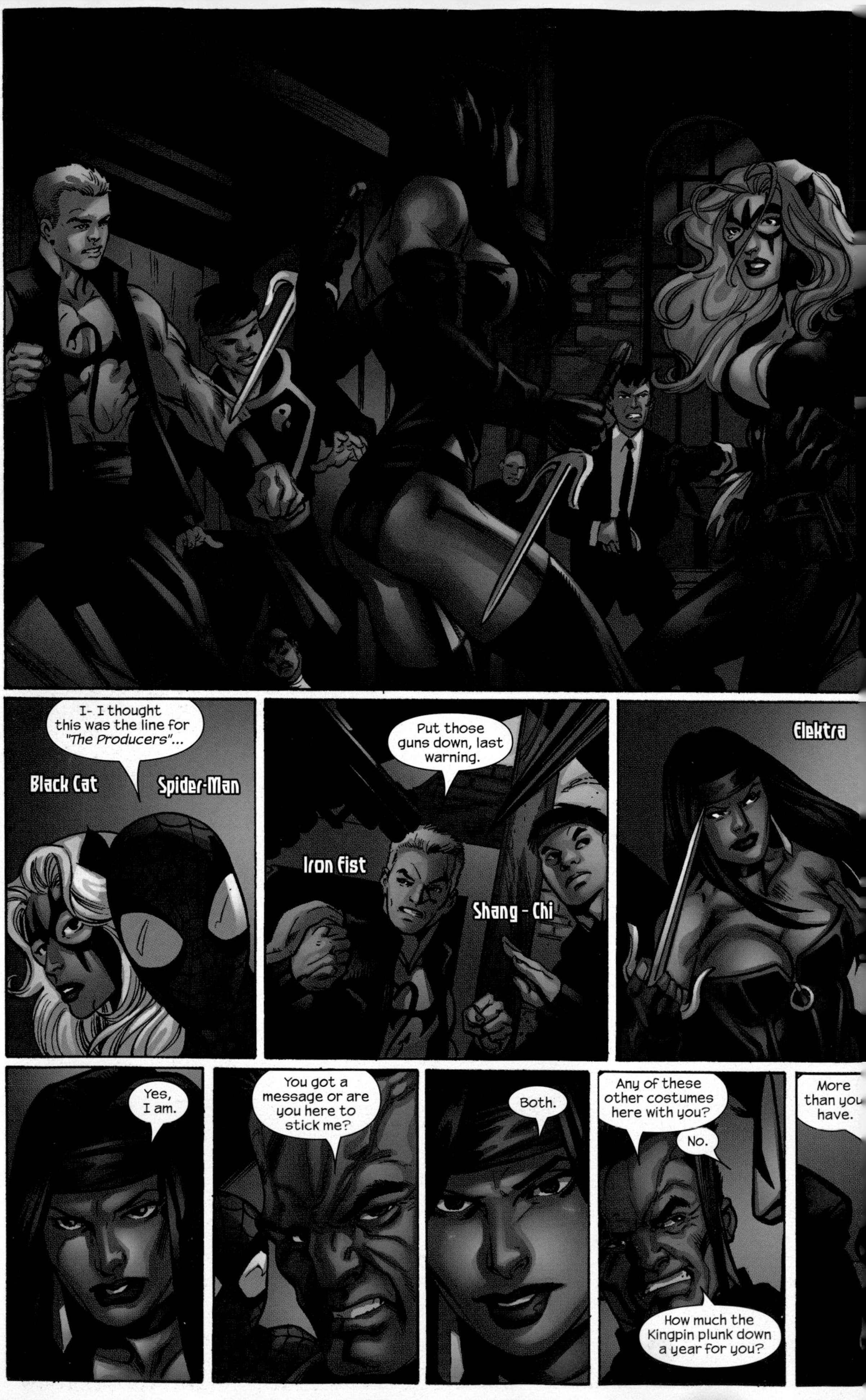

I- I thought this was the line for *"The Producers"*...
Black Cat
Spider-Man
Put those guns down, last warning.
Iron Fist
Shang - Chi
Elektra
Yes, I am.
You got a message or are you here to stick me?
Both.
Any of these other costumes here with you?
No.
How much the Kingpin plunk down a year for you?
More than you have.

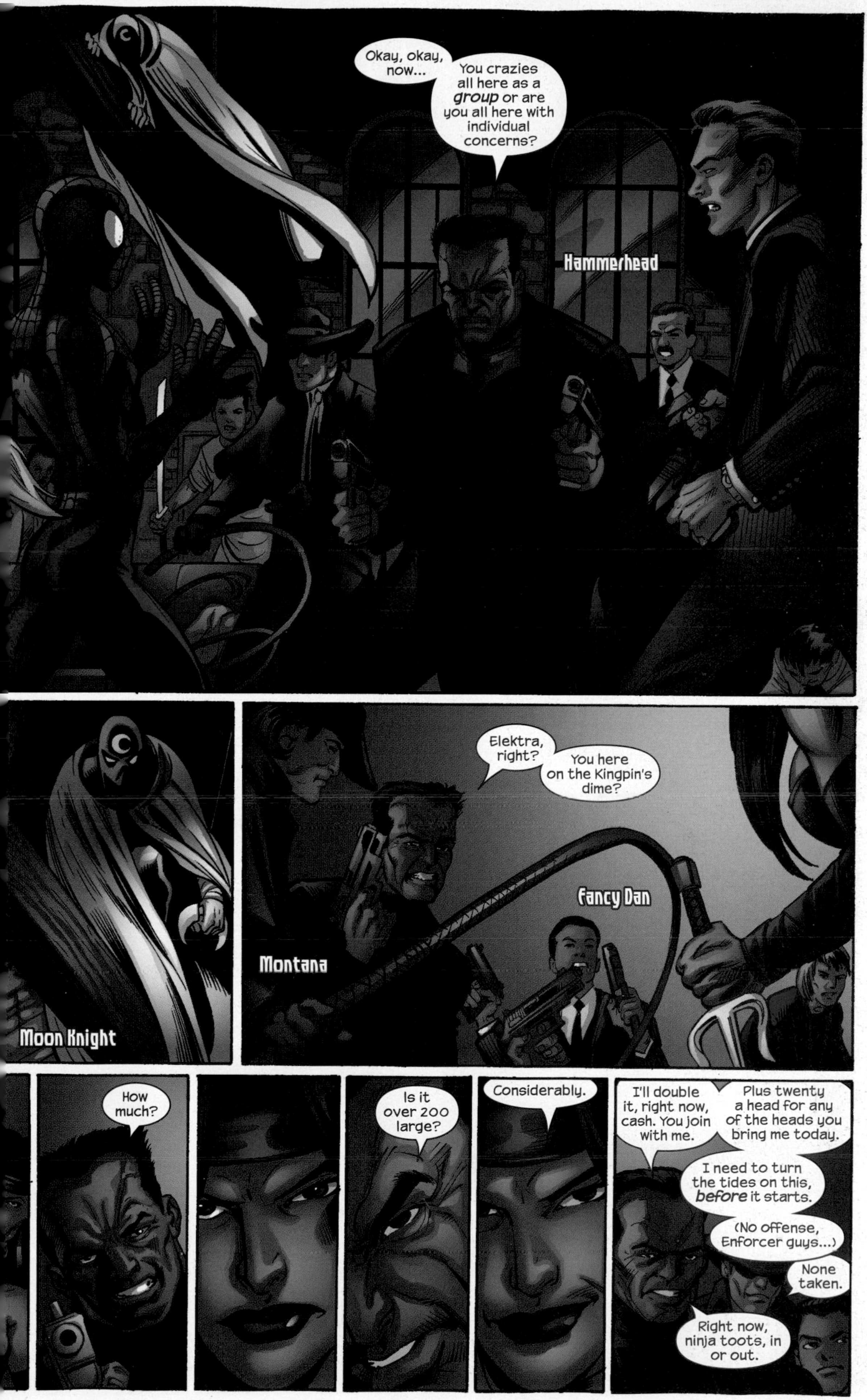

Okay, okay, now...
You crazies all here as a *group* or are you all here with individual concerns?
Hammerhead
Moon Knight
Elektra, right?
You here on the Kingpin's dime?
Fancy Dan
Montana
How much?
Is it over 200 large?
Considerably.
I'll double it, right now, cash. You join with me.
Plus twenty a head for any of the heads you bring me today.
I need to turn the tides on this, *before* it starts.
(No offense, Enforcer guys...)
None taken.
Right now, ninja toots, in or out.

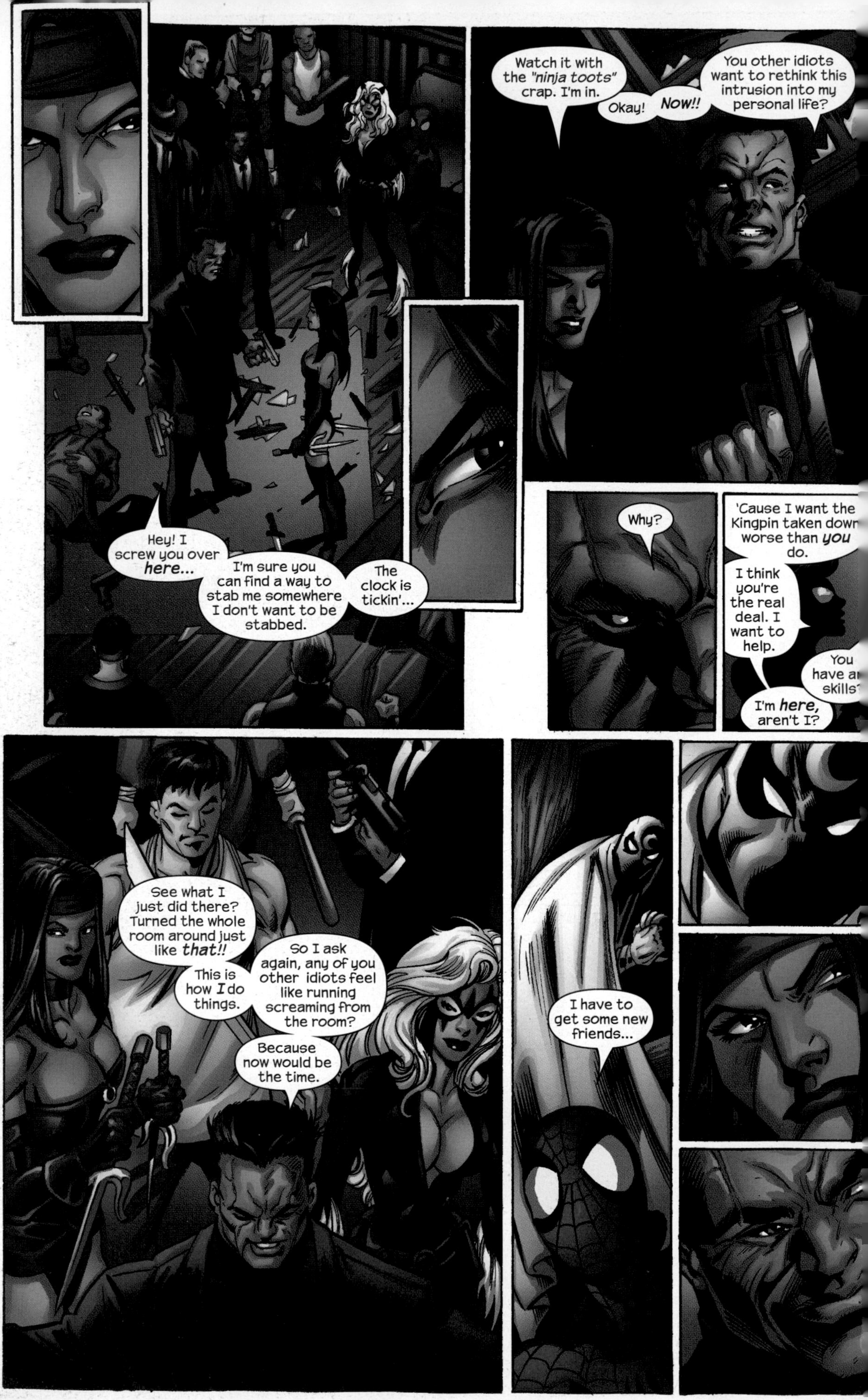

Hey! I screw you over here...
I'm sure you can find a way to stab me somewhere I don't want to be stabbed.
The clock is tickin'...
Watch it with the "ninja toots" crap. I'm in.
Okay!
NOW!!
You other idiots want to rethink this intrusion into my personal life?
Why?
'Cause I want the Kingpin taken down worse than you do.
I think you're the real deal. I want to help.
I'm here, aren't I?
See what I just did there? Turned the whole room around just like that!!
This is how I do things.
So I ask again, any of you other idiots feel like running screaming from the room?
Because now would be the time.
I have to get some new friends...

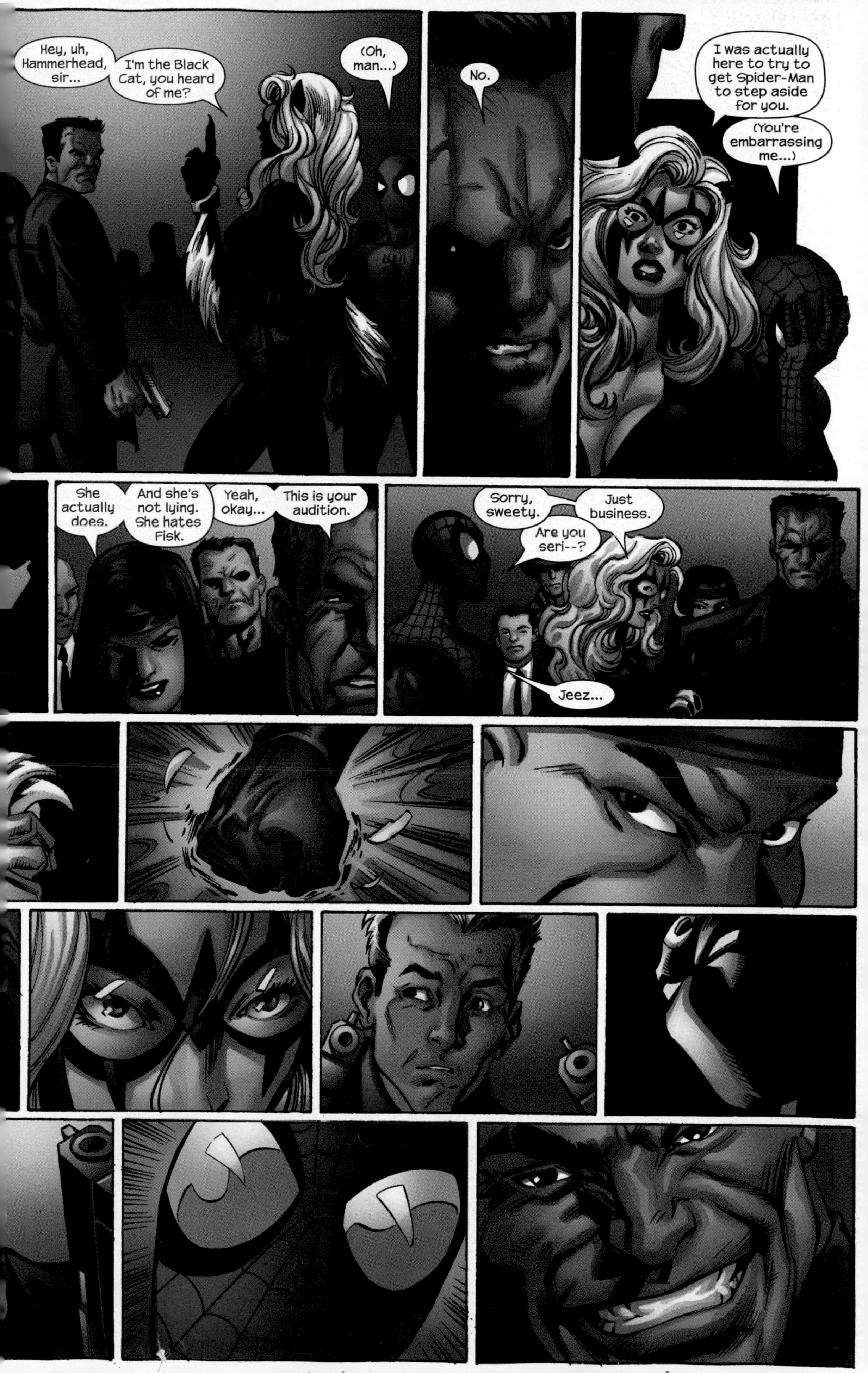
Hey, uh, Hammerhead, sir...
I'm the Black Cat, you heard of me?
(Oh, man...)
No.
I was actually here to try to get Spider-Man to step aside for you.
(You're embarrassing me...)
She actually does.
And she's not lying. She hates Fisk.
Yeah, okay...
This is your audition.
Sorry, sweety.
Just business.
Are you seri--?
Jeez...

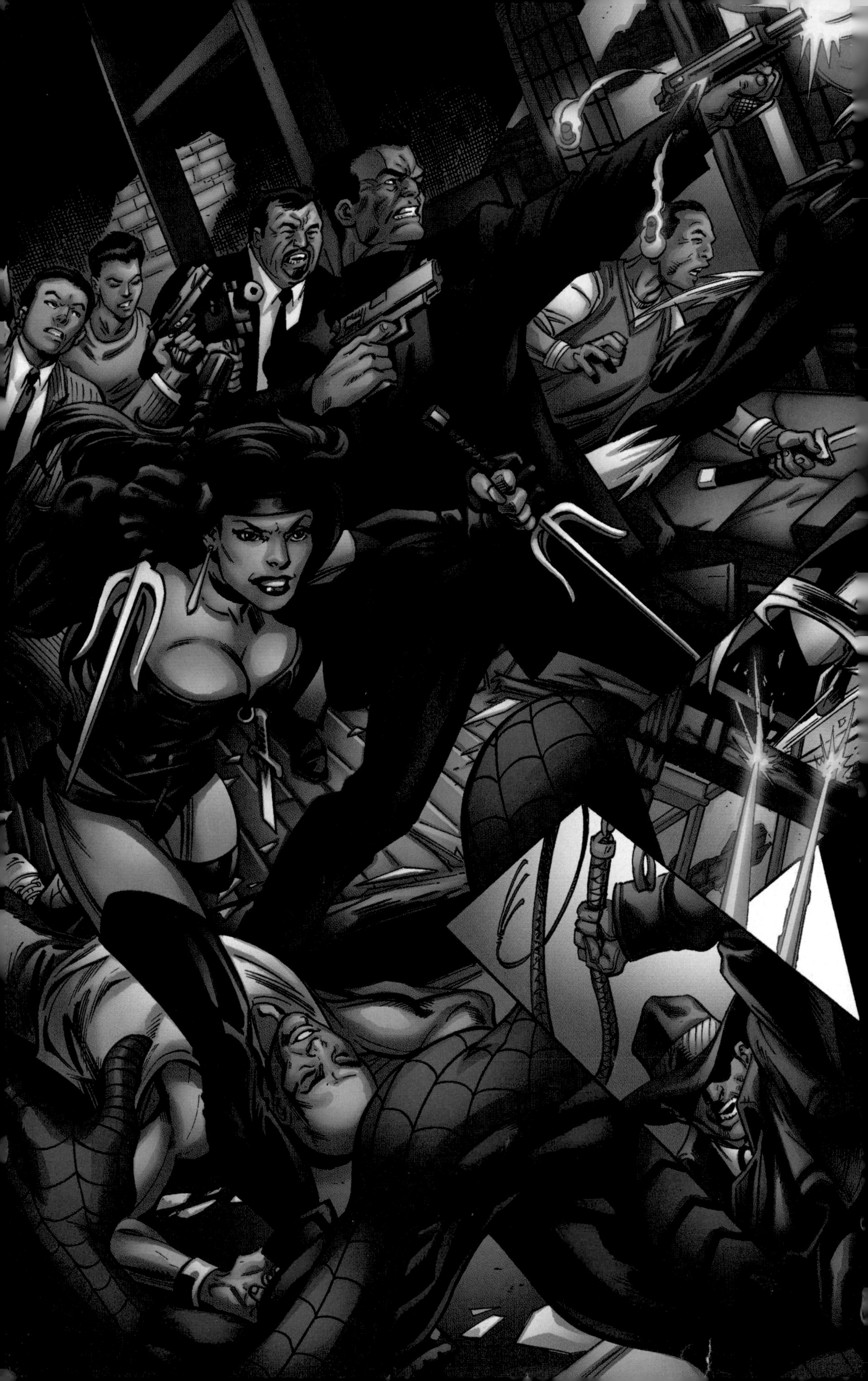

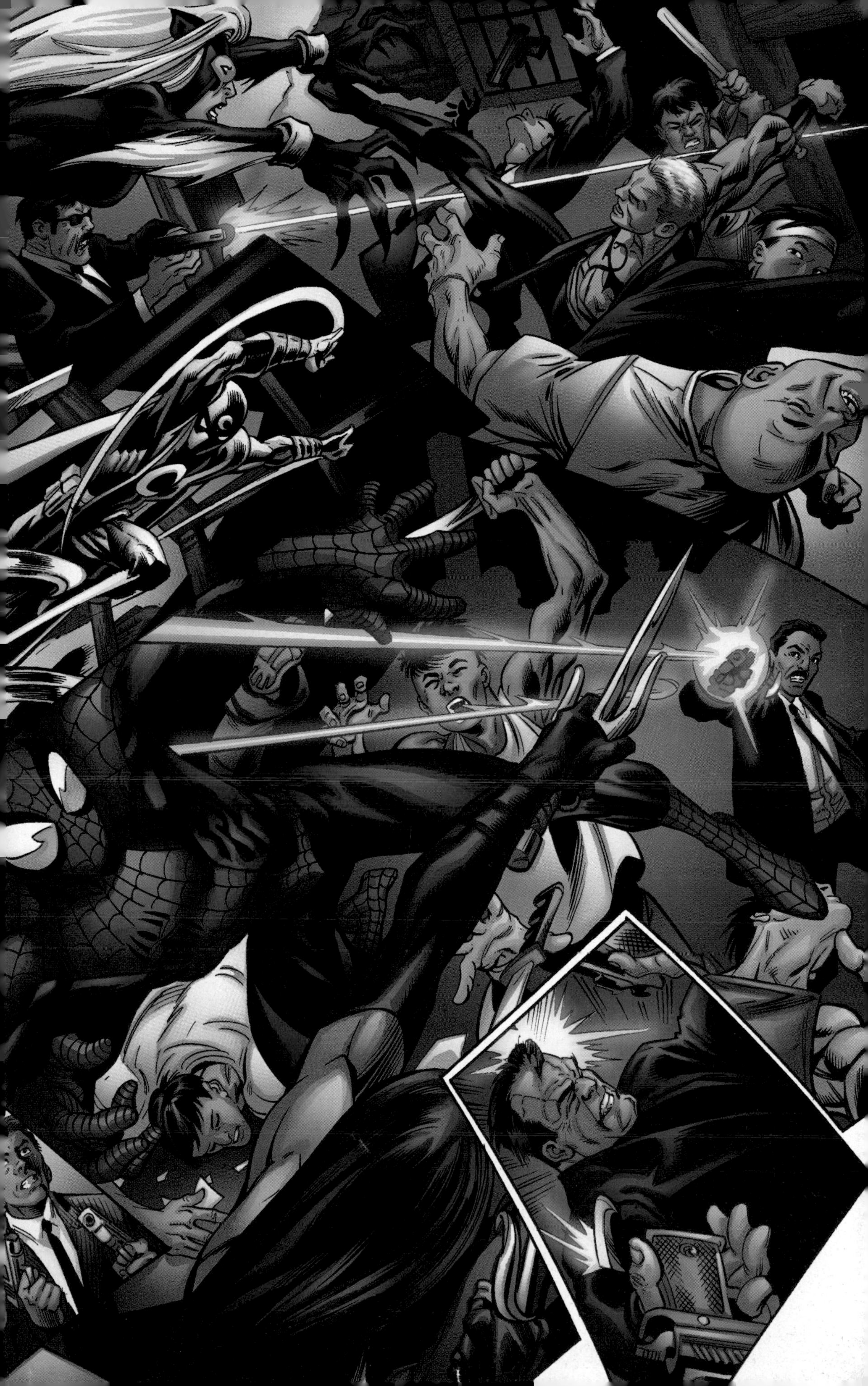

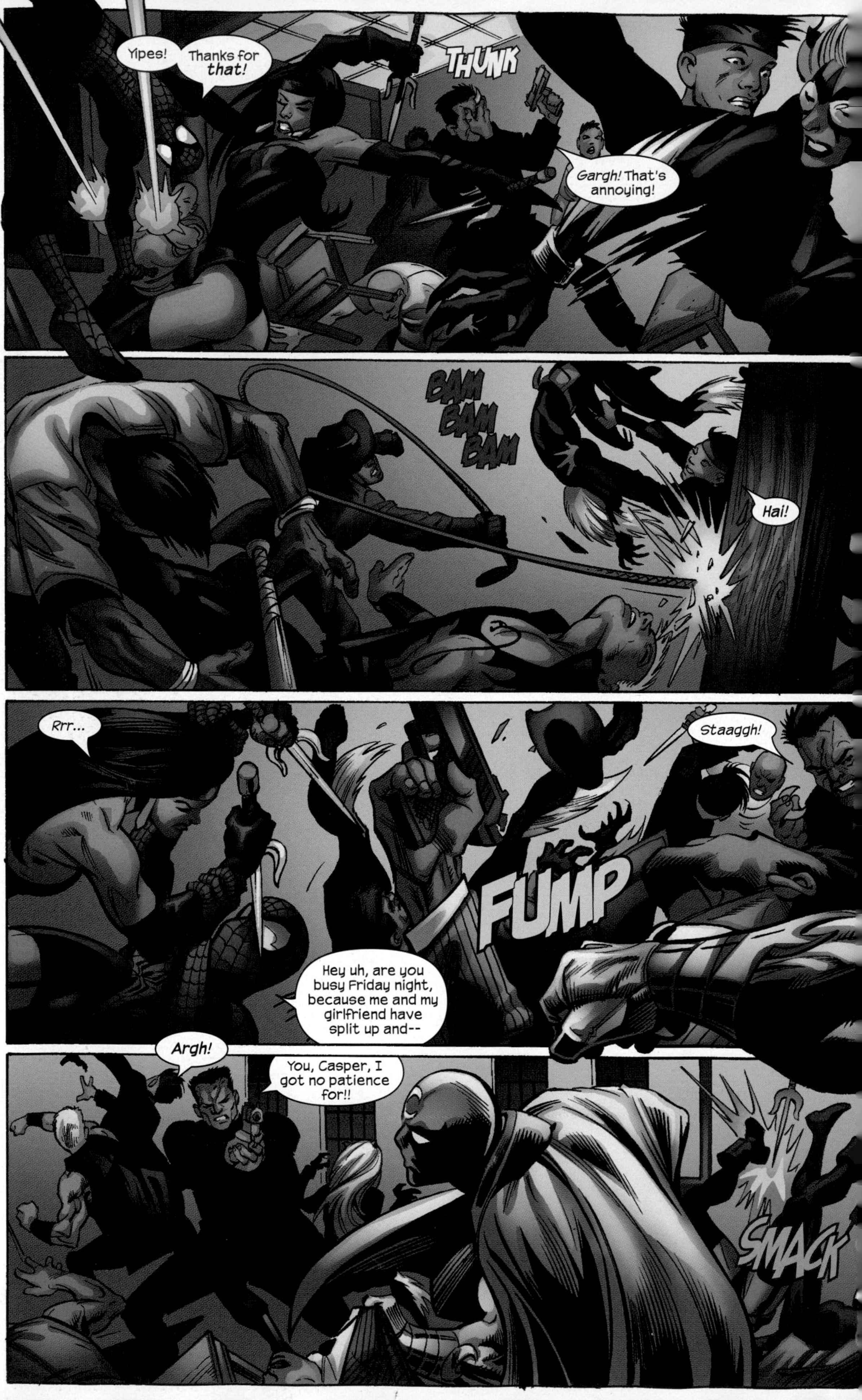
Yipes!
Thanks for that!
THUNK
Gargh! That's annoying!
BAM BAM BAM
Hai!
Rrr...
Staaggh!
FUMP
Hey uh, are you busy Friday night, because me and my girlfriend have split up and--
Argh!
You, Casper, I got no patience for!!
SMACK

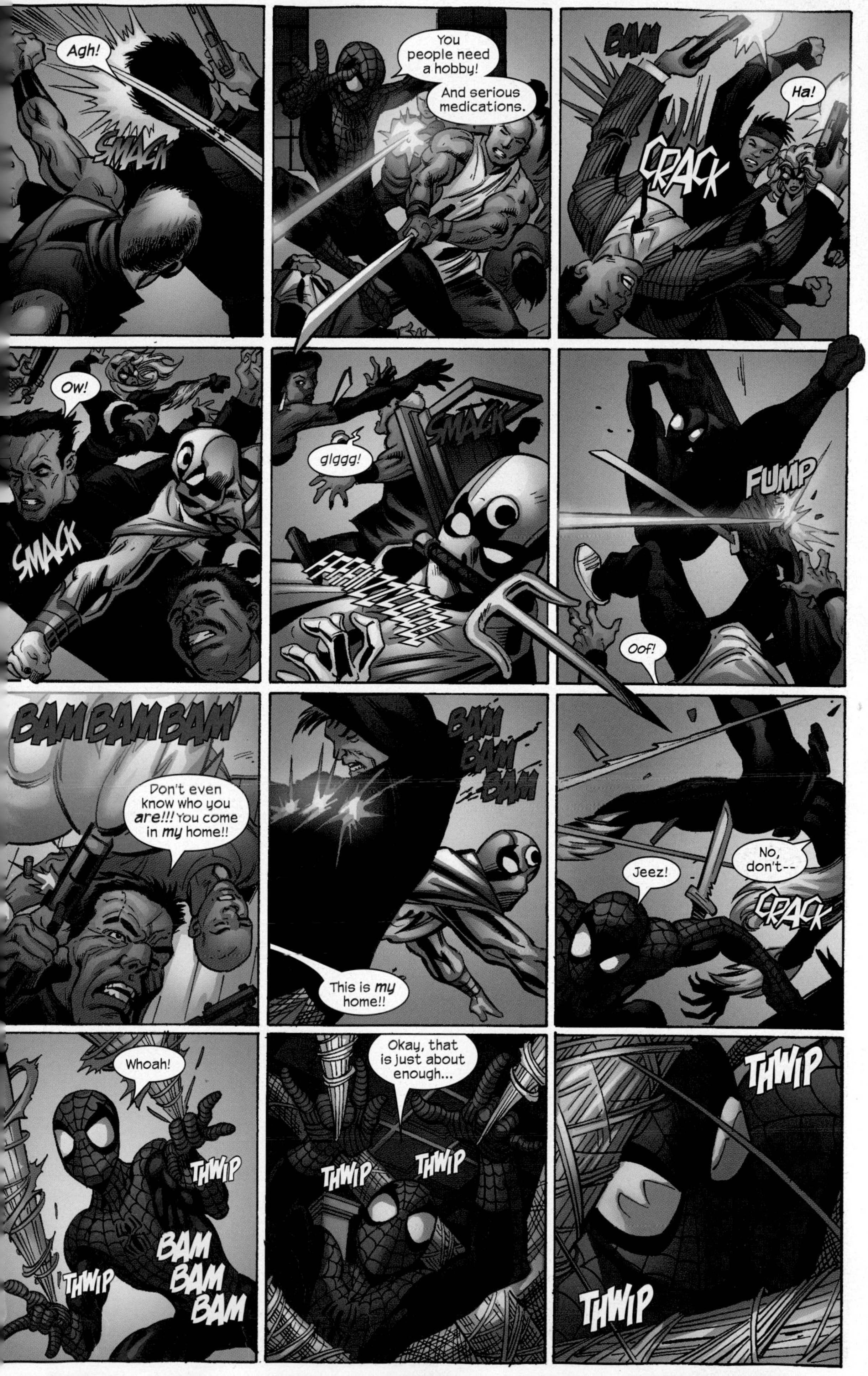
Agh!
SMACK
You people need a hobby!
And serious medications.
BAM
Ha!
CRACK
Ow!
SMACK
glggg!
SMACK
FUMP
Oof!
BAM BAM BAM
Don't even know who you *are!!!* You come in *my* home!!
BAM BAM BAM
This is *my* home!!
Jeez!
No, don't--
CRACK
Whoah!
THWIP
BAM BAM BAM
THWIP
Okay, that is just about enough...
THWIP
THWIP
THWIP
THWIP

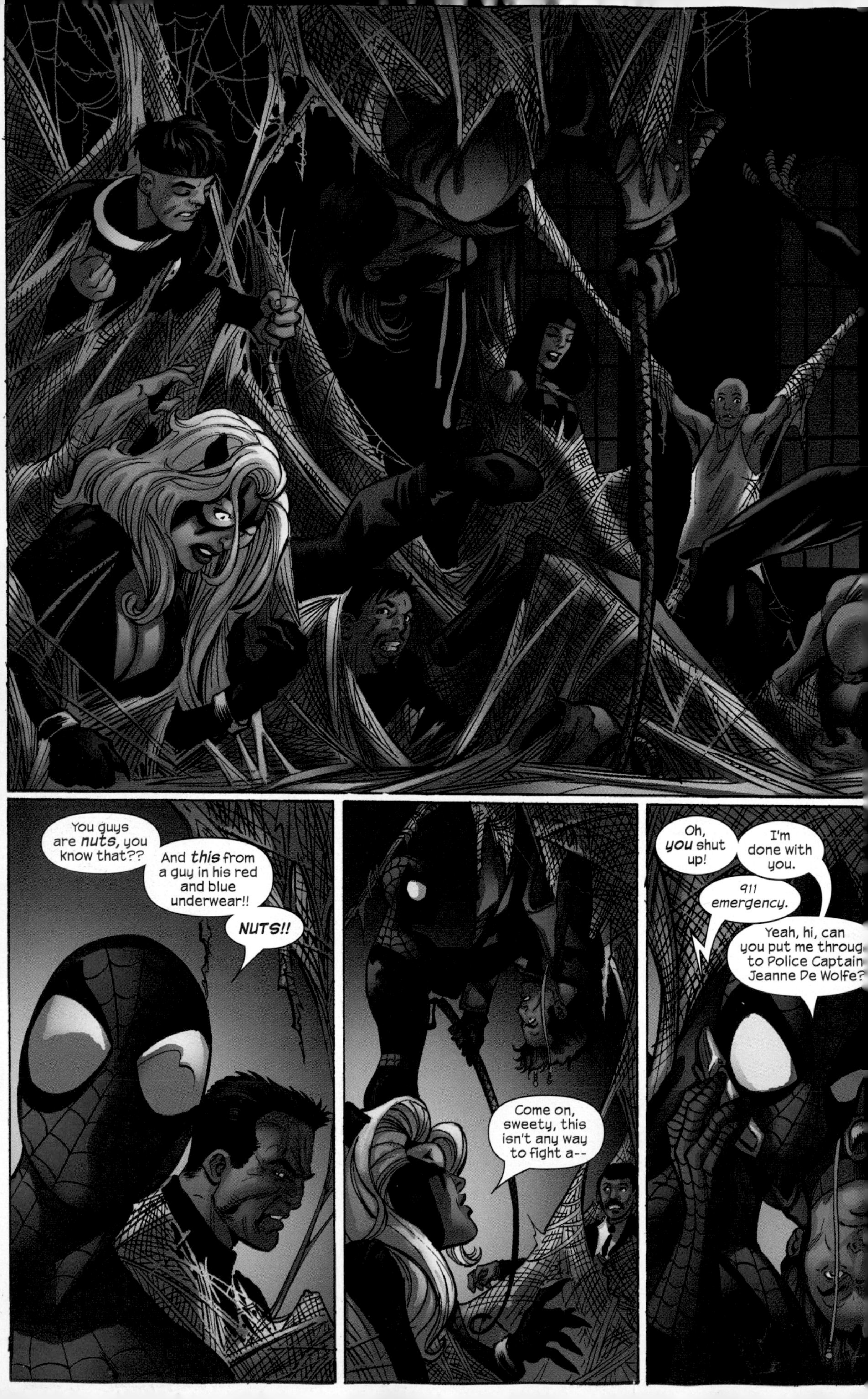

You guys are *nuts*, you know that??
And *this* from a guy in his red and blue underwear!!
NUTS!!
Come on, sweety, this isn't any way to fight a--
Oh, *you* shut up!
I'm done with you.
911 emergency.
Yeah, hi, can you put me throug to Police Captain Jeanne De Wolfe?

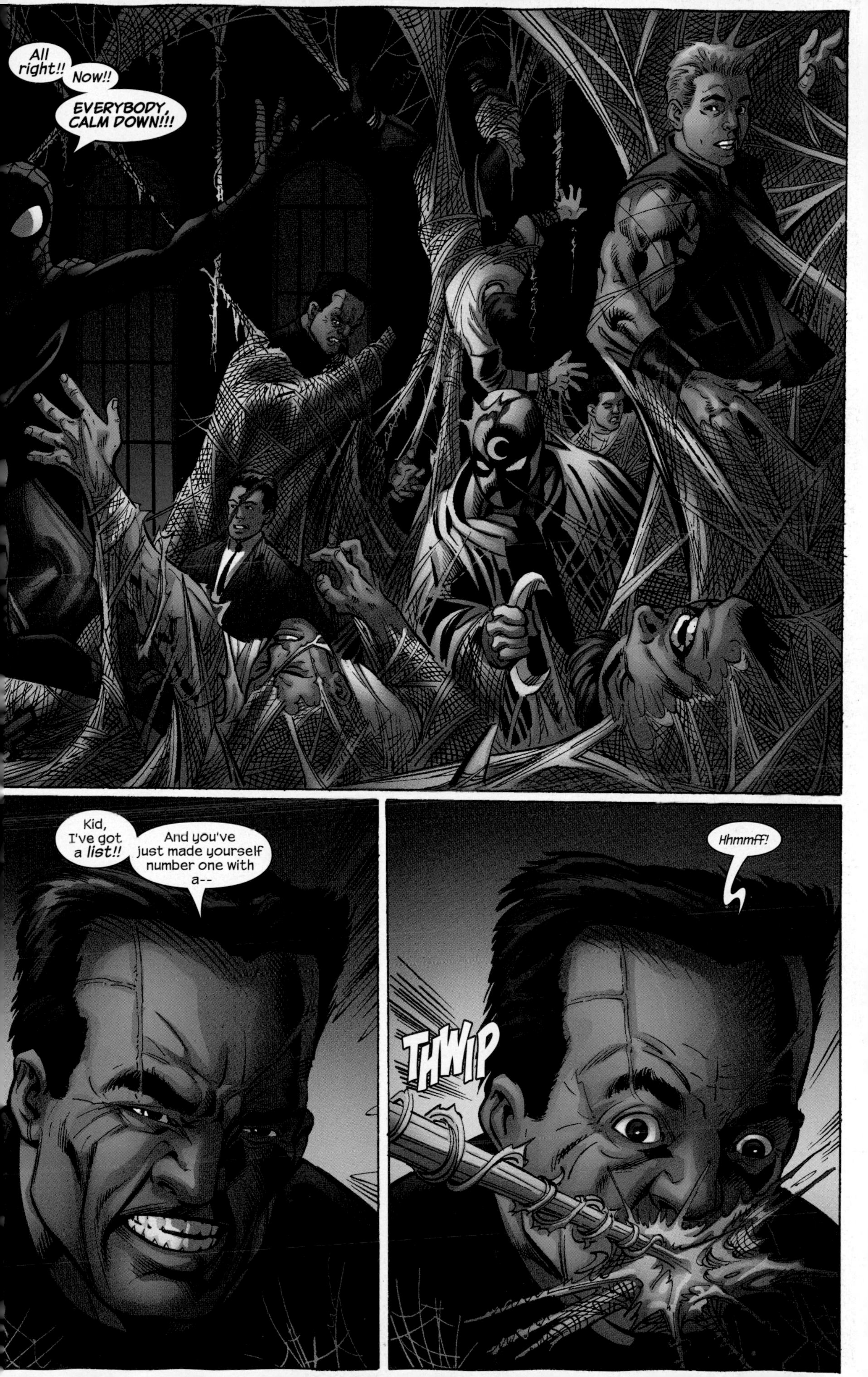
All right!!
Now!!
EVERYBODY, CALM DOWN!!!
Kid, I've got a list!!
And you've just made yourself number one with a--
Hhmmff!
THWIP

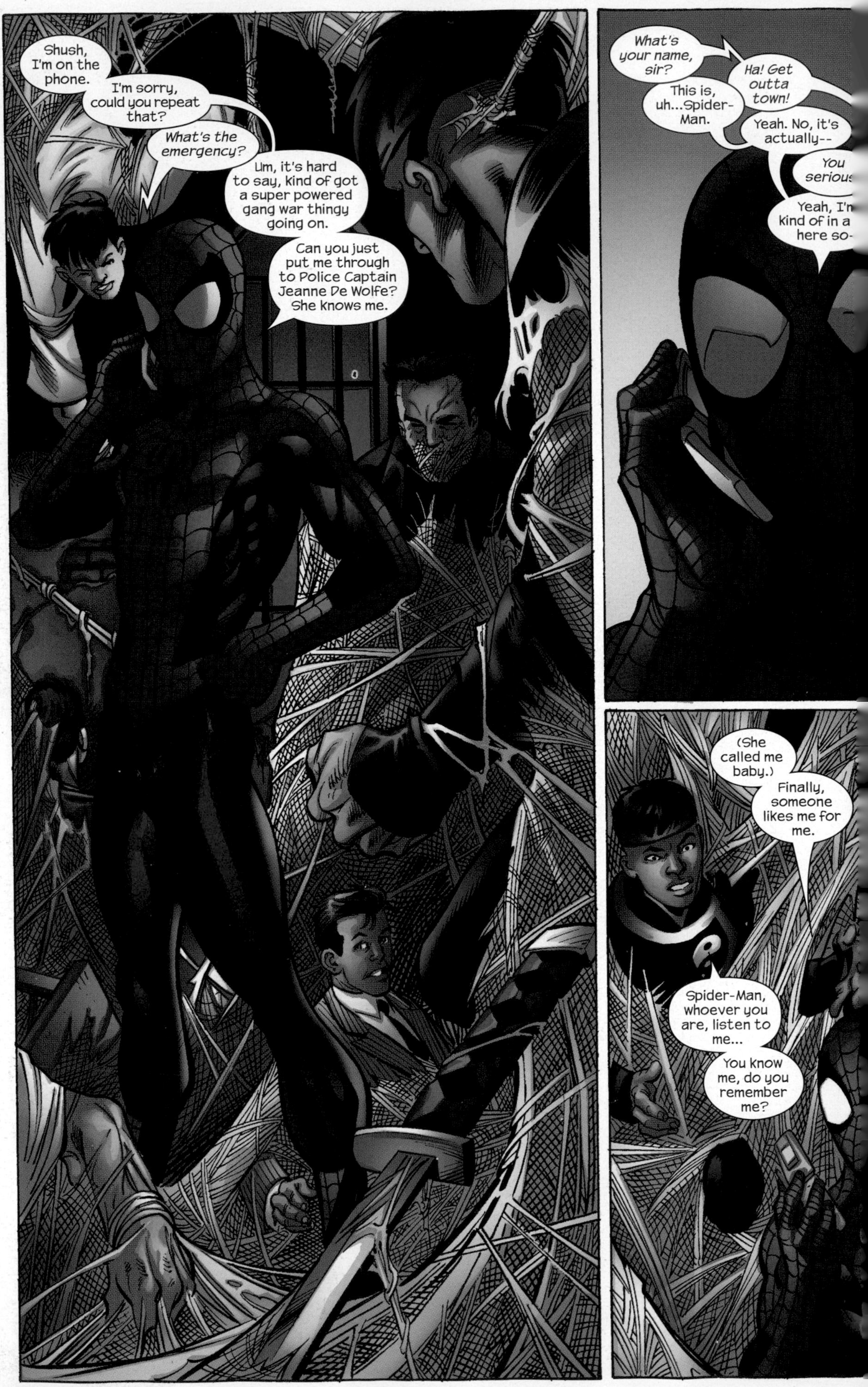
Shush, I'm on the phone.
I'm sorry, could you repeat that?
What's the emergency?
Um, it's hard to say, kind of got a super powered gang war thingy going on.
Can you just put me through to Police Captain Jeanne De Wolfe? She knows me.
What's your name, sir?
This is, uh...Spider-Man.
Ha! Get outta town!
Yeah. No, it's actually--
(She called me baby.)
Finally, someone likes me for me.
Spider-Man, whoever you are, listen to me...
You know me, do you remember me?

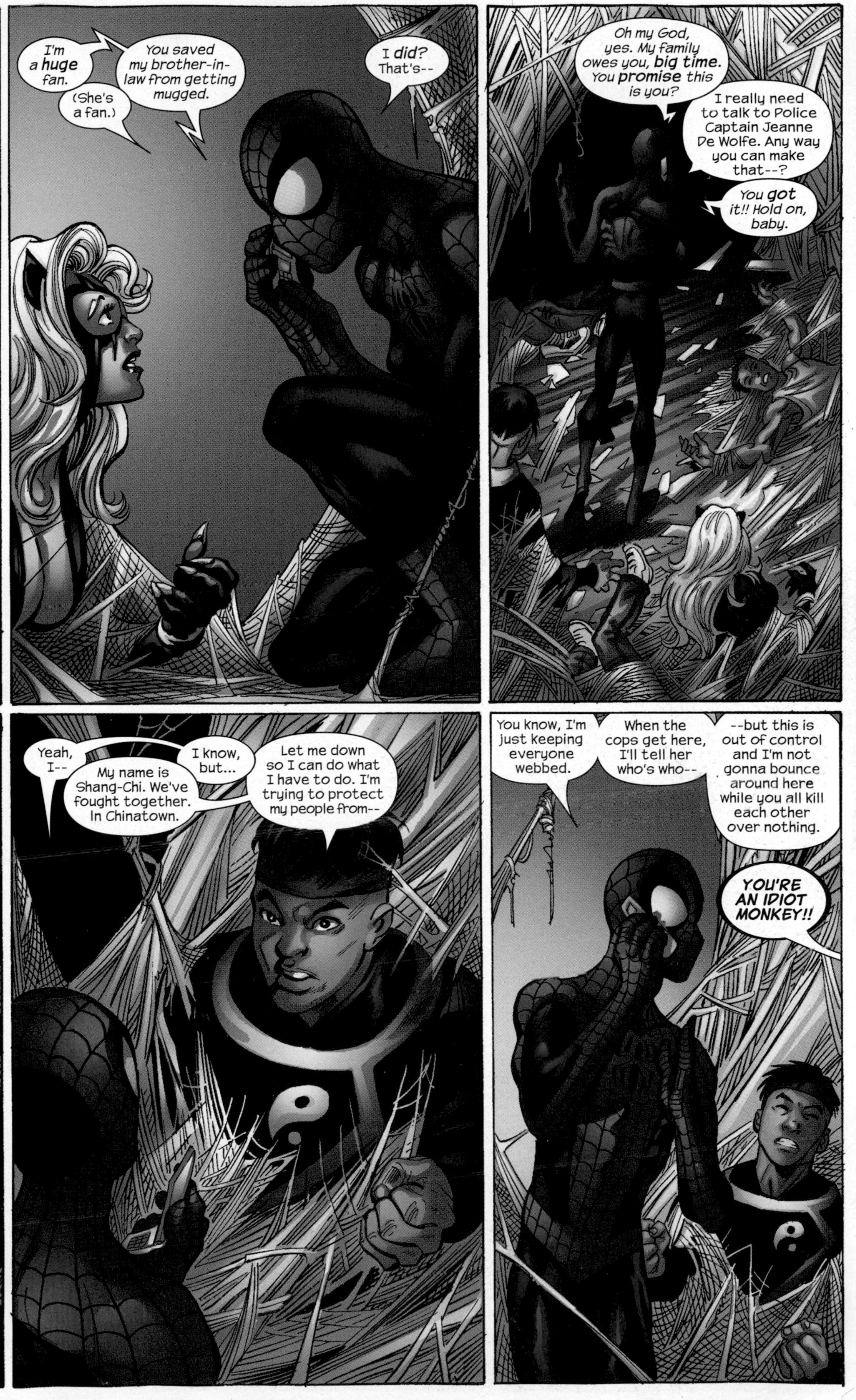
I'm a huge fan.
You saved my brother-in-law from getting mugged.
(She's a fan.)
I did? That's--
Oh my God, yes. My family owes you, big time. You promise this is you?
I really need to talk to Police Captain Jeanne De Wolfe. Any way you can make that--?
You got it!! Hold on, baby.
Yeah, I--
I know, but...
My name is Shang-Chi. We've fought together. In Chinatown.
Let me down so I can do what I have to do. I'm trying to protect my people from--
You know, I'm just keeping everyone webbed.
When the cops get here, I'll tell her who's who--
--but this is out of control and I'm not gonna bounce around here while you all kill each other over nothing.
YOU'RE AN IDIOT MONKEY!!

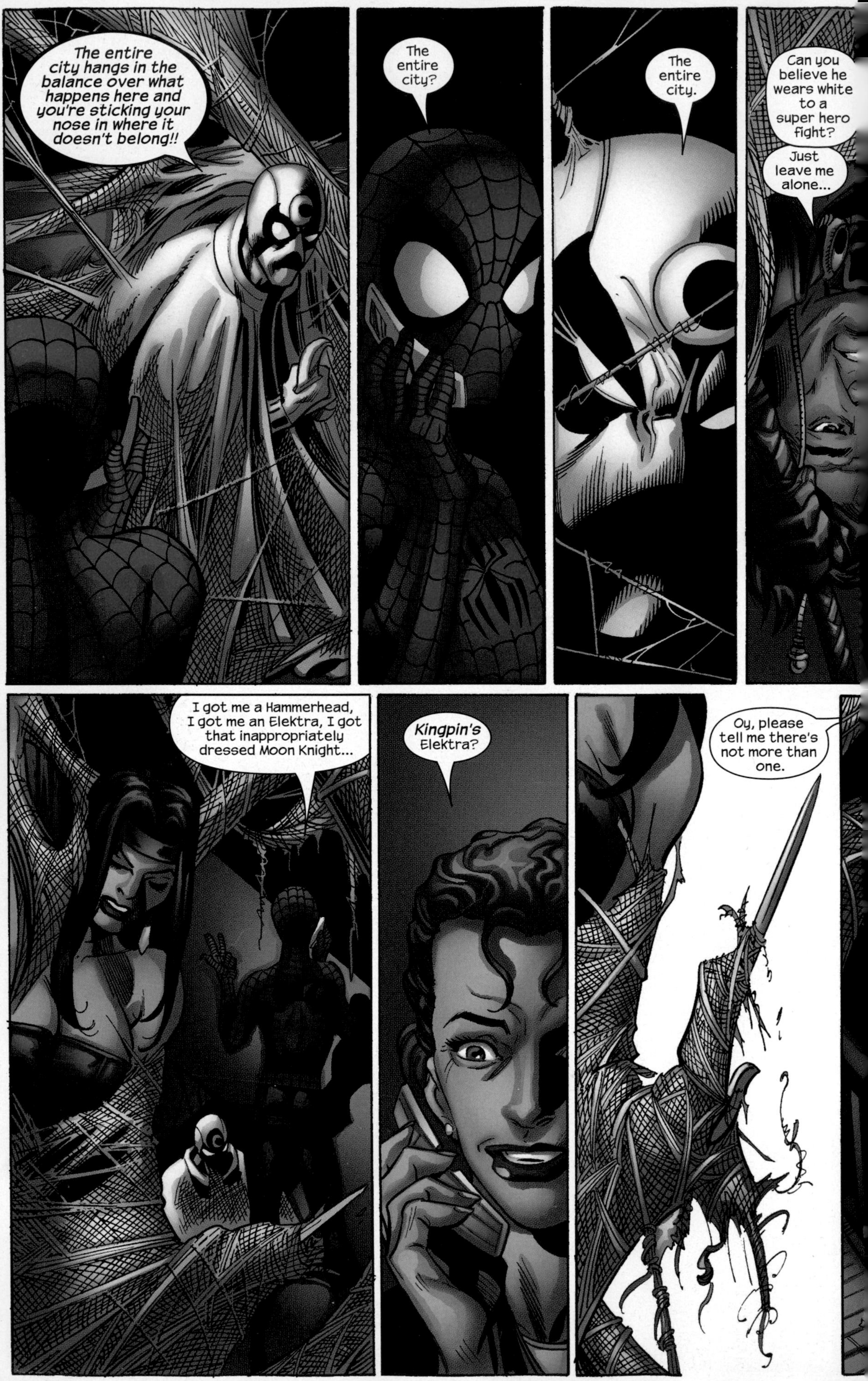
The entire city hangs in the balance over what happens here and you're sticking your nose in where it doesn't belong!!
The entire city?
The entire city.
Can you believe he wears white to a super hero fight?
Just leave me alone...
I got me a Hammerhead, I got me an Elektra, I got that inappropriately dressed Moon Knight...
Kingpin's Elektra?
Oy, please tell me there's not more than one.

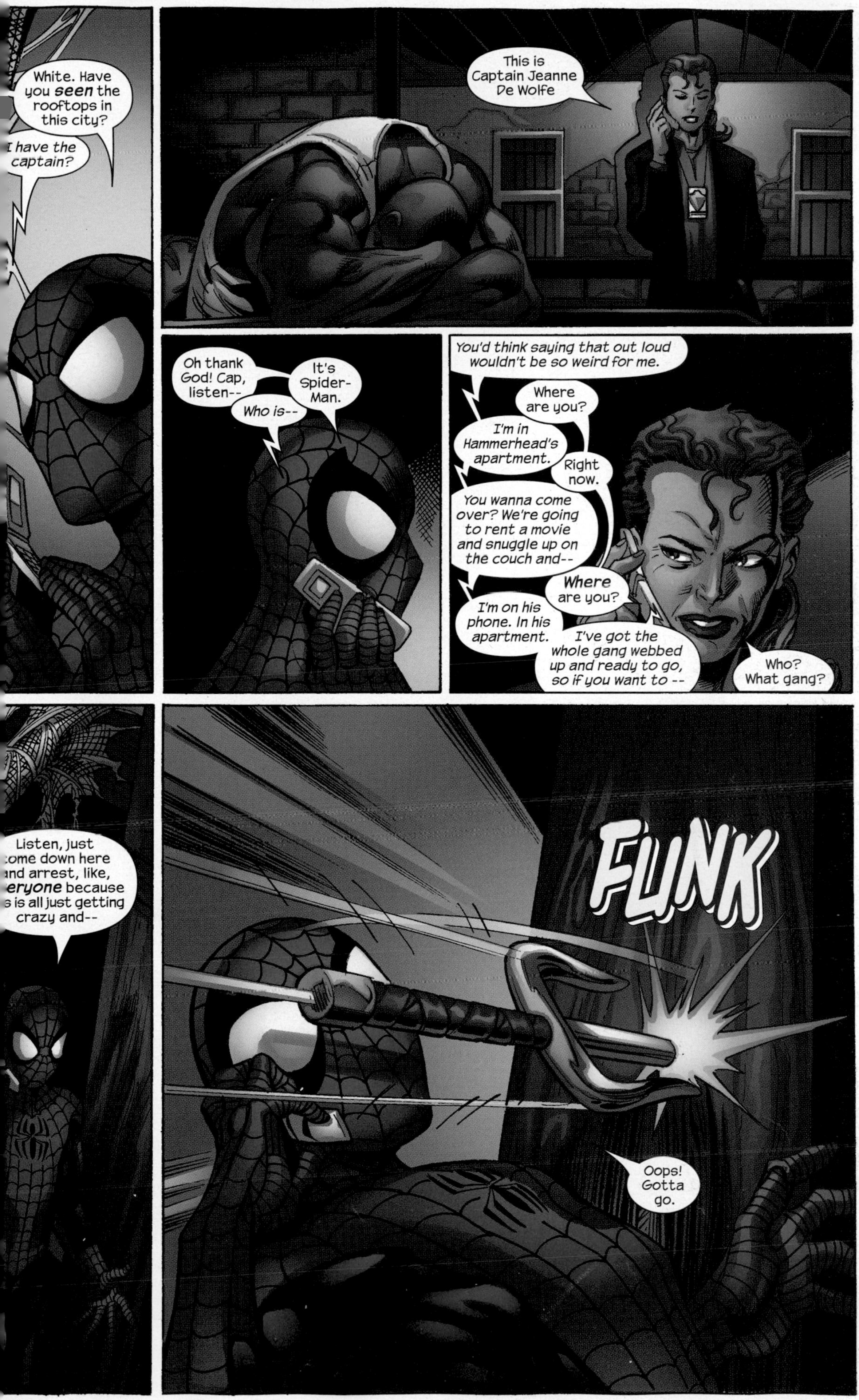
White. Have you *seen* the rooftops in this city?
I have the captain?
This is Captain Jeanne De Wolfe
Oh thank God! Cap, listen--
Who is--
It's Spider-Man.
You'd think saying that out loud wouldn't be so weird for me.
Where are you?
I'm in Hammerhead's apartment.
Right now.
You wanna come over? We're going to rent a movie and snuggle up on the couch and--
Where are you?
I'm on his phone. In his apartment.
I've got the whole gang webbed up and ready to go, so if you want to --
Who? What gang?
Listen, just come down here and arrest, like, ***eryone*** because s is all just getting crazy and--
FUNK
Oops! Gotta go.

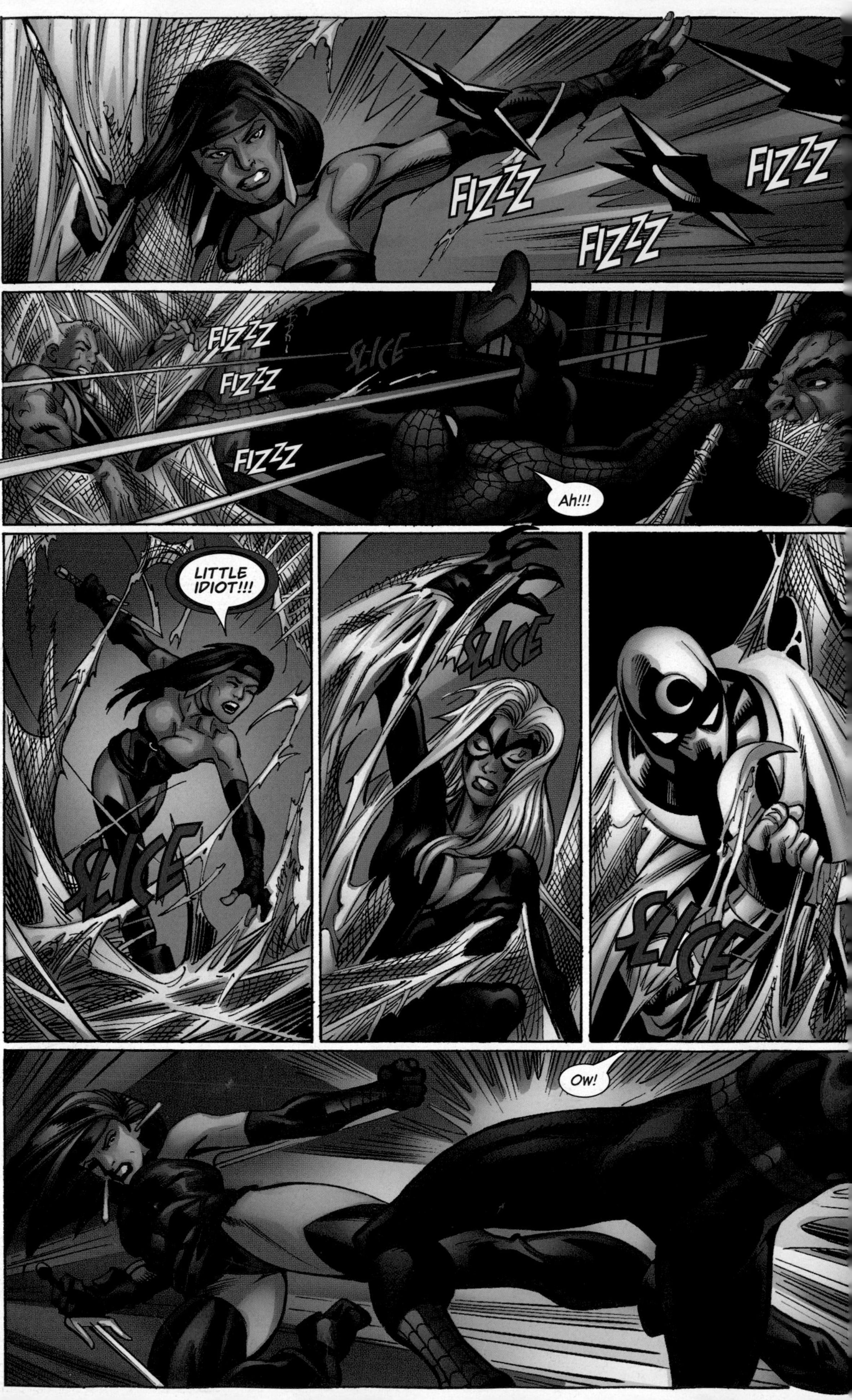
FIZZZ
FIZZZ
FIZZZ
FIZZZ
FIZZZ
SLICE
FIZZZ
Ah!!!
LITTLE IDIOT!!!
SLICE
SLICE
SLICE
Ow!

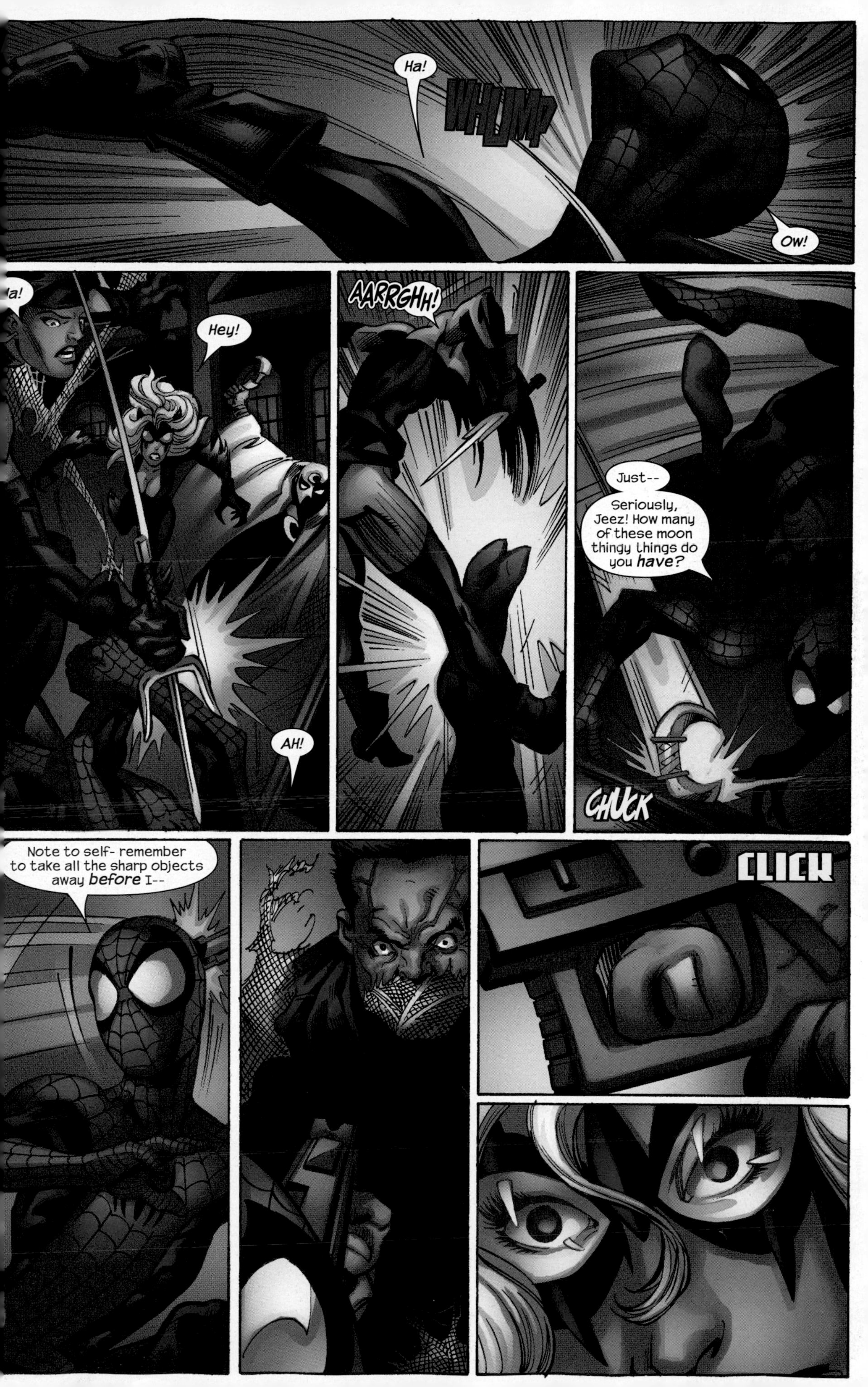
Ha!
WHUMP
Ow!
Ha!
Hey!
AH!
AARRGHH!
Just--
Seriously, Jeez! How many of these moon thingy things do you *have*?
CHUCK
Note to self- remember to take all the sharp objects away *before* I--
CLICK

Mmmfff!!

CLICK
CLICK
CLICK

EEEOOOOWEEEOOOOWEEEOO

Jeez...

Mmff!!

SPOK

Now the police are here and we have nothing to show for this—*argh!*

WHAP

Ggf!

SHUCKKKK

You really shouldn't involve yourself in other people's affairs, mystery man.

Ggkkk...

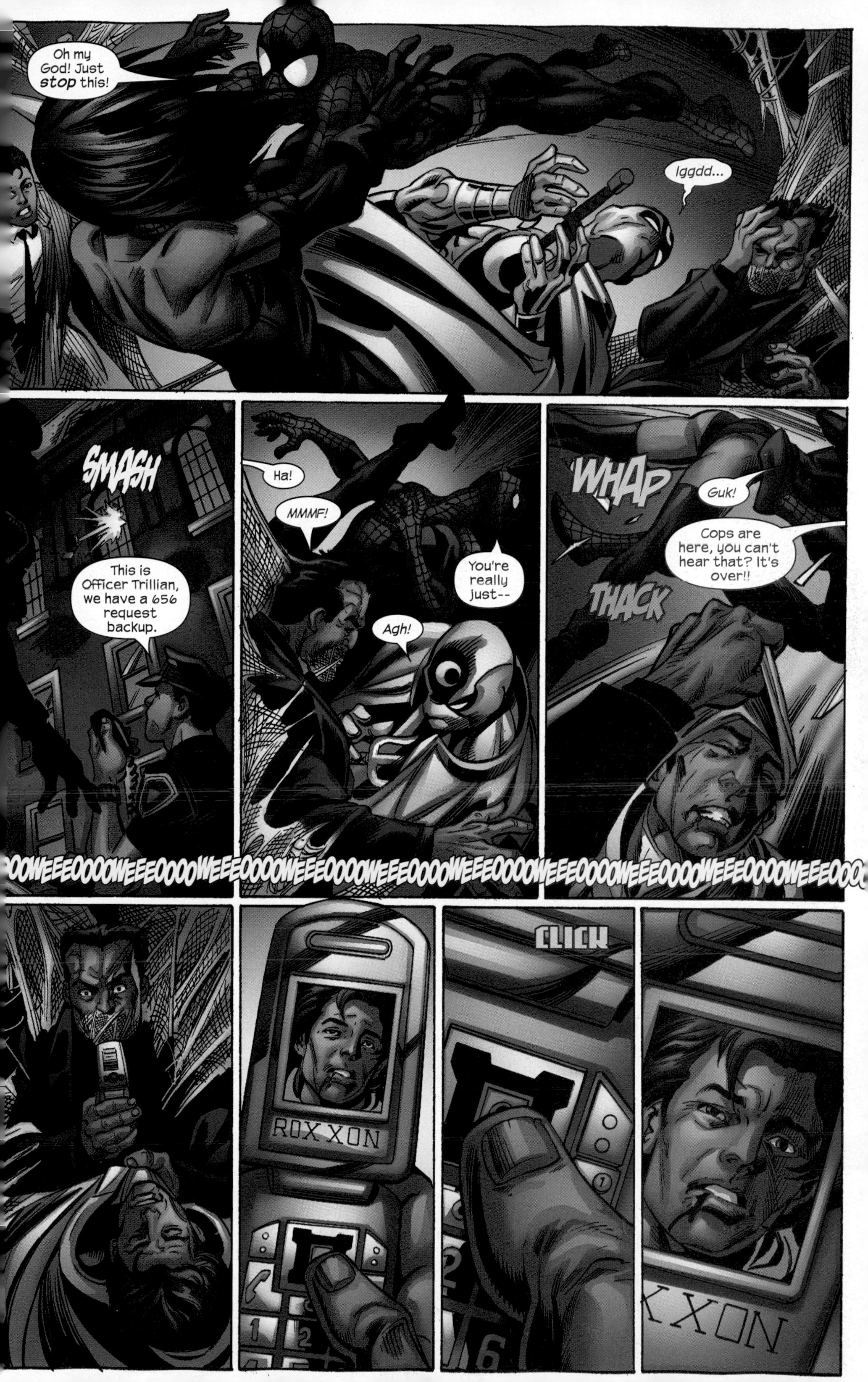
Oh my God! Just stop this!
Iggdd...
SMASH
This is Officer Trillian, we have a 656 request backup.
Ha!
MMMF!
You're really just--
Agh!
WHAP
Guk!
Cops are here, you can't hear that? It's over!!
THACK
OOWEEEOOOOWEEEOOOOWEEEOOOOWEEEOOOOWEEEOOOOWEEEOOOOWEEEOOOOWEEEOOOOWEEEOOOOWEEEOOO
ROXXON
CLICK
XXON

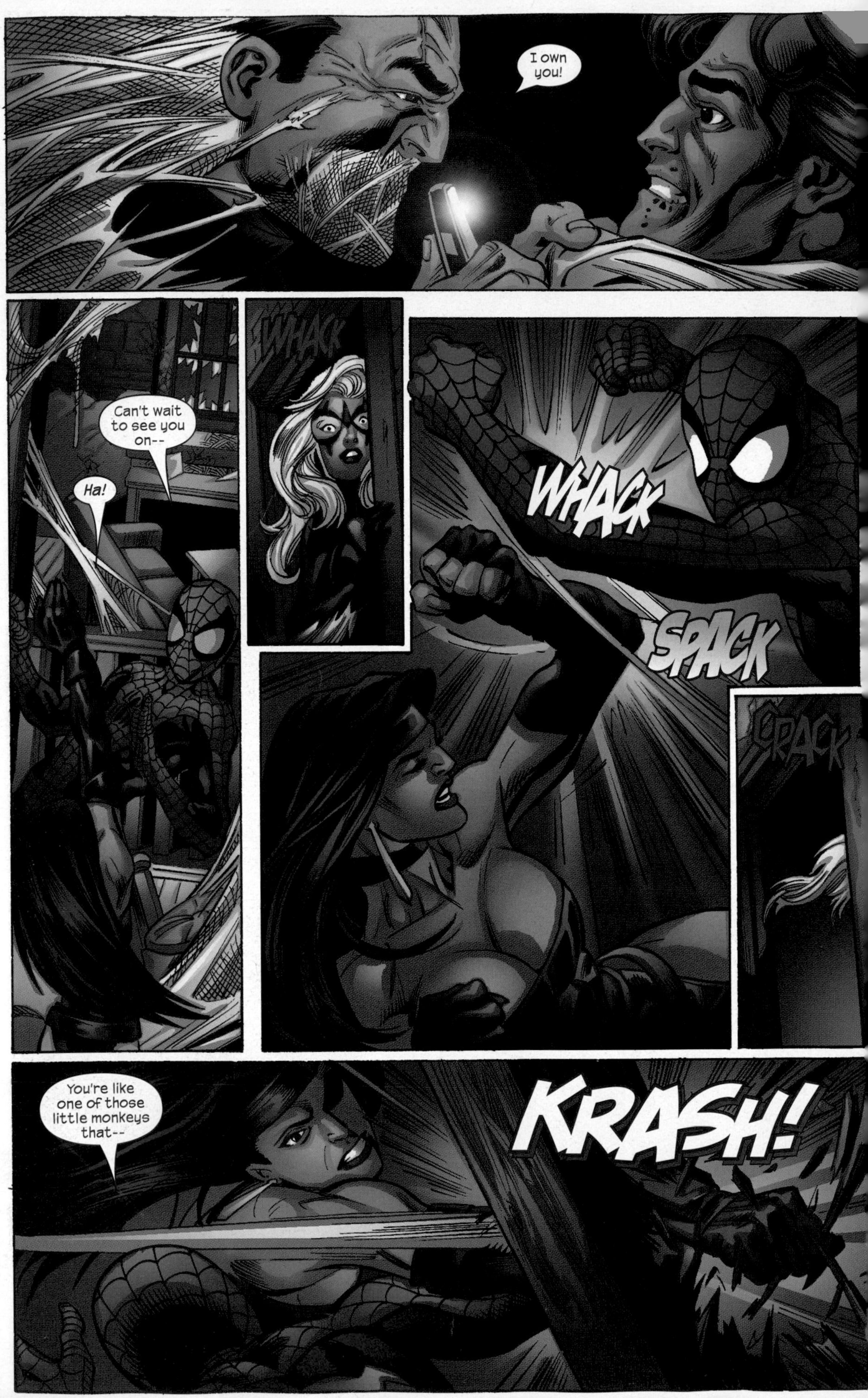

I own you!
Can't wait to see you on--
Ha!
WHACK
WHACK
SPACK
CRACK
You're like one of those little monkeys that--
KRASH!

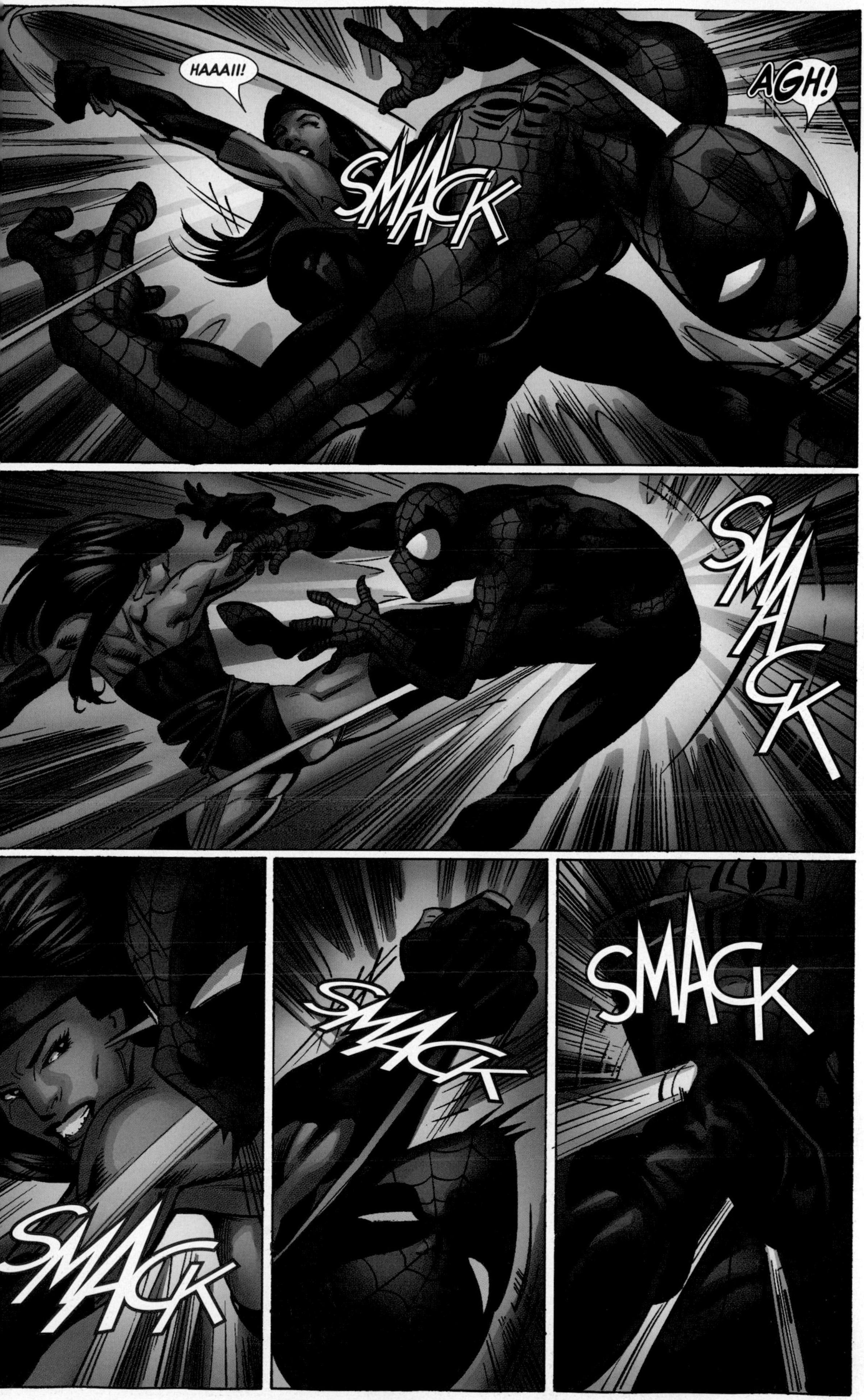
HAAAII!
SMACK
AGH!
SMACK
SMACK
SMACK
SMACK

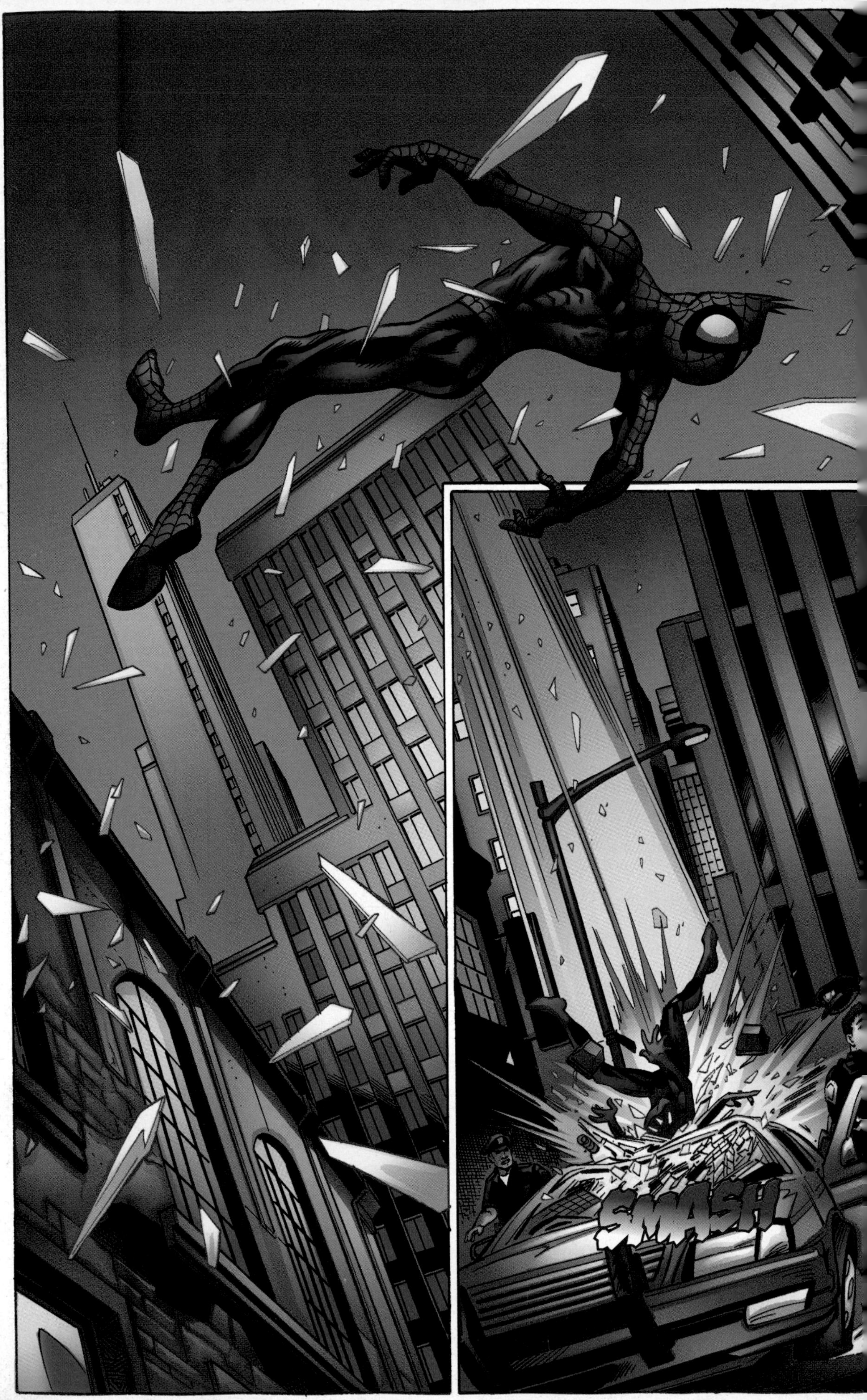
SMASH!

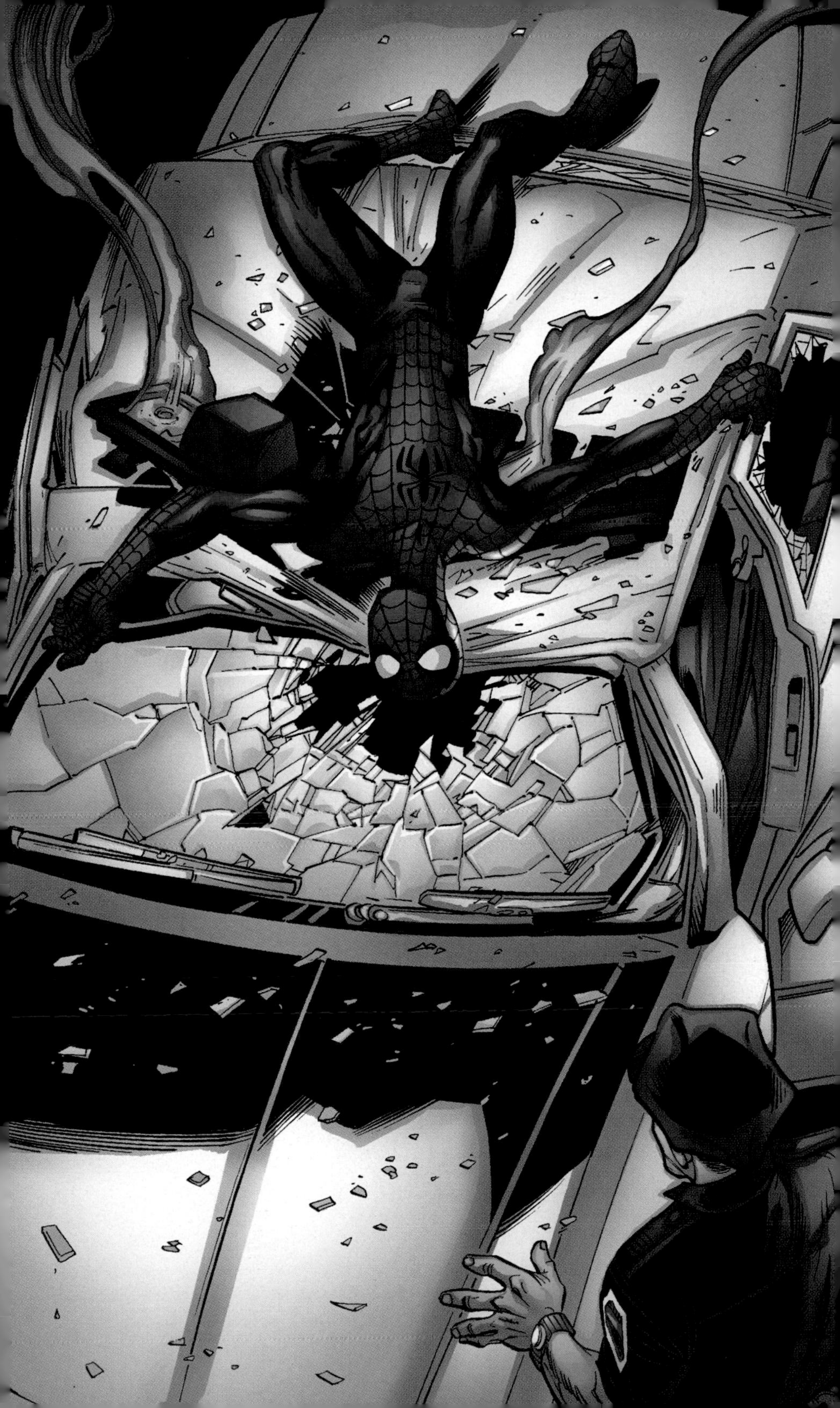

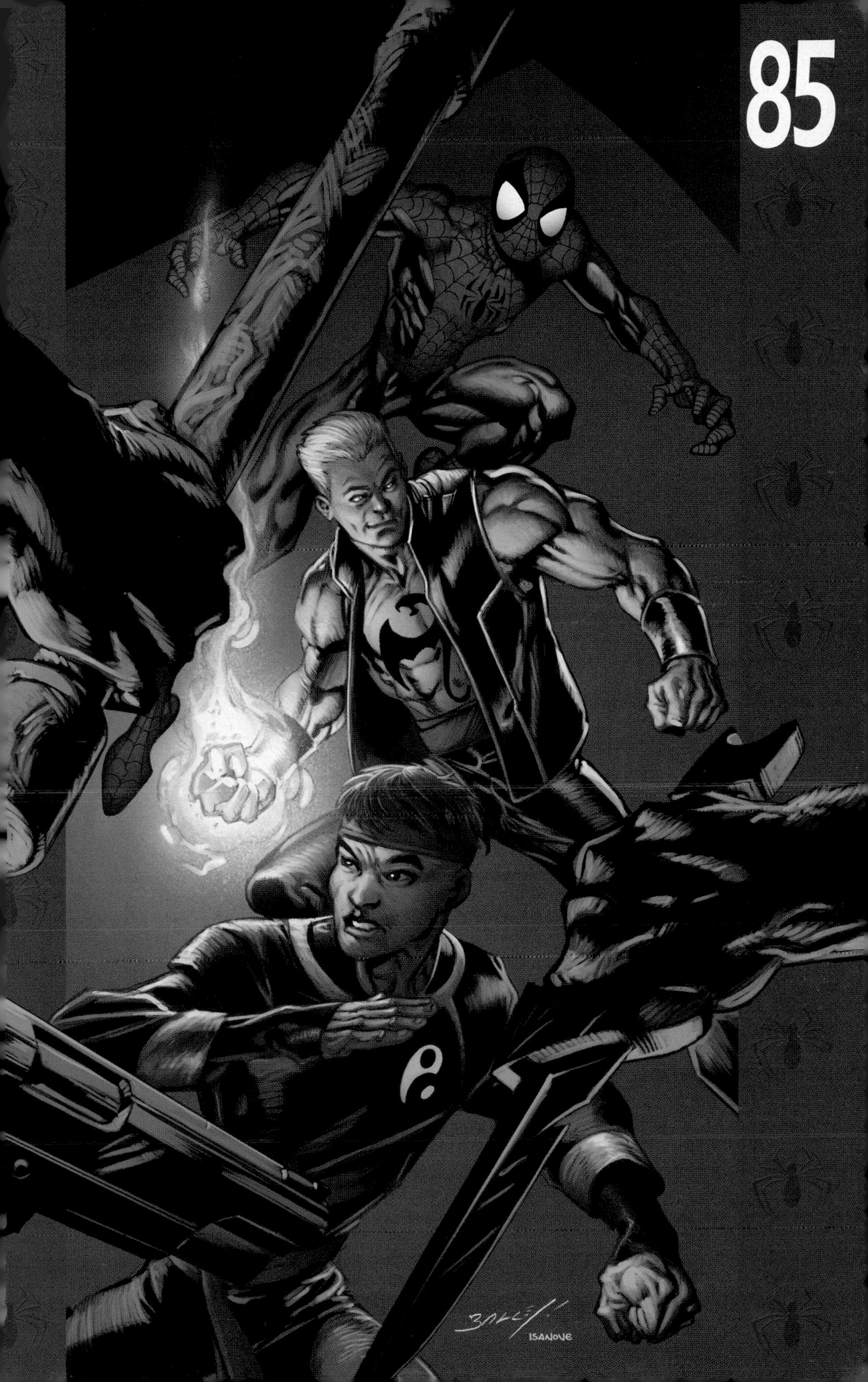
85

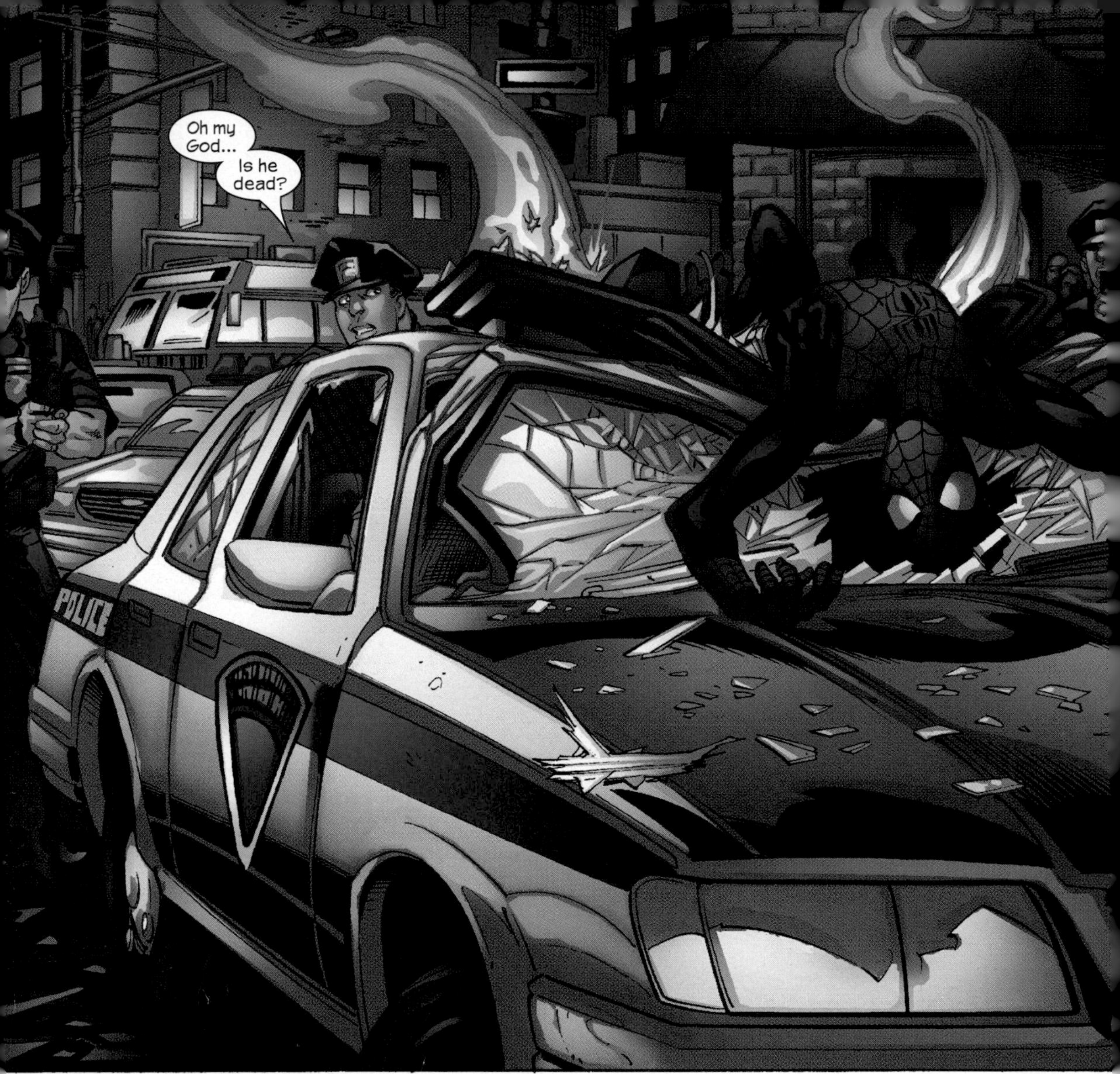
Oh my God...
Is he dead?
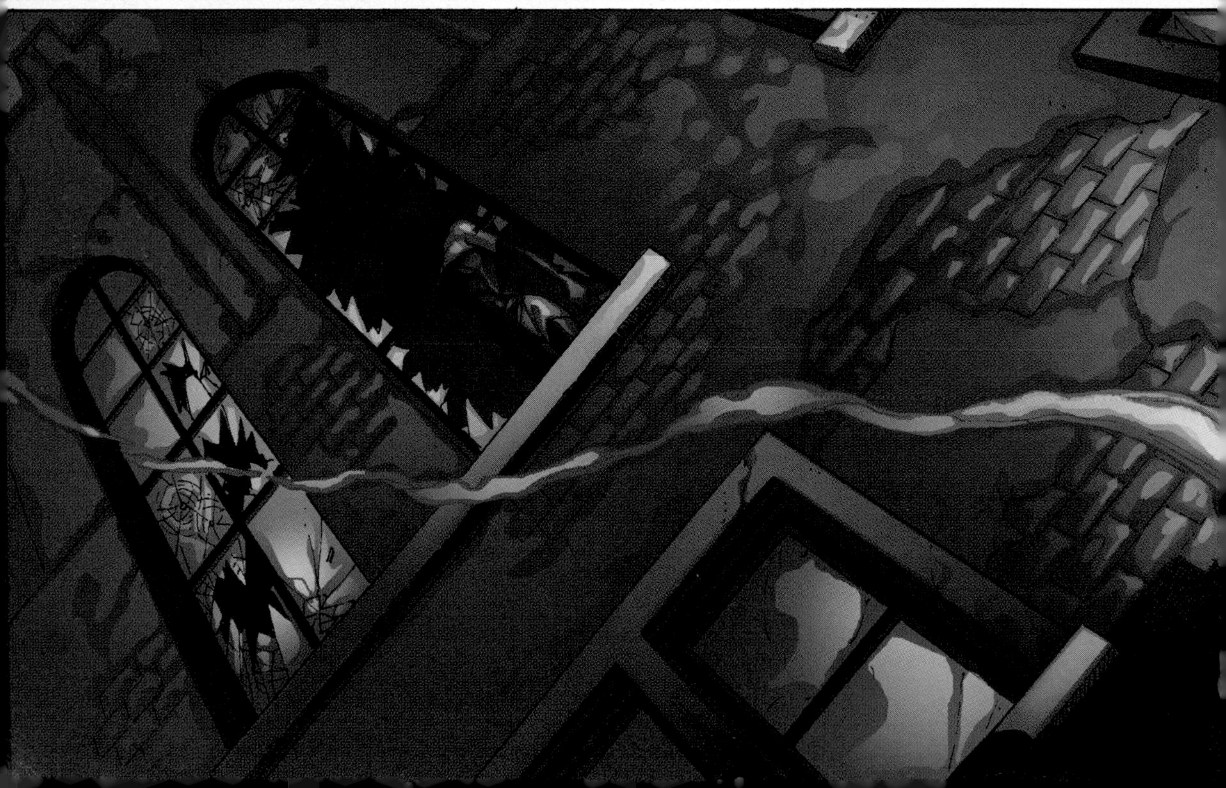

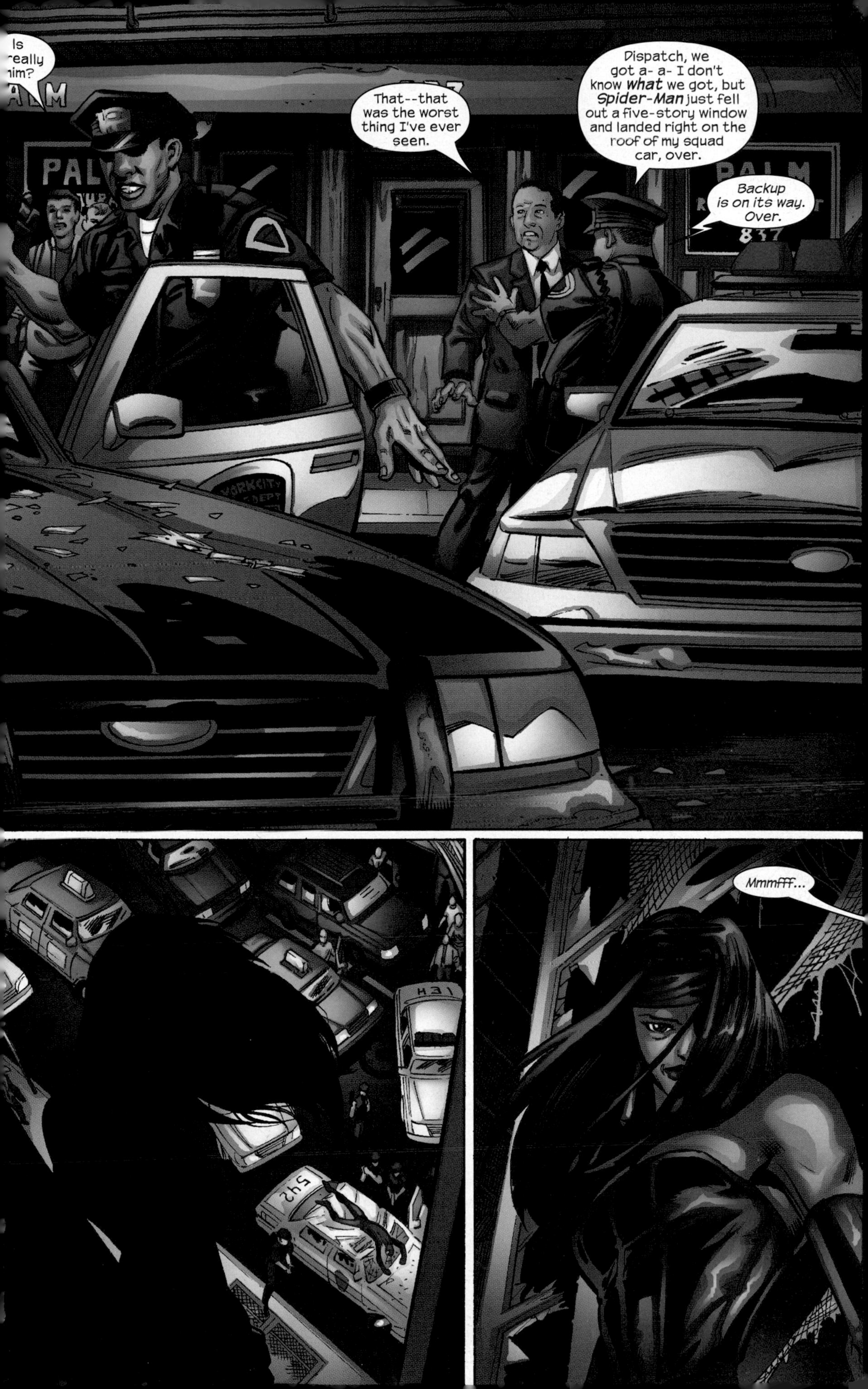

Is really him?
That--that was the worst thing I've ever seen.
Dispatch, we got a- a- I don't know **what** we got, but **Spider-Man** just fell out a five-story window and landed right on the roof of my squad car, over.
Backup is on its way. Over.
Mmmfff...

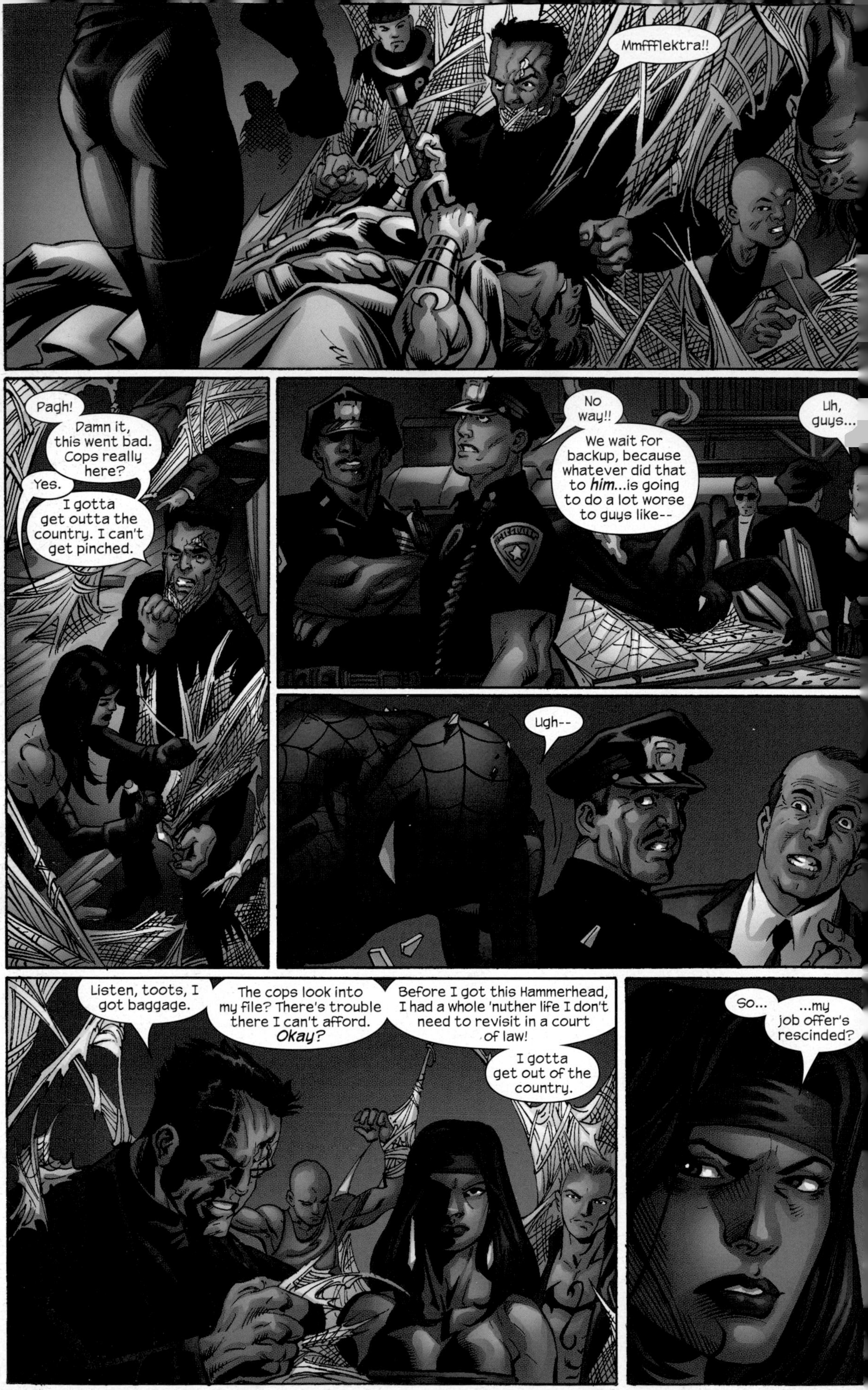
Mmfffflektra!!
Pagh!
Damn it, this went bad. Cops really here?
Yes.
I gotta get outta the country. I can't get pinched.
No way!!
We wait for backup, because whatever did that to *him*...is going to do a lot worse to guys like--
Uh, guys...
Ugh--
Listen, toots, I got baggage.
The cops look into my file? There's trouble there I can't afford. *Okay?*
Before I got this Hammerhead, I had a whole 'nuther life I don't need to revisit in a court of law!
I gotta get out of the country.
So...
...my job offer's rescinded?

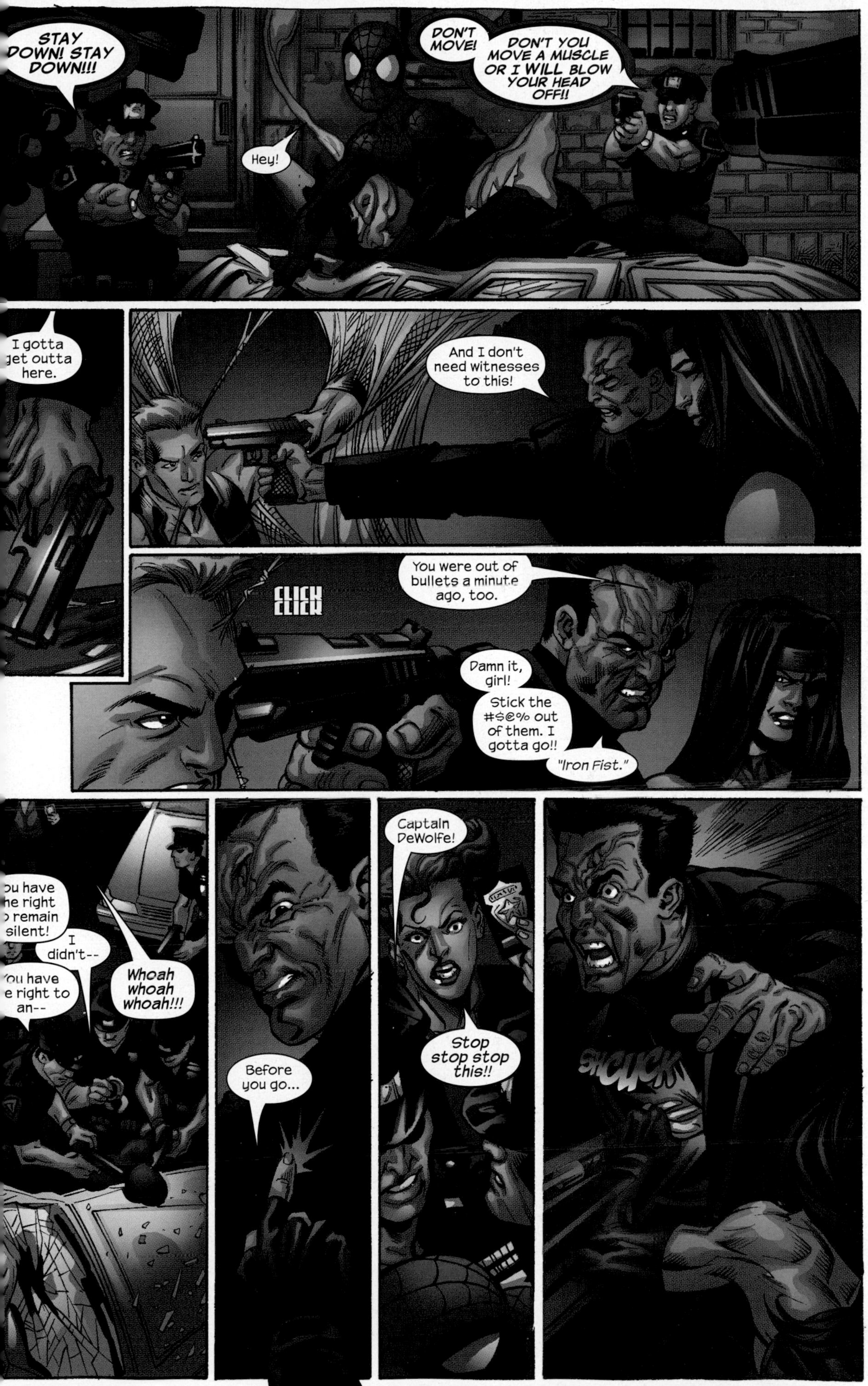

STAY DOWN! STAY DOWN!!!
Hey!
DON'T MOVE!
DON'T YOU MOVE A MUSCLE OR I WILL BLOW YOUR HEAD OFF!!
I gotta get outta here.
And I don't need witnesses to this!
CLICK CLICK
You were out of bullets a minute ago, too.
Damn it, girl!
Stick the #$@% out of them. I gotta go!!
"Iron Fist."
You have the right to remain silent!
I didn't--
You have the right to an--
Whoah whoah whoah!!!
Before you go...
Captain DeWolfe!
Stop stop stop this!!
SHUCK

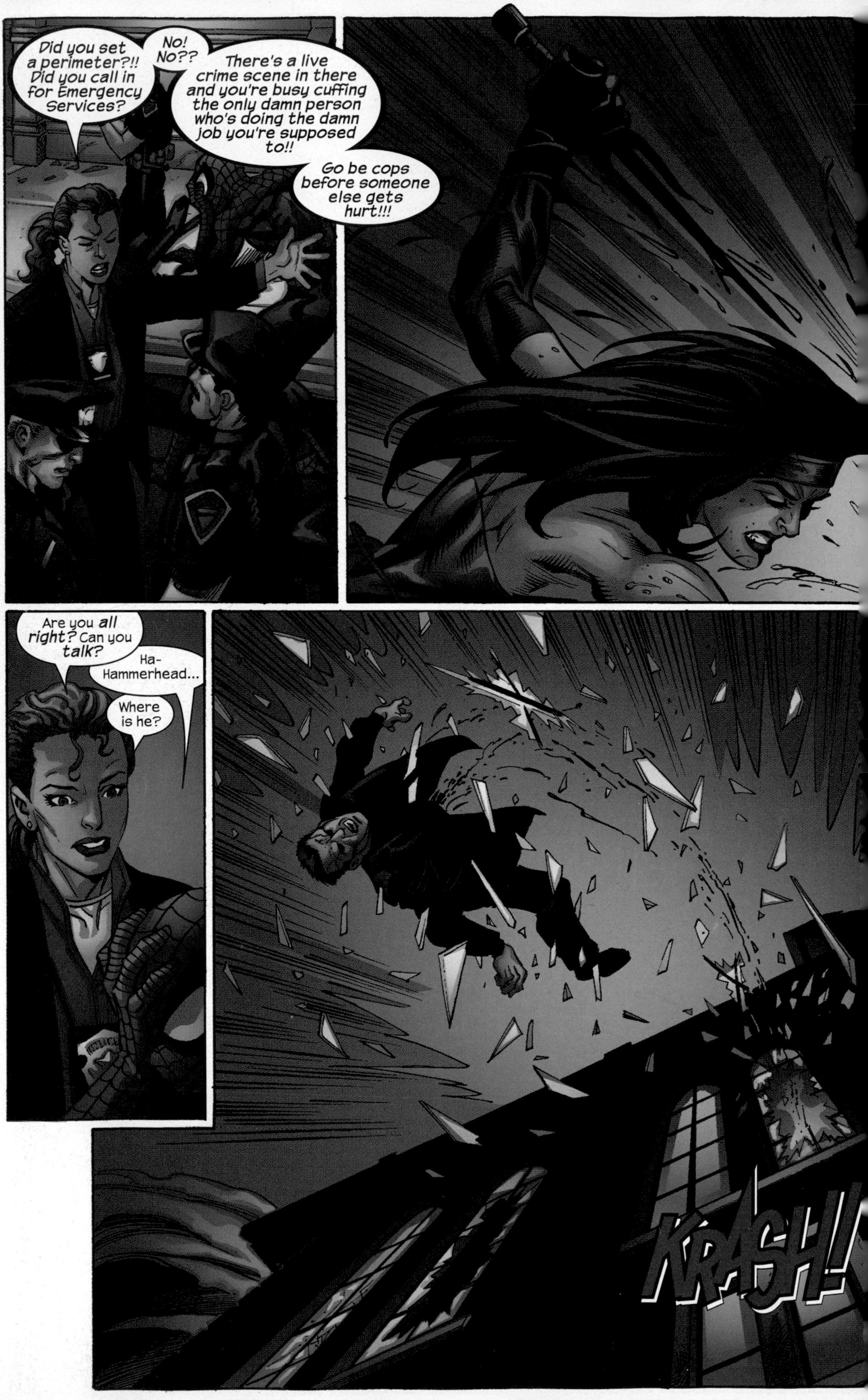
Did you set a perimeter?!! Did you call in for Emergency Services?
No! No??
There's a live crime scene in there and you're busy cuffing the only damn person who's doing the damn job you're supposed to!!
Go be cops before someone else gets hurt!!!
Are you all right? Can you talk?
Ha- Hammerhead...
Where is he?
KRASH!

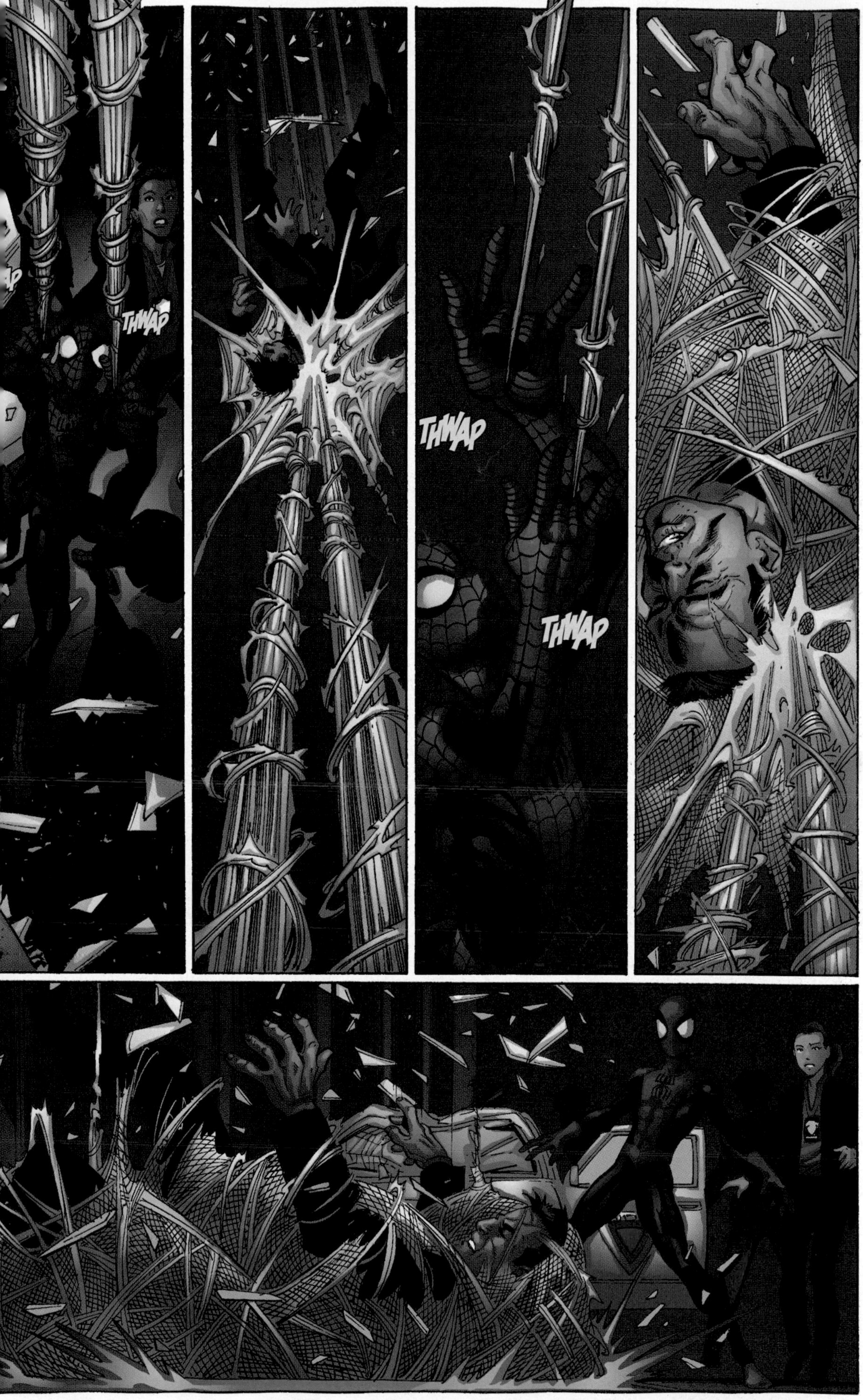
THWAP
THWAP
THWAP

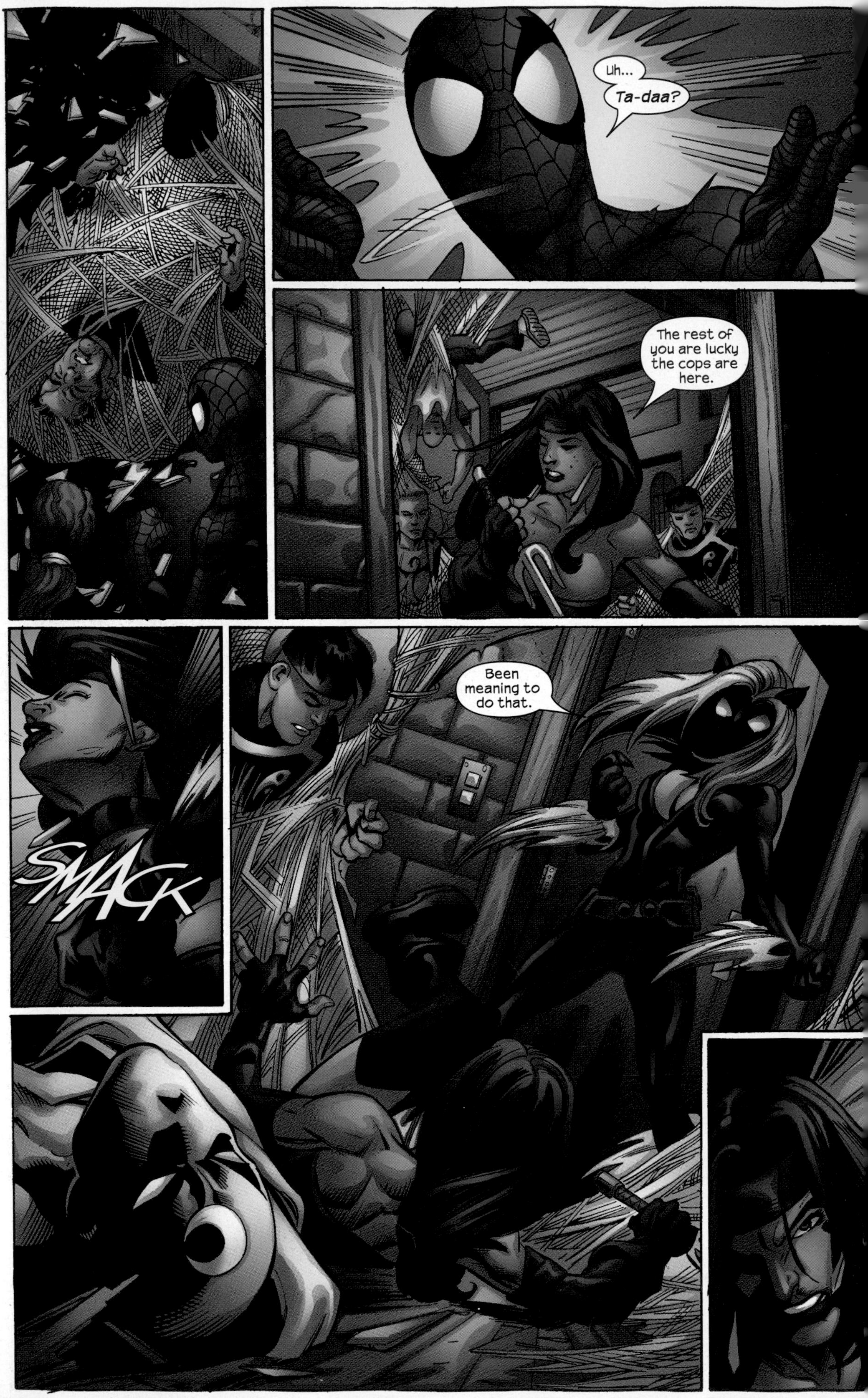
Uh...
Ta-daa?
The rest of you are lucky the cops are here.
Been meaning to do that.
SMACK

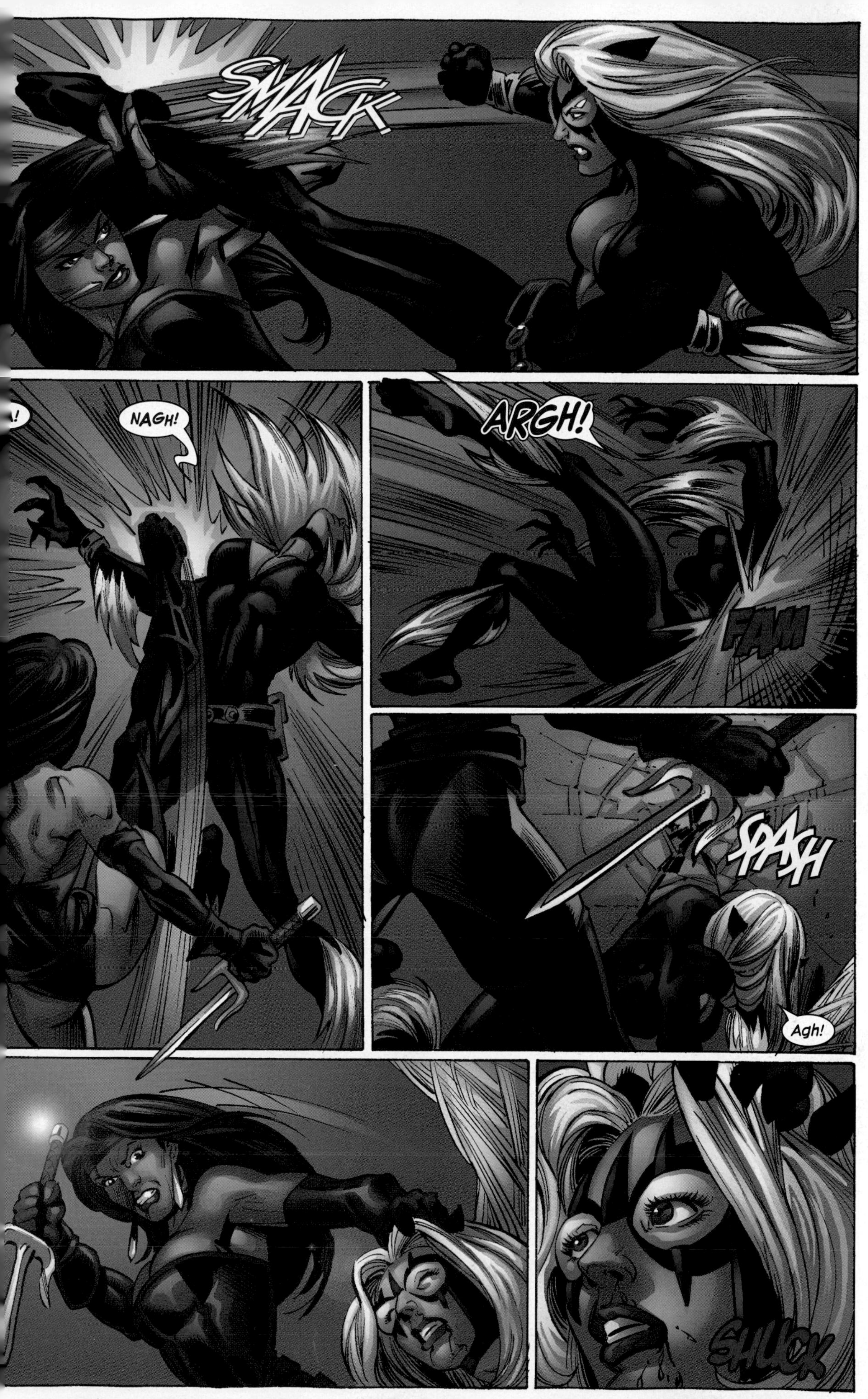
SMACK
NAGH!
ARGH!
FAM
SPASH
Agh!
SHUCK

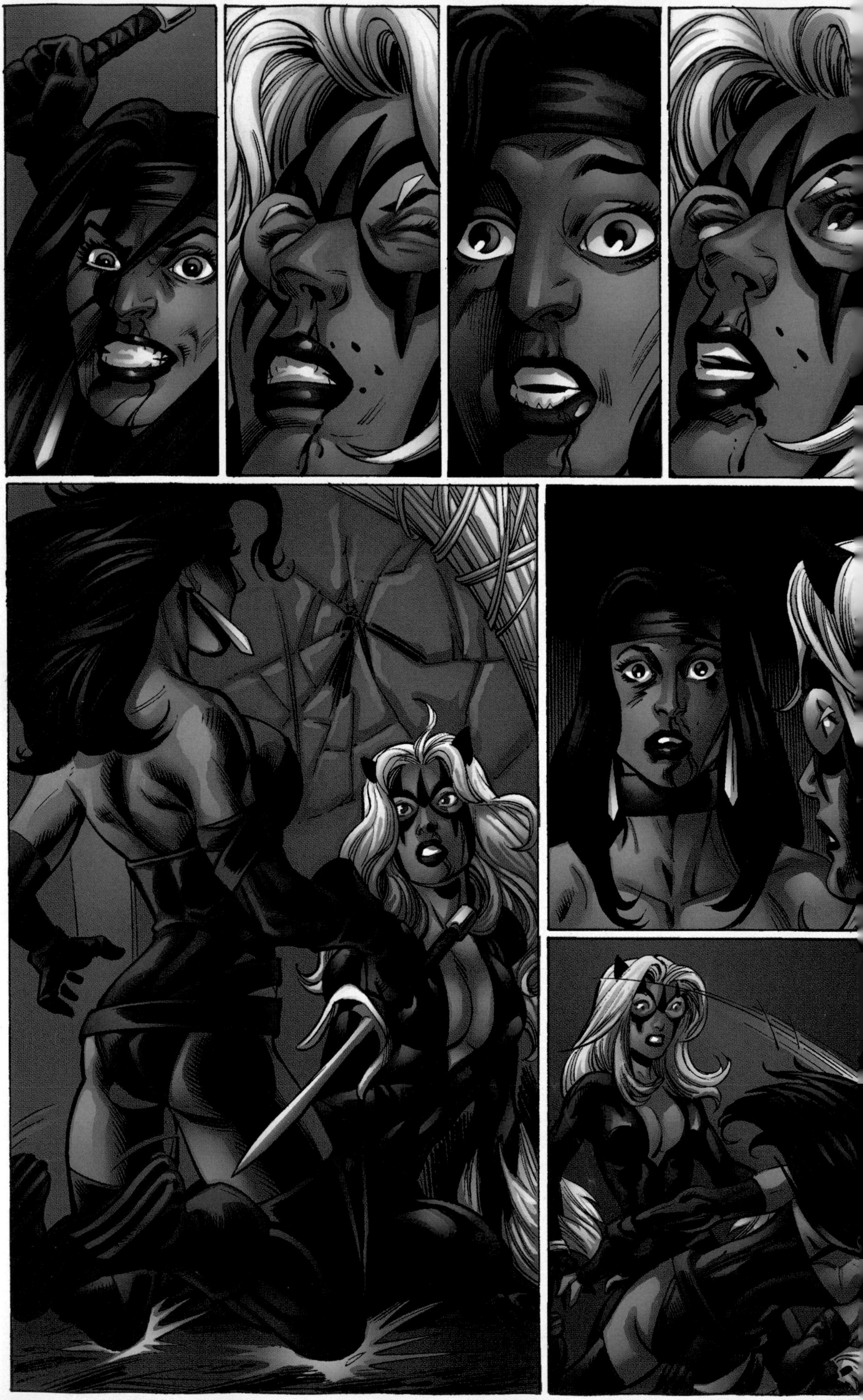

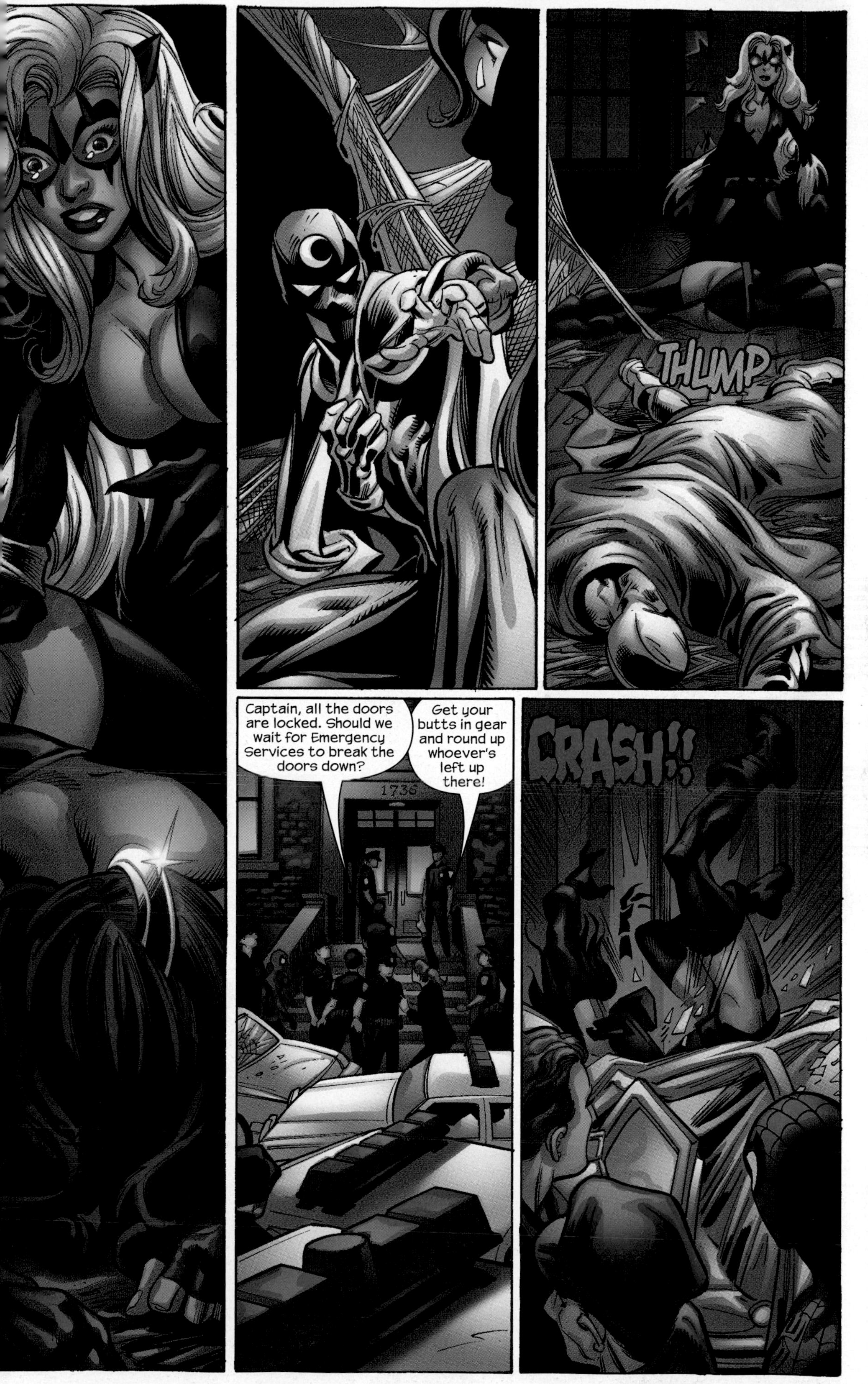
THUMP
Captain, all the doors are locked. Should we wait for Emergency Services to break the doors down?
Get your butts in gear and round up whoever's left up there!
1736
CRASH!!!

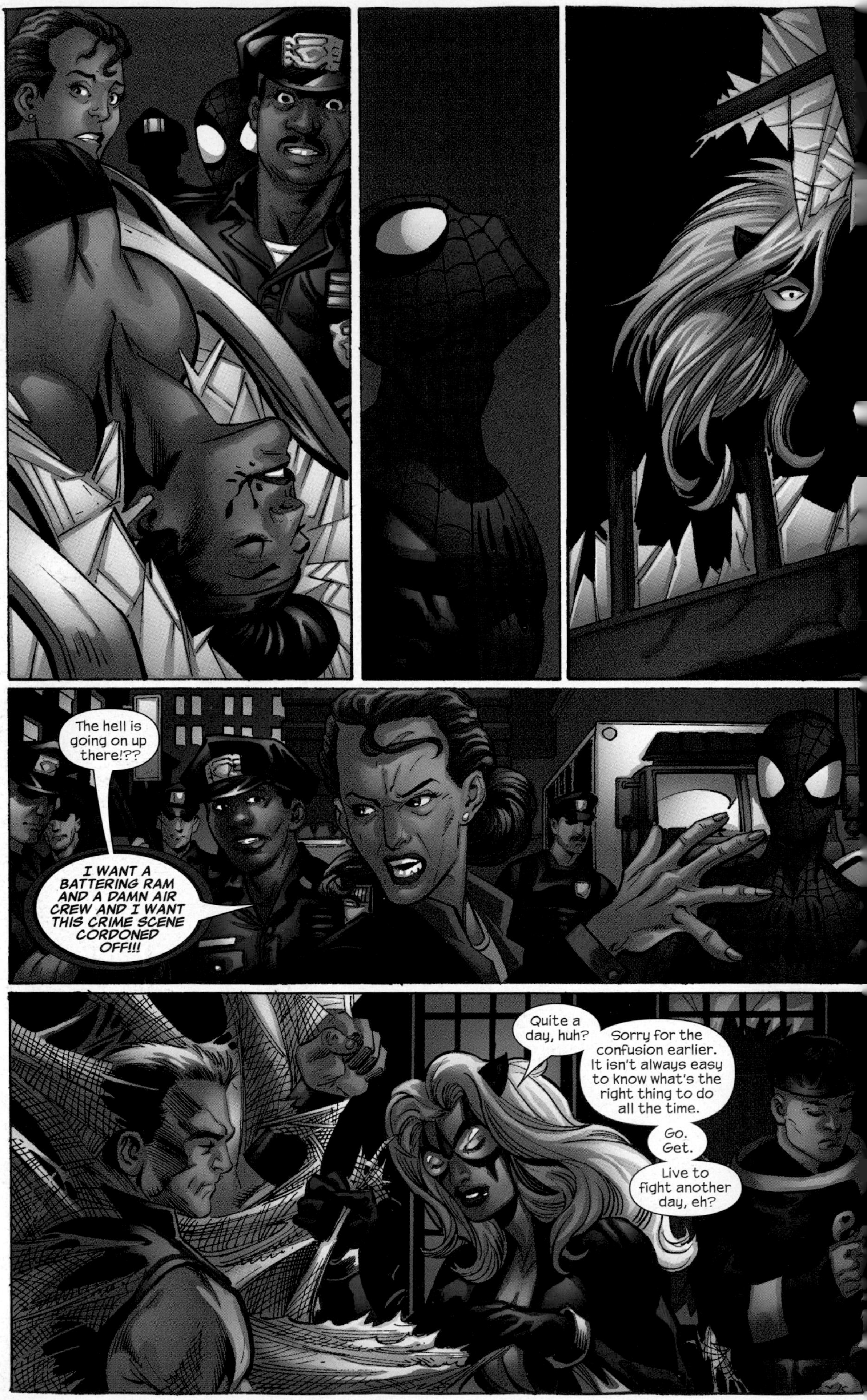
The hell is going on up there!??
I WANT A BATTERING RAM AND A DAMN AIR CREW AND I WANT THIS CRIME SCENE CORDONED OFF!!!
Quite a day, huh?
Sorry for the confusion earlier. It isn't always easy to know what's the right thing to do all the time.
Go. Get.
Live to fight another day, eh?

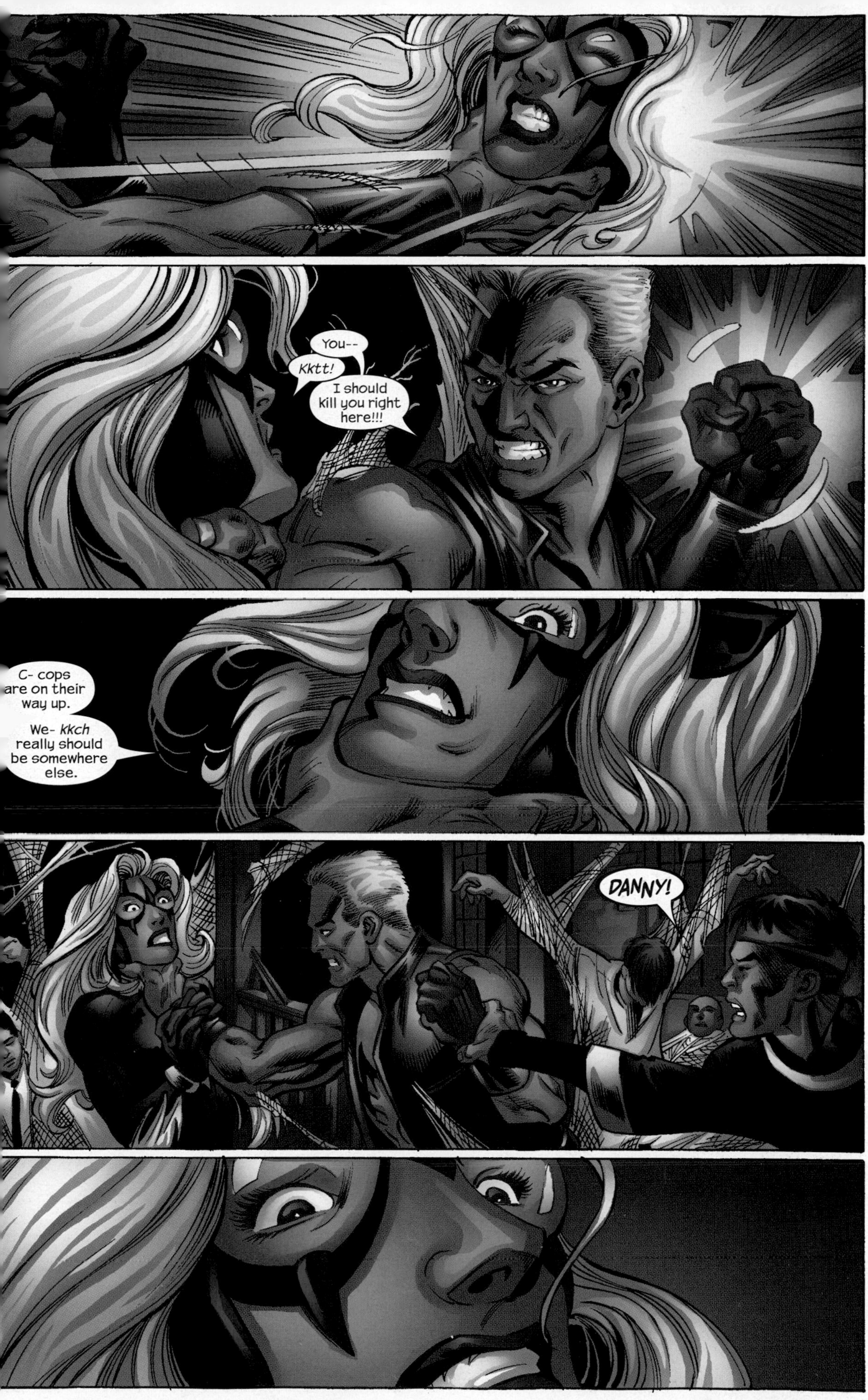
You--
Kktt!
I should kill you right here!!!
C- cops are on their way up.
We- kkch really should be somewhere else.
DANNY!

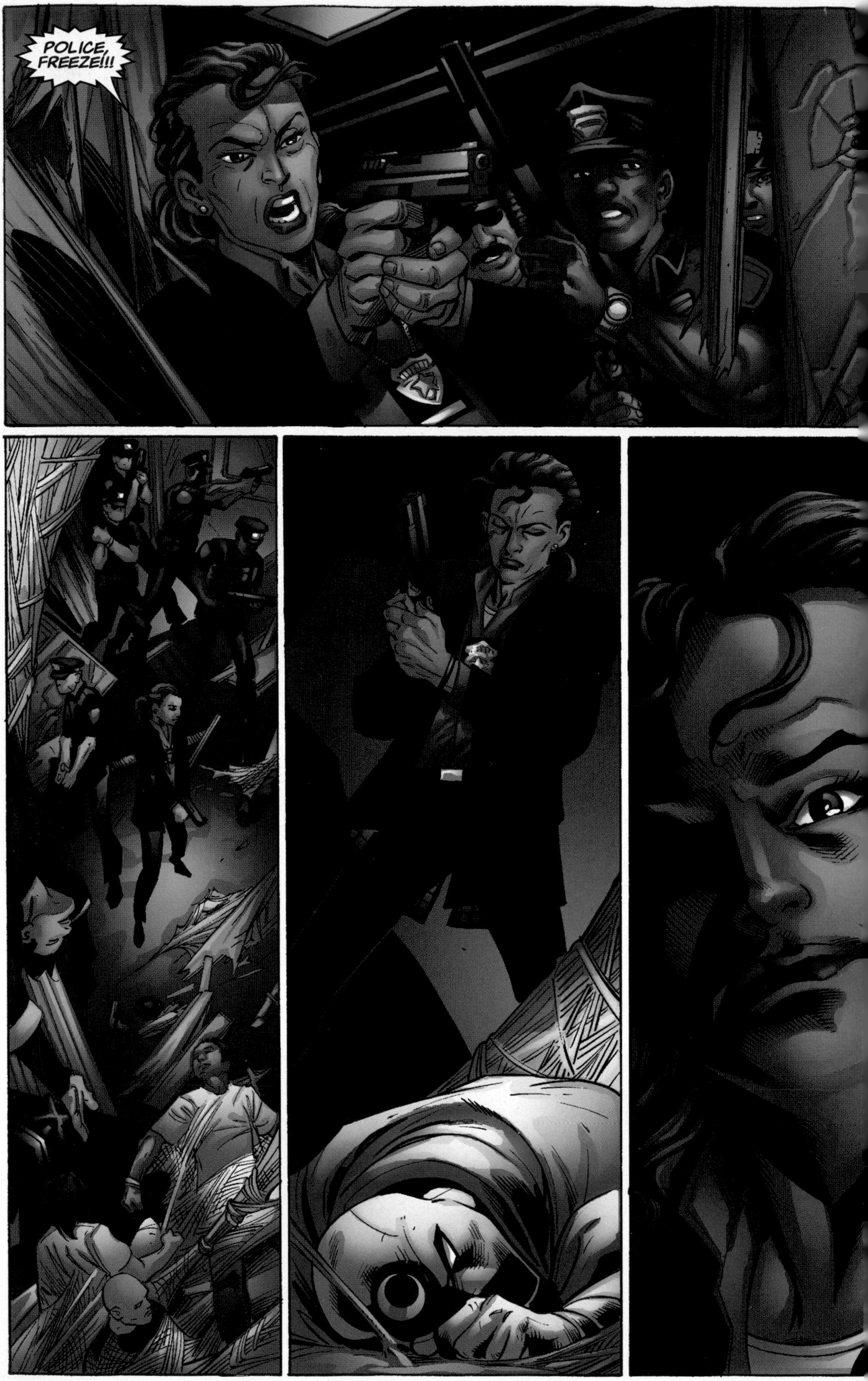
POLICE, FREEZE!!!

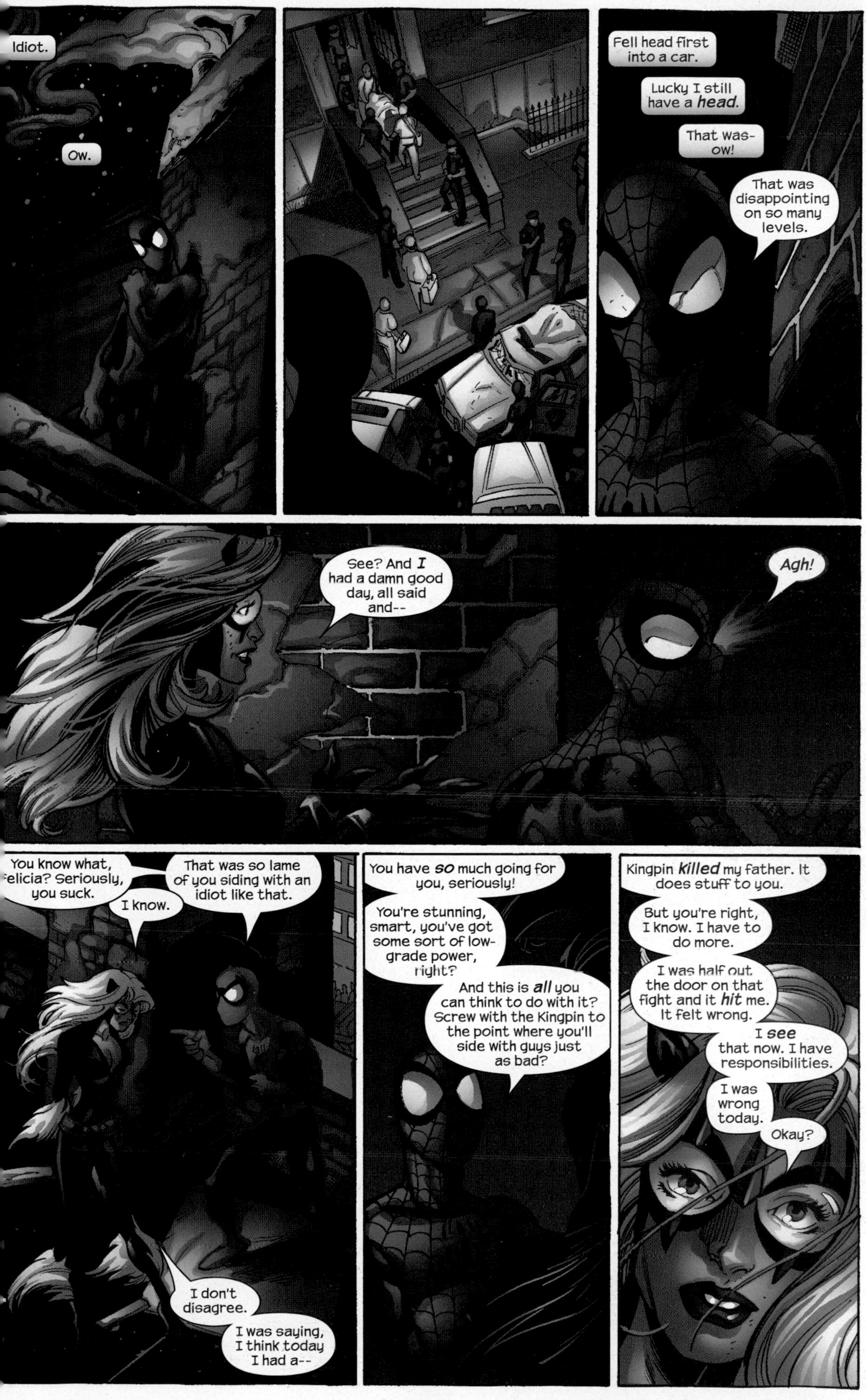
Idiot.
Ow.
Fell head first into a car.
Lucky I still have a head.
That was-- ow!
That was disappointing on so many levels.
See? And I had a damn good day, all said and--
Agh!
You know what, Felicia? Seriously, you suck.
That was so lame of you siding with an idiot like that.
I know.
I don't disagree.
I was saying, I think today I had a--
You have so much going for you, seriously!
You're stunning, smart, you've got some sort of low-grade power, right?
And this is all you can think to do with it? Screw with the Kingpin to the point where you'll side with guys just as bad?
Kingpin killed my father. It does stuff to you.
But you're right, I know. I have to do more.
I was half out the door on that fight and it hit me. It felt wrong.
I see that now. I have responsibilities.
I was wrong today.
Okay?

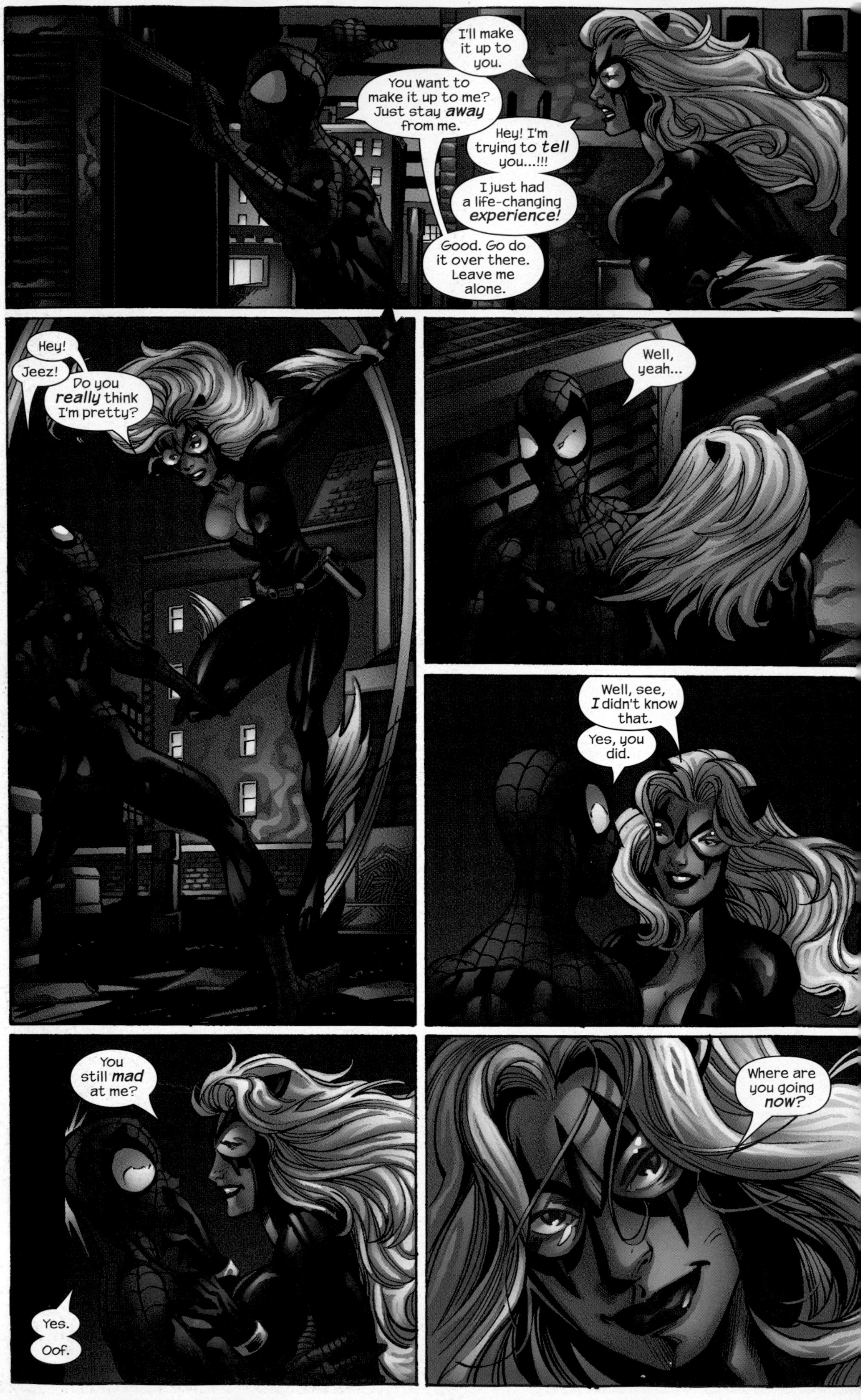
I'll make it up to you.
You want to make it up to me? Just stay away from me.
Hey! I'm trying to tell you...!!!
I just had a life-changing experience!
Good. Go do it over there. Leave me alone.
Hey!
Jeez!
Do you really think I'm pretty?
Well, yeah...
Well, see, I didn't know that.
Yes, you did.
You still mad at me?
Yes.
Oof.
Where are you going now?

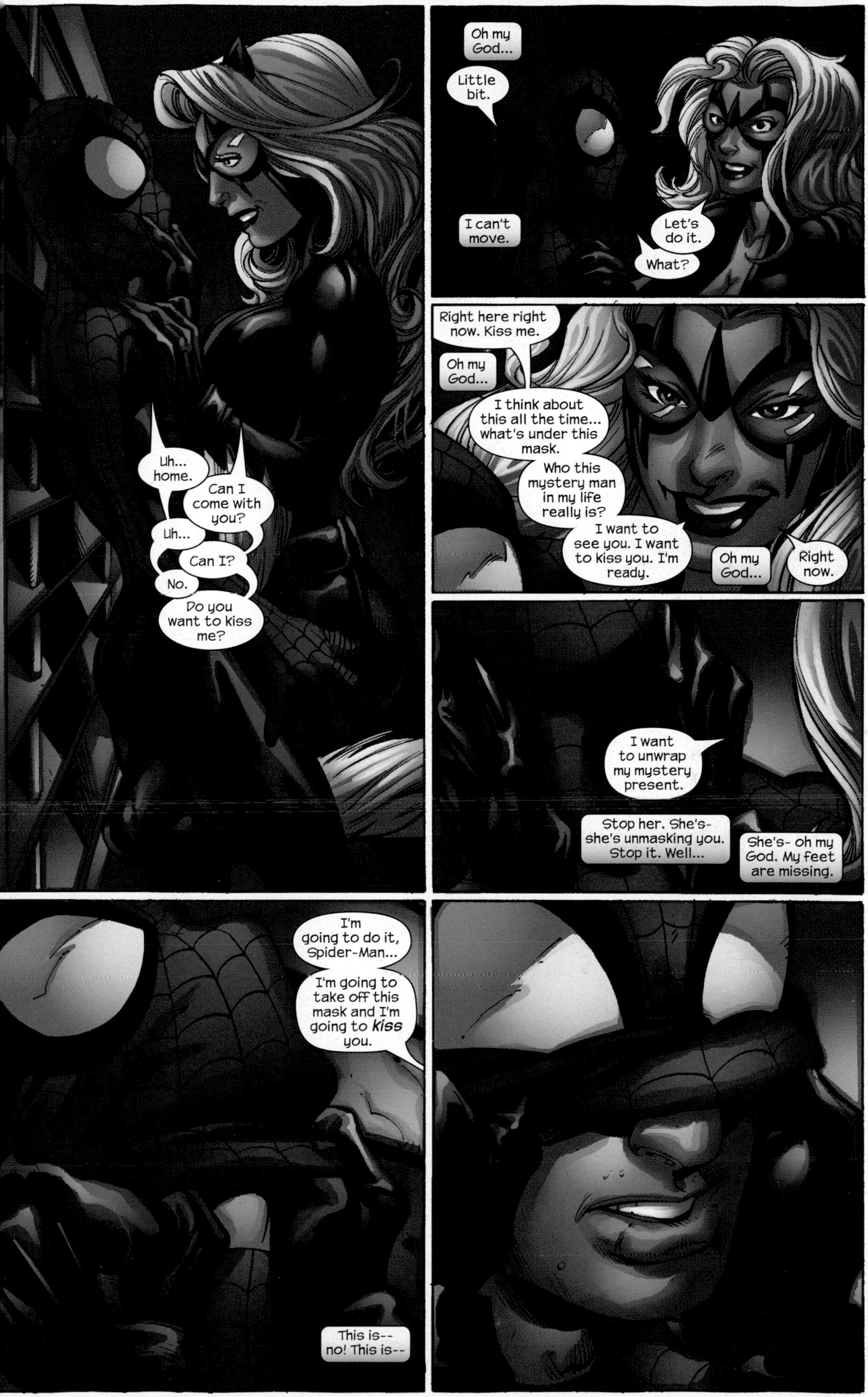
Uh... home.
Can I come with you?
Uh...
Can I?
No.
Do you want to kiss me?
Oh my God...
Little bit.
I can't move.
Let's do it.
What?
Right here right now. Kiss me.
Oh my God...
I think about this all the time... what's under this mask.
Who this mystery man in my life really is?
I want to see you. I want to kiss you. I'm ready.
Oh my God...
Right now.
I want to unwrap my mystery present.
Stop her. She's- she's unmasking you. Stop it. Well...
She's- oh my God. My feet are missing.
I'm going to do it, Spider-Man...
I'm going to take off this mask and I'm going to *kiss* you.
This is-- no! This is--

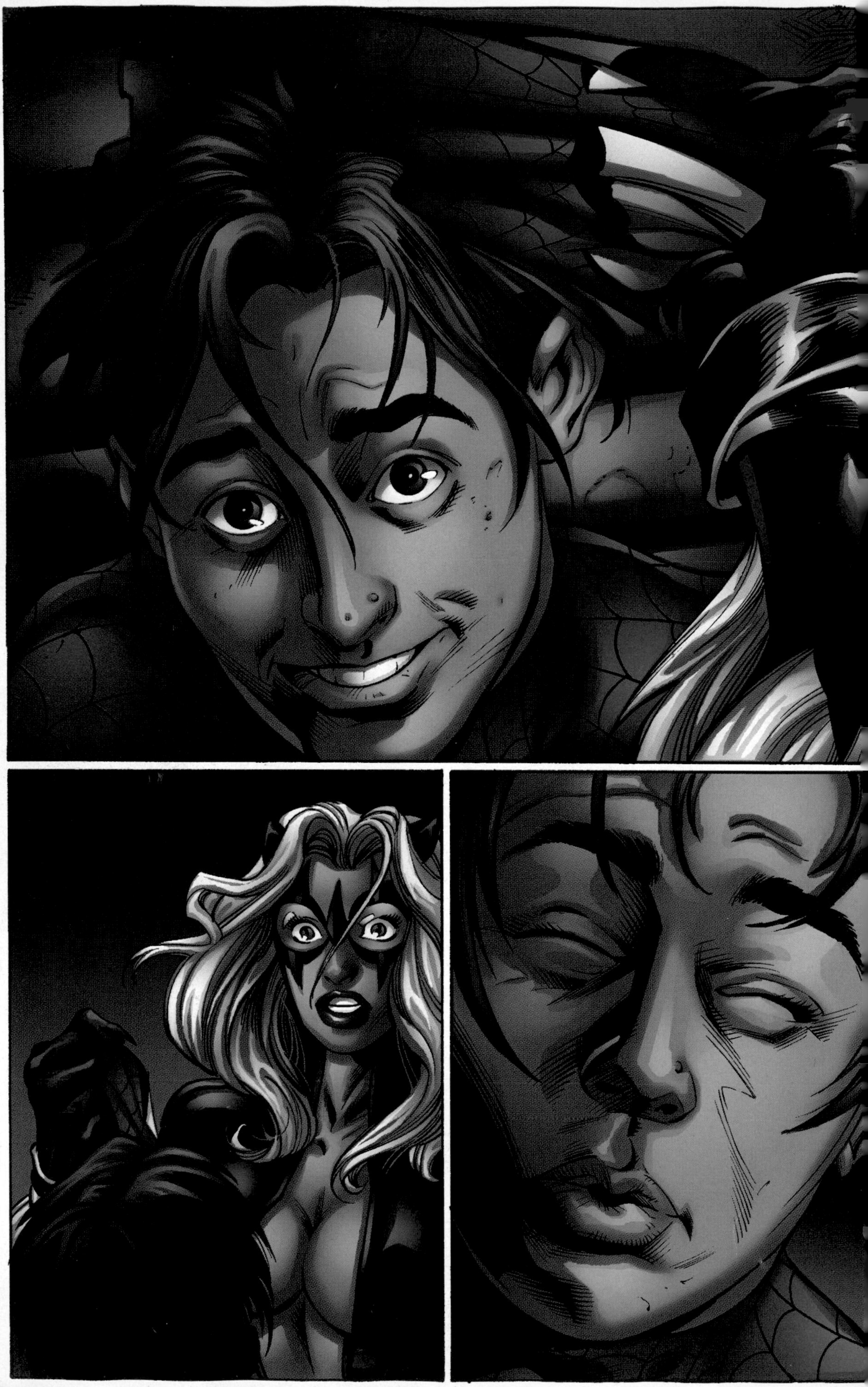

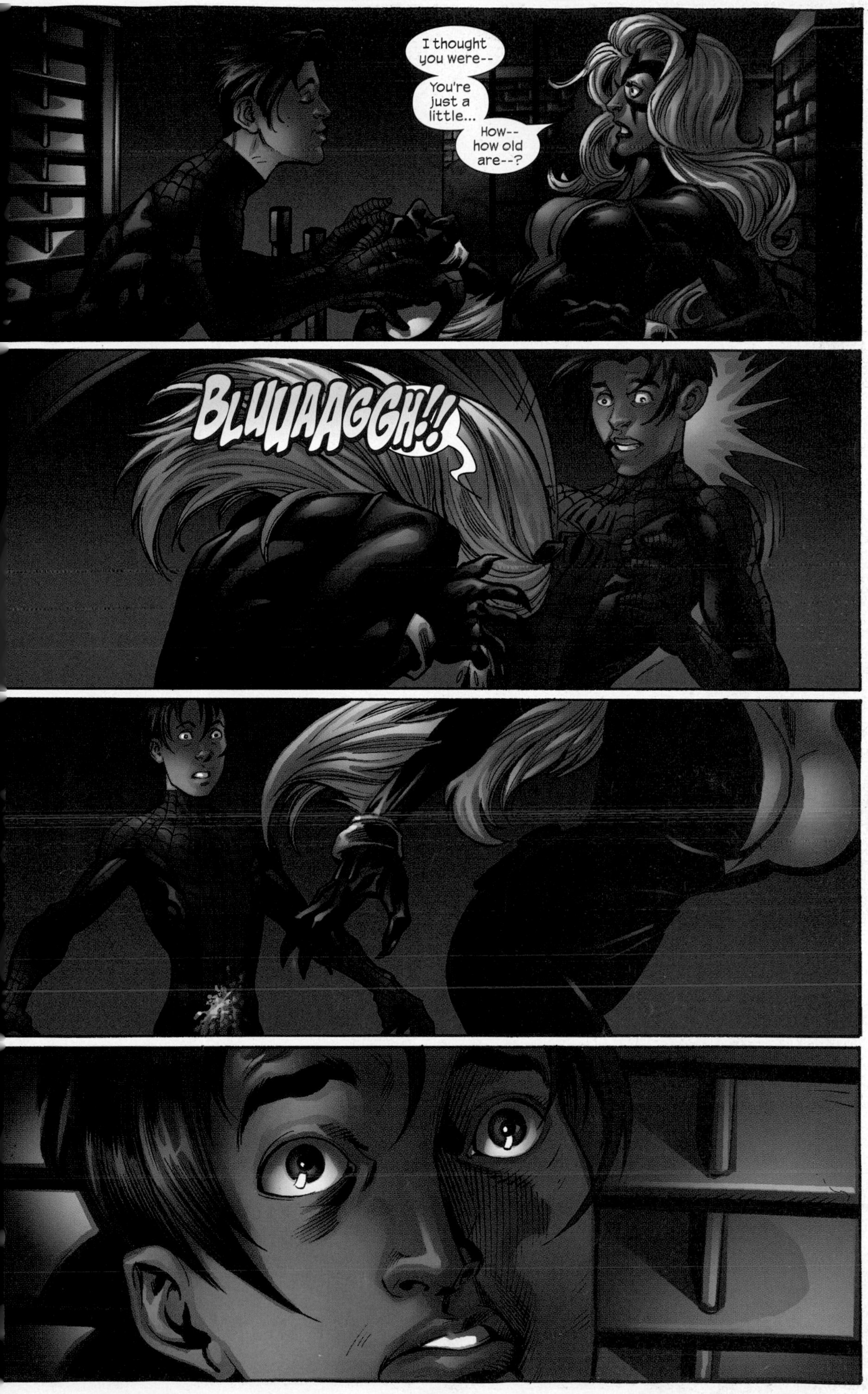
I thought you were--
You're just a little...
How-- how old are--?
BLUUAAGGH!!

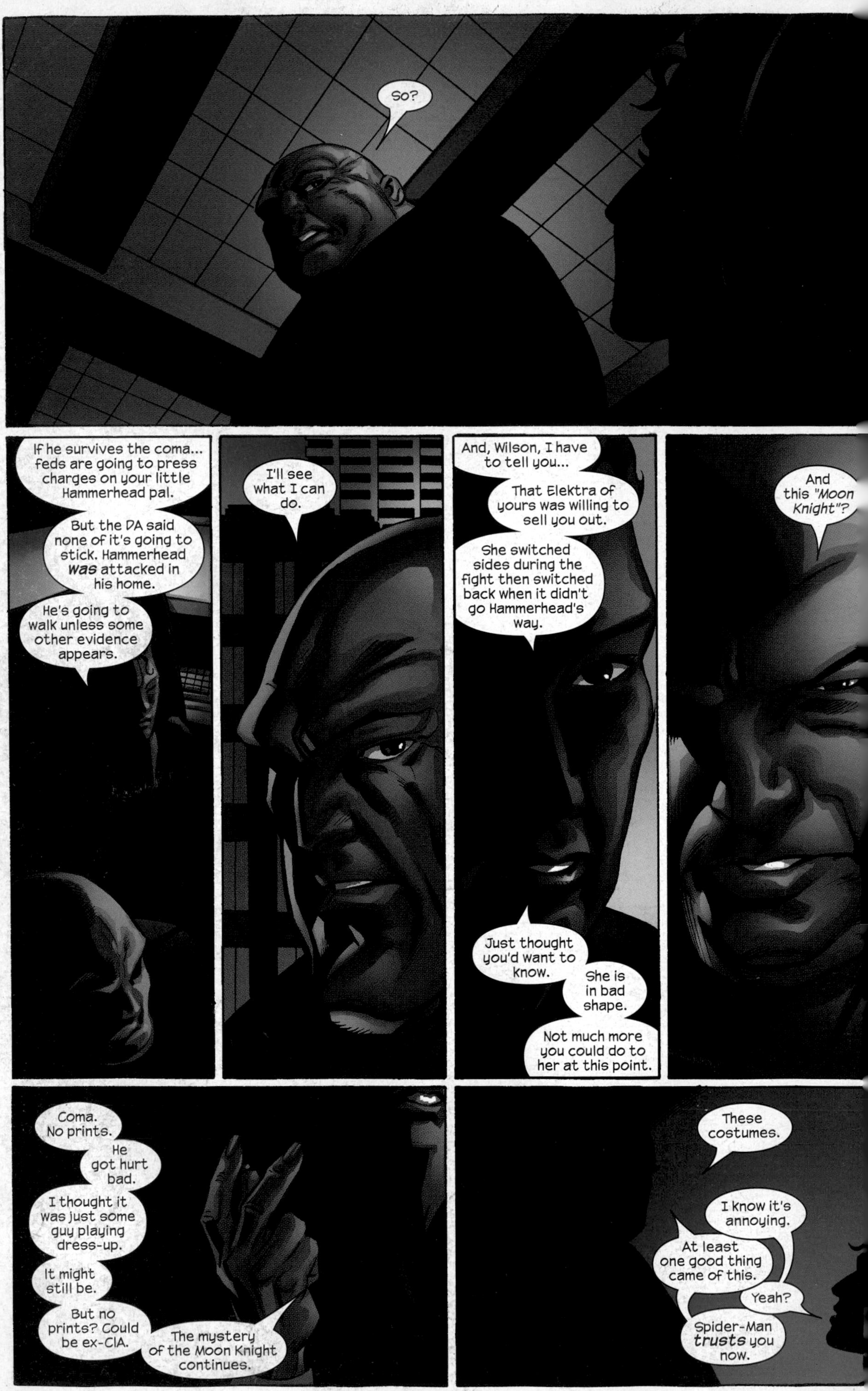
So?
If he survives the coma... feds are going to press charges on your little Hammerhead pal.
But the DA said none of it's going to stick. Hammerhead *was* attacked in his home.
He's going to walk unless some other evidence appears.
I'll see what I can do.
And, Wilson, I have to tell you...
That Elektra of yours was willing to sell you out.
She switched sides during the fight then switched back when it didn't go Hammerhead's way.
Just thought you'd want to know.
She is in bad shape.
Not much more you could do to her at this point.
And this *"Moon Knight"*?
Coma. No prints.
He got hurt bad.
I thought it was just some guy playing dress-up.
It might still be.
But no prints? Could be ex-CIA.
The mystery of the Moon Knight continues.
These costumes.
I know it's annoying.
At least one good thing came of this.
Yeah?
Spider-Man *trusts* you now.

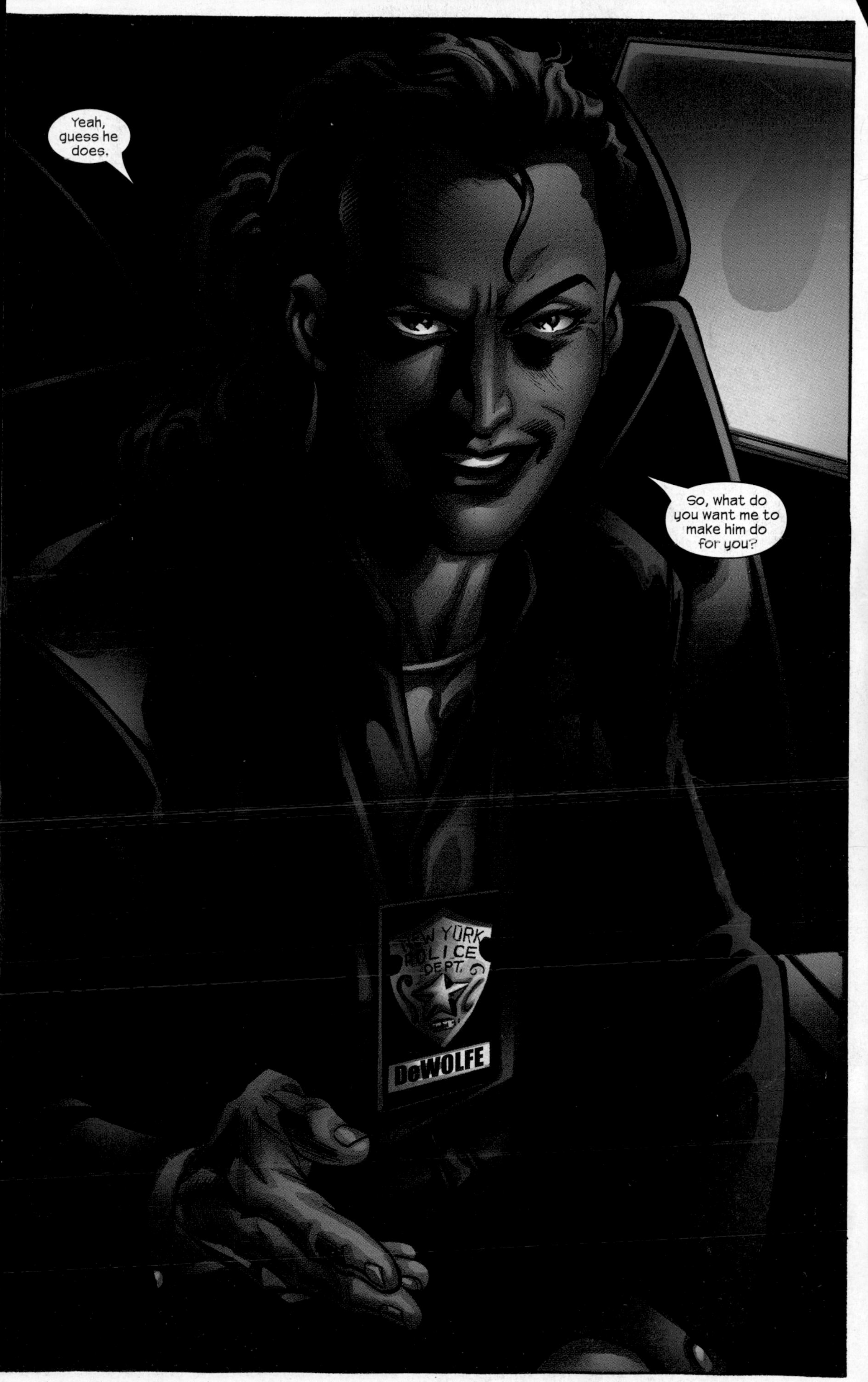
Yeah, guess he does.
So, what do you want me to make him do for you?
NEW YORK POLICE DEPT.
DeWOLFE

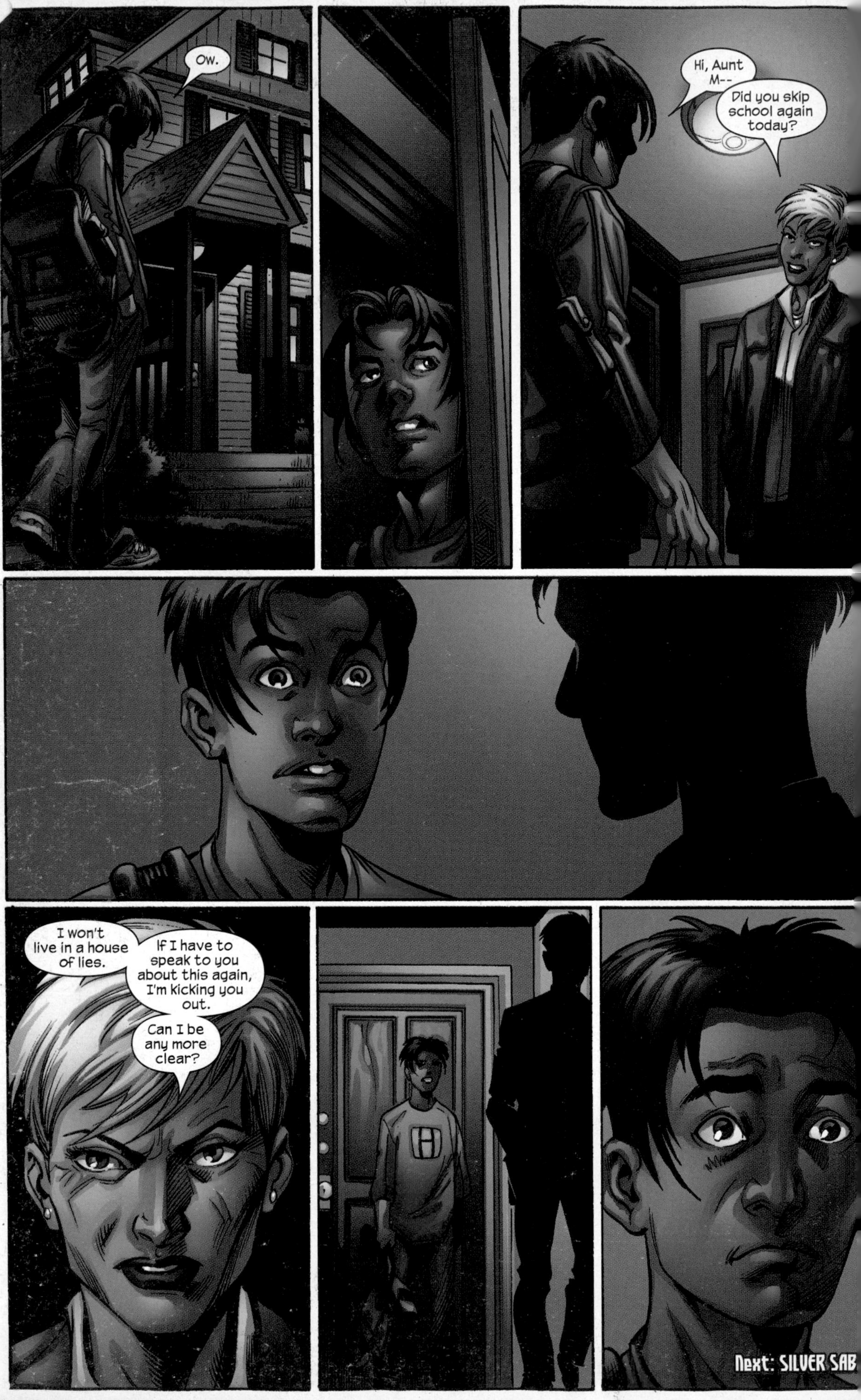
Ow.
Hi, Aunt M--
Did you skip school again today?
I won't live in a house of lies.
If I have to speak to you about this again, I'm kicking you out.
Can I be any more clear?
Next: SILVER SAB